Consultation for Organizational Change

A Volume in
Research in Management Consulting

Series Editor:
Anthony F. Buono

and

Contemporary Trends in Organization Development and Change

Series Editors:
Peter F. Sorensen
Therese F. Yaeger

Research in Management Consulting

Anthony F. Buono
Series Editor

Work and People: An Economic Evaluation of Job Enrichment (2010)
By Henri Savall

Client-Consultant Collaboration: Coping with Complexity and Change (2009)
Edited by Anthony F. Buono, and Flemming Poulfelt

Emerging Trends and Issues in Management Consulting: Consulting as a Janus-Faced Reality (2009)
Edited by Anthony F. Buono

Board Members and Management Consultants: Redefining the Boundaries of Consulting and Corporate Governance (2009)
Edited by Pierre-Yves Gomez and Rickie Moore

Mastering Hidden Costs and Socio-Economic Performance (2008)
Edited by Henri Savall and Veronique Zardet

Socio-Economic Intervention in Organizations: The Intervener-Researcher and the SEAM Approach to Organizational Analysis (2007)
Edited by Anthony F. Buono and Henri Savall

Challenges and Issues in Knowledge Management (2005)
Edited by Anthony F. Buono and Flemming Poulfelt

Creative Consulting: Innovative Perspectives on Management Consulting (2004)
Edited by Anthony F. Buono

Enhancing Inter-Firm Networks & Interorganizational Strategies (2003)
Edited by Anthony F. Buono

Developing Knowledge and Value in Management Consulting (2002)
Edited by Anthony F. Buono

Current Trends in Management Consulting (2001)
Edited by Anthony F. Buono

Contemporary Trends in Organization Development and Change

Peter F. Sorensen
Therese F. Yaeger
Series Editors

Strategic Organization Development: Managing Change for Success (2009)
Edited by Peter F. Sorensen and Therese F. Yaeger

Global Organization Development: Managing Unprecedented Change (2006)
Edited by Therese F. Yaeger, Thomas C. Head, and Peter F. Sorensen

Consultation for Organizational Change

Edited by
Anthony F. Buono
Bentley University
and
David W. Jamieson
Jamieson Consulting Group, Inc.

INFORMATION AGE PUBLISHING, INC.
Charlotte, NC • www.infoagepub.com

Library of Congress Cataloging-in-Publication Data

Consultation for organizational change / edited by Anthony F. Buono and David W. Jamieson.
p. cm. – (Research in management consulting)
Includes bibliographical references.
ISBN 978-1-61735-086-3 (pbk.) – ISBN 978-1-61735-087-0 (hardcover) – ISBN 978-1-61735-088-7 (e-book)
1. Business consultants. 2. Organizational change. I. Buono, Anthony F. II. Jamieson, David, 1946-
HD69.C6.C653 2010
658.4'06–dc22

2010021950

Copyright © 2010 Information Age Publishing Inc.

All rights reserved. No part of this publication may be reproduced, stored in a retrieval system, or transmitted, in any form or by any means, electronic, mechanical, photocopying, microfilming, recording or otherwise, without written permission from the publisher.

Printed in the United States of America

CONTENTS

PART III
REFLECTIONS ON CONSULTING FOR CHANGE

INTRODUCTION

Anthony F. Buono, David W. Jamieson, Peter Sorensen, and Therese Yaeger

This volume is a joint publication in the *Research in Management Consulting* and *Contemporary Trends in Organization Development and Change* series. This dual focus reflects the reality that consulting for organizational change is a special type of management consultation, a complex field of endeavor that requires a broad range of skills and competencies. To be truly effective, change-related consulting requires a unique client-consultant relationship, a special set of consulting skills, an expertise in human and organizational systems, and significant personal qualities. It is in high demand in a world full of change. Yet, we still know relatively little theoretically about this type of consulting and have relatively little empirical evidence about what actually works and why. This theory-practice gap has been an interest of ours for many years, a focus that resulted in two special issues of the *Journal of Organizational Change Management* (Jamieson 1995, 1997).

Although we clearly have much to learn about consulting for organizational change, the field of Organization Development (OD) has a 50-plus-year history dating back to the work of Kurt Lewin. The field has a well developed set of technologies, models of change, and a code of ethics. Still we need to focus on and learn more about the role of an OD consultant as a

Consultation for Organizational Change. pages vii–xx
Copyright © 2010 by Information Age Publishing
All rights of reproduction in any form reserved.

special kind of change agent. This joint volume increases that specific body of knowledge and provides an illustration of much needed collaboration in bringing all possible resources to bear on our understanding of an increasingly critical and essential form of consulting

Part of the difficulty we are faced with begins with what appears to be a relatively straightforward question: "What is consultation?" Although there is a long history of calling most forms of help applied to organizations as "consulting," it is possible to differentiate true "consultation" from other forms of help (see Jamieson, 1996). In addition to the challenge of defining consultation, we are also plagued with questions concerning *who* the consultants are (all different types) and *what* they do. There is a wide variety of products, services, roles, and settings in which a wide variety of players (who are referred to as consultants) operate without a shared body of knowledge. Lalonde (2009) particularly highlights the importance of "context" in consulting work, underscoring the variety of engagements and circumstances that exists and how that makes determining "success" so difficult. Finally, the multiple roles often carried out by consultants (e.g., advocate, ally, adviser, facilitator, leader) produce many paradoxes, further clouding any discussion of what consultants do and what makes a difference (see Whittle, 2006 for a good review of roles and paradoxes). One belief we start with is that consulting effectiveness is determined primarily by client-assessed "value added," which can occur through many mechanisms. Yet, we have relatively little insight and empirical data as to how such value added actually shows up in different consulting approaches, styles, philosophies, roles, and processes.

When we add the target of organization change to our interest in consultation, we enter an even more complex arena with many contributing and hindering factors. Discussions of organization change often presuppose a third-party role (consultant) (Burke, 2008; Lippitt & Lippitt, 1986), yet little is actually known about what these third parties do, contribute, catalyze, or influence that makes a difference for change or how different consulting approaches and processes help to create, support or sustain change. We can, however, propose some of the ways consultation could and/or should add value related to key phases or characteristics of an organization change process.

- *Conditions*: Change theorists have often emphasized the importance of establishing or reinforcing the conditions for change, such as urgency, readiness, commitment and capability (Beckhard & Harris, 1987; Burke, 2008; Kotter, 1996). What do consultants do that influences the urgency, readiness, commitment, or capability of client systems?

- *Content*: Determining the "content" of change (what to do: solutions, alternatives, decisions, tasks) is a reflection of client needs and the focus of the consultation itself. How can consultants use their knowledge and experience to inform questions and answers in a particular client situation?
- *Process*: Providing assistance with the "process" of change (how to go about it: steps, sequence, methods) is sometimes the most important need and focus. Consultants are often required to provide designs or co-develop designs for carrying out change in the client's system. What consulting processes or behaviors bring about effective process contributions?
- *Emotions*: Managing the emotional and psycho-social dimensions of change (conflict, ambivalence, loss, joy, anger, grief, transitions, resistance) are areas where consultants have the potential to add value (Block, 2000; Lundberg & Young, 2001). These situations can occur in individual and group settings, as well as programmatically, across an organization. How do consultants identify and deal with emotional/psycho-social dynamics during change processes? Do these efforts facilitate the change process and, if so, how are they influential?
- *Stages*: Most changes require some forms of planning, discovering or diagnosis, initiating, transitioning, stabilizing, and project management (Beckhard & Harris, 1987; Burke, 2008). How might consultants be useful and provide value in these particular phases? Where do these needs show up and how are they managed by both consultants and clients?
- *Objective Third Party*: As a third party, a consultant *can* bring unique, different or unencumbered perspectives, skills, strengths, and data. How can the consultant use his or her "self" to see, know and do what those in the system cannot? In what ways does the consultant become an instrument in the change process? Can consultants separate themselves from the change processes they are part of?
- *Influence*: Consultants are generally conceptualized as having no formal authority. Yet to be successful they generally need to have impact in the client system. Through what actions or behaviors do we see consultants exercising influence or creating relationships and interactions in which they are granted social power (see French & Raven, 1959)?
- *Client-Consultant Relationship*: The client-consultant relationship has often been highlighted as important to consulting effectiveness and the change process (cf. Block, 2000; Buono & Poulfelt, 2009; Fincham, 1999; Lippitt & Lippitt, 1986; McGivern, 1983; Sturdy, Werr, & Buono, 2009). How do consultants affect the development, modifica-

tion and/or repair of their relationships with clients? What role(s) do clients play in this dynamic?

Clearly, many more issues, concerns and challenges could be raised and explored. Readers are encouraged to seek out other ideas, issues, and evidence in the chapters that follow.

CONSULTATION FOR ORGANIZATIONAL CHANGE

In creating this volume, we sought chapters that would help advance the theory, research, and practice of consulting for organizational change. The book contains fourteen chapters that frame the change challenge, examine different change frameworks and perspectives, and share various reflections and personal insights into the underlying challenges of consulting to bring about organizational change.

Framing the Change Challenge

The first chapter by U.S. consultants David Jamieson and Terry Armstrong takes a critical view of the consulting process, noting that not all consulting assignments necessarily create value. Drawing on the concept of an *engaged relationship* between the client and consultant as a critical characteristic of the process of creating true value and successfully enabling change, Jamieson and Armstrong examine the desired roles and key behaviors underlying this interaction. As they argue, consultants typically fail to truly add value when their attention is focused on attending to distractions involved in correcting flawed roles or behaviors, recovering from relationship potholes, or dealing with deficiencies in interactions with a client. While these behaviors and challenges are often a reality of the consulting process, they rarely add value for the client, the system, or the process of facilitating change.

The chapter draws out the conditions of engagement, common issues that occur when either party performs poorly, and what consultants need to do "on the winding road to engagement." As part of the discussion, Jamieson and Armstrong focus on common problems that undermine the creation of an engaged client-consultant relationship and various actions the consultant can take in response to these difficulties, focusing on achieving presence and creating the necessary roles and behaviors, relationship qualities and interaction characteristics that create a foundation for real value.

The second chapter, by Dutch consultants Léon de Caluwé and Elsbeth Reitsma, examines the tacit knowledge held by experienced management consultants. Drawing on a study of 40 senior consultants, their analysis is focused on understanding these competencies in relation to different contexts and interventions, especially those related to change processes in organizations. Using in-depth interviews, de Caluwé and Reitsma presented each of their subjects with a series of cases in which they assessed the essentials of the case, the approach they would take, the intervention(s) they would use, and the competencies they felt were necessary for success.

While the authors found a core of basic competencies that were seen as important for all consultants, the study suggests that both expert and process-based approaches were valued—though being aware of the choice between them, and when one might be more appropriate than the other was seen as critical. Based on their analysis, for example, in contexts that were characterized by relatively low time pressures and significant conflict or disagreement, the consultants favored a process-oriented approach. Diagnostic skills were also highlighted as the consultants reported that the situation rather than their own style, preferences or personal repertoire determined the intervention. As a way of making these insights more useful to practicing consultants, the chapter concludes with a self-rating instrument.

The final two chapters in this section focus on intervening at the whole system level. Michael Mitchell, an independent organization consultant in the U.S., begins with a comparative assessment of three basic categories of consultation—expert, service provider, and peer/coach—exploring the implications they have for the organization and its members. Although the choice of the different approaches may appear to be relatively straightforward, he argues that there are some underlying dilemmas that can readily complicate the selected engagement, from the "fit" between client and consultant expectations to the typical emphasis placed on a "part-system" perspective.

Suggesting that there is a basic "difference between taking an expert approach to consulting and actually being an expert," Mitchell argues that a continual challenge is to sufficiently observe and understand what the organization is doing in order to recommend interventions that will actually be beneficial to the organization. Yet, despite the reality that organizations are systems, Mitchell underscores that most consulting engagements fall well short of taking a whole-system approach. The chapter examines the challenges inherent in intervening at the whole-system level, focusing on finding a "good" client, contracting effectively for the engagement and its expected outcomes, ensuring the client fully understands and agrees to the crucial conditions that will make success possible, and reaching agreement about needed client leadership support. As the chapter amply illustrates, when interventions are focused on the entire system, the degree of client involvement and collaboration must be particularly high.

The last chapter in this section is by a mix of U.S. internal and external consultants. John Scherer, Gina Lavery, Roland Sullivan, Ginger Whitson, and Elizabeth Vales delve into the consultant's role in helping to create *sustainable* whole-system transformation, especially in terms of "who people become" and "what the system learns." Using the notion of "wholeness" applied to a system, they underscore that the goals are healthy balance, unity and completeness, where the organization's interdependent parts interact with each other and with the environment in such a unified way that a healthier world is created for that system and its stakeholders. As they suggest, whole-system transformation goes beyond simply setting changes in motion that will affect the entire system, and focuses on involving the whole organization in "creating itself anew."

The authors presents a framework for thinking about such whole-system transformation, capturing the process as a dynamic, holistic journey that engages a critical mass of the organization in reinventing itself, creating a "future of aligned and committed action." Beginning with the premise that organizations and individuals are in a state of perpetual change, they argue that the process must begin with the organization's leadership, ensuring that they are aligned with the vision of the new organization. They then turn to the design and execution of a large-group interactive event, drawing on extensive and significant involvement focused on creating a significant shift for the organization. Throughout this self-described journey, they underscore its iterative process of scanning, planning, acting and re-acting, drawing out the "defining moments" that create the possibility of true whole-system transformation.

Change Frameworks and Perspectives

In the first chapter in the second section, consultant Kenneth Kerber and Bentley University professor Anthony Buono explore the challenge of building organizational change capacity—the ability of an organization to change not just once, but as a normal course of events in response to and in anticipation of internal and external shifts. They argue that although many organizations are faced with the challenge of adapting to rapidly changing, often unpredictable environments, the underlying conception of the change process remains relatively simplistic in nature. The authors underscore the need for a diagnostic orientation to conceptualizing and implementing change, focusing on interrelated interventions at the *micro*- (helping people to understand and accept different approaches to change; enhancing willingness and ability to change), *meso*- (creating a change facilitative infrastructure, ensuring appropriate resources), and *macro*- (building a facilitative culture, ongoing strategizing) levels of an organization.

Using a brief case study to illustrate this approach, the chapter includes two "semi-finished" diagnostic questionnaires focused on determining the appropriate change approach (directed, planned, guided) and the level of change capacity that exists in the organization. The case vignette describes the process used to facilitate a senior management team's ability to appreciate the complexity and uncertainty of a key task they were facing, and the understanding that the complexity and uncertainty surrounding that task required a more patient and involving approach to the change process than they had utilized in the past.

The next chapter by Deborah Colwill, a faculty member at Trinity International University, focuses on the use of metaphors in the organizational change process. Noting that metaphors have long been a powerful tool in the hands of persuasive leaders, she argues that they can be used to quickly capture the essence of an organization's current reality and desired possibilities. The chapter draws on two types of organizational metaphors—projecting and eliciting—exploring their potential and limitations in capturing tacit knowledge and attempting to bring about organizational change.

Colwill then turns to four organization metaphors—the machine, organism, human brain, and energy wave—to illustrate how consultants can use metaphor to guide their work, helping to "illuminate the familiar and bring clarity to the unfamiliar." As she suggests, within the change process metaphors can play a steering function and as a way to support organizational uniqueness. Although there are clear limitations as to what metaphors can accomplish, Colwill's analysis points to important dimensions of the change process that are typically not addressed by traditional methods.

Dalitso Sulamoyo, President and CEO of a large anti-poverty network in Illinois, focuses on the potential of peer consulting in the change process. Arguing that the current economic situation and related budget cuts are making it quite difficult for not-for-profits to invest in organizational improvement programs, he underscores the need for a cost-effective approach. Within this context, Sulamoyo examines the mutual benefits of peer consulting as a method of intervention that can facilitate organizational effectiveness and enhance organizational learning. Drawing on the approach used by the Illinois Association of Community Action Agencies (IACAA), the chapter also discusses the learning benefits for the peer consultants themselves and how those benefits can be applied to their respective organizations for continuous improvement.

The chapter details the strengths and limitations of the peer consulting model. Among its many benefits, Sulamoyo points to its potential to provide reciprocal technical assistance and capacity building, ensure empathy and interconnectedness across agencies, and enhance training opportunities as well as create a comprehensive monitoring and technical assistance program in a cost-effective manner. Reflecting on his experience in the community action movement, he also notes a number of ongoing challenges, including a lack of consistency, sub-cultural tensions, and a tendency to focus on problems rather than possibilities and compliance concerns rather than organizational excellence. The chapter concludes with an assessment of the potential of the peer approach as a change model.

Judith Gebhardt, a faculty member at the University of Maryland, explores the similarities and differences between clinical therapy and executive coaching. Noting that even though executive coaching has moved away from its focus on fixing toxic behavior at the top to become an increasingly popular intervention aimed at developing the capabilities of high-potential performers, Gebhardt argues that it is difficult to draw a clear distinction between coaching and counseling. The chapter compares and contrasts the two professions, examining their orientations, educational and licensing requirements, skill sets, values and roles, and ethical considerations as well as the underlying distinctions between "patient treatment" and executive "client session."

Examining the "grey area" between the two professions, she argues that the complexity of change in personal, professional and organizational life has prompted clinicians and coaches to increasingly pursue the same clients, with a blurring of intended outcomes. Potential dangers arise when a behavioral coach slowly drifts toward psychotherapy without making it explicit or when a clinician evolves into a business advisor. As such, she underscores the need to understand the lessons learned from the two fields, noting the potential hazards when one "migrat[es] into the domains of others."

The final chapter in this section by Austrian consultant Kathrin Kordon examines the linguistic challenges involved in international and multicultural consulting processes. She argues that although internationalization has created a growing number of situations that require individuals to "switch" between various "cultures" on a daily basis—including multi-professional teams, interdisciplinary projects, multiple professional identities, and different work places—an overlooked and underappreciated challenge concerns linguistic diversity. She notes that given the widely acknowledged status of English as *the* world language, it has also become the most widely-used language in professional counselling and management consulting in intercultural contexts. Yet, it is rarely English native speakers who prompt a "multilingual" group to speak English. In fact, in many contexts, she argues that although the participants might agree to use English as common code of understanding—the concept of English as *lingua franca*—the reality is that it is not the "mother tongue" for any of them.

Drawing on an interdisciplinary approach at the interface between linguistics and other social sciences, Kordon explores the implications of using English as *lingua franca* (ELF). Following a brief definition of ELF and its ramifications from the perspective of linguists and management consultants, she uses a series of extracts from an audio-recorded intervision group to propose some tentative observations and hypotheses about consulting processes in ELF. Her analysis illustrates that consulting engagements among non-native speakers of English can be carried out successfully despite clear linguistic deviations from native speaker norms. As she concludes, it appears that a high level of proficiency in English (as measured in accordance with native-speakers' norms) does not have to be one of the main prerequisites to work on a global level. The key is to develop sufficient communicative capacity that enables consultants to converse in English with speakers of different cultural and first language backgrounds.

Reflections on Consulting for Change

The final section of the volume contains five chapters that reflect on different dimensions, aspects and challenges in our attempts to bring about organizational change. The lead chapter by Craig Lundberg, who recently retired as the Blanchard Chair of Human Resource Development at Cornell University, posits that while the prevailing rhetoric about management and change is one in which rationality, logic, and analysis dominate, the reality of organizational life is far more "ambiguous, political, emotional and symbolically laden, and constantly changing." As such our views about management, change and consultancy "gloss over the phenomenon of interest" and are in dire need of reconceptualization.

Using a sensemaking approach to conceptualize change and change-related processes, Lundberg presents a series of premises that underlie his conceptualization of change and consultancy. Refocusing organizational change—in terms of sensemaking, mindsets, change recipes and situationally-bracketed projects—he describes change as a series of sensemaking projects involving focusing, analyzing and actioning phases. Change consultancy is also reconceptualized along these lines as a process that provides distress reduction, surfacing, articulating, validating and educating organizational members, and managing the client-consultant relationship. Although Lundberg concludes that "much work remains to be done" with this framework, it promises to enhance our understanding of the complexities of the organizational change process.

The next chapter by Warner Burke, the Edward Lee Thorndike Professor of Psychology and Education at Columbia University, looks at the increased time pressures that shape most consulting interventions today. Noting that "helpful consulting" takes time, he laments the growing reality that clients expect immediate action and instant positive outcomes. Describing his recent consulting experiences as largely "in the moment," working with clients on "one time-limited project after another," Burke briefly explores the growing trend of anti-intellectualism in today's fast-paced corporate world.

The chapter offers a number of suggestions for how to consult in this state of time pressure and delivery demands, in essence conducting one's diagnosis "on the run." Drawing on Kurt Lewin's observation that the best way to understand an organization is to try to change it, Burke shares his thoughts on "real time" diagnosis, "in the moment" executive coaching, and the need to "have a point of view" that helps to explain who we are and how we consult. In the remainder of the chapter, Burke shares his point of view about how organizations work, how to bring about culture change, the dynamics involved in multi-rater feedback processes, talent management, and executive and leadership development.

Continuing a focus on organizational diagnosis and Burke's notion of "helpful" consulting, Dale Ainsworth, a managing partner for a consulting firm in Northern California, describes a methodology that immerses the consultant in the system to uncover highly contextualized and subtle findings. He suggests that this approach is most suitable for situations that are novel, ill-defined, and highly complex. Using the metaphor of "entering into the rabbit hole," he draws on the traditions of cultural anthropologists, ethnographers, heuristic researchers and shamans to examine the principles and practices of immersion as a means to deepen understanding.

The chapter uses a case study of an intervention in a medium-size commercial construction company that underwent a change in ownership to illustrate this approach. The discussion details the different phases of the engagement, from entry and contracting through diagnosis and discovery. As part of the discussion, Ainsworth reflects on the power of "going native" and the process of "climbing out" of the rabbit hole. Through the use of this immersion method, he argues that consultants themselves are transformed along with the systems in which they work—in essence building on the "self-as-instrument" paradigm to include a "self-as-transformed" perspective.

The next chapter by Judith Benson, who has been an internal and external consultant over her career, focuses on healthy closure—helping clients deal with the ending of one part of their career path or company's life so that they are able to regenerate themselves and move on. The chapter provides a framework consultants can use to devise ways to not only help clients, but also themselves as they go through the cycles of their own lives. Comparing the passage through a traumatic event as going through a "ring of fire," Benson explores ways in which we can manage the different levers of loss—how meaning is processed, the need to grieve, inherent conservatism, the pull of the future—and how healthy closure can be achieved.

Using two case vignettes from her consulting practice, Benson illustrates how these processes can facilitate healthy closure. As she suggests, endings, transitions and beginnings are all part of a natural cycle, and, if properly attended to, can result in transformation, adaptation, and resilience rather than more destructive outcomes. The key to success in capturing such healthy closure lies in the consultant's ability to help the client process meaning, manage the tendency toward holding on, and create a space for grieving, while at the same time shoring up the client's pull toward or motivation for the future.

The final chapter in the volume by Pepperdine University professor Kurt Motamedi reflects on the influence that Kurt Lewin's work and ideas have had on our thinking about intervening in organizations and approaches to organizational change and development. As Motamedi notes, as a social activist Lewin strived to improve the human condition and life experience by enhancing our understanding of human relations. Arguing that we are at a pivotal point in the historical progression of human systems development, Motamedi points to Lewin's legacy as a possible foundation in our efforts to advance the humanitarian values and ethics of the consulting field as well as helping to find solutions to the myriad problems we face in the world today.

Noting that Lewin's work was grounded in democratic values, reflective observation, action research and field theory, Motamedi shows how his innovative ideas continue to influence the development of our applied behavioral sciences, contributing to efforts to improve the quality of life and productivity of groups, organizations and institutions. As he suggests, Lewin's work offers a promise to deepen our understanding of the appropriateness of prevailing values, paradigms, purposes and approaches to change and development.

FINAL THOUGHTS

We hope that these contributions will stimulate further practice, research and theory development into the critical questions and issues raised in this volume. Particular emphasis should be placed on more exploration of the role(s) consultation plays in creating and sustaining successful organization change, and how different approaches to consultation affect the processes and outcomes associated with organization change.

We would like to thank the book's contributors for their good-natured colleagueship, patience and willingness to accept constant queries and prodding in moving this volume to completion. As with all the volumes in the *Research in Management Consulting* and *Contemporary Trends in Organization Development and Change* series, our goal is to continue to add insight into the complex, ever-changing fields of management consulting and organization development.

REFERENCES

Beckhard, R. & Harris, R. (1987). *Organizational transitions: Managing complex change.* Reading, MA: Addison-Wesley Publishing Company.

Block, P. (2000). *Flawless consulting* (2nd Ed.). San Francisco, CA: Jossey-Bass/Pfieffer.

Buono, A. F. & Poulfelt, F. (Eds.). (2009). *Client-consultant collaboration: Coping with complexity and change.* Charlotte, NC: Information Age Publishing.

Burke, W. (2008). *Organization change* (2nd Ed.). Thousand Oaks, CA: Sage Publications, Inc.

Fincham, R. (1999). The consultant-client relationship: Critical perspectives on the management of organizational change. *Journal of Management Studies, 36*(3), 335–351.

French, J., & Raven, B. (1959). The bases of social power. In D. Cartwright (Ed.), *Studies in social power* (pp. 150–167). Ann Arbor, MI: University of Michigan.

Jamieson, D. (1995). Guest editor, Special issue on Consultation for organization change. *Journal of Organizational Change Management, 8*(3).

Jamieson, D. (1996). Let's get serious about consulting. *Consultants News.* July/August.

Jamieson, D. (1997). Guest Editor, Special issue on consultation for organization change. *Journal of Organizational Change Management, 10*(3).

Kotter, J. (1996). *Leading change.* Cambridge, MA: Harvard Business School Press.

LaLonde, C. (2009). *Challenging some universal success criteria in management consulting: When practice meets prescription.* Paper presented at the Changing Paradigm of Consulting Conference, 4th International Conference on Management Consulting, Management Consulting Division, Academy of Management, Vienna, Austria, June.

Lundberg, C. & Young, C. (2001). A note on emotions and consultancy. *Journal of Organizational Change Management, 14*(6): 530–538.

Lippitt, G & Lippitt, R. (1986). *The consulting process in action* (2nd Ed.). San Diego, CA: University Associates.

McGivern, C. (1983). Some facets of the relationship between consultants and clients in organizations. *Journal of Management Studies, 20* (3), 367–386.

Sturdy, A., Werr, A. & Buono, A.F. (2009). The client in management consultancy research: Mapping the territory. *Scandinavian Journal of Management, 25*(3), 247–252.

Whittle, A. (2006). The paradoxical repertoires ofmanagement consultancy. *Journal of Organizational Change Management, 19*(4), 424–436.

PART I

FRAMING THE CHANGE CHALLENGE

CHAPTER 1

CONSULTING FOR CHANGE

Creating Value through Client-Consultant Engagement

David W. Jamieson and Terry R. Armstrong

Not everything that is called "consulting" really is "consulting." Some of what passes for consulting is really "task for hire," "an extra pair of hands," or "buying expertise." In these cases the consultant works for the client to complete a specified task(s), provide some information, give answers, or achieve some bounded results. Within this context, determining "value" is generally determined by completing the task in a satisfactory manner or achieving certain outcomes.

In contrast, we prefer to consider "real" consulting (Jamieson, 1996) to be characterized as:

- working with a client in a relationship;
- not knowing the answers or exactly what you'll even do at the start;
- guiding and influencing the client's work and decisions (rather than doing it for them);

Consultation for Organizational Change. pages 3–13
Copyright © 2010 by Information Age Publishing
All rights of reproduction in any form reserved.

- expertise being transferred and getting used with and through others;
- client learning, growing insight and capability; and
- continuous diagnosis and customized intervention content, methods and timing.

While these distinctions are derived primarily from an organization development (OD) orientation, where there has historically been an emphasis on the client-consultant relationship and how consultation is carried out, they apply equally to all forms of consulting and help to distinguish consulting from other forms of helping.

Particularly in situations of consultation for change, the purpose and contract need to be different because:

1. much of the critical work will occur with the client;
2. the client is part of the system being changed; and
3. the client has a special role in leading the change.

In these cases, much of the consultation occurs in the relationship and the nature of the client-consultant relationship becomes both more critical to the outcomes and more important to the change process. In these situations, real "consulting" needs to occur and creating value is both very important and more difficult to determine.

While multiple and differing types of clients may become involved or emerge during a project, our primary emphasis in this chapter is on what Schein (1997) has referred to as the *primary client*—the primary leader one works with in conducting the change. It is this relationship that becomes the critical medium through which value will be created.

OUR GUIDING PREMISE

The basic premise underlying this work is that the best results occur in *engaged* client-consultant relationships and that, as a consultant, one may need to add or do many different things to develop an engaged relationship and that the real value comes when operating *within an engaged relationship*. Real value is determined by the client and will therefore vary across situations. However, it generally involves what the consultant does or says that enables the client or client system to do or change something they were not previously able to accomplish or something desirable or beneficial gained by the client or system through the consultation. The medium for adding value is in the relationship with the client—in the interaction, transfer, and influence. Without an engaged relationship, one is less likely to add value. In fact, you don't really add value if you are attending to the distractions involved in correcting flawed roles or behaviors, recovering from relationship potholes or dealing with deficiencies in interactions with a client. These may all be necessary requirements of the consulting process, but rarely what add value for the client, the system, or what facilitates change.

This premise suggests that the first order of business for the consultant is building an engaged relationship with the client and, it is possible, that the client and consultant may never get past this challenge. In such a case, the consulting work may not add value. When the client and consultant are in a truly engaged relationship, however, then the resources that each brings to the change situation—which are valuable to the work—can be applied to the change work and to related information flows, strategic thinking, learning, collaboration and difficult conversations that will be needed.

An Engaged Relationship

Engagement in a client-consultant relationship is about achieving minimum critical specifications, that is, certain conditions that then allow the consultation and change work to proceed. There are 4 dimensions to engagement and both the client and consultant need to contribute to meeting these conditions:

1. presence;
2. desired roles and behaviors;
3. the nature of the relationship; and
4. quality of the interaction.

Presence

Presence—by both parties—is characterized by showing up, emotionally connecting, being attentive and available, participating, and noticing what *has not* been said. The client's body language and what is not said often tell more than what is said. Covert and unspoken concerns and issues can quickly derail a consultation. Helping the client surface covert behaviors, theories, and concerns can save the consultant and the client a lot of grief and often leads to substantial learning (Marshak, 2006). "Being present" and not judgmental is critical to developing an engaged relationship. Establishing such presence is not easy. It often means taking "quiet time" for 20 or 30 minutes before meeting with the client in order to shut out the noise and demands of the day. If clients appear hurried, it is often necessary to slow them down so they can become engaged rather than being bothered with pre-occupations. Sometimes we ask to "sit in silence" for five minutes so that we can both gather ourselves before beginning the session. Just taking a few minutes of silence can often help us both to be more present to each other and the situation.

Desired Roles and Behaviors

There are a number of roles and behaviors that are necessary for both the client and consultant to execute for the work to be able to progress and engagement to be possible. First, it is critical that the client is the one *in the lead*, not abdicating that role to the consultant. This includes, in particular, visibility in the work, being the primary communicator and making decisions when needed. Secondly, the client must communicate and act in ways that *show commitment and ownership*. For example, it is important that clients express their personal belief in the vision, goals and work, meeting deadlines, and spending time in important project activities. Third, the client needs to be a *strategic thinker* and *understand systems*. They need to be able to see impacts, interdependencies, and how decisions will affect their strategy. They also need to recognize how their business is affected by the external environment in which it operates. Finally, the client has to be able to *imagine a desired future* and *communicate that future as a vision and expectations* to other critical people in the system. It is important for change leaders to translate desires into concrete, organization-specific language, and action and to be able to communicate these as expectations among various stakeholders.

For the consultant's role, it is important to *act as an equal*. One has to be comfortable in *using influence* without being in charge. Consultants cannot be intimidated by clients' power or act in ways that express a greater or lesser position. They need confidence in what they bring to the situation. Consultants need to develop credibility with their clients in order for the clients to provide them with equal power. Second, real consultation requires consultants to *operate as an educator*, identifying client learning opportunities and transferring expertise. Many situations arise that allow for the consultant to use questioning in the service of client learning, provide explanations coupled with actions, help clients develop similar capabilities or coach a client through certain actions instead of doing it themselves. The consultant needs to be interested in actual learning and transfer by allowing the client to initiate more, having reflective conversations with the client on what they see and how they understand what's going on. Effective education needs to show up. Third, consultants also need to be *strategic thinkers* and *understand systems*. They also need to see strategic implications of actions or decisions to operate as an equal and recognize systems connections across the organization in order to help improve how the organization operates.

It is also important for consultants to bring *particular skills and knowledge* to the relationship, especially about change in human systems, organization diagnosis, intervention design, and group and process facilitation. This knowledge and insight needs to be integrated with the client's skills and knowledge in the content and processes of their organization's environment, industry or sector, mission and design. Finally, consultants must be able to *ask clear, reflective questions* based on what they have noticed about the organization, its dynamics and its leaders. These questions are both diagnostic and purposeful. Often, an observation posed as an inquiry, helps the client to see a dynamic differently or re-consider something generally taken for granted. It has been our experience that clients are biased towards action. They often act without thinking and seldom question their assumptions. We have found that to get the client to slow down and examine why they do what they do will often lead them to stop doing it or consider a new direction.

The Nature of the Relationship

The relationship between the client and consultant needs to be characterized by and built on trust, openness, authenticity, directness, truth, a sense of partnership, low ego involvement, and shared goals, means, and values. This foundation in the relationship is critical to the openness, sharing, vulnerability, and honesty that will be necessary during change work. This foundation is similar to that found with close friends in life, where the operable norms engender feelings of safety, belief in the welfare of each other and the outcomes and enough overlap of values that being aligned and in-sync is most prevalent.

Quality of the Interaction

Interactions between consultant and client need to be characterized by a spirit of inquiry, openness to learning, sharing of information and feedback, collaboration, constructive confrontation, challenge, support, professional respect, power balance, integrity, enjoyment, and energy. Both the consultant and client must develop respect for and value each other, yet be able to confront or challenge each other on any issues that could be hindering the work. They also have to experience working together as stimulating and not burdensome. This can be accomplished by careful listening and asking questions that demonstrate the consultant understands the client's world. By taking actions that prove the consultant has heard the clients concerns can also go a long way in building rapport and trust. It also helps if each party minimizes assumptions and righteousness, operates with a desire to learn and understand and uses respect to gauge their feedback, confrontations and challenges.

VALUE IN CONSULTATION

Defining value for consulting and determining whether it is present are highly subjective and qualitative judgments, because what constitutes value for different people and in different situations will vary. Value is generally determined by the client, but it is one of the elements for discussion and agreement during initial or subsequent contracting.

Value can also emerge during an engaged relationship and show up in unexpected ways. For example, sometimes clients find new value in being asked the right question, having their anxiety reduced or confidence improved, or from something specific they learn from a project. Sometimes, clients develop an enlarged picture of their reality or new frames for understanding what they are experiencing. Value can also accrue through changed mindsets where new ideas or perspectives are integrated with existing ways of looking at a situation, or through facilitation that helps them to better deal with a difficult, key relationship.

Consider the following scenario. In a recent situation in a non-profit agency, a client had determined that board roles and relationships were in need of development and clarification in order for them to effectively execute their mission (which they were not currently doing). While technically this was correct and needed, the consultant was also aware of their low commitment, energy, and engagement with their work. Thus an underlying goal was to help them to see and understand the role of vision and how it was missing in their system. By including work on this missing link, board members and the primary client "came alive" and made connections between tasks and mission, and between their own values and emotions and the work of the organization. The short-term effects showed up in improved attendance, more outward signs of commitment, higher levels of support for organization activities and more engaged meetings—in essence, value that occurred, but was not initially envisioned by the client.

In another consultation, in a retail environment, the consultant used questions to surface a client's series of assumptions about poor attendance by staff at team/communication meetings. Using these data on assumptions, the consultant designed a different structure and process, focused on engaging the members in the launch of a new initiative. An empowering invitation and attraction process was used that included greater responsibilities for the staff in the new initiative and more choice in how they will receive future communications. After a couple of well-attended meetings run this way, the client managers and team members adopted the new format, changing attendance norms, participation, quality of information, and decision-making.

Asking Questions

In both instances, asking the appropriate questions led to value for the client. Most consultants, of course, know that asking the "right" question is often critical, but even seasoned consultants inquire about how to formulate good questions. Generally a consultant does not ask the "right" question out of the blue. Skilled consultants typically follow a pattern of question asking, building their inquiry in a systematic fashion, while intently listening to the client and noticing what is not said as well as what is said. Using the stated and unstated input, the next questions are formulated.

Before questioning the client, consultants need to ask themselves questions that raise consciousness about intent and value potential, such as: Why am I asking these questions? What is my objective? What do I hope to accomplish by my questions? Would this question(s) help me if I were in the client's situation? Consultation has a better chance of creating value if one starts with open-ended questions such as: What have you learned from the experience? How do you feel about *X*? When did you first notice *Y*? If you could do anything to solve this issue what would you do?

Building on initial open-ended queries, more specific questions, intended to refine one's understanding and facilitate the client's thought process, are then formulated: Are you assuming something about the way ______ is behaving? Have you checked it out with ______? What would you like to see changed? The next stage is to "tighten" the precision of the questions, which also guides the client's understanding and awareness: What precisely do you need to have changed? Why haven't you done that already? When do you expect to be finished? The question sequence is generally:

1. broad, open-ended questions;
2. still open-ended, but more specific questions; and
3. tighter, converging questions.

The consultant can also use theory and known models to help formulate questions. For example, one might use the principles of the *Johari Window* (Luft & Ingham, 1955) to help formulate questions to learn about the client (e.g., Can you tell me something about yourself? Is this a new feeling or have you experienced it before? How do others generally describe you?). Another approach is Weisbord's (1976) *Six Box* model to gain information about the organization (e.g.,What is your vision for the organization? How are you rewarded for your work? Do you have the necessary tools and resources to achieve your objective? How do you accomplish *X*?)

Inquiring consultants are able to put themselves in the client's shoes, often including empathic statements coupled with questions. For example, "I felt angry when I lost my first big client. How did you feel when ...?" "I noticed you flinched at your boss's comment. Did it make you uncomfortable?" "How did my question make you feel?" As part of this process, consultants should also ask "reflective" questions intended to generate self-searching and self-awareness for the client: Why do you think you responded the way you did? What is the most important thing you learned from the experience? What will you do differently next time?

Finally, consultants should not back away from probing, challenging, or confrontive questions when they need to be asked, for example, "How long have you been doing it this way? Are you really ready to change? Why will it take you two weeks to complete the project?"

If we follow a motto similar to the physician's oath, "First, Do No Harm," we would be forced to think more consciously about the value *for the client* and *his or her system* in the choices we make and the things we do and say in consultation. As an example, if our motto were, "First, Be Helpful," we would need to question if something we are doing, asking, or suggesting is actually helpful for *this* client. We are often supported by the fact that clients can experience value in a wide variety of ways, a reality that allows for a myriad of options to use ourselves, as instruments. An illustration is provided by a consultant who was faced with a client who was poorly and irregularly communicating with him. Since he generally avoided conflict, he fretted about it for awhile, but said nothing. Finally, deciding he also needed to use himself differently, he confronted the client about this communication behavior, how it affected him and their work, and inquiring as to the intention and motivation. What ensued was probably one of their most valuable discussions during the consultation. The client had no negative intentions toward the consultant, but was unsure of some aspects of their project and its visibility and impact within the organization. This feeling led the client to think about how vulnerable he could be in this situation. It turned out that the lack of communication was this client's method of dealing with anxiety, uncertainty and fear. And the behavior experienced by the consultant was the same behavior often experienced by others in the organization. Through the consultation, the client was able to build more confidence, make better choices, learn to keep communication open and regular, and improve his presence and impact with work colleagues.

THE PATH TO AN ENGAGED RELATIONSHIP

If the first order of business in consulting—especially consultation focused on bringing about change—is developing an engaged relationship, then consultants, more than the clients, will need to manage the development of the underlying processes and confront any hindering issues along this path. As summarized in Table 1.1, there are some common classes of needs and problems in *getting to* an engaged relationship. These issues must be dealt with for truly effective consultation, for when we have an engaged relationship, the medium for adding value is in place. Time and attention are no longer needed for building the relationship or for dealing with issues along the path. Now it is possible to be fully heard, influence one another, bring

Table 1.1. Common Needs or Problems in Getting to an Engaged Relationship

Common Needs or Problems	Suggested Consultant Actions
Poor Client Presence:	
• Unreliable showing up • Distracted with other agendas • Passive • Impersonal	• Dedicate time in contracting to setting expectations of presence • Create openings requiring client responses • Dedicate early time to getting to know each other more personally • Confront client behavior • Explain how client's behavior affects the work
Poor Consultant Presence:	
• Low energy • Scattered in client meetings • Passive	• Ask yourself about motivation, interest and valuing of client/system • Use quiet time before meetings for getting focused
Client Role & Behavior Issues:	
• Weak leadership/decision-making • Weak in strategic and systems thinking • Weak in communicating; inspiring • Not taking front role • Ambiguous in statements of commitment • Weak in conceptualizing future • Consultant dependence	• Informally educate • Recommend courses or development • Question motivation, confidence, concerns of client • Structure work on vision and message • Consider adding another resource to augment leader • Clarify roles on the project & key activities • Organize agendas with decisions
Consultant Role & Behavior Issues:	
• Intimidated; passive • Falls into pseudo-leading • Frustrated by not getting through to client • Too much operational involvement • Jumping to conclusions • Naïve about change dynamics • Unclear in communications • Telling, not asking • Doing, not educating	• Self-awareness • Be sure of career interest in consulting role • Development; further education • Shadow consultant help • Focus on role boundaries
Client-Consultant Relationship Issues:	
• Low trust • Guarded communications • Lack of disclosure of information relevant to work • Self-interest; ego intrusion • Misaligned goals, values, processes, etc. • Independent actions	• Dedicate time in a meeting and contracting to sharing values, beliefs, expectations, goals and roles • Discuss hopes and fears; strengths & vulnerabilities on project • Share successively deeper data on who you each are

(*continued*)

Table 1.1. Continued

Common Needs or Problems	Suggested Consultant Actions
Client-Consultant Relationship Issues: (cont.)	
• Interpersonally unattractive	• Build equality by discussing what each brings to the work • Build in periodic feedback and relationship checks • Role & involvement agreements
Client-Consultant Interaction Issues:	
• Too much certainty • Inconsistent information sharing • Power imbalance • Questionable integrity • Lethargy • Withholding of concerns, differences, frustrations • Lack of faith & confidence • Lack of reliance & support • Style clash	• Structure norms for interaction • Provide periodic feedback on interaction experience • Confront specific aberrant behaviors • Keep asking why you're doing this • Clarify what each of you want and need • Discuss fears in project & relationship • Build in inquiry practices

your separate resources to bear on the work, and be really useful in the service of change, without unrelated distractions.

Through the creation of truly engaged relationships, the myriad ways that clients experience value comes alive. For example:

- With more free flowing information and openness, you can together redefine the system's reality.
- With less defensiveness or passivity, new perspectives can emerge or new ways to understand what needs to change can become clear.
- If the client needs to change as part of the process, he or she might be better able to hear and take in the feedback.
- With less intimidation and/or fear, learning can occur.
- Confidence can replace anxiety and both clients and consultants can perform their needed roles for the change.
- With presence and attentiveness, it is possible to better understand the client and what will really add value.
- The use of questions has a better chance of shifting mindsets and influencing client learning.
- The client is more likely to handle resistance and difficult situations directly.
- With more trust and honesty, there are fewer covert dynamics.

Regular checkpoints can be a useful practice to see what value the client is experiencing and how effectively the consulting is moving towards the agreed upon outcomes. Just because the consultant thinks he or she is helping, does not mean it is the case. If the client is not learning new behaviors or taking needed actions, or if something in the consultation is getting in the way of achieving such outcomes, then it may be time to sit down with the primary client and discuss how he or she sees the value of the work and the process of the consultation. These periodic checkpoints also provide an excellent opportunity to surface changed expectations or needs and to re-contract. Clients generally appreciate these prearranged discussions. As consultants, these discussions also help us get feedback and new insights into what works and why.

"First, Be Helpful." Think about the underlying responsibility of such a statement. It requires creating value in the subjective mind of the client. Without an engaged relationship, however, any value is illusive. The work of the client and consultant is fragmented, distracted or focused on recovering from "potholes." Until they both achieve presence, the necessary roles and behaviors, the relationship qualities and the interaction characteristics discussed in this chapter, real value is unlikely to emerge and develop. The potential for learning and changing is thus undermined... and so is the consultation itself.

NOTE

An earlier version of this chapter was presented at the Academy of Management, Management Consulting Division's Third International Conference on "Client-Consultant Cooperation: Coping with Complexity and Change," at the Copenhagen Business School, June, 2007.

REFERENCES

Jamieson, D. (1996). Let's stop calling everything we do 'Consulting.' *Consultants News,* (July–August), 1.

Luft, J., & Ingham, H. (1955). *The Johari Window: A graphic model for interpersonal relations.* Berkley: University of California Western Training Laboratory.

Marshak, R. (2006). *Covert processes at work.* San Francisco: Berrett-Koehler Publications.

Schein, E. (1997). The concept of "client" from a process consultation perspective: A guide for change agents. *Journal of Organizational Change Management, 10*(3), 202–217.

Weisbord, M. (1976). Organizational diagnosis: Six places to look for trouble with or without a theory. *Group & Organization Management, 1*(4), 430–447.

CHAPTER 2

COMPETENCIES OF MANAGEMENT CONSULTANTS

A Research Study of Senior Management Consultants

Léon de Caluwé and Elsbeth Reitsma

Drawing on our earlier studies examining the relationship between consultancy context, objectives and interventions (see de Caluwé & Vermaak, 2003; Reitsma, Jansen, van der Werf & van der Steenhoven, 2003; Reitsma & van Empel, 2004), the chapter looks at these relationships in the context of consultant competencies. The basic focus of our investigation is on those competencies that management consultants need to be able to execute different interventions, especially those related to change processes in organizations. The results of this study promise to give insight into the skills and capabilities that management consultants should have and the resulting ramifications for training, development, professionalization, and selection of management consultants. Although the International Association of Management Consultants has developed a body of knowledge and

Consultation for Organizational Change. pages 15–40
Copyright © 2010 by Information Age Publishing
All rights of reproduction in any form reserved.

skills (ICMCI, 2004), as far as we know, there are no empirical data supporting this work.

The study examines the practice theories (interventions) that experienced management consultants use in practice. Experienced management consultants use implicit and explicit rules, heuristics, and models to diagnose situations, and to decide which approach or intervention will fit the situation. In most cases, this knowledge is "hidden" inside their heads, in essence, part of their tacit knowledge. Our goal was to investigate this collective experience, delving into the relationships and insights that are developed in practice—in other words, we attempted to "empty" the heads of 40 highly experienced management consultants.

The research design is based on the contemporary literature in this area. Lists of interventions and competencies were compiled from existing sources and literature and were used to structure the interviews with the consultants. We also documented remarks and insights that were not categorized in these lists. The interviewees were given two, three, or four cases that represented a broad variety of problem situations. The respondents were asked their views on the problem, the essential elements in the case, which interventions they would choose, and which competencies would be needed. The results provide us with new insights and new research questions for further investigations, which are discussed at the end of the chapter.

RESEARCH MODEL AND THEORETICAL FRAMEWORK

A goal of this study as to make explicit the relations between:

1. the context in which the change took place;
2. the general approach that was applied; and
3. the interventions that were chosen; and the competencies that the consultant needed to undertake the intervention.

The research model that guided this work is captured in Figure 2.1.

The rationale for this choice is as follows. A change takes place in a specific situation—the context (i.e., the combination of objectives of the change and characteristics of the situation). On the basis of this context, the consultant decides on an approach and related interventions. To be able to execute these interventions, a consultant needs certain competencies. Some of these competencies are intervention specific (i.e., they are coupled to the intervention) and some are basic competencies (i.e., they are always needed, independent of the context or specific intervention). The approach that a consultant chooses, the interventions that he or she utilizes and the required competencies are related to background characteristics of the consultant. As an example, one can think of the type of train-

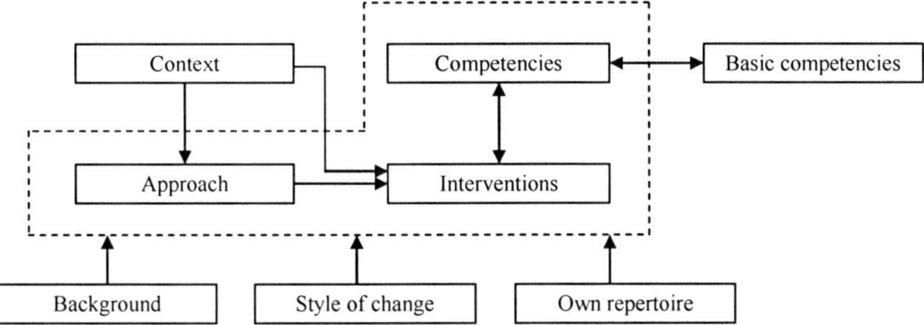

FIGURE 2.1. Research Model: Competencies of Management Consultants in Change Processes

ing that the consultant followed. The same holds true for the personal style of change that the consultant embraces and the repertoire of interventions and competencies that the consultant thinks he or she has mastered (i.e., their own repertoire).

Operationalization of Context

We define context as the situation in which the consultants does interventions or in which the change take place. Thinking about context has its roots in Lawrence and Lorsch's (1967) contingency thinking. The essence of this approach is that the best way to organize is specified by the situation. The "right" way to intervene in organizations is derived from (a cluster of) variables that play a dominant role in the situation. We assume that two main variables play a significant role in establishing the context: 1) the objectives of the change; and 2) the characteristics of the situation in which the change will take place (see, for example, de Caluwé & Vermaak, 2003).

Objectives of the Change

There are several theories that categorize the objectives or content of change. We have chosen 4 types of objectives:

1. strategy and structure;
2. products, services and processes;
3. culture, interaction and leadership; and
4. knowledge, skills and attitudes (e.g., Cummings & Worley, 2005; de Caluwé & Vermaak 2003, 2004).

We wanted to build in a variety of objectives in the research; therefore we constructed four cases in which this variety of objectives was reflected.

Context Variables

The literature has a range of variables that are suggested to influence the choice of a specific intervention. For the purpose of the present study, we searched for a theory that was viewed as rather complete, with assumptions on the relationships between the variables, but without an overwhelming number of variables. We selected Otto's (2000) framework with eight variables, in which each of these variables has a certain value and the variables are related. Otto also provides "rules of thumb" about the connection of the variables and the degree in which certain change strategies are possible (or impossible). The value of each of these variables (and especially the configuration of these variables, combined with the objectives of the change) influences the choice of an intervention. This theory and its eight variables were used as the framework for our research (see Table 2.1). We wanted to explore whether there was empirical evidence for the relationships between the objectives, these context variables and the choice for intervention.

TABLE 2.1. Context Variables and Their Meaning

Context Variables	Variable Meaning...
1. Time pressure	What is the deadline that something must be solved? Is it close to the deadline already? Time pressure can be great or absent, but there can also be no time to work on the problem because all the energy goes to daily operations.
2. Escalation	Is there tension between parties? How intense is it? Are parties capable of collective reflection?
3. Power differences	Does one party have possibilities to influence the behavior of others? Is there a power center or equilibrium between centers? Is approval needed by one of the power centers? Can someone make the decision?
4. Dependencies	Are the persons involved in their work strongly dependent upon each other? Can they work independently?
5. Rules	Are there rules and procedures for decision making? Are the authorities clearly described?
6. Identification with the organization	Does one identify with the organization? Do many people act as spectators?
7. Capabilities for reflection	Is there opportunity for reflection? Is it present or absent? High or low?
8. Knowledge and skills	Does one have all the knowledge and skills to cope with the problem? Is outside expertise needed?

TABLE 2.2. Example of a Case: Variables in Context

A consultancy firm has experienced poor financial results. Inside the company there is an investigation as to what the causes might be. This investigation is carried out among the senior consultants through intensive talks.

From these conversations it becomes evident that the strategy of the firm is obsolete and that the internal structure does not fit with the developments in the market. The senior consultants argue that the firm needs to reconsider its strategy and adapt its internal structure.

Financial results, however, go down further. Management is faced with a fast decision, because the firm will not survive if the situation continues. There is a lot of unrest within the organization and many of the consultants do not have enough work. Most of them feel very involved in the firm and do not leave. But the situation is precarious. People start looking at each other: do you spend enough time on client acquisition and marketing? Are you doing too much internal work? Are we looking enough to the outside world?

The various groups engage in self assessments, focusing on what they can do to confront the situation. They analyze the market and their conversations focus on what each person can do to clear up this situation. Most of the people are experts in the area of strategic assessment and in the area of the target groups they typically work for.

The discussions are very interesting and valuable. But they do not result in a new strategy or structure. The management does not know how to cope with this problem and is considering turning to external help.

Objective:	Strategy and structure
Context variables:	Time pressure: Yes
	Escalation: High
	Power differences: Small
	Dependency: Low
	Identification with the organization: High
	Capability for reflection: High
	Knowledge and skills: Extensive

Four cases were constructed in which the variables in Table 2.1 were systematically incorporated. These four cases create the context for the study. Each of the interviewees was asked to respond to these cases, focusing on their assessment of: the problem, its essential elements, which intervention(s) they would choose, and which competencies would be necessary. Table 2.2 provides an example of one of these four cases.

Operationalization of Consultancy Approaches

We define approach as generic coping with the (problem) situation. There are several categorizations of these approaches in the literature. Each one has different assumptions about change, different ways of steer-

TABLE 2.3. Scheme of Change Approaches

Author	Approaches				
Boonstra & Vink (2004)	Design		Develop		
Beer & Nohria (2000)	Theory E		Theory O		
Weick & Quinn (1999)	Episodic/Planned change		Continuous/Emergent change		
Huy (2001)	Commanding	Engineering	Teaching	Socializing	
Chin & Benne (1970)	Power/ coercion	Empirical-rational	Barter/ rewarding	Normative-re-educative	
De Caluwé & Vermaak (2003)	Yellowprint	Blueprint	Redprint	Greenprint	Whiteprint

ing the change process, and different actors that are involved (see Table 2.3). The study makes a clear distinction between two approaches: design of change and development of change. The first is a planned process with a lot of influence from the change manager and experts, without much attention to interaction and participation. The second is a more evolving and emerging process, with a lot of actors who can exert influence and a high degree of attention to interaction and participation.

Examining the different categories of interventions, we discovered that for all interventions one could choose both of these approaches. For instance, one could undertake a strategy intervention as the expert, in a small group, on the drawing table. But one could also approach the same challenge through a participative process, in a large group setting, as an emergent process. We refer to this as a generic approach.

Our study uses this dichotomy in the degree of participation on a ten point scale, ranging from the expert approach (i.e., expert judgment or proposal, small group) to a more process-oriented approach (i.e., participative, involving large numbers of employees (see Figure 2.2).

Expert approach		**Process approach**
One or small group	1 ———————— 10	Participative
Judgment or proposal by expert		Involvement of employees

FIGURE 2.2. Operationalization of the General Approach

Operationalization of Interventions

We define interventions as one or a series of intended change activities aimed at improving the functioning of the organization (Cummings & Worley, 2005; de Caluwé & Vermaak, 2003, 2004). While interventions can be aimed at the individual, group or organizational level, the study emphasized the group and organization level.

The literature on this subject is abundant and we were inspired by several authors (Boonstra, 2004; Cummings & Worley, 2005; Keuning, 2007; Kubr, 2000; Schein, 1969, 1999). Based on this work, Table 2.4 presents a categorization of these interventions, capturing the relevant authors and their main thoughts related to this categorization. Table 2.5 lists the interventions, definitions and examples that were used in the study.

Operationalization of Competencies

Similar to Hoekstra and van der Sluijs (2003), we define competence as something that someone is good at. Although this definition appears simple, there is a lot of discussion and confusion about the concept. Does competence refer to skill, expertise, attitude, capabilities or knowledge? Competences have to do with generic characteristics of a person, with skills and attitude. The concept is not clear in detail, but we wanted to use this language to be able to communicate with our interviewees about the essential capabilities of a consultant. We collected several theoretical notions and lists of competencies from the literature and compiled them into a list of competencies that might be important in the execution of a change process. This list is a taxonomy that is based on the domains and competencies proposed by Hoekstra and van der Sluijs (2003); Volz and de Vrey (2000); Yukl, (2002); and Yukl, Fable, and Youn (1993). We have also used many of their definitions. The list used in the present study is presented in Table 2.6.

Operationalization of Other Variables

Three variables were used to delineate the background of the consultant. First we documented characteristics of the interviewee: gender, age, experience, specialization, and market sector expertise. Second we gave the interviewees a test that measures their change preferences (referred to as the "puntentest"). This twelve-item (forced choice) test measures individual preferences and feelings of irritations for five theories of change. The result is an individual profile of one's score on these five theories in terms of preferences, blind spots and feelings of irritations. Finally, we asked the

TABLE 2.4. Categories of Interventions

Interventions focused on:	Cummings & Worley	Schein	Kubr	Keuning	Boonstra
Orientation and awareness			Organizational diagnosis and problem solving techniques		Learning and research in action
Strategic questions and images of the future	Strategic programs			Strategy formation	
Adaptation of the structure or ways of cooperation	Technostructural		Structural arrangements Compaign type, action-oriented change programs	Design of organization structure	Structuring organizations
Improvement of business performance and business processes	Technostructural		Compaign type, action-oriented change programs		Business performance

Motivation of employees (with HRM instruments)	Human resources management		Compaign type, action-oriented change programs	HRM-instruments	Employee motivation
Governance and control				Directive tasks	
Training and development	Human process	Coaching and counseling	Training and developing people		Leadership and culture
Processes (social) between people	Human process	Agenda setting interventions Feedback Structural suggestions	Organization development techniques		Group dynamics
Continuous learning and changing by means of interaction					Inquiring, dialogue and narrative; Learning and research in action

Table 2.5. Interventions, Descriptions, and Examples Per Intervention

Interventions focused on:	Description of the intervention and examples
Orientation and awareness: The acknowledgement of the nature and cause of a problem and the awareness of the need for change.	SWOT analysis: mapping the strengths, weaknesses, opportunities and threats of the own achievements and that of the competitors and to know the developments in the environment and to decide upon the strategy.
	Benchmarking: comparing own achievements with those of the best competitors to see on which parts the organization can improve.
	Balanced Score Card: mapping or measuring indicators for performance on finance, business processes, innovation and customers to see on which parts the organization performs according the expectations.
	Causal loop diagrams: mapping cause-effect relations to see repetitions and patterns. The diagrams show which factors can be influenced easily or only in a very complicated way.
	Other examples: Porter's model; Environment scan.
Strategic questions and images of the future: The formation of images of the future of the organization and sharing of the images.	Strategic change plan: making of a plan with objectives and means to realize a desired long term positioning of the organization in its environment, starting from where we are now.
	Search conference: using a conference method (large scale intervention) to create a well-considered desired and reachable future.
	Strategic culture change: developing a strong and shared collective culture that is different of what we have now, but is important for the continuation of the organization
Adaptation of a structure or way of cooperation:	Project organization: a person, group or entity that executes a clear defined assignment within the organization.
The making of provisions and circumstances, fitted to make changes possible.	Temporary groups: task forces that have clear defined tasks (developing new ideas; making priorities).
	Pilot project: experimenting on a small scale with one or some changes.
	New organization entities: the creation of one or more new parts of the organization for example to offer new services
	Adaptation of the structure: the clarification and adaptation of the division of tasks, responsibilities and mechanisms for coordination.
	Outsourcing: placing activities that were executed within the organization outside.
	Other examples: mergers, joint ventures, reorganizations

(*continued*)

Table 2.5. Continued

Interventions focused on:	Description of the intervention and examples
Improvement of business performance and business processes: Changing the business processes in order to improve results.	Business process redesign: a (large) shift or change in the working processes. Total quality: a permanent process to raise customer satisfaction by systematic work on the improvement of products or services. The conference model: using a conference method to reconsider working processes and to improve the relations with customers, following the strategy of the organization
Motivation of employees with HRM instruments: Enhancing the motivation of workers to improve the flexibility or the achievements of the organization.	Rewarding system: a system to improve the performance and satisfaction of employees and to decrease undesired behaviour by rules for rewards and promotion. Selection: placing the right man or woman on the right place. Career development: supporting people in their careers in the organization and the formulation of career goals. Task enlargement: expand parts of tasks on the same level. Task enrichment: expand parts of tasks with higher level work and more room for decision making.
Governance and control: Developing insight in the progress, quantity and quality of the work.	Control: see to it that the work is done properly. Report: making and giving reports on the performance or progress of activities for a certain period. Time sheets: reporting on how much time is spent on activities.
Training and development: Learning of new thoughts, concepts, skills or insights.	Training: learning of skills by managers or employees. Workshops: making people sensible for the need to change, for trends, for different options or for certain methods or concepts. Feedback: letting individuals, groups or the organization see what the effect is of their behavior or performance on others. Coaching or counseling: giving individuals feedback to improve the personal effectiveness, to create more self confidence and to provide them with knowledge and skills. Gaming/simulations: experiencing through gaming what consequences or effects one's own behavior has. Survey feedback: gathering information and knowledge in an active process about problems and solutions and then execute activities based on that information Other examples: 360 degrees feedback

(*continued*)

Table 2.5. Continued

Interventions focused on:	Description of the intervention and examples
Processes (social)between people: Improving social processes in organizations—interpersonal relations, functioning of a team, the relations between teams	Process consultation/teambuilding: helping a group to analyze its own functioning, to find solutions for dysfunctional group processes.
	Search conference: an organization wide meeting in order to find important values and to develop new ways to solve problems.
	Process management: facilitating decision making in complex situations.
	Third party: an independent third party helps the interaction and problem solving between parties.
	Other examples: T-groups; Organization confrontation meeting; intergroup relations; agenda setting.
Continuous learning and changing by means of interaction:	Action learning: creating a context in which one can learn with others. Essential is the exchange of experiences and collective reflection.
Keeping up the process of interaction and communication.	Action research: creating cooperation between researchers and other actors to do research and to learn together.
	Dialogue: creating various ideas about reality, sharing them and constructing new realities on the basis of interaction.
	Narratives/ story telling: creating and finding stories, looking for different views and contradictions, reading between the lines and so creating new stories.

respondents about the interventions and competencies that are part of their own repertoire. The underlying assumption is that these preferences might influence their choice of interventions and competencies.

METHODOLOGY

The study draws on four case vignettes, which were constructed on the basis of two main variables: 1) the different objectives of the change; and 2) the eight variables in the context/situation (see Table 2.1). These four cases (see Table 2.2 for an example) provide a wide variety of problem situations that management consultants might encounter. As noted earlier, for virtually all interventions there is the fundamental choice between an expert approach and a participative approach, captured on a ten-point scale with each approach as polar opposites (see Figure 2.2). As summarized in Table 2.5, we compiled a list of interventions under 9 main categories, with examples and definitions. Finally, the same approach was used to construct a

Table 2.6. Consultant Competencies: Domains, Competencies and Descriptions

Domain	Competencies	Description
Enterprising	1. Boldness	Taking certain risks in order to gain expected long-term benefits.
	2. Individuality	Seeking opportunities and taking action to exploit them. Acting on one's own initiative rather than passively awaiting events.
	3. Independence	Acting on the basis of one's convictions rather than on a desire to please others. Steering one's own course.
	4. Entrepreneurship	Identifying business opportunities and undertaking action, including calculated risks, to take advantage of them.
	5. Market oriented	Being well informed about developments in the market and technology. Using this information effectively in actions.
Showing resilience	6. Adaptability	Acting appropriately by expedient adaptation to changing environments, tasks or responsibilities and to different people.
	7. Flexibility	Changing one's style or approach when new opportunities require such a change.
	8. Stress tolerance	Performing steadily and effectively under time pressure, regardless of setbacks, disappointments or opposition. Reacting calmly and in proportion to the significance of the issue at hand.
	9. Restraint	Being able to adequately control one's emotions and react effectively to those of others, even in emotionally taxing situations. Avoiding undesirable commitments and escalations.
Organizing	10. Monitoring progress	Effectively monitoring progress in one's work and that of others, given the available time and resources, anticipating future developments and taken appropriate timely measures.
	11. Planning	Determining objectives and priorities effectively, planning timely measures in order to attain stated goals.
	12. Organizing ability	Identifying and recruiting people and other resources in order to carry out a plan; allocating them in such a way that the intended results are achieved.
	13. Making coalitions	Seeking and using support, help and sponsors to convince a person or a group.
Performing	14. Result orientation	Focusing one's actions and decisions on intended results and giving priority to the realization of stated objectives.
	15. Attention to details	Paying attention to detail; being able to focus on and deal with detailed information in a sustained way.
	16. Persistence	Sticking to a chosen approach or position until the intended results have been achieved
	17. Quality orientation	Setting high demands with respect to the quality of one's own work and that of others, striving continuously for improvements.
	18. Energy	Being able to be extremely active for long periods when necessary. Working hard; having stamina.
	19. Ambition	Demonstrating an aspiration to be successful in one's career; investing in personal development in order to achieve this.

(*continued*)

Table 2.6. Continued

Domain	Competencies	Description
	20. Legitimating	Showing the legitimacy of a request by the authority or claiming the right to do the request or showing that the request is in accordance with the policy, the rules or traditions in an organization.
	21. Problem solving	Signalizing of (potential) problems and solving these one self or with others.
Analyzing	22. Analytical skills	Breaking a problem down into its component parts; describing its source and structure. Seeking possible causes and gathering relevant data.
	23. Conceptual thinking	Providing wider or deeper understanding of situations or problems by applying another frame of reference or by connecting them with other information.
	24. Learning orientation	Showing an interest in new information, taking in new ideas and developments and applying them effectively.
	25. Creativity	Suggesting original solutions for problems related to one's work; devising new ways of doing things.
Considering	26. Balanced judgment	Comparing possible courses of action and assessing available information, applying relevant criteria. Making realistic judgments and decisions based on such assessments.
	27. Awareness of the external environment	Keeping well informed about societal and political developments and relevant issues in the environment; using this knowledge to the advantage of the organization.
	28. Generating vision	Identifying the main direction for the organization in relation to its environment; formulating long-term objectives and strategies.
	29. Innovating	Creating new and original ideas, ways of working and applications by combining formal and informal information, existing and new solutions and approaches.
	30. Awareness of organizational context	Demonstrating an understanding of how things work in an organization, taking the consequences for one's own organization and that of the customer into account in one's action.
Facilitating	31. Customer orientation	Enquiring about the needs and wishes of customers and clients and showing that one's thinking and actions reflect them.
	32. Coaching	Supporting others in the execution of their work. Motivating others and making them think about improving their own behavior. Being a partner for talking and listening.
	33. Co-operation	Contributing actively to achieving a common aim, even when this is not in one's personal interest; fostering helpful communication.
	34. Listening	Picking up important signals and messages in oral communication and giving space to others to express themselves, paying attention to their reactions, responding appropriately and, where necessary, asking further questions.
	35. Sensitivity	Showing that you recognize feelings, attitude and motivation of others and be open for it. Understanding one's own influence on others and taking that into account.

(*continued*)

Table 2.6. Continued

Domain	Competencies	Description
	36. Accuracy	Acting careful and punctual, aimed at the anticipation of failures. Detailed execution of activities.
	37. Inspiring	Creating enthusiasm for a request or proposal by evoking values, ideals and aspirations of a group or person or showing that a person or group has the qualities to do a task or achieve a goal.
	38. Awareness of costs	Taking into account returns and costs in short and long term. Recognize costs.
	39. Personal appeal	Making a personal appeal upon the loyalty or sympathy of a person or group.
Influencing	40. Communication	Communicating ideas and information clearly and correctly so that the essential message comes across and is fully understood.
	41. Presentation	Presenting oneself in such a way that the first impression is positive, turning such an impression into lasting respect or sympathy.
	42. Persuasion	Presenting ideas, points of view or plans convincingly to others so that they agree and approve, even after initial hesitation.
	43. Sociability	Making contacts easily and maintaining relations with others, when required for work purposes; mixing easily with all kinds of people.
Managing	44. Decisiveness	Making decisions by taking action or expressing an opinion, even when the situation is unclear or inherently hazardous.
	45. Leadership	Giving direction in an inspiring way. Being a role model. Encouraging and bringing about teamwork and maintaining good cooperation to achieve an intended goal.
	46. Delegation	Assigning clearly delimited tasks and responsibilities to the appropriate individual(s) when necessary, being able to entrust one's work to others.
	47. Communicating vision	Communicating the direction in which the organization is developing in an appealing way and creating support for strategic objectives.
	48. Consultation	Letting people participate in the strategy, activity and change when support and assistance of them is required. Changing a proposal in such a way that interests and suggestions are taking in.
	49. Negotiating skills	Acting in the interest of one's own unit or organization in direct contacts with counterparts, in such a way that profitable results are attained without loss of mutual respect.
	50. Diplomatic	Capability to recognize interests of others, to assess them and take them in account tactfully.
	51. Awareness of risk	Recognize and assess risks and hindrances. Assessing the influence of them on persons, organization or environment.
	52. Networking	Developing and maintaining contacts and cooperation with others.
Integrity	53. Integrity	Maintaining social and ethical standards at work, even when under pressure to be less particular. Inspiring confidence in one's professional integrity.

(*continued*)

Table 2.6. Continued

Domain	Competencies	Description
	54. Reliability	Keeping to arrangements and promises and accepting their consequences. If things don't work out, taking responsibility for their consequences and, whenever possible, avoiding a negative impact on others.
	55. Loyalty	Complying with the policies and interests of the organization and group to which one belongs. In situations where there are conflicting interests, supporting the position of one's own group or at least avoiding damage to that position.
	56. Creating a favorable atmosphere	Giving compliments, seducing, being friendly or helpful to create a good mood with a person or a group.

list of competencies, with 10 domains and each domain having several competencies (56 competencies; see Table 2-6). The background characteristics of the interviewees, their change preferences, and their own repertoire of interventions and competencies were also measured.

Selection of Respondents

The 40 management consultants who were interviewed were selected from the list of members of the Dutch Association of Management Consultants and from the network of the researchers themselves. A reputation method for the selection was used: a minimum of 10 years of experience was needed; and all respondents had to have a solid reputation in the field and in the country. Consultant reputation was based on responses from an independent group of professional peers when asked for names of the best consultants in the country. No one who was approached refused to cooperate, and most of them were flattered that they were asked for their cooperation. Together the consultant respondents represent more than 900 years of consultancy experience.

Interviews

The interviews took each 1.5 to 2 hours. Depending on the available time and pace of the interview, we did 2, 3 or in some instances 4 cases per interviewee. After the respondents had read a case, they were asked:

1. what they saw as the essentials of case;
2. the approach they would choose;
3. which intervention(s) they would use; and
4. what competencies were needed for success.

This process was repeated for each case. Finally we asked the respondents for their views on the basic competencies of a consultant and their own self-reported repertoire of competencies.

Processing and Analyzing the Data

Three methods were used to process the data. Responses from the interviews were coded and analyzed (quantified). The answers and choices the interviewees gave reflected their general approach (see Figure 2.2) and the lists of interventions (see Table 2.5) and competencies (see Table 2.6). These responses are quantitative data. These data were analyzed through counting and correlating the variables through the SPSS program. The interview transcripts were coded with the help of Atlas.ti. We then used the method of "snow cards" (Geurts, de Caluwé, & Stoppelenburg, 2000). Parts of the coded sentences were combined under similar concepts or categories, which were both quantitative (how many times they appeared) and qualitative (what was exactly meant). Representative quotes and examples were also taken from the interviews as illustrations.

RESULTS AND ANALYSIS

Using SPSS we looked for significance and strength of relationships between the variables. Figure 2.3 summarizes the significant relationships ($p < 0.05$) between the variables. The solid lines reflect over 60% of the respondents mentioning this relationship. The arrows give the direction of the relationship.

Most of the relationships depicted in Figure 2.3 were expected. One interesting finding was that there was no direct relationship between approach and intervention. Based on the views of the consultants in the study,

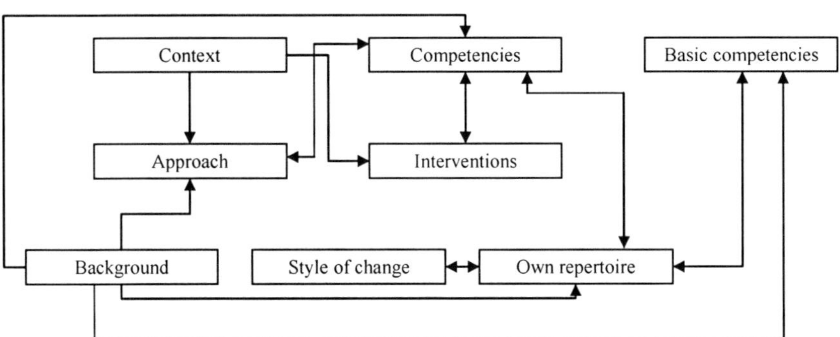

FIGURE 2.3. Overview of Significant Relationships in the Research Model

TABLE 2.7. Basic Competencies of Management Consultants

Domain	Basic Competency
Enterprising	-
Showing resilience	Flexibility
Organizing	-
Performing	-
Analyzing	Analytical skills
	Conceptual thinking
	Learning orientation
	Creativity
Considering	Balanced judgment
	Awareness of external environment
	Generating vision
Facilitating	Listening
	Sensitivity
Influencing	Communication
	Presentation
	Persuasion
	Managing
Inspiring confidence	Integrity
	Reliability
	Loyalty
	Creating a favorable atmosphere

it appears that the choice for a generic approach and an intervention is tenuous. As noted earlier, most interventions can be done in either an expert-based or process-oriented approach.

Competencies

We began with the assumption that there are basic competencies that every consultant should have—without any distinction by age or experience. The respondents were asked which competencies management consultants (independent from their experience and from specific interventions) need with respect to the ability to deal with change processes. Table 2.7 provides a summary of the basic competencies mentioned by at least 40% of the respondents. The basic competencies belong to six of the ten domains:

TABLE 2.8. Competencies Consultants Need in Expert and Process Approaches

Approach	Competencies
Expert approach	Boldness, Independence, Entrepreneurship, Market oriented, Result orientation, Quality orientation, Analytical skills, Conceptual thinking, Generating vision, Persuasion, Leadership, Consultation, Awareness of risk, Reliability, Loyalty, Creating a favourable atmosphere
Process approach	Restraint, Organizing ability, Making coalitions, Energy, Conceptual thinking, Learning orientation, Awareness of organizational context, Coaching, Listening, Sensitivity, Personal appeal, Decisiveness

showing resilience, analyzing, considering, facilitating, influencing and inspiring confidence. There were no basic competencies mentioned in the enterprising, organizing, performing and managing domains.

There were several relationships between approach and competencies (see Table 2.8). The expert approach and the process approach have relations with some of the basic competencies as mentioned in Table 2.10 and they have relations with other competencies (not mentioned as basic competencies) as well. The latter we call "approach-specific competencies." In Table 2.8 the expert approach has sixteen competencies. Nine of them are approach-specific competencies: entrepreneurship, market oriented, boldness, independence, result orientation, quality orientation, leadership, consultation and risk awareness. From the competencies that consultants need in a process approach, eight of the twelve competencies are approach-specific competencies: restraint, organizing ability, making coalitions, energy, awareness of organizational context, coaching, personal appeal and decisiveness.

Table 2.9 provides a summary of the competencies that management consultants need for the execution of interventions, containing the nine interventions (see Table 2.5) in seven rows because some of the interventions (structure, business process, HRM-instruments) have a relationship with the same competencies. These so called *intervention-specific competencies* are planning, organizing ability and being result oriented. Some of the other listed interventions are related to basic competencies, intervention-specific competencies and mostly both of them. Intervention orientation and awareness is only related to basic competencies (analytical skills, conceptual thinking, listening and sensitivity). In other words, orientation and awareness seems to be an intervention that every consultant should be able to practice.

There were three patterns in the relationship between interventions and competencies:

TABLE 2.9. Competencies Needed for Different Interventions

Intervention	Competencies
Orientation and awareness	Analytical skills, Conceptual thinking, Listening, Sensitivity
Strategy and images of the future	Analytical skills, Generating vision, Awareness of organizational context
Structure, Business process HRM	Planning, Organizing ability, Result orientation
Governance and control	Boldness, Planning, Result orientation, Attention to details, Problem solving
Training and development	Coaching, Inspiring
Processes between people	Awareness of organizational context, Listening, Sensitivity
Continuous learning and changing	Coaching, Sensitivity, Inspiring

- The "hard" interventions, which are more instrumental (in the area of structure, business processes, HRM instruments, governance and control) correlated with competencies from the Organizing and Performing Domains.
- The interventions aimed direction seeking (strategy) and processes between people correlated with competencies from the Analyzing, Considering and Facilitating Domains.
- The "soft" interventions (training and development and continuous, processes between people and learning and changing) correlated with the Considering and Facilitating Domains.

Summary: Basic Competencies, Approach-Specific Competencies and Intervention-Specific Competencies

Combining Tables 2.7 to 2.9 provides an overview of the competencies that management consultants need as basic competencies and for the execution of different approaches and interventions (see Table 2.10).

TABLE 2.10. Overview of Basic Competencies and Approach- specific and Intervention-specific Competencies

Approach-specific Competencies	Intervention-specific Competencies
• ***Expert approach***: Entrepreneurship, market oriented, boldness, independence, result orientation, quality orientation, leadership, consultation and risk awareness • ***Process approach:*** Restraint, organizing ability, making coalitions, energy, awareness of organizational context, coaching, personal appeal and decisiveness	• ***Strategy and processes between people***: Awareness of organizational context • ***Structure, processes and HRM***: Planning, organizing ability en result oriented • ***Governance and control***: Boldness, planning, result oriented, attention to details and problem solving • ***Training, development and continuous learning and changing***: Coaching and Inspiring

Basic Competencies

- **Showing resilience:** Flexibility
- **Analyzing:** Analytical skills, Conceptual thinking, Learning orientation, Creativity
- **Considering:** Balanced judgement, Awareness of external environment, Generating vision
- **Facilitating:** Listening, Sensitivity
- **Influencing:** Communication, Presentation, Persuasion
- **Inspiring confidence:** Integrity, Reliability, Loyalty, Creating a favourable atmosphere

At the bottom of Table 2.10 are the basic competencies that every consultant needs. At the left are the two generic approaches: expert and process. The competencies needed for these approaches are listed. At the right are the four clusters of interventions that we found, with the competencies needed for each of these clusters:

- Strategy and images of the future and processes between people;
- Structure, business processes and HRM instruments;
- Governance and control; and
- Training and development and continuous learning and development through interaction.

In Table 2.10 the basic competencies are not listed in the approach-specific and intervention-specific clusters anymore.

Context Variables

Based on the analysis of the coded interview data, it appears that in contexts with low time pressure and high escalation the consultants recommended a process-oriented approach. When there is a lack of pressure and when there is much conflict or disagreement, the process model seems the only way out. People need to be captured (on a voluntary basis) in an arena where they want to come to agreement. In contrast, an expert approach was preferred in contexts with high time pressure, reasonable degree of escalation, great power differences, high dependencies and low identification, low ability to reflect, and low knowledge. Then there is no time for much discussion, there is an (accepted) locus of power which can act and people are not inclined to come to action themselves and they miss the capabilities to do so.

It also appears that the management consultants in the study always look especially for two of our eight variables: time pressure (i.e., if not present, there is not a problem!) and power differences (i.e., if there is not a powerful management, the consultant cannot help). Escalation is sometimes a relevant variable, especially when escalation is high: at this point something needs to be done, because the organization itself is not capable to do so. The other context variables were not seen as relevant.

DISCUSSION AND CONCLUSIONS

Overall, this study was a learning experience. The conceptualization of the study itself was a discovery trip through the relevant literature and concepts. The construction of the cases and compilation of the lists of interventions and competencies were also enormous learning processes. In addition, most of the interviews produced learning moments for the respondents as well.

Competencies

Is every consultant capable of using all approaches and interventions? Are there clusters of competencies that are needed for certain interventions and certain types of consultants?

The respondents felt that the basic competencies were important for all consultants. They should, therefore, be part of every training program for consultants. The study suggests that consultants need to know both approaches—the expert and process-based approaches—being aware of the choice between them, and when one might be more appropriate than the other. This suggestion does not mean that one has to be strong in both approaches: one can choose not to execute certain change processes, because one knows already that one's effectiveness is likely to be low.

Most interventions require competencies that are specific for a particular intervention. These competencies are related to clusters of competencies and interventions and thus to profiles of consultants. In this way we discovered on an empirical basis four clusters of interventions and related competencies. These clusters can be seen as a typology of four kinds of consultants: Strategy and Futuring-consultants; Improving the Business-consultants; Governance and Control-consultants; and Training and Learning-consultants, each with its own set of interventions and competencies (see Table 2.10).

What type of consultant do you need for which kind of problem and for which context?

Certain contexts ask for specific approaches, interventions and competencies. Although we found strong relationships between these factors, we do not have simple prescriptions or recipes. The overview Table 2.10 provides is the clearest picture we can make. The typology that develops from these relationships refers to different consultants with specific interventions and competencies. We also discovered that consultants all need certain basic competencies.

Do background characteristics of the consultant influence the choice of an approach or intervention?

It appears that this is not the case. Based on the views of this group of experienced consultants, the choice of an intervention is situational. They choose interventions, independent from their own style, preferences or repertoire. They tend to make similar choices in similar situations, suggesting that there is a professional body of knowledge within consulting.

Can we develop a typology of profiles for consultants with related competencies?

Yes, a key point that is an outcome of this study. We found basic competencies that everybody needs: young, old, experienced, and new consultants. Every consultant needs to know the two generic approaches and, if possible, have the ability to execute them. Every consultant should also have one or more dominant (clusters of) interventions in his or her repertoire, with the related competencies that are needed for these to be successful. However, it is also clear that the ability to master all interventions and competencies could very well be an impossible task, even for skilled consultants. In other words, consultants need to specialize.

Limitations and Future Research

In the four cases used in the study not all the competencies were mentioned. Nevertheless we maintained the list of 56 competencies for two reasons. First, the four cases are a selection that does not cover all the possible problem situations for consultants. Second, we want to gain some more experience with the present list of competencies and reconsider a possible reduction in a later phase of this work.

A major limitation of this research is that it studies espoused theory (i.e., what consultants say that they are going to do, not what they actually do). We have tried to minimize this disadvantage through the use of real practice-based cases, stimulating the respondents to paraphrase the text in their own words and understandings. We noticed that all of the respondents could see the cases as real. In a future study we want study consultants in a simulated environment, in which the consultancy process is done by role play. This design might enable us to focus on what consultants actually do in practice.

The study is also based on highly-experienced consultants, with a goal of "emptying the heads" of these individuals. This selection, however, could also reflect a truncated range in the consulting world, a potentially biased view from older consultants who were trained "in the past" and in the Dutch tradition. The younger generation or a consultant working in a different culture might have quite different perspectives.

Implications for Practice

We expect that this study can be used by consultants, consultancy training institutions and consultancy firms. Many aspects of this study can also be used for learning purposes—a through introspection: duo-learning, intervision (i.e., a form of collegial feedback between individuals), coaching, action research, reflective talks, assessments, and so forth. To support this, we created a Self Test based on the materials in this research. The Self Test is a 360-degree feedback instrument (see Figure 2.4). A consultant fills in the lists of interventions (based on Table 2.5) and competencies (Table 2.6) and questions for reflection (e.g., have I executed this intervention and/or do I have this competency? Can I develop it?). The consultant would then ask a colleague, his boss and/or his employees to fill out the same information on him or her. By comparing the lists and by opening the dialogue about the differences and similarities, one can explore strengths and weaknesses and discover chances and points for development and learning.

The data in the study also allow us to create a categorization of the competencies in terms of how they can be developed and learned. Some

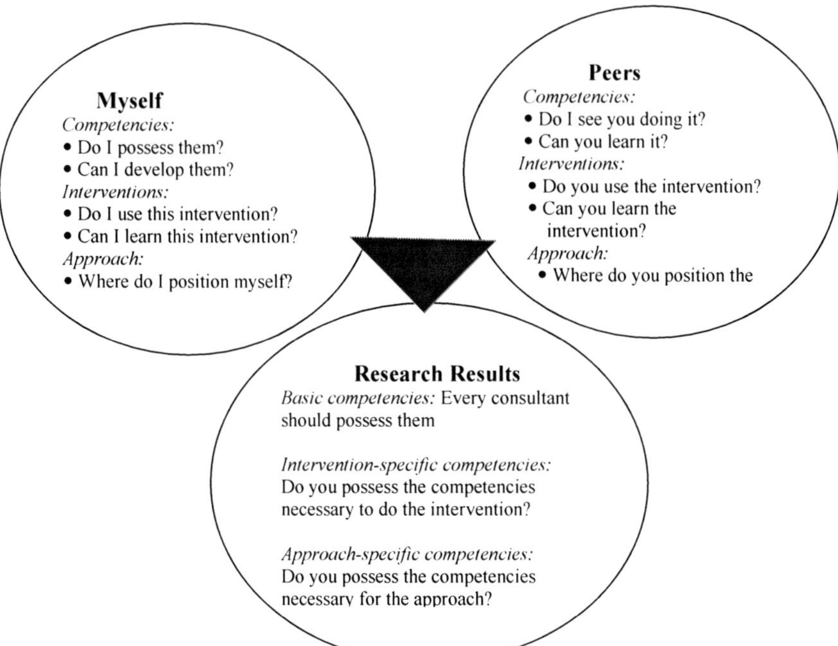

FIGURE 2.4. The Self Test

of them, for example, can be learned in school. It is basically a question of studying and applying the theory. The Analyzing competency is an example. Other competencies can only be learned in practice. Feedback, assessments, duo-learning, and supervision are ways to develop this type of competencies, for example, Listening and Building Coalitions. Still other competencies might be far more difficult to learn, as they are an inherent part of the talent and disposition of a person. If you have these talents—for example, the ability to create a favorable atmosphere—you might just have the capability to become a good consultant.

REFERENCES

Beer, M. & Nohria, M. (Eds.)(2000). *Breaking the code of change.* Boston, Harvard Business School Press.

Boonstra, J. J. (2004a). *Lopen over water, over dynamiek van organiseren, vernieuwen en leren* [*Walking on water, about dynamics of organizing, innovating and learning*]. Amsterdam: Vossiuspers.

Boonstra, J. J. (2004b). Conclusion: Some reflection and perspectives on organizing, changing and learning. In J. J. Boonstra (Ed.), *Dynamics of organizational change and learning* (pp. 447–475). Chichester, UK: John Wiley & Sons.

Chin, R., & Benne, K. D. (1976). General strategies for effecting changes in human systems. In W. G. Bennis, K. D. Benne, R. Chin, & K. E. Corey (Eds.), *The planning of change* (3rd ed.). (pp. 22–45). New York: Holt, Rhinehart and Winston.

Cummings T. G., & Worley, C. G. (2005). *Organization development and change* (8th ed.). Mason, OH: Thomson/South-Western.

de Caluwé, L., & Vermaak, H. (2003). *Learning to change. A guide for organization change agents.* Seven Oaks, CA: Sage Publications.

de Caluwé, L., & Vermaak, H. (2004). Change paradigms: An overview. *Organization Development Journal, 22*(4), 9–18.

Geurts, J., de Caluwé, L., & Stoppelenburg, A. (2000). *Changing organisations with gaming/simulation.* The Hague: Elsevier.

Hoekstra, H. A., & van der Sluijs, E. (2003). *Managing competencies: Implementing human resource management.* Assen, The Netherlands: GITP, Van Gorcum.

Huy, Q. N. (2001). Time, temporal capability, and planned change. *Academy of Management Review, 26*(4), 601–623.

International Council of Management Consulting Institutes. (2004). *Professional standards: Competency model and competence framework UK.* Vancouver: ICMCI.

Keuning, D. (2007). *Management: A European perspective.* Groningen: Wolters-Noordhoff.

Kubr, M. (Ed.) (2002). *Management consulting: A guide to the profession* (4th ed.). Geneva: International Labour Office.

Lawrence, P. R., & Lorsch, J. W. (1967). *Organization and environment: Managing differentiation and integration.* Boston: Division of Research, Graduate School of Business Administration, Harvard University.

Otto, M. (2000). *Strategisch veranderen in politiek bestuurde organisaties [Strategic change in organizations steered by politics].* Assen, The Netherlands: Van Gorcum.

Reitsma, E., Jansen, P., van der Werf, E., & van der Steenhoven, H. (2003): *Report project change.* Amsterdam: Vakdirectoraat Consultancy Deloitte/Center for Research in Consultancy.

Reitsma, E., & van Empel, F. (2004). *Wegen naar verandering [Routes for change].* The Hague: Academic Service.

Schein, E. H. (1969). *Process consultation: Its role in organization development.* Reading, MA: Addison-Wesley.

Schein, E. H. (1999). *Process consultation revisited: Building the helping relationship.* Reading, MA: Pearson Education/Addison-Wesley.

Volz, A., & de Vrey, M. (2000). *Competentiemanagement sjabloon [Patterns of competency management].* Amersfoort: Twynstra Gudde.

Weick, K. E., & Quinn, R.E. (1999). Organizational change and development. *Annual Review of Psychology, 50,* 387–418.

Yukl, G. (2002). *Leadership in organization.* Upper Saddle River, NJ: Prentice-Hall

Yukl, G., Fable, C. M., & Youn, J. Y. (1993). Patterns of influence behaviour for managers. *Group and Organization Management, 18,* 5–28.

CHAPTER 3

WHOLE SYSTEM CONSULTING

Michael D. Mitchell

Consulting is one of those words like communication or motivation—it has many meanings to different people. Over the years I have spent as an organization consultant, I have practiced my "elevator speech" so that I can succinctly explain to people who ask what I do. I am still practicing; it isn't easy to compose a short description that makes it clear what organization consultants do in practice. Part of the problem is that there are a great many activities that clients and consultants alike label as consulting—and these depictions vary considerably. I won't attempt to describe all the things that are perceived as consulting, but I will offer a simple way to categorize consulting activities into broad categories.

CONSULTING TYPES

Consulting can be broken down into three basic categories—"expert," "service provider," and "peer/coach." As each of these approaches has pros and cons, advantages as well as disadvantages, it is not the intent of the chapter to suggest that one is necessarily better than the others. Instead, the focus is on exploring some of the implications that different types of consultation have for the organization and its members.

Consultation for Organizational Change. pages 41–55
Copyright © 2010 by Information Age Publishing
All rights of reproduction in any form reserved.

The Expert

Primarily, consultants who serve as experts tend to offer clients knowledge and/or packaged products. They provide specialized information about markets, competitors, options for action, diagnostic information about the client system, and solutions to problems. They may survey the organization's operations and then recommend a course of action that they may or may not apply. Their work is complete when they have provided the requested information or recommended course of action. They are typically not involved in the organization past delivery of the contracted information or action.

The benefit of using experts is that they can introduce new ideas or options to their clients—ideas and options that the clients themselves lack or have failed to consider. If these ideas are then acted upon by the client organizations, they have the potential to exert a valuable effect on their clients. The negative aspect of drawing on experts is that clients are typically not involved in the diagnosis and action planning to resolve organization issues. As such, clients are typically no more skilled or capable of solving future issues than they were prior to employment of the expert(s).

The Service Provider

Consultants who serve as an "extra pair of hands" typify this approach. They are not likely to be involved in the diagnosis of client issues, but are brought in to implement a client-decided solution. Many organizations today are involved in out-sourcing, which is a case of using service providers to perform actions which the client organization desires but does not have the expertise or resources to perform on its own.

The benefits of hiring service providers or out-sourcing are that the organization doesn't need to add staff to accomplish desired results. Selected services can be purchased and, when no longer needed, the contract can be terminated. Moreover, the provided services can be delivered at a high level of quality by experienced providers. The negative side of using service providers is that the services provided may not be in line with the client's actual needs. The client, in self-diagnosing his or her organization, is often unaware of the actual causes of problems. It has been my experience that clients do not understand the causes or natures of their problems; if they did, they would probably have already solved them and moved on. Burke (2002) speaks to this when he cites the difference between the "presenting problem" and the actual problem.

Peer/Coach

Consultants who operate from this perspective join with the client in diagnostic efforts, selection of alternatives, and, often, the application of solutions. Consultants who take this approach perceive their work as helping the client to grow stronger through learning about his or her organization, working to identify critical issues, developing solutions, and applying them. The consultant may both coach the client on what to do and work "shoulder to shoulder" with the client in moving through the problem-solving process.

The benefits of this approach are that clients have maximum opportunity to learn and grow in this consulting relationship, and to be in a better position to deal with future problems. Additionally, since organizations are complex entities, both the client and consultant can begin the consultation without a commitment to the action to be taken; the action is determined by the joint efforts to understand the organization's functioning and needs. The negative aspect of this approach is that many clients do not perceive themselves as individuals who are involved in problem-solving, seeing themselves instead as individuals who direct others to solve the problems that they have identified. Additionally, not all clients want to be learners, involved in identifying how the organization actually functions.

Consulting Approaches and Dilemmas in Practice

Although the choice of the different approaches appears fairly straightforward, the dilemma is often one of "fit," where both the client and consultant are comfortable with the same approach. Clients whose preferences are not met by the consultant's may become disappointed or angry, and may fire the consultant for failing to deliver according to client expectations. Consultants, on the other hand, who feel forced to perform in a manner they deem ineffective or inappropriate, may feel both frustrated and ethically challenged.

Client Preference

One of the dilemmas in consulting revolves around the client's choice of consulting approach. Clients unconsciously choose the type of consultants hired, based on their own needs. As noted above, not all clients wish to work on a peer basis with a consultant, preferring instead to bring in experts or service providers to carry out actions consistent with the client's view of the organization and its needs. The classic opening line from potential clients—in essence, confusion of a problem with a solution—is something along the line of, "We have a problem; we need training!" Experienced consultants take such an opening with a "grain of salt," suspecting that something is not going well in the client organization, with the client deciding that the perfect solution to fix whatever is not going well is to train the affected individuals.

Part-system View

A second dilemma is that clients rarely take, nor do they ask their consultants to take, what organization development (OD) practitioners frequently espouse, a whole-system view. If the problems are in manufacturing, then it can easily be argued that manufacturing is where the work should take place. As such, clients identify sub-systems and specific areas of perceived need as the "itches that need to be scratched." It is most uncommon for clients to take a systems perspective, that everything that goes on in the organization is connected and that an intervention in one sub-system has an effect on other sub-systems. The consequence is that consultants are often put to work in a limited number of sub-systems, without access to the larger system.

Consultant Limitations

A third dilemma is the understandable leaning of consultants toward issues and content with which they are most familiar. If they are strong in financial analysis, the issues addressed often tend to be financial in nature. For organization consultants, there is an often unconscious tendency to perform as a management consultant (focused primarily on supporting and/or changing management behavior), rather than as an organization consultant.[1] This is often due to the fact that many organization consultants have been trained in the behavioral sciences and are largely unfamiliar with or uninterested in the work processes employed in client organizations.

As a consequence, these individuals often opt for a focus on working with the human systems of the organization, making the assumption that well-aligned human systems will lead to a better application of technical systems. And, since the client is typically a manager, this perspective leads to focusing consulting efforts on improving the systems of management. An alternate view is that it is the system, the organization, that is the client, and it is the work of the consultant to aid the system to function more effectively.

A Personal Perspective

As an organization development consultant, I have always considered OD to be a form of consulting that should take the peer approach. I have always believed that my efforts should be directed at helping the client become more effective, and, in essence, to work myself out of a job. In my experience, the peer approach does this best.

There is also a difference between taking an expert approach to consulting and actually being an expert. It is the business of OD consultants to be experts in a number of areas: coaching, process intervention, providing feedback, training, team-building, process improvement, and knowledge of potential organization interventions, among others. Being an expert in those aspects of consulting provides consultants with the needed expertise to work effectively as peers and coaches to help clients become better at their roles in their organizations.

INTERVENING IN ORGANIZATIONS

When one is working with a client to make the organization more effective, it is a continual issue for the consultant to observe what the organization is doing so that the consultant can search for potential interventions that will move the organization in the direction of improved performance. This focus on interventions requires the consultant to have a wide view of potential interventions as well as a sense of the results that these interventions engender. I think of interventions as means of prodding the organization in the right place at the right time, so that the organization alters its course to head more in the client's desired direction. Some interventions are simple and take only a moment to undertake, and some require a considerable amount of time and effort to accomplish. And, some interventions work as predicted, and some have an entirely unpredictable (even disastrous) result. I tend to label these as "diagnostic experiences" because they tell me that there was something about the organization that I misread completely. Explaining failed interventions to clients is easiest if you have contracted ahead of time not to be required to be perfect.

Reflecting Back: The Choices I Have Made

When I began my career as an OD consultant, I didn't experience any dissonance about the orientation I would take (expert/service provider/peer/coach), and elected to operate from the peer perspective. Part of this was instinct, but it was also the case that I was no expert, and had no unique expertise to offer. In addition, I was not predisposed to accepting clients' self-diagnoses, because it seemed to me that clients were often wrong in their assessments of problems, causes, and appropriate solutions.

I did, however, fall easily into operating as a management consultant, particularly in the early stages of my career, when any offer of employment of my services was exciting and desirable, and when clients tended to expect management consultation rather than organization consultation. In addition, my background in the behavioral sciences led me unerringly in the direction of focusing on the human systems (and not the technical systems) of the client organizations.

The Focus of this Chapter

There would be little point in writing a chapter that simply repeated what others have said and will say again about consulting and organizational change. Instead, the focus is on exploring some of the implications of consultation from the perspective of an uncommon intervention. The intervention is one I have developed and refined over several decades, and represents the best approach that I know to helping an organization become vastly more successful at doing whatever it does.

I ask you to assume modesty on my part when I say that this intervention is successful beyond the wildest dreams I ever had in my early years as an organization consultant; it is the intervention itself that yields results, not my own enlightened form of consultation. In describing this approach, I will set the stage by explaining how I came to this intervention and what caused me to depart from traditional organization consulting.

When referring to an intervention as successful, I am referring to the speed, low cost, and lack of recidivism that clients experience in increasing bottom line performance by factors of anywhere from 4 to 25. These are amounts of performance improvement, measured in dollars, which I never saw in the many years of working as a behavioral-focused organization consultant. It breaks with traditional results in yielding large and measurable improvements in all aspects of value. The standard joke about results goes something like this: "Do you want it fast, cheap, or good? Pick two." The approach that follows generates all three results: faster results, lower costs, and better quality.

Problems Experienced

In my early years, despite the view that organizations were systems, I accepted offers to consult with part-systems, largely because I did not encounter any clients that asked for me to take a whole-system approach. Looking back, I did many years of "good" work with clients of those partial systems, only to observe too many cases of deterioration of implemented solutions due to the resistance and backward pull of the larger systems in which my clients were imbedded.

Working as a peer with clients was a rewarding and satisfying process, in which, as a consultant, it was possible to aid the clients' growth, as well as experience a great deal of self-growth. Over time, however, I began to feel guilty that I had encouraged clients to take risks that were not long supported in their organizations; I had raised hopes only to see them dashed later.

After several decades of OD consulting, I had amassed a great deal of experience, created many useful interventions, and learned a lot about how to avoid many of the problems that beset the field. However, I had also experienced a severe period of consultant burnout, plenty of frustration about successes that didn't last, and saw that, in many cases, I was figuratively shoveling against the tide in the work that I was doing. I saw employees develop trust and a willingness to take risks to get better results, only to observe new managers who abused that trust and reinforced the typical perspective of employees that the OD work we did was just another fad. In hindsight, I had done a lot of good work, but no great work. The results, in terms of financial success and improved human processes, were laudable, but few systems remained better and more effective.

The net result of this experience was that I decided to give up consulting for a while. I took a sabbatical of sorts, dropping my consulting practice to do something completely different (build houses) while I thought about what I wanted to do in the future. The sabbatical convinced me that if I were to return to consulting, it would need to be sufficiently different for me to consider it effective. I decided that I would only do work that helped whole systems to become more successful as defined by bottom-line figures, more viable over the long term, and committed to being better places to do meaningful work.

I also saw that I had failed to recognize the importance of the technical systems in organizations, the methods and processes for doing the organizations' work. To be more effective as a consultant, I would need to put behavioral science in second place and focus instead on finding "the right work" of organizations, the work that added value and thus sustained the organizations in their marketplaces. It had always been my belief, as a consultant, that it was crucial to understand the objective of the consulting before contracting with the client, and that a continued focus on the objective was needed at all stages of consultation. Taking a whole-system perspective made that focus all the more important.

WHOLE-SYSTEM INTERVENTION

I had no illusion that most organizations would be looking for whole-system consulting[2] or that my consulting peers would embrace this approach. However, the sabbatical had made clear to me what kind of consultant I was and the type of consulting that I wanted to do, with a focus on delivering more effective consultation. It was also obvious that for me to be successful

I would need to contract with the right clients and create a "stacked deck" of conditions that would favor consulting success.

The "Good" Client

Every person in business knows from experience that there are better and worse customers or clients, but not everyone believes it is feasible to exclude the worst clients and work only with the desirable ones. Yet, decades of organization experience had convinced me that working with the wrong clients was a hopeless situation, one in which the results were often less than successful, and moreover, one in which my own sense of fulfillment was lacking. My years of reflection had left me with a strong resolve to work only with clients with whom I could be successful in significant and meaningful terms.

Based on over 20 years of experience with all sorts of clients, I came to believe that a "good" client is one who is:

- secure in his or her leadership, and is not a control freak;
- a good manager and leader;
- open-minded about potential change if it leads to better performance;
- neither strongly authoritarian nor laissez faire, but involved;
- honest and willing to share information with employees;
- able to allow others to solve problems differently than he or she does;
- focused more on the results than the methods;
- trustworthy, and will do what he or she says; and
- can partner with the consultant.

This definition of a good client leaves out a lot of potential clients, but there are a lot of potential clients out there, and one can't work with them all anyway. Selecting the client is paramount to success if one is to do the kind of peer/coach consulting described below.

Intervening at the Whole-system Level

The whole-system intervention outlined below is designed to move all employees of an organization to action in making the organization more effective in meeting its goals.[3] It differs from other approaches described as "whole-system" because it involves *all* employees, not representatives, not tiger teams, not selected groups. All employees are involved in learning about the organization, what all other employees do, and the core processes of the organization, from initial contact with clients to completed client satisfaction and/or payment. The intervention is based on the concept that all organizations are in existence to add value in one way or another, whether clients define value in terms of speedy performance, high quality of products, or low prices. Value can be identified several ways: it is the change of raw materials into a useful product, it is a service delivered better or easier than a customer can do it, or it is something for which a customer is willing to pay.

The basis for the intervention is a search for "waste" of the organization's resources, although other bases are possible. The reason that waste is used is that it is basic, not debatable, and something that all employees can understand. Whether the wastes are in time, materials, excess inventory, or lost sales opportunities, all employees can identify examples in the workplace. The aspect of value chosen as a focus is of minor importance, because the ultimate goal is to move all employees to action. In the process of identifying wastes, problems of quality, slow processes, and so forth all come up and are addressed, because they all have related wastes attached, as in re-work, penalties for late deliveries, and lost proposals.

Organizing the intervention so that all employees, including managers, are away from their normal jobs and tasked only with exploring the work of the organization with an eye to wasted resources eliminates turf battles, silo wars, and management resistance. Continual visible support from the client enhances the process of letting go of sacred cows, territorial fiefdoms, and favored but non-productive work methods.

The power of the intervention is immense, because it engages all employees in a search for how to make not only the organization more effective, but each position more effective. It is a strong belief on my part that all employees want strongly to see themselves as competent at work. The notion of sharing increased profits with employees links the drive for effectiveness with tangible rewards for success. Once employees see improved effectiveness resulting in shares of bottom line results, the drive for continued improvement is fueled.

How To Do It

There are four critical steps to take in creating the potential for success. The first is to find a "good" client. The next step is to contract effectively for what you (as the consultant) will do and the results being sought. The third step is to ensure that the client fully understands and agrees to the crucial conditions that make success possible. The fourth step is to get agreement about the conditions for the work you will do in terms of client leadership support.

Organizational Conditions

For this approach to be truly successful, the organization must commit to three core tenets. First, it is necessary for everybody in the organization to be involved in the performance improvement process; no one is "too important" to be involved in working on finding the right work of the organization. Sales people, for example, often claim that they are too important to be part of the improvement process, but their participation is essential. Second, there *must* be a gain-sharing system so that employees share financially in improved profits. The amount and method of distribution can be worked out later, but there must be some form of gain-sharing so that employee efforts can be related to increased income for all employees. Finally, employment *must* be guaranteed, so that improved performance does not lead to employees working themselves out of jobs. No one should be let go, unless it is a result of poor performance, even as would be the case in a normal work environment. However, jobs themselves may change, as work methods are improved.

Leadership Commitment

The client must agree to several ground rules. First, is that *anything* found to be blocking better performance can be changed. Second, nothing should be regarded as sacred. Third, the client must be willing to change the organization's structure and management methods as needed. Fourth, the client must support the notion that *everyone*'s job will change as a result of successful whole-system change.

The client must be actively involved, not simply a "check-signer." This commitment means sitting in on problem-solving meetings, answering questions about the process in which the organization is involved, taking action on problems, and so forth. Such involvement also involves partnering with the consultant to monitor progress. It will be necessary for the client to act in ways that support analysis and involve the whole system; this means that no part of the organization is allowed to operate without regard for its effects on other parts of the organization. All interactions must be based on trust and honesty as the organization moves through the change process.

Underlying all of this is the requirement that the organization lives up to its promises to employees. The quickest way to derail this type of whole system intervention is to say one thing and do another.

Creating a Process Schedule

The process itself is quite straightforward. First, the organization's employees should be divided into diagonal groups of about 20 to 25, so that, as much as possible, all functions are represented in each group. Managerial personnel should also be dispersed within the groups, and managers are encouraged to take off their management "hats" and join in the work of the groups; it also inhibits manager-to-manager conflict that can occur with multiple managers in the same unstructured group. Second, the physical space for the exercise should be conducive for exchange and interaction. Arrange for a "classroom" in which employee groups can meet, away from the working floor and with lots of wall space on which the paperwork of each group can be displayed, so that all groups can see the work of the other groups. Reserve the classroom for the groups' use alone. If one doesn't exist, arrange for the client to create, or even rent one.

Plan a schedule that allows each group to meet twice a week for about 1¼ to 1½ hours over a 10-week period. Thus, an organization of 400 employees would have 16 to 20 groups, each group meeting twice a week. Depending on shifts, it might be feasible to meet with diagonal groups on four days of the week, and reserve the mid-week day for working with the client and spending time on the work floor observing and interacting with workers. This makes for long consulting days, but the work is very energizing.

It is also important to plan with the client that he or she will attend as many group meetings as possible the first few weeks. The consultant should expect to coach the client to be prepared to answer questions about the importance and value of the meetings so that all employees hear that the meetings are not time away from work. It should also be emphasized that the sessions are work meetings—whose purpose is to find better ways to meet the goals of the organization. When the consultant inaugurates the classroom meetings, he or she needs to encourage all employees to interact and participate in the activities of the meetings. Among the tasks the consultant must undertake, is to observe any problems and discuss these with the client, and to develop plans for resolving the problems. One should expect disbelief, skepticism, resistance, and testing behavior in the early stages. The consultant must speak to problematic behavior, ensuring that the process allows employees to freely identify problems in the workplace and supporting them in their efforts to develop plans that they will implement to eliminate those problems.

The activities of the classroom meetings move through four phases:

1. discovery (i.e., discovering what the organization actually does);
2. analysis (analyzing wasted resources);
3. solution (developing solutions that conserve resources and add value); and
4. implementation (applying solutions).

Once the employees have identified the wasted resources and the cost of those wastes, they self-select into temporary teams that focus on significant amounts of wasted resources and develop cost-benefit solutions. I routinely set a goal for each team to find and eliminate $100,000 of waste for a capital cost of no more than $5,000. When the teams self-select, I ask them to identify problems for which they have passion and some knowledge. In that way, groups form based on a personal desire to eliminate problems that affect their work or for which they can imagine solutions. Setting the $100,000 goal requires that they thoroughly research the problems they tackle to identify the actual impact of the problems. It is also high enough that success will be real and measurable. The teams then develop their proposed solutions, which will be presented to the client. As part of this process it is useful for the consultant to work with team members in developing proposals, and in practicing presentations. In the practices, team members critique the ideas and delivery of each presentation.

The client should be coached to respond favorably to the proposals—unless there are holes in logic or if more data and analysis are needed. If this is the case, the group should be sent back to get the necessary information and then re-present its ideas. The goal is for all teams to have their presented solutions accepted and given the "okay" for implementation. The ultimate goal is for all employees to begin to take an active role in making the organization run better. The intent is not to simply achieve instant savings, though initial financial success will occur and will tend to energize everyone in the organization. The best case result is the installation of a continuous improvement process.

The consultant should assist the teams along the way, however help is needed—working to problem-solve, identify potential options, develop a cohesive presentation, overcome obstacles in implementation, and so forth. Meeting briefly at the beginning of classroom time in the implementation phase is a time to review team progress, before teams are turned loose to implement. It is useful to review progress with the client and the teams about half-way through implementation, identifying any resources that are needed along the way and arranging for them to be made available.

Finally, the consultant must aid the client in creating a structure reporting directly to the client. This structure should be installed after the implementation process, to support new teams coming up with new proposals, and to provide an avenue for the teams to bring their proposals to the attention of the client. This will provide a path for continuous improvement that doesn't require approval by any of the "silos" or levels of management.

Intervention Effectiveness: The Importance of the "Good" Client

The process described above is one that can only be accomplished through a peer relationship with a client, and requires the client to be highly involved with the change process. The client must not only attend work sessions, but be highly visible in the workplace so that organizational members can get reassurance that the promises of continued employment and gain-sharing will be kept. In addition, the client must look for opportunities to confront old practices that inhibit individual initiative and resist change.

An illustration is provided by the following conversation, which took place after a client observed an employee mumbling and cursing as he struggled to align an overhead machine with its mate below.

Employee (complaining out loud): This would be a whole lot easier if only we had a laser attached to the top machine.
Client (walking over to the employee): Why isn't there a laser on the machine if it would help?
Employee: Because engineering won't let me attach anything to it.
Client: What does a laser cost?
Employee: About $10, and they make them next door.
Client: (To the consultant) Come on, let's take a trip.

Visiting the company adjacent to the firm, the client purchased the laser and gave it to the employee, asking him if he could attach it to the machine.

Employee: Sure, but what about engineering's reaction?
Client: Just do it and let *me* handle engineering.

Although this vignette may not appear to be a major act, it "went miles" toward supporting the notion that anything that supports improved performance was fair game.

Another client discovered that a supervisor, who was on one of the problem-solving teams, had wadded up and thrown into the trash one of the team member's papers showing a solution to the problem that the team was addressing. The supervisor was apparently asserting his power over his subordinates. The client called the supervisor into his office, quizzed him on his behavior, explained that it was completely inappropriate, and relieved him of his supervisory responsibilities. This action was a clear statement of the importance of the process in which the organization was engaged, ending what might be thought of as supervisory tyranny.

A third client, while roaming the work floor, came upon a group of employees busily talking. His initial temptation was to tell them to get back to work. Instead, he asked what they were doing. One of his female employees, who had been resistant to believing that the process was "real," told him that the group was solving a problem with one of the machines. She continued, "stopping us to ask us questions will only slow us down." The client laughed and told them to let him know if they needed help, but to otherwise go ahead and solve the problem.

These examples illustrate the degree to which clients need to have a hands-on role in the whole-system intervention. It is also clear that close coaching by and support of the consultant are critical. Changing a system cannot be a program, a project, or a fixed format intervention. It is entirely dependent on a step-by-step learning process that requires the client to learn, along with other employees, how the organization truly does its work. The reality is that managers rarely understand the details of the work that is actually done, though few will admit this is the case. The client's support for a spirit of learning is important, reinforcing the notion that finding wastes is a good thing, not a cause for embarrassment or blame.

CLIENT INVOLVEMENT: CONSULTING AND CONTRACTING

It is my belief that client involvement needs to be greater in peer/coach approaches to consulting than in expert and service provider approaches. In the latter two, the client needs to understand what efforts the consultant will make in the organization, in order to authorize and evaluate the interventions. What is not required is a great deal of involvement in the details of the intervention process. When, however, the consultant takes a peer/coach role, the client must be much more involved in the diagnosis, objective-setting, solution choices, and often, the intervention action. When the intervention is whole-system, as illustrated in this chapter, the degree of client involvement must be particularly high.

What follows then is that the greater the client's involvement, the greater the need for consultant interaction and coaching with the client. For that coaching and interaction to be effective, the consultant needs to do a more thorough and exacting job of contracting with the client. This process guides the client, identifies actions that the client should be prepared to take, structures legitimate interactions and involvement of the consultant in the organization's business, and sets the ground rules for the intervention and consulting relationship. Done well, contracting about roles and conditions for success will go a long way towards guaranteeing consulting success and client satisfaction.

NOTES

1. Organization consultants tend to view the whole system as the client for change. Clearly, managers play a large role in organization performance, but the whole system view shifts the focus from management behavior to the work the whole organization does to achieve its collective goals.
2. There are other approaches to improving these aspects, such as re-engineering, fast cycle time, "lean" manufacturing, Work Out, and so forth, but I do not know of any use of these approaches employed in or as a truly whole-system strategy. Work Out may be the closest in methodology, but it differs in critical

aspects; freedom of employees to select issues to address and to implement solutions, representation vs. all-employee participation, manager-directed vs. client-directed follow-up, and the absence of the promises of employment and gain-sharing. Work Out is a process and issue-oriented approach; the approach I describe here is system-oriented.

What will be evident to anyone examining the approach outlined in this chapter is that there is little that is unique or innovative in terms of techniques; rather, it is the combination of *conditions*, in alignment with the techniques, that produces the major results associated with this approach.

3. It is a reasonable question to ask if this approach can be used with large systems. It can, but it involves multiple consultant-facilitators, and a bit of careful interlinking of the teams and groups; there is no reason it cannot be applied to large systems. However, it has been my observation over the years of consulting that the motives of owner-leaders of small and medium-sized organizations tend to be different than those of the typically professional leaders of large systems. Owner-leaders tend to see the benefit of improving their organizations in very personal terms; if their organizations perform better, employees are more secure, retirements are secure, and the life of the organization is prolonged. Professional leaders may have none of those motives, given that their tenures may be short, their personal incomes and power may have more to do with their sense of success than success of the organization, and they may be too "important" to spend any time learning about what really goes on in the organization. It has been my choice in the last two decades to work more with small and medium-sized organizations for the above difference in motives.

REFERENCES

Burke, W. W. (2002). *Organization change: Theory and practice.* Thousand Oaks, CA: Sage.

Dannemiller Tyson Associates. (2000). *Whole-scale change: Unleashing the magic in corporations.* San Francisco: Berrett-Koehler Publishers.

Hammer, M., & Stanton, S. A. (1995). *The re-engineering revolution.* New York: Harper.

Myers, C. (1993) *Fast cycle time: How to align purpose, strategy, and structure for speed.* New York: Free Press.

Schonberger, R. J. (1982). *Japanese manufacturing techniques: Nine hidden lessons in simplicity.* New York: Free Press.

Slater, R. (2000). *The GE fieldbook: Jack Welch's battle plan for corporate revolution.* New York: McGraw-Hill.

CHAPTER 4

WHOLE SYSTEM TRANSFORMATION

The Consultant's Role in Creating Sustainable Results

John J. Scherer, Gina Lavery, Roland Sullivan, Ginger Whitson and Elizabeth Vales

Anyone who has ever attempted a large-scale planned change initiative knows the disappointing truth of what can happen shortly after you and your consultant colleagues leave the building:

- The busy-ness of people's daily work diminishes—or even neutralizes—the changes that were agreed to at the end of the kick-off celebration.
- Three months (or maybe even three weeks) later, leaders and employees alike are thinking—or saying, "What was *that* all about?"
- The "We-are-changing-everything-around-here" t-shirts, so proudly worn for a while, go back in the dresser drawer as people realize it was not really about changing anything fundamental. Things are pretty much the same, only different.

Consultation for Organizational Change. pages 57–77
Copyright © 2010 by Information Age Publishing
All rights of reproduction in any form reserved.

- The bottom line: your change process has "dropped like a marble in a bowl of oatmeal," making hardly a ripple in the on-going effectiveness and practice of the system.

What happened? Why do so many large-scale change initiatives fail to create lasting change in the system that badly needed it—especially when all those involved thought they had created it?

SUSTAINABLE WHOLE SYSTEM TRANSFORMATION

Based on our experience in participating in transformation initiatives with a wide variety of client organizations, we believe there is a clear set of principles that make up a kind of "recipe" for what we refer to as sustainable whole system transformation (WST).[1] Our experience also suggests that following these principles enhances the likelihood of actually transforming the organization, not simply changing it. In most instances, what we do may feel good and even lead to some change, but it is not likely to result in sustainable whole system transformation with deep, lasting impact on the client organization's processes and people.

Sustainable

By using the term "sustainable" we are not inferring that a change remains in place *forever.* This scenario is highly unlikely, regardless of what you do. Life moves on. The world changes. What is right for one moment becomes a drag on the organization later on. As Weisbord (2004, personal communication) has noted,

> "Sustainable transformation" is a philosophical dilemma and an oxymoron, since nothing lasts forever, regardless of the method used. Leaders come and go. There are many variables out of our control or even ability to influence. Pressure from Wall Street or shareholders can demand a return to business-as-usual. We can help people build transformed organizational cultures for *today and maybe tomorrow,* but not for the ages.

Even though many—or even all—of the specific operational changes set in motion during our WST interventions fade with time, we have often seen that something lasting does "stick" within the system. Perhaps what is sustainable are *who people become*—effective leaders and unleashed employees—and *what the system learns* about cross-functional teamwork, breakthrough thinking, and about the process of transformation itself. Sometimes a critical mass of people is able to hold on to what Weisbord (2004, personal communication) calls "the capacity to do things together that everyone values and they could not do alone."

In the context of the framework presented in this chapter, the "sustainable" part of whole system transformation means assisting people in the development of a *replicable and evolving enterprise-wide capability to transform the way they do things again and again in a chaotic, ever changing world.*

Whole System

The scientific worldview, held by Chaos theorists and thinkers like Wheatley (1992) and Capra (1975), emphasizes that we must no longer look at the world as a machine with isolated, separate parts that need to be "fixed." Chapter co-author John Scherer uses the image of a *clothesline* to describe a system: "Pull on the socks and the underwear jumps." Roland Sullivan likes a *cooking* metaphor: change one thing in a recipe and that changes everything, because all the ingredients, even the smallest, are interacting with each other in the process of becoming the meal. What happens in one part of a system, no matter how small or isolated it may appear, has an effect on every other part of that system.

We are also not just referring to a system but to a *whole* system, and that additional word is extremely important. Our word "whole" comes from the Old English root *hool,* which meant healthy, unhurt, entire. *Whole,* therefore, is more than a quantitative word referring to "all of something." It has a *qualitative* sense of a healthy balance, unity and completeness. When the term "wholeness" is applied to a system, it refers to the interdependent parts interacting with each other and with the environment as a unified whole, so that a more healthy world is created for that system and its stakeholders.

Whole system transformation goes beyond simply setting in motion changes that affect the entire system. WST means the *whole organization is involved*—as a system—in *creating itself anew.*

Transformation

There is change and there is transformation. *Change* is altering something within the given parameters of the situation, but keeping the fundamentals basically the same, like going faster in first gear. Some examples include changing to a new Performance Management Process, installing a different Information Technology platform, sending everyone through a training program, merging two organizations, or reducing the workforce. These interventions are often necessary—but are rarely sufficient to transform an entire system. Something else may be needed—not "more-of-the-same-only-different," which is change, but something *entirely* different—like shifting into another gear, or as a more powerful analogy, leaving your car to use a plane to get where you are headed.

We use the image of the *quantum leap,* which is what happens when an electron makes a shift to another state within an atom (Zukav, 1979). The actual shift from one "shell" to the next does not happen gradually over time. It is discontinuous. One moment the atom is in one state with a certain configuration among its electrons; the next instant it is in another state, which dramatically alters the nature of the atom. In the vernacular, "quantum leap"' has come to mean a relatively small "jump" that makes a huge difference, and happens all at once.

This jump is what we refer to as transformation. *Transformation* is a sudden shift that is so profound that the old situation and the way you saw that situation are either left behind or are subsumed into a new way of seeing and doing things. It is actually a new way of *being* that alters the system's relationship to what is happening. Chapter co-author Gina Lavery refers to it as the "birth" of a new view because it can be painful, uncomfortable, messy and unpredictable.

Transformation means "going back to zero" and re-thinking the fundamental principles and paradigms on which you are basing what you do and how you do it. When you make a *quantum (transformational) leap,* there is a shift in the way the world occurs for people, such as:

- The strategic intention or the "Big Idea" behind the enterprise is understood and embraced by a majority of the organization.
- Employees start working together in completely new ways.
- A sense of accountability and "ownership" becomes personal and present at all levels in the system.
- Leaders lead from a more authentic, related, and integrated stance.
- Decision-making becomes more collaborative, and conflicts are handled instead of avoided.
- Communication becomes more honest, especially *up* the organization.

Change is always embedded in transformation, but the opposite is rarely the case.

Implementing WST Processes

In virtually every request for transformation, some or all of the following elements are present. First, there is an awareness among a few key leaders that "things are not working," that there are forces and/or factors at work in the organization's world that must be reckoned with, and that some units—or the entire system—would benefit from breakthroughs that lead to higher levels of effectiveness or performance.

Second, those same leaders have had some kind of a transformational experience that allows them to see that the normal ways the system addresses situations like this are not likely to work, and that they must take a radically different approach. It is important to have a senior leader in the system who *sees* or *wants* transformation for the organization, and is well-positioned and willing to be a strong "champion" in making it happen.

Finally, the notion that the "answers" or "'solutions" are already in the system somewhere, rather than existing only in the reports of expert external consultants—or in senior management. The developed leadership core must realize that there is a lot more potential to be actualized.

THE WST MACRO-MODEL

The whole system transformation journey is a dynamic, holistic process designed to help leaders engage a critical mass of the organization in reinventing itself and creating a future of aligned and committed action (see Figure 4.1).[2] Starting at the center of the diagram, organizations and individuals are in a state of perpetual change. The process begins with transforming the leader and his or her team so they are aligned both intellectually and emotionally with a new vision. They must be ready to move forward with one heart and one mind in order to sustain the kind of committed action required to succeed with the new vision.

Once leadership is aligned, then and only then can the process move into transforming a critical mass of the organization. This is accomplished through the design and execution of a powerful large-group interactive event where enough people within the system participate to drive a significant shift for the organization. They emerge more aligned with leadership and the new vision.

The *change foci* can be any number of things. To name a few, the journey can be focused on a new strategy, change in culture, or aligning the organization to take advantage of new opportunities in an ever-changing market place. Throughout the transformation journey there needs to be an enterprise-wide *communication* effort that keeps a multi-directional information flow alive. In today's environment it is not enough to just meet or even exceed customer expectations. In order to obtain new and retain existing customers, organizations today must continuously find new and innovative ways to *thrill the people* who purchase their products or services.

Kathy Dannemiller used to say if you have gone through a large-group interactive event and have to find a way to *measure the outcomes*, the event

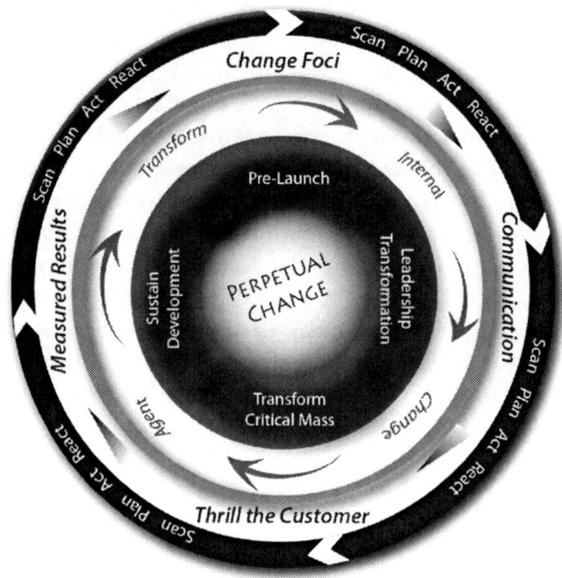

FIGURE 4.1. WST Macro-Model

failed. Cost effective measurement methodologies need to be established to compare intended results with actual results. Throughout the journey the process of *scan, plan, act, and re-act* is applied. Planning consists of convening the right people from the system to review the data and collaboratively develop action plans and commitments. Act and re-act go hand-in-hand. Re-evaluation is necessary during the process in which the organization implements the plan and re-actions are required to respond to new realities and unanticipated obstacles.

The WST conceptual methodology described above has several crucial *action* elements. The first is *gathering data* on the system's culture and functionality of its operations and processes. Information can be obtained through a mix of interviews, surveys, observation, public data, and so forth. When there is conflicting data, go with your findings from face-to-face interviews, especially from front-line performers. This usually gives you the best "read" on both the "hard" and "soft" data needed for diagnosis and planning.

The next step is to *share the data* with the senior leader, then the leadership group, facilitating the implication derivation process, where they *see* what is happening and are moved by what they realize it means. In our experience, taking an Appreciative Inquiry approach helps leaders digest tough data, turning problem statements into energizing descriptions of how it *could* be. This means asking questions like:

1. What is a recent *high point* for you and/or the system—when you were at your very best and it worked?
2. What do you *value most* about what your unit contributes to the organization's objectives?
3. What is a *core* attribute or quality that must be central to your development?
4. As you picture your unit performing brilliantly, what do you need to: start doing, stop doing, build on?

The Leadership Alignment Session

It is then important to *align* the senior leadership group so they are powerfully holding a vision of what Lindaman and Lippitt (1979) called a "preferred future"—and committing their unconditional support for what will be required to transform the organization. The senior leadership group must set aside enough time (we find that three days is the minimum) to embrace the future they are choosing, to discuss the business reasons for that future, to understand the whole system transformation process, and to let go of "sacred cows," such as programs, procedures, or processes that are not in alignment with that preferred future. By the end of this series of conversations, complete with arguments and changes of position, the leadership team is more ready for the role they need to play in the process as participants (and facilitators) and not as drivers of what happens.

The overall purpose of this session is to create alignment among the members and the team leader, and to engender their commitment to show up as "one voice." Specific objectives include:

1. bonding as a team by establishing an environment of authenticity and support;
2. chartering the team by agreeing on the organization's and the team's critical commitments, guiding values, common purpose, shared accountabilities and how the team will organize to accomplish them;
3. creating and establishing alignment among team members and ownership for the organization's transformation roadmap; and
4. becoming "one voice."

The session is highly experiential (more interaction, less presentation) and designed to create a space where the leadership team can engage in deep dialog in order to develop trust in one another and a deep commitment to their shared vision of the future. The "secret sauce" is that the facilitator(s) must engage the group at the heart level, not just the head level. This can be quite uncomfortable for leaders (and consultants) who are accustomed to living inside their plans and concepts. Once they enter the "heart space", they find they all really want the same things, both from each other and from own their work as leaders. This opens them up to the possibility of working in a synchronous and supportive manner.

Although the leadership alignment session can do wonders in terms of transforming the top team, they need to be vigilant about continuing to allow themselves to be open with each other as the process unfolds. In our experience, this is a challenge, because when leaders leave the safe and transformational space of the offsite and re-enter the world of work, they have a tendency to shift back into their heads and their former patterns of interaction. It helps to have a consultant who is there through re-entry to help the top team internalize this new way of working.

Transforming the Leadership Core

Now that the senior leadership team is *aligned* ("on board") and motivated to champion the process, the next phase involves *transforming* the (larger) leadership core. *Alignment* is each leader seeing and committing to what needs to happen, and what each of them needs to do next or differently. *Transformation* is a dramatic shift in who the leaders are "being" with each other. Co-Author Gina Lavery explains it this way: Quite often it is the shedding of the old, dysfunctional, more superficial ways of interacting with each other, resulting in a fundamental shift in trust, deepened relationships, and increased comfort in sharing deeper truths about who they are and what they want. This shift is often characterized by leaders as a "softening" towards each other, with a surge of compassion, understanding and respect. In a three-day experience, this shift usually occurs on the morning of day three. A hallmark of the transformation is a spontaneous and positive emotional release at the group level, often evidenced by tears, laughter, celebratory shouts, or standing ovations. The shift in energy can be felt by anyone who is physically located in the room.

Who comprises the leadership core? Once the senior leadership team becomes aligned and transformed, it is necessary to involve *other* natural leaders throughout the system. This is an expanded group of natural leaders representing every level and from every department or division who have been selected by the senior leadership team for their potential influence on the initiative. It is essential to invite a few "nay-sayers" to participate, especially those skeptical or cynical members who have a "constituency" in the system and need to be represented. This group needs to come together and for a three-day experience that aligns them around the "preferred future," the whole system transformation initiative, and their own experience of transformation. Since people in organizations tend to "look up" to see what is important, as they see the example set by the senior leadership team and the leadership core, this begins to energize, encourage, and empower them to trust the process and engage in the transformation initiative.

Transformation in this context often looks like some or all of the following shifts taking place in the members of the leadership core:

1. A fundamental shift from self-centeredness to a heightened awareness of colleagues and concern for their welfare—and their organizational unit.
2. A fundamental shift from avoiding or deflecting responsibility for mistakes to taking 100% personal responsibility for whatever happens to anyone on the team.
3. A fundamental shift from "looking good" (or looking better than anyone else) to "lifting up" colleagues and wanting everyone to be their best.
4. A fundamental shift from holding on to information as a source of power *over* others, to sharing information as a source of power *with* others.
5. A fundamental shift from playing it safe—by doing what has been done before (and maybe making a few small changes)—to seeking entirely new ways of doing things (breakthrough thinking).
6. A fundamental shift from trying to have control *over* everything that happens (in an attempt to make it conform to their personal agenda) to having power *through* what happens, regardless of what that might be.

A critical part of the process is *involving* the entire system in a minimum of 2 days over 3 days (3 days and 3 nights is better) in "max-mix" (representative) gatherings to deeply engage in exploring the vision for the organization. Participants should be encouraged to dream and share their vision of a preferred future, unleashing the spirit of the organization to "live the vision." As an example, a recent client vision was "*Mobilizing all our economic and human power to thrill the customer.*" Sometimes mundane, the actual *language* of the vision does not have to be magical; the powerful and profound personal *ownership* of those words is where the transformational power comes from. As part of the discussion, people also begin to uncover things that need to change in order to achieve the vision. Deepening the vision in the hearts, minds and spirits of the participants, attention should move toward creating robust *action plans* for shifting the organization from its current state to the preferred future state. Small cross-functional teams can also be used to prioritize breakthrough ideas and develop plans to convert them into action.

The final steps involve *connecting* and *applying* the work of the teams to the day-to-day work of the system to ensure the preferred future comes alive in the real world, and *soliciting feedback* continuously from the system, in essence, adjusting what is happening based on what is learned. How many breakthroughs created at the offsite are actually being followed up on? What are the early signs that a breakthrough idea is having a positive impact on its intended "target"? What kind of resistance are decisions running into, and what kind of leadership may be needed to free the "logjam" and move things forward?

Core Ingredients in Sustainability

In order to ensure the sustainability of the project, it is critical to create a sense of ownership of the problem and solution, tap the energies that exist in the system, and touch the spirits, hearts, and minds of those involved.

Ownership

"Getting the whole system in the room," as Weisbord (1987, 2004) has made clear, is the fastest way to transform a system. Once you and the client have figured how best to do that, for example, how to create a strong sense of ownership among all key stakeholders of what happens, including the design of the process, the breakthrough possibilities that get addressed, and the decision-making that finally moves the system in real-world, day-to-day ways.

This type of transformation requires everyone in a critical mass to be *very* self-aware and system-oriented, starting at the top of the organization. When the individuals in a system are *self-aware,* they come to see that they need to get beyond their habitual ways of thinking, doing and being. When people are *system-oriented,* they are able to appreciate *all* the stakeholders (including suppliers and customers), not just their department. Combine the two and everyone involved can see how they relate to each other and to the outside environment, resulting in a healthy system that knows what to do next and is capable of acting quickly.

More important, though, is that their self-awareness enables participants to understand how they, themselves, are collectively responsible for what is happening in the current system. This awareness brings a keen understanding that the *system* will not transform until they *personally* transform. When that "moment" comes, when people clearly see their system-at-work, often like a thunder clap, a whole new range of possibilities emerge, along with the necessary energy and focus to enable them to succeed, now and over time. Experiencing such newness, like learning to ride a bike, never goes away.

Tapping the Energy of Polarities

Johnson (1992) has pointed the authors toward a powerful source of indestructible sustainability that is inherently present in every system: its ability to keep moving through an "infinity energy loop" that flows around and between two poles (ways of doing things). When a system becomes enamored with one pole, say *change*, to the exclusion of the opposite pole, *stability*, this attachment is guaranteed to bring on a sinking into the downside of the preferred pole. People begin to experience uncertainty and exhaustion and yearn for more stability. If the movement toward stability is resisted, the system gets "stuck" in a less-than-optimal place, and the natural flow of energy is blocked.

As illustrated in Figure 4.2, as long as the system continues to move back and forth between these two poles (which are both valid and deserve to have their "time"), the system is alive and well. Such a system is able to tap the benefits inherent in the unavoidable, constant, infinite energy flow around the polarities. WST empowers that flow.

Touching Spirits, Hearts and Minds

When a system begins to experience difficulty, the "trouble"' usually manifests "above-the-waterline" at the operational level, where important numbers begin to fall, like customer satisfaction, market share, revenue, speed to market, and so forth. However, leaders who understand WST prin-

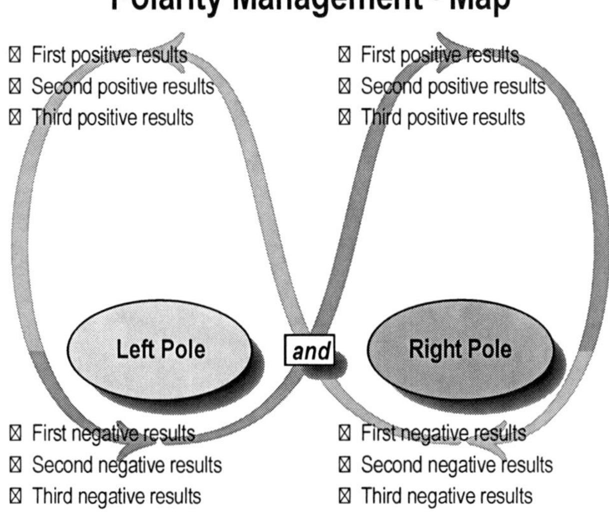

Figure 4.2. The Polarity Infinite Energy Loop

ciples realize that the response to falling numbers has to involve shifting the way things are happening "below-the-waterline," inside and between people and organizational units. They know the long-term "solution" lies in awakening, unleashing, and focusing the spirit of the system (Scherer, 2009).

"DEFINING MOMENTS" THAT CREATE THE POSSIBILITY OF WST

Figure 4.3 provides an overview of the typical flow of events in the WST process. We have identified a handful of moments in a change initiative that hold great leverage in creating sustainable whole system transformation with clients.

WST Starts in the Contracting Conversation

If you want to do sustainable whole system transformation, you need to be clear and committed to what it takes from the very first interaction with the client. What you are proposing will almost certainly be different from

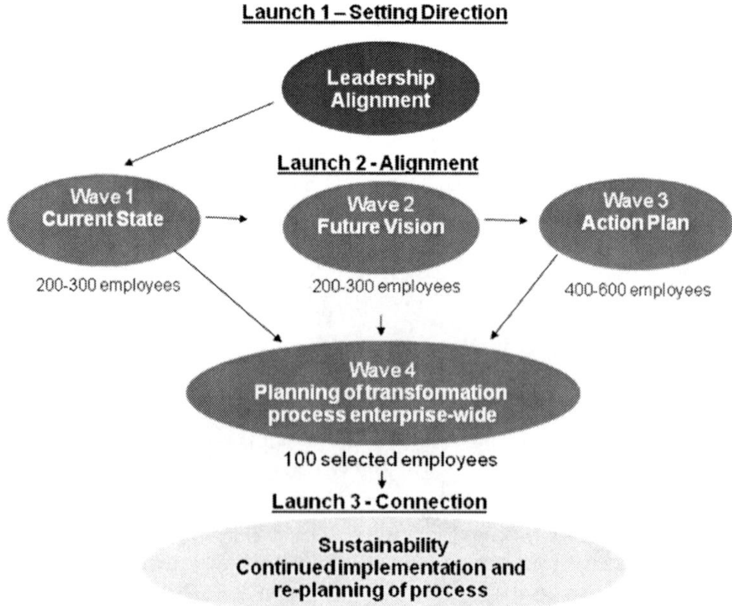

FIGURE 4.3. Whole System Transformation Process

the way the organization and its leaders currently go about things, otherwise they would not be in their situation. It is a natural paradox: leaders need to do things in radically new ways, yet they instinctively protect the status quo and the old ways of working together.

As a result, the client is likely to have an urge to "negotiate" or remove things from the process that scare them, like allowing front line people to participate in making decisions regarding what to do, or having to experience personal transformation themselves. The consultant must hold his or her ground and help them see the logical connection between their situation and the breakthrough potential of what is being proposed. WST must not be allowed to become another leadership flavor-of-the-month that people can "hunker down and outlast." Even though the process appears to be a series of events that can be scheduled on a calendar, WST is beyond a program. It is a journey, a new "way" of working together that never ends. Chapter co-author Lavery likes the metaphor of learning to ride a bicycle: once you have learned how, *you cannot un-learn it.* It is with you forever. As soon as you *get* the experience of balance, the whole world is different, and you will never go back. Like riding a bike, people cannot un-learn transformation. Once people and the system learn how to be an organization that renews itself, this capability does not end, and is so compelling they do not *want* to go back to the way it was before.

The Leadership Core Must Experience Transformation First

After the contracting phase, WST begins with a "Leadership Alignment Intensive" for the leadership core, where they come to understand transformation by experiencing a personal quantum leap in the way they relate to themselves, to each other, and to the system. Without this deep and often dramatic increase in self-awareness, when the pressure is on leaders can "bail out" and abandon the process. Within this context, the *leadership core* goes beyond top or senior leadership, extending to the leadership that exists throughout the system (e.g. union and other informal leaders).

The primary objective is a leadership core that is aligned around a single intention—the creation of a "preferred future," developed in collaboration with front line employees, that is more productive and more alive. For this to happen, leaders at every level must be willing to let go of control, trust the process, and share control with their people. At this point, the senior leadership team may not realize what they have agreed to. Transformation is about to rock their world, but without a committed "thumbs-up" from the senior leadership team, WST is very difficult or impossible to achieve.

In an interview, WST colleague Jennifer Todd puts it this way:

> In hierarchical organizations, the results from WST are made possible by the leadership core's commitment at the heart level and their actively and visibly shifting their behaviors and '"way of being'" to align with the transformation.

> The organization will continuously test them to see if they really are willing to do the work themselves personally: "Are they for real this time?" The depth of the personal transformation the leadership team is willing to take on will be proportionate to how much and how deep the front line people will feel safe in going. Leadership has the power to make or break the success of transformation, particularly in its early stages when the system is still forming itself anew and stepping into its new paradigms.

How do you transform the leadership core? Any of several designs will work here, but the Leadership Alignment Experience, referred to earlier, usually includes these elements:

- Staff: Two external consultants (male and female is recommended) take the lead, shadowed by (1 or 2) internal people who have been selected to be trained to lead certain aspects of the WST initiative from inside.
- The first order of business is to guide the group in identifying tangible business challenges confronting the organization and to feel a common sense of urgency in addressing them. Each member of the leadership core needs to "own" the system's situation, and commit to the co-creation of breakthroughs via a process of discovery and action carried out with front line people as colleagues.
- Leaders need to experience a shift in their relationship with each other so they end up speaking with one voice. They also need to be assisted in what Scherer and Yeoell (2001) calls "facing the tiger," discussing what they need to discuss in ways they have not done before: "If you are not facing your tigers, they are already eating you."
- One important outcome is experiencing greater trust in themselves, in their leader, in each other, and in the consultants.

A key concept that surfaces at the Leadership Alignment Session is that everything that happens in the up-coming WST initiative must be understood as happening "in stereo," with attention being paid to both operational (above the waterline) and human factor (below the waterline) dimensions. WST is based on the principle that sustainable transformation occurs when *both* of these domains are acknowledged and addressed.

The leadership core also needs to understand that, rather than the traditional "un-freezing, changing, and re-freezing" model (Beckhard, 1969; Lewin, 1951), WST is a conscious and continuous un-freezing of the organization so that, like water, it can *flow*. Frozen water is rigid and cannot flow or adapt to changes in the environment. Today there is no room for re-freezing. The older change model may give temporary advantages—and a feeling of some control for managers—but it drives the system to repeat the past as soon as things change again, which is happening constantly.

A Truly Integrated Team of Internal and External Facilitators

We cannot emphasize enough that, unlike other change management models, WST is not primarily about the external consultants. It's about the system transforming itself, led by a small team of capable internal people who are "joined at the hip" with each other and with the externals. These dual roles make it possible for the process and its results to be "owned" by all key stakeholders in the system. Without *internal* consultants, the process is unlikely to succeed, as the system becomes dependent on the external resources and fails to learn how to do what is needed. Without *external* people helping to guide, stimulate and inspire what happens, the initiative is less likely to create transformation, since the culture will instinctively try to "domesticate" the process and its output, "taming it down" to fit within existing paradigms.

In many traditional planned-change models, the initiative is managed by a team of external consultants, working closely with top leadership. There may be a small group of internal people appointed to "'work with the consultants," but everyone knows they have little or no influence over what happens. In WST, this pattern is reversed. People soon realize that what happens is being obviously planned and carried out by internal people, trained and assisted by a small team of external consultants who are experienced in WST.

The work in a typical WST initiative is divided between the external consultants, internal resources, and both groups working together. External consultants, working alone, typically:

1. manage the initial contracting conversations with the client;
2. undertake the initial briefing and coaching of the WST Sponsor;
3. model transformation for everyone else (e.g., letting go of control and sharing the limelight with others);
4. create the initial design for the Leadership Core and their subsequent transformation experiences;
5. guide the Transformation Management Team's (TMT) work; and, as outside content experts, from time to time they may be invited to address the gatherings and provide a context for transformation (e.g., an industry expert or someone experienced with a particular issue being addressed).

An organization's internal resources fulfill a number of key supporting roles. One key role is *intelligence and reconnaissance*, in essence serving as the "eyes and ears" of the team, asking their sources around the organization what the "buzz" is about the process. Part of this role is ensuring that the external consultants understand political "landmines" and other hidden hazards to be avoided. *Communication* should also come from within the organization, sharing updates on what is happening via internal communications like newsletters, emails, strategic conversations, and so forth. Insiders also have the knowledge and insight to ensure *coordination*, managing subteams, handling scheduling, and making sure the right people are included in all phases, logistics and other matters. Another function that insiders should provide is ensuring that all existing change efforts are *connected* and *aligned* "under the WST tent," building bridges to other improvement initiatives that are underway to ensure they do not interfere with each other and generate synergy wherever possible. Since external consultants rarely have the necessary historical knowledge about the organization, insiders can also *link to history and reality,* helping externals to understand where the organization has been and ensuring that what is planned is connected with the daily life of the organization. Finally, an underlying intent of WST is for the external experts to train and empower the internal TMT to *lead and facilitate* as much of the process as possible, depending on their level of competence and confidence.

Working together, the two groups—the external consultants and internal resource people— typically: design and facilitate the Leadership Alignment and Transformation Experiences (again depending on the skill and experience of the Internals on the TMT); help to facilitate the Whole-System-in-the-Room experiences; facilitate TMT planning and debriefing meetings; and guide the selection of who needs to be included in the process and how such inclusion should be carried out.

Shared Power and Decision-Making

Radical in the 1950s when it was introduced, our OD ancestors invented what they called "planned change," where front line performers were invited by top management into a process that generated ideas for improving things, which then went back to top management for consideration (see Beckhard, 1969; Lippitt, Watson, & Westley, 1958). This approach was picked up by large consulting firms and dubbed "change management." Unlike the application of planned change by our OD ancestors, which involved front-line employees, these top-down, consultant-driven change-management programs sold to so many corporations simply have not worked. The literature often reports that upwards of 75% of such initiatives fail. Successful WST is less about imposing change on an organization from *above* (management-driven change) or from *outside* (consultant-driven change), than it is about enabling and empowering the system to transform itself.

In WST, there is a blurring of the line between 1) who is identifying areas that need work and thinking up ideas for action, and 2) who is deciding what gets done. In WST, managers join front-line performers in developing breakthrough ideas, and front-line performers join managers in making decisions. As consulting colleague Bob Kline noted in a recent conversation:

> Rational management thinking must still be prized, but it alone simply cannot provide the *energy* needed for the long march that is transformation. What is needed is an empowered system where the empowerment does not come solely from the benevolence of positional authority, but also from a genuine sense of shared commitment to take initiative and be accountable for reaching larger goals.

Everyone involved, especially senior leaders and the consultants, both internal and external, need to practice what Buddhists call "passionate non-attachment." This means investing your all yet being willing to live in the "muck" of ambiguity and allowing a new organization and a new way of working to unfold. Transformation is not only a quantum leap—it is, as the current (millennial) generation might say, a "jump of faith." As chapter co-author Lavery describes it, "They just get it! It's as if they have been waiting for this all along!"

While consultants can facilitate and create a safe "container" that allows for WST, no one can force transformation to happen. Acts of force stop the natural evolutionary process of *discovery*. This requires a great deal of responsible and responsive leadership with a strong trust in both people and process. The seeds for this are planted back at the beginning, at the initial offsite for the senior leadership team. This is where the consultant(s) must remind leaders of their commitment to see the process through and not interrupt it out of fear or allow the old paradigms to defeat the emerging breakthroughs taking shape. There is often a lot of "hand-holding" of leaders by the consultants behind the scenes to keep them from stepping in and either stopping things or telling people what the right answer is. We might say something like this to a leader we sense is about to assert their authority: "Let the process unfold. Stay still, just a little while longer. Wait and see what happens next. You will be respected even more for doing this—and more likely to get that preferred future you say you want."

At a well-designed WST event, you will not see the external consultants dominating the process from the front of the room with their magic markers and PowerPoint slides. What you will see are internal people from across the organization and from many levels working with the externals in guiding the agenda. For many external consultants, this kind of "letting go"' is almost unthinkable. "What happens if they mess up?" is the rationale for taking charge. In the service of creating greater ownership—and therefore greater sustainability—it is more important for people in the system to see "their own" leading than it is to have everything absolutely perfect. In those places where the internal team cannot be trained to handle a crucial aspect of the agenda, the external consultants step forward. What a powerful signal this sends to the system—and to leaders—who all have a chance to see their people in a more powerful, responsible and surprising way. As a CEO client recently put it, "Wow! I never knew our people cared so much, or were so smart about our situation!"

Getting the Whole System in the Room

Somehow the consultant must find a way to "get the system in the room" (Weisbord, 1987, 2004). In a small organization that is able shut down for three days, you could gather the entire system and do it in one go. This is rarely possible, so alternative methods must be created. One approach we use often is bringing together cross-functional, quasi-representative groups of from 64 to 2,000 people for that three-day/three-evening off-site, and repeating the process to ensure the involvement of everyone in the system.

You will almost always get "push-back" on the three-day off-site requirement. "Can't we do what we need to do in a half-day?" a client may ask. The answer is, "Not if you truly desire to create sustainable transformation." The optimum schedule starts at 6:00 p.m. on Day 1 and ends at around 1:00 p.m. on Day 4. Given how long the system has been "perfecting" what it is doing now (that is not working), three days of hard work seems a small price to pay to create a quantum leap.

A typical WST Intensive event for the whole system will usually include these kinds of elements in the agenda:

- *Setting the context:* The CEO says, "We are here because we need to. . ."
- *Acknowledging history:* "We will be building a new structure on the old foundation, which includes. . ."
- *Ventilation:* People get a chance to complain about the way things are. "Complaints are actually stuck energy patterns. Underneath the complaint is an undeclared commitment, and a whole lot of energy yearning to be released" (Chapter co-author Lavery). In an appreciative inquiry model of WST, complaints get converted into what is working well and what can be learned from these successes.
- *Visioning:* Everyone is involved in a process to generate words that have compelling power and heart for them and the organization.
- *Moving forward:* "What do we want to *hold on to, let go of,* and *learn or develop* in order to move toward that vision."
- *Action and Heart-Felt Commitment* (at the level of the individual, department, inter-department, whole system, and customer): Cross-functional, "stakeholder-rich" breakthrough teams formed and tasked.
- *Send-Off* by CEO and TMT Members.

Tracking and Reporting Results

In a typical WST process, participants go back to their organization "fired up" and focused on specific tasks that are directly connected with creating performance breakthroughs: new operational procedures, processes and people systems. It is imperative to track these initiatives in terms of real-world business results, which is, after all, the main reason for the WST effort. Measuring and reporting results—using the system's own hard numbers—provides ongoing impetus and validity to the WST process as people see how their efforts are making a difference in the real world.

Staying the Course

Transformation usually happens both within an individual and an organization in a "thunder clap" moment, but it does not stop there. In fact, when a quantum leap occurs in an organization's way of operating, learning, and adapting, transformation continues indefinitely, punctuated by times of stability and times of change (see Figure 4.2, the infinite energy loop of Polarity Management.) Once WST is initiated, the system must engage in many smaller change initiatives inside the larger transformational context that has been created. *Now* things like training and performance management and new procedures make sense, and connect directly to the bottom line. These change projects will become the focus of attention until the system realizes that it needs to once again engage in transformation, enabling the system's energy to continue to flow. As one of our clients said about a recent WST initiative, "It's important to see this as a new way of being rather than a program with an end. Even after two years, we're still on the journey. I suspect that transformation *is* our new state of being."

In a recent discussion, Jennifer Todd reflected on taking an organization on the WST journey: As a leader or consultant, if you are considering taking on WST for your organization, get ready for a ride. If your heart is open, this process will pierce you in unimaginable ways. You will experience the real pain of generations and cries for relief from thousands of people who have worked and worked in difficult, even impossible, situations. You will also have the honor of seeing the heart and soul of your organization emerge as the true desires, creativity, power and passion of people gets unleashed. And all the while you will be wrestling with yourself—the shifts and changes in your own head and heart as you go through your own transformation. This WST process is hugely challenging, invigorating and deeply rewarding. If you are leading it and truly experiencing it, *you don't get a hall pass.* It guarantees to change you from the inside out.

CONCLUSION

We believe WST is a concept whose moment has arrived. Although it does not take that much more *time* or *effort* to carry out, it does require a major shift in the *attitude, courage,* and *authenticity* of the consultant—as well as those sponsoring and leading the process. As great teachers have said over the centuries, "You can't take people where you haven't been yourself." WST cannot be led by a consultant who has not experienced—and who does not continue to experience—transformation in their life and their practice.

As opposed to the traditional planned change approach, WST accomplishes what is needed by most organizations today that require significant shifts in the way they do their work in the real world. Planned change is popular in part because of the amount of control exercised by top management in an incremental process and the sense of safety that comes with it. Ironically, it is that same attachment to safety and control by top management that prevents the effort from leading to the extraordinary results they seek, primarily because it has not connected with the human spirit. *Unleashing the spirit of an organization to create performance breakthroughs* is what WST is all about.

John Parker, Executive Sponsor of WST from a highly-successful company committed to "thrilling the customer," sums it up this way:

> Whole System Transformation fosters deep change. It requires personal transformation on everyone's part. It also requires courage to take an organization through this type of change. The impacts are extraordinary, one of which is the expanded capability for change in the organization. The employee engagement that results is an unbelievable thing to see and feel. It is worth it! It is hard work, emotional, draining, and miraculous. It is magic! And yes, very rewarding.

What our world needs now is organizations and institutions that know how to continue to adapt and learn how to be whole systems that are continually transforming. And that requires more consultants who can do what we have attempted to lay out here—creating sustainable whole system transformation.

NOTES

1. The concept of whole system transformation was coined by Roland Sullivan in 1974. See Rothwell and Sullivan (2005), Dannemiller and Cady (2005), and Dannemiller-Tyson Associates (2000).
2. The WST schematic was developed by our colleague, Tom Dick. He can be reached at: tom_dick@msn.com.

REFERENCES

Beckhard, R. (1969). *Organization development: Strategies and models.* Reading, MA: Addison-Wesley.

Capra, F. (1975). *The Tao of physics.* Boulder, CO: Shambala.

Dannemiller, K., & Cady, S. (2005). Whole system transformation™: Five truths of change. In W. Rothwell & R. Sullivan, (Eds.) *Practicing organization development* (pp. 440–455). New York: Wiley.

Dannemiller-Tyson Associates. (2000). *Whole-scale change: Unleashing the magic in organizations.* San Francisco: Berrett-Koehler, 2000.

Johnson, B. (1992). *Polarity management.* Amherst, MA: HRD Press.

Lewin, K. (1951). *Field theory in social science.* New York: Harper & Row.

Lindaman, E., & Lippitt, R. (1979). *Choosing the future you prefer.* Ann Arbor, MI: HRDA Press.

Lippitt, R., Watson, J., & Westley, B. (1958). *The dynamics of planned change.* New York: Harcourt Brace & World.

Rothwell, W. J., & Sullivan, R. (2005). *Practicing organization development.* San Francisco: Pfeiffer/John Wiley, 2005.

Scherer, J. J. (2009). *Five questions that change everything: Life lessons at work.* Fort Collins, CO: WordKeepers Press.

Scherer, J .J., & Yeoell, M. (2001). *Facing the tiger: How to turn conflict into positive change.* Amherst, MA: HRD Press.

Weisbord, M. (1987). *Productive workplaces: Organizing and managing for dignity, meaning and community.* San Francisco: Jossey-Bass.

Weisbord, M. (2004). *Productive workplaces revisited: Dignity, meaning and community in the 2lst century.* San Francisco: Jossey-Bass.

Wheatley, M. (1992). *Leadership and the new science.* San Francisco: Barrett-Kohler.

Zukav, G. (1979). *The dancing Wu Li masters.* New York: William Morrow.

PART II

CHANGE FRAMEWORKS AND PERSPECTIVES

CHAPTER 5

INTERVENTION AND ORGANIZATIONAL CHANGE

Building Organizational Change Capacity[1]

Kenneth W. Kerber and Anthony F. Buono

A basic reality of the 21st century is that organizations and their management are faced with unrelenting demands for change. Companies in literally every industry are increasingly being challenged to both respond to and anticipate continuously changing competitive, market, technological, economic, and social conditions to the point where change is described as the "new normal" (Jørgensen, Owen, & Neus, 2008). Yet, despite this reality, and a virtual explosion of research and managerial attention devoted to conceptualizing and empirically testing a range of change management practices (cf. Abrahamson, 2000; Armenakis & Harris, 2002, 2009; Beer, Eisenstat, & Spector, 1990; de Caluwé & Vermaak, 2002; Higgs & Rowland, 2005; Kerber & Buono, 2005; King & Wright, 2007; Kotter, 1996; Kotter & Cohen, 2002), successful organizational change often remains an elusive

Consultation for Organizational Change. pages 81–112
Copyright © 2010 by Information Age Publishing
All rights of reproduction in any form reserved.

quest. A global business study by McKinsey underscores this problem, noting that only one-third of organizational change initiatives were viewed as successful by their leaders (Meaney & Pung, 2008). As a recent IBM white paper study suggests, the "change gap" (i.e., the gap between an organization's expectation of change and its history of successfully managing it) has increased significantly over the past few years (see Jørgensen, et al, 2008).

On a general level, managers have grown increasingly comfortable with planned change, as organizational leaders rather than external specialists have taken on increasingly active roles in bringing about change (cf. Aiken & Keller, 2007; Kotter & Cohen, 2002; Nadler, 1988). Indeed, more and more managers have become skilled at reacting to external forces, conceptualizing a preferred future state, and implementing the subsequent "plan" for achieving that well-defined end. In this context, however, change is largely viewed as linear and mechanistic, as a series of discrete and, at times, traumatic events that need to be controlled to enable the organization to achieve its goals. Given the onslaught of changes that a growing number of organizations now face, however, this carefully planned, change-specific approach is quickly becoming inadequate as success in rapidly changing environments often demands experimentation, improvisation and the ability to cope with unanticipated occurrences and unintended repercussions (see, for example, Gersick, 1991; Meyer & Stensaker, 2006; Wheatley, 1992). In essence, companies increasingly face the challenge of sustaining continuous movement—sometimes fast, sometimes slow interspersed with brief periods of constancy (e.g., Leana & Barry, 2000)—toward a largely unknown, emergent future state.

BUILDING A CAPACITY FOR CHANGE

The literature has a number of discussions of "change readiness," a mental state that typically focuses on the extent to which organizational members' beliefs, attitudes and intentions reflect and recognize the need for a particular change at a specific point in time (e.g., Armenakis, Harris & Mossholder, 1993; Cawsey & Deszca, 2007; Miles, 1997; Neves, 2009; Smith, 1996). As this literature notes, attempts to enhance change readiness encompass a number of factors, including clarifying the underlying message for the change (needs, anticipated effects), mobilizing collective support for the change across the organization, and encouraging active participation in the change process.

Since such readiness is seen as fundamental to the successful management of change, given the constant state of flux in the current business environment some observers have suggested that it might be more successful to focus on facilitating *continuous* change readiness rather than on implementing and managing specific change efforts (By, 2007; By, Diefenbach & Klarner, 2008). Given this emphasis, it is important to differentiate change readiness with respect to the ability to implement a specific change, from *change capacity*—the ability of an organization to change not just once, but as a normal course of events in response to and in anticipation of internal and external shifts, constantly adapting to and anticipating changes in its environment (see, for example, Klarner, Probst, & Soparnot, 2008; Myers & Stensaker, 2006; White & Linden, 2002). Change capacity, which in essence is a broader concept, requires a much more extensive set of interventions. Such capacity implies a focus on multiple, often iterative and over-lapping, changes over time, which is different from the traditional view of change as a series of isolated events (Meyer & Stensaker, 2006). Change capacity is thus an ongoing capability that reflects (1) a dynamic process of continuous learning and adjustment, enabling the organization to thrive on ambiguity and uncertainty, and (2) the ability to implement those changes (Klarner, et al, 2008; Staber & Sydow, 2002).

Drawing on our observations and consulting experience over the past twenty years, the paper focuses on the challenge of building organizational change capacity, enhancing an organization's ability to successfully navigate an array of changes in response to and in anticipation of ever shifting market conditions, customer demands, competitive pressures and societal conditions. As illustrated in Table 5.1, building organizational change capacity includes three primary dimensions reflecting change-related processes, an organizational context that facilitates change, and organizational learning (cf. Gravenhorst, Werkman & Boonstra, 2003; Klarner, et al, 2008). It requires focused intervention at the:

1. *micro-* (understanding and acceptance of different approaches to change; enhancing willingness and ability to change):
2. *meso-* (creating a change facilitative infrastructure, ensuring appropriate resources); and
3. *macro-* (building a facilitative culture, ongoing strategizing) levels of the organization.

In essence, building change capacity involves a systemic approach to developing the organization in ways that tap into people's natural capacity to change by supporting change and making it a basic part of organizational life.

Intervening at the Micro-level

An important first step in building organizational change capacity is to understand the nature of change and the various ways in which it can be

Table 5.1. Building Organizational Change Capacity

Level	Focus	Illustrative Actions
Micro	Developing an understanding and acceptance of different change approaches	• Adopt a common, enterprise-wide framework for thinking and talking about change • Develop widespread knowledge about different approaches to change and when each is appropriate • Develop deep expertise about change in the organization • Provide change coaching and consulting services • Establish change agent networks to share best practices, tools and insights about changing • Debrief change initiatives with a focus on learning from experience
	Enhancing willingness and ability to change	• Select, hire, evaluate and reward people based on their ability to thrive on change • Form diverse teams to encourage innovation and creativity • Develop, reward and promote supervisors and managers who enable change • Enhance the personal credibility of organizational leaders • Listen to, encourage, and reward mavericks and trailblazers • Create a climate of trust, honesty, and transparency
Meso	Building a change-supportive infrastructure	• Hold frequent meetings to identify and critically assess opportunities • Encourage low-cost experiments with new ideas • Recognize and reward those who support, encourage, lead and share learning about change • Maintain a fluid structure that allows the easy formation of new groups • Create systems to share knowledge, information and learning across boundaries • Provide responsive and proactive training and education
	Providing appropriate resources	• Designate an owner of the goal to develop change capacity • Devote resources to continually scanning the environment for new ideas • Encourage external contact with stakeholders, especially with customers • Appoint committed change sponsors for specific initiatives • Target key change initiatives with enough resources to get public successes • Shelter breakthroughs with their own budgets and people

(*continued*)

Table 5.1. (continued)

Level	Focus	Illustrative Actions
Macro	Creating a change-facilitative culture	• Emphasize learning and information sharing • Encourage questions and experiments • Value alternative viewpoints • Support people who take risks • Tolerate mistakes in the interest of learning • Value conflict
	Ensuring ongoing strategizing	• Create a shared purpose • Think dynamically and systemically so that strategies can change quickly • Examine future markets, competitors, and opportunities • Factor future scenarios into today's decisions • String together a series of momentary advantages • Create and communicate a change friendly identity, both internally and externally

dealt with, with the goal of enhancing the willingness and ability of organizational members to change.

Conceptualizing Different Approaches to Change

From a conceptual vantage point, there are three basic, interrelated approaches to implementing organizational change: directed change, planned change and guided changing (Kerber & Buono, 2005; see Table 5.2). *Directed change* is driven from the top of the organization and relies on authority, persuasion and compliance. Leaders create and announce the change and seek to convince organizational members to accept it based on business necessity, logical arguments (rational persuasion), emotional appeals, and the leader's personal credibility. Directed change reflects a quick, decisive approach to introducing change in an organization.

Planned change, which has become an increasingly popular approach to change management, may arise from any level in the organization but ultimately is sponsored by the top. Change leaders and implementers seek involvement in and commitment to the change by making extensive use of specific actions, identified through research and experience, which mitigate the typical resistance and productivity losses associated with directed change (e.g., Beckhard & Pritchard, 1992; Beer & Nohria, 2000; Kotter, 1996; LaMarsh, 1995). Underlying most planned change efforts is the Lewinian three-stage process of unfreezing, changing, and refreezing:

1. unfreezing or releasing the organization from its current patterns;

2. transitioning the resulting, more malleable, organization from its current patterns to more adaptive ones; and then
3. refreezing the organization into a new set of patterns by weaving them into the fabric of the organization (Lewin, 1947, 1951; Weick & Quinn, 1999).

Thus, instead of simply creating and announcing a change, planned change provides a "roadmap" that outlines a project management approach to the change process. It attempts to create the conditions for people to become more involved in the change process, identifying and encouraging key stakeholders to participate in both the form and implementation of the change.

A very different approach to implementing change is *guided changing*, an emergent process that can start at any location within the organization. It is based on the commitment of organizational members and their contributions to the purpose of the organization. In the context of the over-lapping changes that are characteristic of today's hypercompetitive environment, this approach attempts to take full advantage of the expertise and creativity of organizational members, as organic changes emerge and evolve, reconfiguring existing practices and models, and testing new ideas and perspectives. As illustrated in Figure 5.1, guided changing is an iterative process of initial interpretation and design, implementation and improvisation, learning from the change effort, and then sharing that learning system-wide, leading to ongoing re-interpretation and redesign of the change as needed. The resulting spiral of learning, innovation and development contributes to both continuous improvement of existing change efforts as well as the ability to generate novel changes and solutions.

As suggested above, each of these approaches has certain advantages but each one has disadvantages as well. For example, when directed change

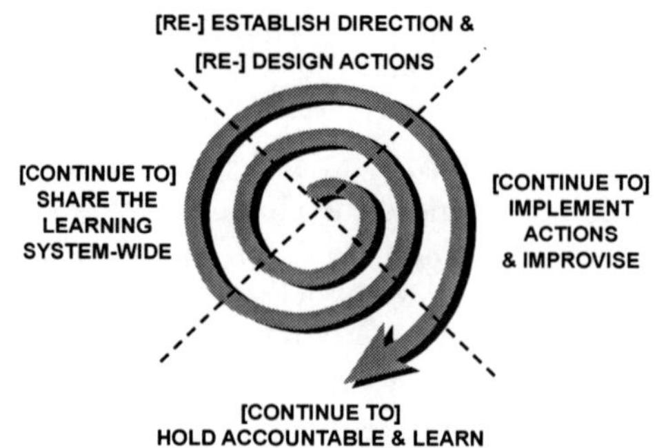

FIGURE 5.1. The Guided Changing Spiral

is used inappropriately organizational members are forced to cope with the well-known and expected reactions of the recipients of the imposed change—denial, anger, bargaining, sadness and loss (e.g., Kubler-Ross, 1969; Marks, 2003; Nalbandian, 1985). Similarly, while planned change creates an important capability in today's organizations, used inappropriately it can still result in significant reductions in productivity, overwhelm organizational members with its complexity, and alienate key stakeholders as a result of limited participation and true influence in the process. A related limitation with planned change is a lack of flexibility in the face of changing conditions. As experience has illustrated, planned change efforts often constrain the ability of the organization to achieve its intended goals (e.g., Abrahamson, 2000; By, et al, 2008; Kerber, 2001). Moreover, the burden for initiating and sustaining the change is still placed directly on organizational leaders, from identifying the need for change and creating a vision of desired outcomes to deciding which changes are ultimately feasible. Finally, our experience suggests that guided changing, if used inappropriately, can contribute to organizational chaos, as continuous changes and transitions confuse and frustrate rather than enlighten organizational members and other key stakeholders. The need to constantly adapt and adjust—the idea of "living in beta" (Wilson, 2008)—can be a daunting experience. A related resource issue is that repeated iterations could easily burn up a fair amount of time and other resources without necessarily "finishing" the process and moving on to the next change. Many people ultimately want organizational change to end, rather than experience changing as a way of doing business that, in essence, never ends.

Acceptance of Different Approaches to Change

Given the reality that each of these approaches has certain advantages and disadvantages, developing true change capacity entails the ability to move back and forth among these change management approaches as dictated by the situation. There are two key factors that influence the appropriateness of each of these approaches to change: business complexity and socio-technical uncertainty (Kerber & Buono, 2005).

Business complexity refers to the intricacy of the system, in essence, the number of different components and extent of differentiation in the organization in which the change is to be implemented. While there are no precise demarcation points between low and high business complexity, indicators include such factors as organizational size and geographical dispersion, the nature of interdependencies and related technology, the number of products and services, and the array of critical stakeholders. The degree of business complexity increases:

1. the more an organizational change cuts across different hierarchical levels, different work units and different geographic locations;
2. involves reciprocal or team interdependence;
3. affects a range of products and services; and
4. requires the buy-in of a number of internal and external stakeholders.

Thus, the focus is on the relative complexity of implementing the change solution and what it will take to successfully introduce and sustain the change overtime.

Socio-technical uncertainty refers to the amount and nature of information processing and decision making required for the change based on the extent to which the tasks involved are determined, established, and/or exactly known. Some tasks are clearly analyzable, where work processes can be reduced to repeatable steps. In these instances, organizational members can be directed to follow objective, standardized procedures based on technical knowledge and managerial expertise. As the change challenge and its solution become less clear and the appropriate solution is far more difficult to identify, such directed or planned approaches begin to break down. In these instances, there is no organizational repertoire of suitable techniques or procedures, and organizational members must draw on their own judgment, intuition and expertise. While no precise demarcation points appear between low and high socio-technical uncertainty, situations can be described as varying in the extent to which there are:

1. clearly known ways to approach the situation;
2. an understandable sequence of steps that can be followed; and
3. an identifiable set of established procedures and practices (see Daft, 2001; Perrow, 1970).

In low socio-technical uncertainty situations, the solution to the change challenge is known, while in high socio-technical uncertainty contexts the solution is not known or even fully understood. When socio-technical uncertainty is high, the problem itself is not fully described or clearly understood, meaning that the search for a solution occurs simultaneously with the search for a clear definition of the problem.

As illustrated in Figure 5.2, when thinking about appropriate approaches to implementing organizational change, the primary driver of the shift from directed change to planned change is increasing business complexity, while the shift to guided changing is driven by increasing socio-technical uncertainty. As the dynamics of a particular situation change—and the relative business complexity and/or socio-technical uncertainty shift—the approach to implementing the change should also evolve. As an example, once an appropriate solution to a guided changing challenge has emerged

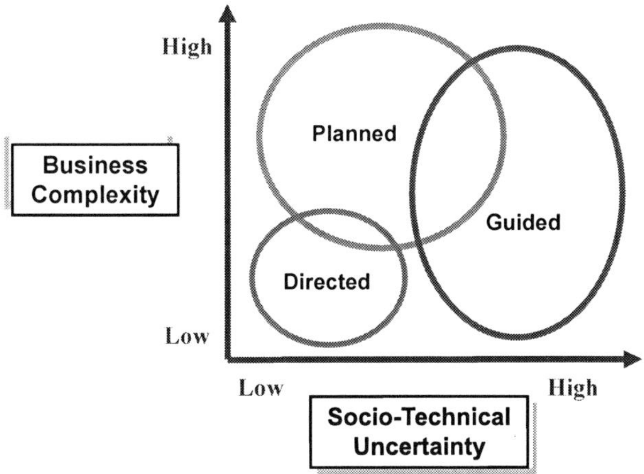

FIGURE 5.2. Complexity, Uncertainty and Approaches to Change

(in essence, decreasing the socio-technical uncertainty involved), implementation should then shift to either a planned or directed change approach based on the relative business complexity of the situation and urgency of the required change.

Enhancing Change Willingness and Ability

Much like the idea of emergent change itself, it is more effective to have the motivation to seek out different approaches to change come from the organization and its members. While managers may have the ability to undertake such change, many are often not willing to accept nor are comfortable with the idea of ongoing iteration and improvisation. Thus, in getting managers to think more fully about the challenges associated with organizational change, it is typically most effective to begin where they are likely to be most comfortable—by enhancing organizational understanding of how to successfully lead planned change in their specific context. As part of such discussions, managers typically begin to see the need for a more iterative approach to change as they wrestle with problems and issues that are not clearly defined.

In prompting the reasons underlying their frustration, organizational members typically point to situations from their own experience that start with little more than a general direction, *without* a clearly defined end state, because the solution (or outcome) is generally not determined, established or exactly known. As organizational members discuss the nature of the problems they face, they also begin to question the limits of planned change. One of the ways this process can be facilitated is through the completion of a diagnostic questionnaire focused on the nature of the problem the organization is facing (see Appendix 5.1: Assessing Appropriate Approaches to Change). At this point, it is useful to prompt managers to think about the challenges and skills necessary to "move forward" in dealing with highly complex and uncertain problems—reinforcing the ways in which *business complexity* and *socio-technical uncertainty* shape and influence change management dynamics (see Figure 5.2).

Moving from directed change to planned change to guided changing—and back and forth as needed—involves significant competence transfer from executives and managers to organizational members as the latter become, in effect, the new change leaders. The transition from directed or planned change to guided changing, in particular, can pose a significant challenge for executives and organizational members, who are both accustomed to having the former lead change. While resistance is clearly related to instances where people feel change is being thrust upon them—especially when that change is associated with loss (Nalbandian, 1985)—a downside of carefully orchestrated planned change is that it might create an artificial sense of security among organizational members that could limit reflection (Werr, Stjernberg, & Docherty, 1997) and, as a result, suppress the type of learning and improvisation necessary for successful guided changing. Organizational members may also be reluctant to accept responsibility for identifying the nature of a required change—there is a certain comfort in having leaders say, "Here is the problem and the solution." At the same time, one of the greatest challenges to the implementation of this type of emergent, guided changing may be the unwillingness of upper-level managers to let go of tight management control and embrace a messy, dynamic process that can involve the entire organization (Buono & Kerber, 2008; see also By, et al, 2008).

In an effort to enhance the willingness and ability of organizational members to embrace change, companies can place greater emphasis on selecting, hiring, evaluating and rewarding people based on their ability to thrive on change. As a way of encouraging innovation and creativity, firms can also create and support highly diverse teams—prompting, listening to, and rewarding mavericks and trailblazers, so-called "positive deviants" who "transcend the conventional wisdoms, discovering new and innovative ways to function *without* creating conflict" (Seidman & McCauley, 2008). Finally, as part of an effort to enhance the personal credibility of organizational leaders, it is important that organizations create a climate of trust, honesty and transparency. Persuasive and ethical communication is critical, ensuring both the clarity of the message and the honesty and trustworthiness of managers and executives. If organizational members do not trust the change implementer and his or her message, their acceptance of the change is unlikely.

Intervening at the Meso-level: Building a Change-Supportive Infrastructure

Directed change involves telling people what to do and how to do it, with little or no opportunity for input about or modification of the change goal or process. In such instances, the infrastructure supporting the change and the resources that are required for successful change tend to be minimal. Even so, an important dimension of directed change communication is the ability to respond to the "so that" question— "We are changing X *so that* we will be able to accomplish Y"—making certain that organizational members fully understand the reason, rationale and expected outcome of the change (see Ulrich, Zenger, & Smallwood, 1999). Yet, while this approach is effective in low complexity/low uncertainty situations, it can severely limit the development of an organization that is faced with more complex and uncertain changes.

In confronting these latter instances, guided changing involves identifying an overall direction and then giving people the opportunity to modify and re-define both the change goal and the change process as needed. For this approach to be successful there must be open and lavish communication across individuals and groups, with flexible systems and processes to allow for and support improvisation and iteration, cross-boundary meetings to identify and critically assess new opportunities, and responsive and proactive training and development that provides organizational members with the requisite skills for such continual learning and experimentation. It is also important to have a sufficiently fluid structure that allows groups to be easily formed and ended as needed, encouraging an open sharing of information, knowledge and learning across departmental and work unit boundaries. Traditional planning and communication strategies, which typically serve as the basic mechanism for work group-related coordination, fall short of supporting the type of dynamic interactions and adjustments that contribute to the ongoing collaboration required for more iterative processes (see Rico, Sanchez-Manzanares, Gil & Gibson, 2008). The infrastructure should also encourage low-cost experimentation with new ideas. Sometimes referred to as "no-budget knowledge management" (Hardy, 2007), emphasis is placed on carrying out multiple initiatives that simultaneously improvise, test and iterate solutions and new directions. Once a breakthrough emerges, however, it is important to shelter the effort with its own budget and people.

Within this context, appropriate resources to support the change are critical for such emergent change to be successful. As illustrated in Table 5.2, in addition to sufficient time, people and financial resources, mindshare is critical. When people feel over-loaded and overwhelmed by organizational tasks and responsibilities, they are often reluctant to engage in the

Table 5.2. Differentiating Approaches to Managing Change

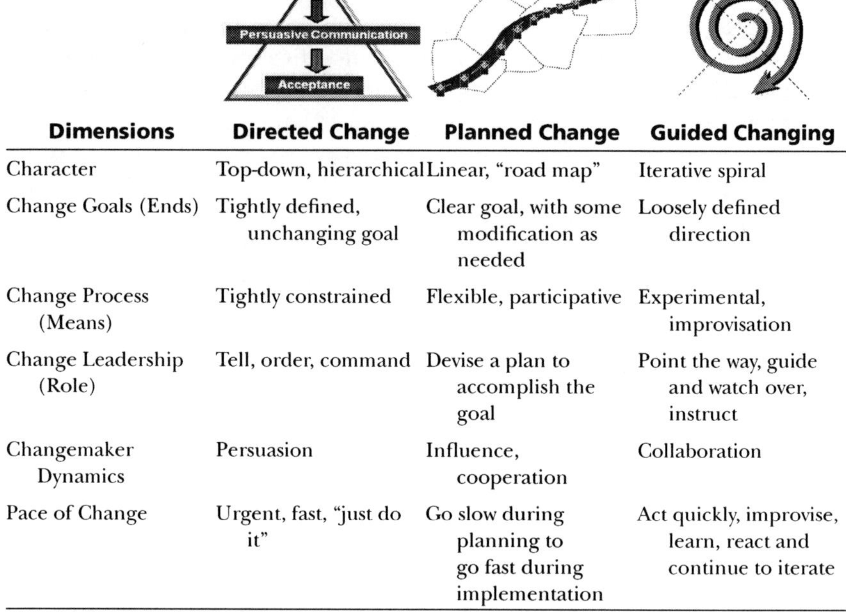

Dimensions	Directed Change	Planned Change	Guided Changing
Character	Top-down, hierarchical	Linear, "road map"	Iterative spiral
Change Goals (Ends)	Tightly defined, unchanging goal	Clear goal, with some modification as needed	Loosely defined direction
Change Process (Means)	Tightly constrained	Flexible, participative	Experimental, improvisation
Change Leadership (Role)	Tell, order, command	Devise a plan to accomplish the goal	Point the way, guide and watch over, instruct
Changemaker Dynamics	Persuasion	Influence, cooperation	Collaboration
Pace of Change	Urgent, fast, "just do it"	Go slow during planning to go fast during implementation	Act quickly, improvise, learn, react and continue to iterate

type of experimentation, improvisation and learning that is characteristic of guided changing. As part of this process, it is also useful to designate an "owner" of the goal to develop organizational change capacity, a role that not only serves as change champion but one that can ensure appropriate sponsorship for different initiatives as well. Resources must also be available for continually scanning the environment for new ideas, encouraging contact with external stakeholders (e.g., customers).

Intervening at the Macro-level: Creating a Culture of Change

While organizations typically emphasize stability, predictability and execution, a change-facilitative organization culture is one that embraces fluidity, openness and learning (see Lawler & Worley, 2006; McLagan, 2003). The ability to break free of organizational traditions and move away from familiar rules and operating procedures, of course, is not easy to do. Indeed, the power of custom and the status quo reinforce cultures that forestall the types of adjustments—especially in terms of agility and flexibility—that organizational members need to embrace in unstable environments (see Thompson, 1994). At the same time, a change-facilitative culture recognizes that more traditional approaches to change may still be appropriate in certain circumstances. It is imperative, therefore, that all organizational members become better informed about the advantages and limitations of different approaches to change as well as the broader context for the change itself as they develop a shared framework for thinking and talking about change. In essence, the organization must strive to create a shared purpose supported by a common language about change.

As part of this process, managers at all levels should be encouraged to embrace a stakeholder orientation that emphasizes learning and information sharing, encourages questions and experiments, values alternative viewpoints and tolerates mistakes in the interest of learning. A focus on simply getting things done—and done right the first time—can quickly crowd out the type of reflection and experimentation that is increasingly vital to success in today's rapidly changing, hyper-competitive environment (see Edmondson, 2008).

A related macro-level factor that affects organizational change capacity involves the organization's approach to strategy. In contrast to traditional approaches to strategy, Lawler and Worley (2006) emphasize the importance of making "strategizing" the normal condition. This approach to strategy involves thinking dynamically, focusing on the future, and stringing together a series of momentary advantages, rather than attempting to achieve a sustainable competitive advantage. Although a high change capacity organization certainly requires a shared purpose to provide overall direction, strategies for achieving that shared purpose can change quickly based on scenarios involving future markets, competitors, and opportunities. Combined with the type of change-facilitative organizational culture discussed above, this dynamic approach to strategizing encourages the organization to keep pace with, if not anticipate, external changes that are critical to business success.

It is important that organizations work to create a shared understanding through which organizational members are:

1. encouraged to think dynamically and systemically so that strategies can change quickly;
2. supported in their efforts to think about future markets, competitors, and opportunities; and
3. prompted to factor future scenarios into today's decisions.

In general, an underlying goal is to create and communicate a change friendly identity both internally and externally.

A Case Illustration: Building Change Capacity

An example of this approach recently occurred in a client organization, a multi-billion dollar global technology leader (GlobalCom) focused on information infrastructure technologies, services and solutions, that was faced with a long-term, complex problem with uncertain dimensions. During a workshop in which different approaches to change were examined (see Table 5.2), the senior management team wrestled with how to best implement a large-scale planned change that would revamp the process through which GlobalCom's services are delivered to customers. Drawing on the questionnaire noted earlier (see Appendix 5-1: Assessing Appropriate Approaches to Change), in discussing the business complexity involved in such a massive undertaking, it became increasingly clear that they were also dealing with a higher level of socio-technical uncertainty than initially realized. As they shared the results of the questionnaire (see Figure 5.3) and worked through the process, it became more and more apparent that a planned change approach would fall short of what they needed to do, especially in terms of gathering input from their global field-based workforce, assessing local practices and preferred service delivery strategies, evaluating and assessing this information in light of customer needs and workforce expectations, and determining an appropriate cost structure and level of service uniformity. During the discussion, the group re-visited the idea of guided changing—initial interpretation and design, implementation and improvisation, learning from the change effort, sharing that learning system-wide, then moving to reinterpretation and redesign and so forth—using the iterative process to think through how the new service delivery model could be created and better integrated across all of the key areas of the company. Emphasis was placed on supporting improvisation and shared learning throughout the organization.

As part of their analysis, the senior management team further examined GlobalCom's overall capacity for change, noting that the constraints they were operating under fell short of the change demands of the situation (see Figure 5.3). Based on their assessment of GlobalCom's change capacity (see Appendix 5.2: Organizational Change Capacity Questionnaire), they drew on the illustrative actions in Table 5.1 to guide their thinking about how they could begin to solidify a foundation that would facilitate an organization-wide commitment to the integrated services delivery change as well as other changes that would likely follow. This questionnaire was intended as a "semi-finished" instrument (see Lobnig, 2009), with the goal of stimulating deep, on-going conversations between team members, pushing toward new learnings, new mindsets, and new skills about change and how they could build greater change capacity within their organization. The underlying objective was to help the management team frame the complexity they were dealing with, assisting them in translating the related uncertainty into grounded, concrete actions. As others have noted (e.g., Armenakis, et al, 1993; Armenakis & Harris, 2009; Gravenhorst, et al, 2003), such question-

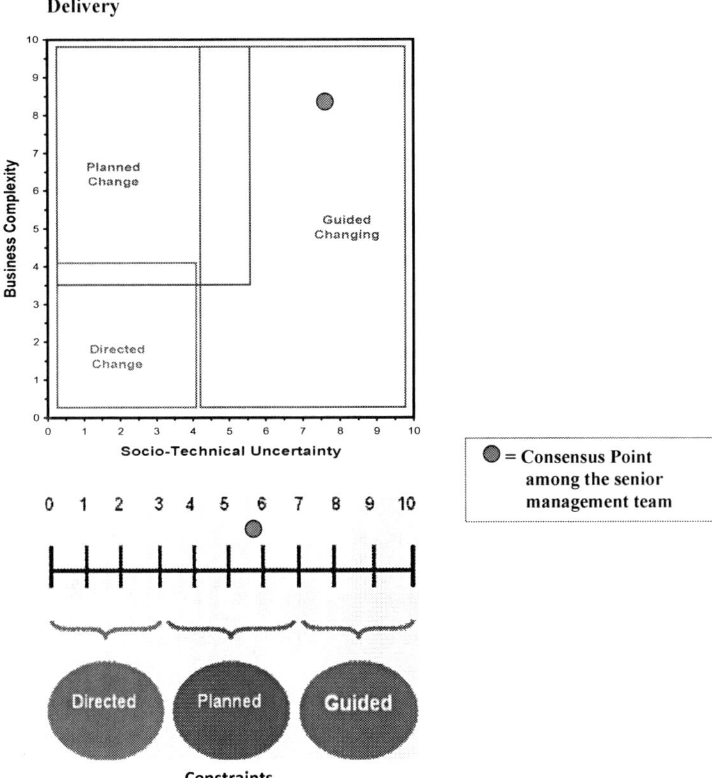

FIGURE 5.3. Assessing the Change Challenge at GlobalCom

naires can be very useful in change-related assessments, for discovery as much as confirmation purposes.

Drawing on this assessment, an important part of the senior management team's commitment to the change effort was to develop a plan to track the progress of the change and continually assess the extent to which GlobalCom was building appropriate micro-, meso-, and macro-levels of support for the initiative. These assessments would then be used to guide the planning for additional interventions to build the organization's capacity for both large-scale and ongoing change.

Returning to the micro-level, a next step was to create a series of workshops and webinars on "Mastering Change" that would capture this way of thinking, disseminating it to its world-wide workforce, encouraging middle-managers and the field-based service delivery personnel to explore, test and capture leading practices, and share that learning on a system-wide basis. The workshops were also used to encourage organizational members to think more analytically about the organizational change challenges that they faced in their work. Participants assessed which approach to change they thought was most appropriate for the challenge(s) they were personally facing. By assessing the relative business complexity and socio-technical uncertainty associated with their particular situation, and the concomitant infrastructure and culture needs at the meso- and macro-level, the managers were quite capable of determining how they should approach the change in question. Discussion also focused on working at the boundaries, as the types of change challenges and strategies often blur together in practice.

At this point, the intervention and process of creating the new services delivery model and way of thinking about organizational change are still in progress. To date, however, workshop participants have reported success in using this approach to conceptualize, plan, and implement change within their sphere of influence. With respect to GlobalCom's senior management team, beginning with an understanding and application of planned change, where they initially felt most comfortable, they began to realize *from their own experience* that planned change, while necessary and effective in many situations, was not necessarily sufficient for all situations. At the same time, they realized that as the plan for the new integrated service delivery system was created through this iterative process, once the uncertainties were resolved it would most likely take a planned change approach to ensure world-wide implementation, with the need to continually re-visit possibilities as their markets, resources and customer needs continued to evolve. In essence, they foresaw an ongoing iteration between guided changing and planned change in formulating new approaches and ensuring their implementation on a system-wide basis. Through their analysis, the senior management team also began to realize that the ability of the organization to accept and implement these different approaches to change required appropriate resources, a change-supportive infrastructure, and a culture that emphasized the importance of ongoing strategizing and changing.

INTERVENING TO BUILD CHANGE CAPACITY

Organizations and their management are quite capable of creating a sustainable foundation for implementing change if they focus the appropriate attention and resources on enhancing their change capacity. As discussed in this paper, this effort requires focused intervention at the micro-, meso-, and macro-levels of the organization. Based on the framework presented in the paper, our experience suggests that once organizational members begin to understand the various approaches to change and the concept of organizational change capacity, they are quite capable of determining the appropriate change approach—moving back and forth between directed and planned change and guided changing as necessary—*if* given the opportunity and support.

The approach and intervention described in the paper helped GlobalCom's senior management team to more fully appreciate the complexity and uncertainty of the task they were facing and understand that the complexity and uncertainty surrounding that task required a more patient and involving approach to the change process than they had utilized in the past. More often than not management teams approach highly complex and uncertain tasks with the same mindset and approach they "always use," which often leads them to underestimate the difficulty of the resultant change and, as a result, under-resource the change in terms of time, money, support, and so forth.

As one moves from directed change to planned change to guided changing, however, managers must be willing to give up control based on rules, procedures and tight supervision and substitute an approach based on overall direction, principles, values and commitment. At the same time, as the socio-technical uncertainty involved in the change is gradually resolved, organizational members must be willing to accept follow-on planned or directed changes as dictated by the business complexity and urgency involved. A shared purpose, supported by a common understanding and language about organizational change, can readily facilitate such transitions.

Unfortunately, organizations are all too frequently overly constrained by infrastructures, cultures and strategies that are based on needs for control and predictability rather than what is required by the rapidly changing environment. Companies and their management, however, can no longer afford to rely on ad hoc approaches to managing change that are controlled from above, in essence creating "self-sabotaging traps" that undermine their ability to effectively bring about needed changes in their organization (cf. Edmondson, 2008; Jørgensen, et al, 2008). The key is to encourage and support managers to broaden their change implementation repertoire by developing a common understanding of the dynamics of organizational change, building a change-supportive infrastructure, and creating and nurturing a change-facilitative culture. Although successful organizational change may seem to be an elusive quest, the ability to execute change on a sustainable basis is an achievable goal if organizations and their management invest in developing their change capacity.

NOTES

1. An earlier version of this paper was presented at the 2009 Academy of Management Meeting

REFERENCES

Abrahamson, E. (2000). Change without pain. *Harvard Business Review, 78*(4), 75–79.

Aiken C. B., & Keller S. P. (2007). The CEO's role in leading transformation. *Management Quarterly, 48*(2), 30–39.

Armenakis, A. A., & Harris, S. G. (2002). Crafting a change message to create transformational readiness. *Journal of Organizational Change Management, 15*(2), 169–183.

Armenakis, A. A., & Harris, S. G. (2009). Reflections: Our journey in organizational change research and practice. *Journal of Change Management, 9*(2), 127–142.

Armenakis, A. A., Harris, S. G., & Mossholder, K. W. (1993). Creating readiness for change. *Human Relations, 46*(6), 681–704.

Beckhard, R., & Pritchard, W. (1992). *Changing the essence.* San Francisco: Jossey-Bass.

Beer, M., Eisenstat, R., & Spector B. (1990). Why change programs don't produce change. *Harvard Business Review, 68*(6), 158–166.

Beer, M., & Nohria, N. (2000). Cracking the code of change. *Harvard Business Review, 78*(3), 133–141.

Buono, A. F. & Kerber, K. W. (2008). The challenge of organizational change: enhancing organizational change capacity. *Revue Sciences de Gestion,* (65), 99–118.

By, R. T. (2007). Ready or not ... *Journal of Change Management, 7*(1), 3–11.

By, R. T., Diefenbach, T., & Klarner, P. (2008). Getting organizational change right in public services: The case of European higher education. *Journal of Change Management, 8*(1), 21–35.

Cawsey, T., & Deszca, G. (2007). *Toolkit for organizational change.* Thousand Oaks, CA: Sage.

Daft, R. (2001). *Organization theory and design.* Cincinnati, OH: South-Western/Thomson.

de Caluwé, L., & Vermaak, V. (2002). *Learning to change: A guide for organization change agents.* London: Sage Publications.

Edmondson, A. C. (2008). The competitive imperative of learning. *Harvard Business Review, 86*(4), 60–67.

Gersick, C. (1991). Revolutionary change theories: A multilevel exploration of the punctuated equilibrium paradigm. *Academy of Management Review, 16,* 10–36.

Gravenhorst, K. M. B., Werkman, R. A., & Boonstra, J. J. (2003). The change capacity of organisations: General assessment and five configurations. *Applied Psychology: An International Journal, 52*(1), 83–105.

Hardy, B. (2007). Linking trust, change, leadership and innovation. *Knowledge Management Review, 10*(5), 18–23.

Higgs M., & Rowland D. (2005). All changes great and small: Exploring approaches to change and its leadership. *Journal of Organizational Change Management, 5*(2), 121–151.

Jørgensen, H. H., Owen, L., & Neus, A. (2008). *Making change work.* IBM Corporation. <www.ibm.com/gbs/makingchangework> Accessed November.

Kerber, K. W. (2001). Change in human systems: From planned change to guided changing. In A. F. Buono (Ed.), *Current trends in management consulting* (pp. 145–169). Greenwich, CT: Information Age Publishing.

Kerber, K. W., & Buono, A. F. (2005). Rethinking organizational change: Reframing the challenge of change management. *Organization Development Journal, 23*(3), 23–38.

King, S. B., & Wright, M. (2007). Building internal change management capability at Constellation Energy. *Organization Development Journal, 25*(2), 57–62.

Klarner, P., Probst, G., & Soparnot, R. (2008). Organizational change capacity in public services: The case of the world health organization. *Journal of Change Management, 8*(1), 57–72.

Kotter, J. P. (1996). *Leading change.* Boston: Harvard Business School Press.

Kotter, J. P., & Cohen, D. S. (2002). *The heart of change: Real-life stories of how people change their organizations,* Boston: Harvard Business School Press.

Kubler-Ross, E. (1969). *On death and dying.* New York: Macmillan.

LaMarsh, J. (1995). *Changing the way we change.* Reading, MA: Addison-Wesley.

Lawler, E.E. & Worley, C. (2006). *Build to change.* Palo Alto, CA: Kantola Productions, Stanford Executive Briefings.

Leana, C., & Barry, B. (2000). Stability and change as simultaneous experiences in organizational life. *Academy of Management Review, 25*(4), 753–759.

Lewin, K. (1947). Frontiers in group dynamics. *Human Relations, 1*(1), 5–47.

Lewin, K. (1951). *Field theory in social science.* New York: Harper & Row.

Lobnig, H. (2009). *Strategy work in an international setting: Entangling top-down and bottom-up approaches via continuous conversations, learning cycles and semi-finished instruments.* Paper presented at the 4th International Conference on Management Consulting, Vienna, Austria (June).

McLagan, P. A. (2003). The change-capable organization. *Training & Development, 57*(1), 51–57.

Marks, M. L. (2003). *Charging back up the hill: Workplace recovery after mergers, acquisitions, and downsizings.* San Francisco: Jossey-Bass.

Meaney, M., & Pung, C. (2008). McKinsey Global Results: Creating Organizational Transformations. *McKinsey Quarterly,* (August), 1–7.

Meyer, C. B., & Stensaker, I. G. (2006). Developing capacity for change. *Journal of Change Management, 6*(2), 217–231.

Miles, R. H. (1997). *Leading corporate transformation: A blueprint for business renewal.* San Francisco: Jossey-Bass.

Nadler D. A. (1988). Organizational frame bending: Types of change in the complex organization. In R. H. Kilmann, T .J. Covin, and Associates (Ed.), *Corporate transformation: Revitalizing organizations for a competitive world* (pp. 66–83). San Francisco: Jossey-Bass.

Nalbandian, J. (1985). Human relations and organizational change: Responding to loss. *Review of Public Personnel Administration, 6*(1), 29–43.

Neves, P. (2009). Readiness for change: Contributions for employee's level of individual change and turnover intentions. *Journal of Change Management, 9*(2), 215–231.

Perrow, C. (1970). *Organizational analysis: A sociological approach.* Belmont, CA: Wadsworth.

Rico, R., Sanchez-Manzanares, M., Gil, F., & Gibson, C. (2008). Team implicit coordination processes: A team knowledge-based approach. *Academy of Management Review, 33*(1), 163–184.

Seidman, W., & McCauley, M. (2008). Positive deviants rule! *Cutter IT Journal, 21*(7), 16–20.

Smith, D. K. (1996). *Taking charge of change.* Reading, MA: Addison-Wesley.

Staber, U., & Sydow, J. (2002). Organizational adaptive capacity: A structuration perspective. *Journal of Management Inquiry, 11*(4), 408–424.

Thompson, L. (1994). *Mastering the challenges of change.* New York: American Management Association.

Ulrich, D., Zenger, J., & Smallwood, N. (1999). *Results-based leadership: How leaders build the business and improve the bottom line.* Boston: Harvard Business School Press.

Weick K. E., & Quinn R.E. (1999). Organizational change and development. In J.T. Spence, J.M. Darley, & D.J. Foss (Eds.), *Annual review of psychology* (pp. 361–386). Palto Alto, CA: Annual Reviews, .

Werr, A., Stjernberg, T., & Docherty, P. (1997). The functions of methods of change in management consulting. *Journal of Organizational Change Management, 10*(4), 288–307.

Wheatley, M. (1992). *Leadership and the new science.* San Francisco: Berrett-Koehler.

White, S., & Linden, G. (2002). Organizational and industrial response to market liberalization: The interaction of pace, incentive and capacity to change. *Organization Studies, 23*(6), 917–948.

Wilson, A. (2008, November). *Innovation tools for an innovation society.* Presentation at the 2008 Copenhagen Innovation Symposium, Copenhagen Business School, Copenhagen, Denmark.

APPENDIX 5.1.
ASSESSING APPROPRIATE APPROACHES TO CHANGE

Part 1: Questions

Circle one number on each of the following 0 to 10 scales with reference to your change initiative.

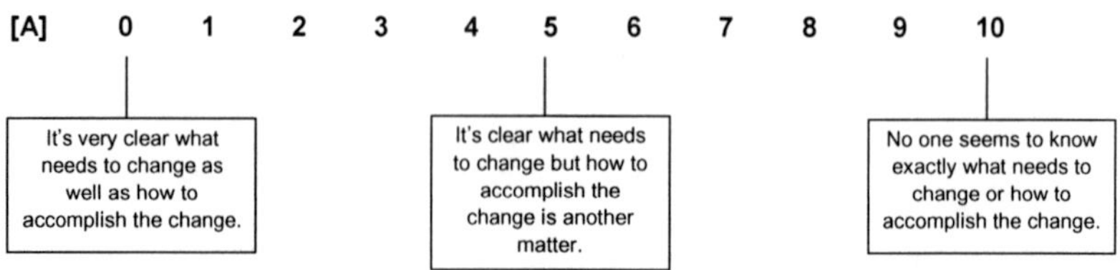

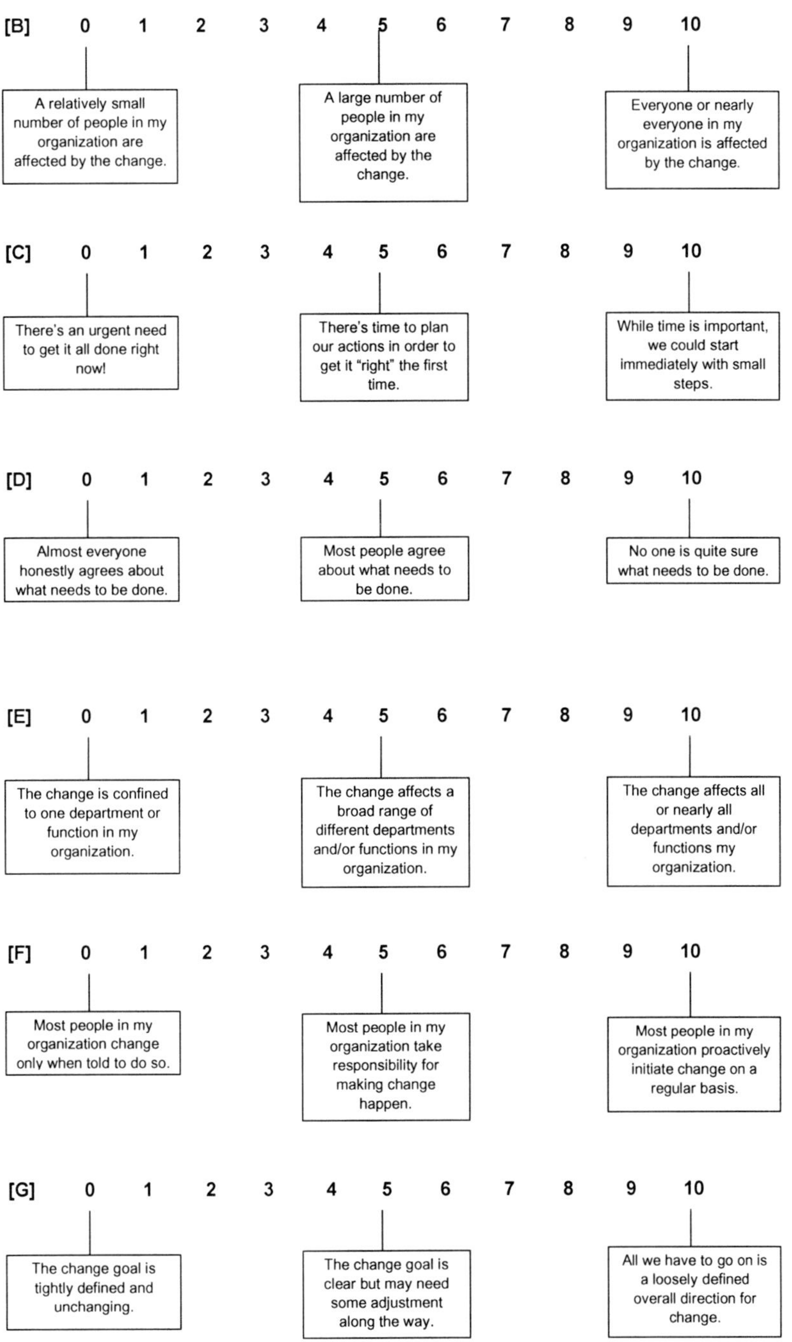
[B] 0 1 2 3 4 5 6 7 8 9 10
A relatively small number of people in my organization are affected by the change.
A large number of people in my organization are affected by the change.
Everyone or nearly everyone in my organization is affected by the change.
[C] 0 1 2 3 4 5 6 7 8 9 10
There's an urgent need to get it all done right now!
There's time to plan our actions in order to get it "right" the first time.
While time is important, we could start immediately with small steps.
[D] 0 1 2 3 4 5 6 7 8 9 10
Almost everyone honestly agrees about what needs to be done.
Most people agree about what needs to be done.
No one is quite sure what needs to be done.
[E] 0 1 2 3 4 5 6 7 8 9 10
The change is confined to one department or function in my organization.
The change affects a broad range of different departments and/or functions in my organization.
The change affects all or nearly all departments and/or functions my organization.
[F] 0 1 2 3 4 5 6 7 8 9 10
Most people in my organization change only when told to do so.
Most people in my organization take responsibility for making change happen.
Most people in my organization proactively initiate change on a regular basis.
[G] 0 1 2 3 4 5 6 7 8 9 10
The change goal is tightly defined and unchanging.
The change goal is clear but may need some adjustment along the way.
All we have to go on is a loosely defined overall direction for change.

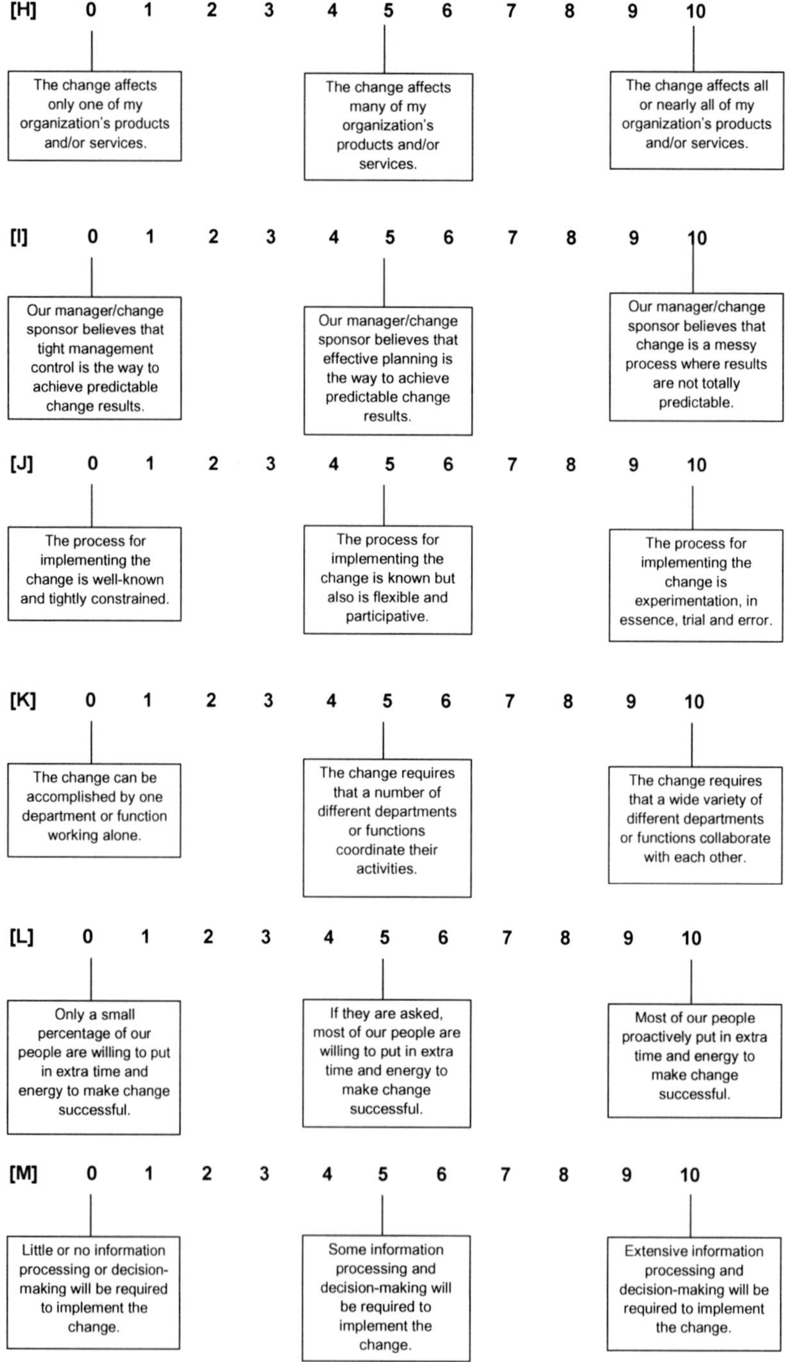
[H] 0 1 2 3 4 5 6 7 8 9 10
The change affects only one of my organization's products and/or services.
The change affects many of my organization's products and/or services.
The change affects all or nearly all of my organization's products and/or services.
[I] 0 1 2 3 4 5 6 7 8 9 10
Our manager/change sponsor believes that tight management control is the way to achieve predictable change results.
Our manager/change sponsor believes that effective planning is the way to achieve predictable change results.
Our manager/change sponsor believes that change is a messy process where results are not totally predictable.
[J] 0 1 2 3 4 5 6 7 8 9 10
The process for implementing the change is well-known and tightly constrained.
The process for implementing the change is known but also is flexible and participative.
The process for implementing the change is experimentation, in essence, trial and error.
[K] 0 1 2 3 4 5 6 7 8 9 10
The change can be accomplished by one department or function working alone.
The change requires that a number of different departments or functions coordinate their activities.
The change requires that a wide variety of different departments or functions collaborate with each other.
[L] 0 1 2 3 4 5 6 7 8 9 10
Only a small percentage of our people are willing to put in extra time and energy to make change successful.
If they are asked, most of our people are willing to put in extra time and energy to make change successful.
Most of our people proactively put in extra time and energy to make change successful.
[M] 0 1 2 3 4 5 6 7 8 9 10
Little or no information processing or decision-making will be required to implement the change.
Some information processing and decision-making will be required to implement the change.
Extensive information processing and decision-making will be required to implement the change.

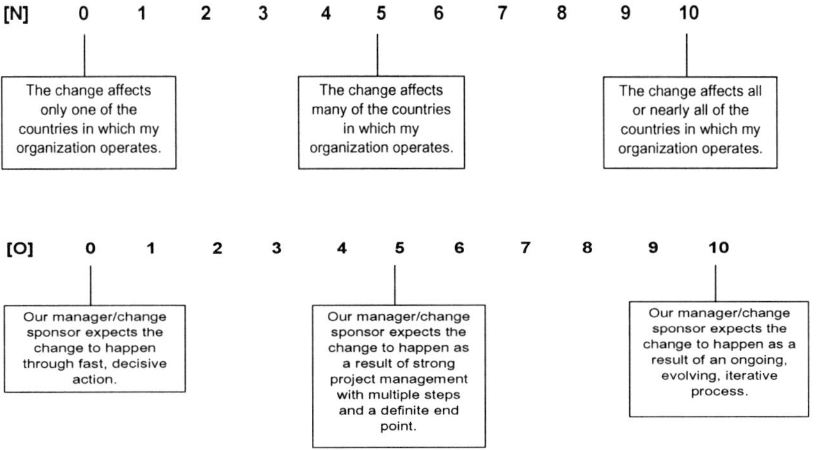

Part 2: Scoring

Next to each item below, write the rating that you gave that item on the questionnaire. After you have entered your rating for each item, calculate the average score for each column.

Item Score	Item Score	Item Score
B.__________	A.__________	C.__________
E.__________	D.__________	F.__________
H.__________	G.__________	I.__________
K.__________	J.__________	L.__________
N.__________	M.__________	O.__________
TOTAL = _____	TOTAL = _____	TOTAL = _____
$\frac{\text{Total}}{5}$ = _____	$\frac{\text{Total}}{5}$ = _____	$\frac{\text{Total}}{5}$ = _____
Business Complexity	***Socio-Technical Uncertainty***	***Constraints***

Business complexity refers to the intricacy of the system, i.e., the number of different components and extent of differentiation in the organization in which the change is to be implemented. The degree of business complexity increases the more an organizational change cuts across different hierarchical levels, different work units and different geographic locations;

involves reciprocal or team interdependence; affects a range of products and services; and requires the buy-in of a number of internal and external stakeholders.

Socio-technical uncertainty refers to the amount and nature of information processing and decision making required for the change based on the extent to which the tasks involved are determined, established, or exactly known. Socio-technical uncertainty increases to the extent that there are no clearly known ways to approach the situation, no known sequence of steps that can be followed, and no identifiable set of established procedures and practices. In low socio-technical uncertainty situations, the solution to the change challenge is known, while in high socio-technical uncertainty contexts the solution is not known or fully understood. In fact, when uncertainty is high, the problem itself is not fully described or clearly understood, meaning that the search for a solution occurs simultaneously with the search for a clear definition of the problem.

Constraints refer to the extent to which the parameters of the change situation are clearly defined with little or no room for modification versus broadly defined with room for interpretation. In highly constrained situations there is little time to accomplish the change, people resist change, and the change sponsor seeks to tightly control the change process. In highly unconstrained situations, the time pressure to accomplish the change is not as great, people contribute readily to the change process, and the change sponsor has flexible expectations about the change process and outcomes.

Part 3: Identifying the Approach to Change

A. **Plot your results (Total/5) for *Business Complexity* and *Socio-Technical Uncertainty* on the grid, below.**

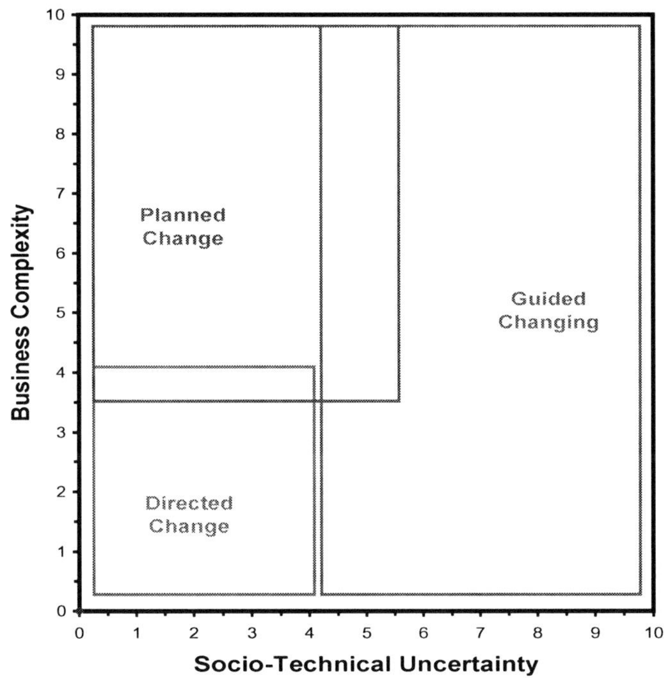

B. **Plot your results for *Constraints* on the continuum, below.**

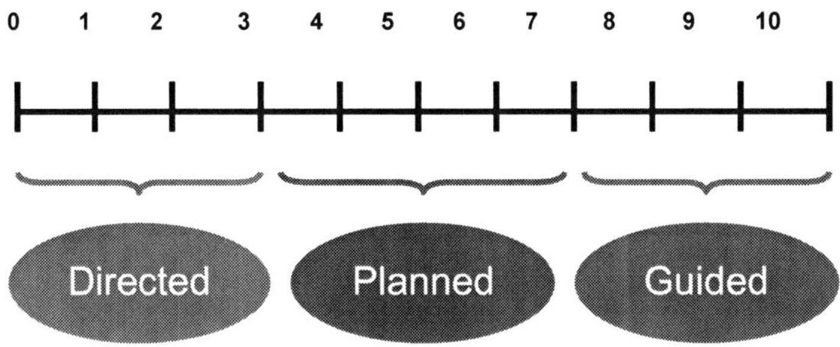

APPENDIX 5-2
ORGANIZATIONAL CHANGE CAPACITY QUESTIONNAIRE

Part 1: Questions

Circle one number on each of the following 0 to 10 scales with reference to your organization.

1. We place a strong emphasis on learning and information sharing.

   0 1 2 3 4 5 6 7 8 9 10

   Never —— Sometimes —— Almost Always

2. We hold meetings in all functions that focus on identifying and critically assessing new business opportunities.

   0 1 2 3 4 5 6 7 8 9 10

   Never —— Sometimes —— Almost Always

3. We use a common, organization-wide framework for thinking and communicating about change.

   0 1 2 3 4 5 6 7 8 9 10

   Never —— Sometimes —— Almost Always

4. We communicate an enduring, shared purpose that is well understood by everyone in the organization.

   0 1 2 3 4 5 6 7 8 9 10

   Never —— Sometimes —— Almost Always

5. We designate and hold accountable an owner of the goal to develop our organization's change capacity.

   0 1 2 3 4 5 6 7 8 9 10

   Never —— Sometimes —— Almost Always

6. We select, hire, evaluate, and reward our employees based, in part, on their ability to thrive on change.

   0 1 2 3 4 5 6 7 8 9 10

   Never —— Sometimes —— Almost Always

7. We encourage everyone in the organization to ask questions and speak the truth, especially when people perceive problems or obstacles.

0 1 2 3 4 5 6 7 8 9 10

Never ——————— Sometimes ——————— Almost Always

8. We conduct low cost experiments with new ideas.

0 1 2 3 4 5 6 7 8 9 10

Never ——————— Sometimes ——————— Almost Always

9. The people in our organization understand there are different approaches to change and when each is appropriate.

0 1 2 3 4 5 6 7 8 9 10

Never ——————— Sometimes ——————— Almost Always

10. We encourage people to think dynamically and systematically so that strategies can change quickly.

0 1 2 3 4 5 6 7 8 9 10

Never ——————— Sometimes ——————— Almost Always

11. We devote resources to scanning the external environment in search of new ideas for our business.

0 1 2 3 4 5 6 7 8 9 10

Never ——————— Sometimes ——————— Almost Always

12. We create teams with maximum diversity to encourage innovation and creativity.

0 1 2 3 4 5 6 7 8 9 10

Never ——————— Sometimes ——————— Almost Always

13. We encourage everyone to empathize with and value alternative viewpoints.

0 1 2 3 4 5 6 7 8 9 10

Never ——————— Sometimes ——————— Almost Always

14. We recognize and reward people who support, encourage, lead, and share learning about organizational change.

0	1	2	3	4	5	6	7	8	9	10

Never ——— Sometimes ——— Almost Always

15. We focus on developing deep expertise about how to implement organizational change.

0	1	2	3	4	5	6	7	8	9	10

Never ——— Sometimes ——— Almost Always

16. We thoroughly examine future markets, competitors, and business opportunities.

0	1	2	3	4	5	6	7	8	9	10

Never ——— Sometimes ——— Almost Always

17. We encourage our employees to have lots of external contact with stakeholders, especially with customers.

0	1	2	3	4	5	6	7	8	9	10

Never ——— Sometimes ——— Almost Always

18. We develop, reward, and promote supervisors and managers who enable change.

0	1	2	3	4	5	6	7	8	9	10

Never ——— Sometimes ——— Almost Always

19. We support people who take risks and apply innovative ideas.

0	1	2	3	4	5	6	7	8	9	10

Never ——— Sometimes ——— Almost Always

20. We maintain a fluid organizational structure that allows the formation of new groups as needed.

0	1	2	3	4	5	6	7	8	9	10

Never ——— Sometimes ——— Almost Always

21. We provide change coaching and consulting services to our people and departments.

0 1 2 3 4 5 6 7 8 9 10

Never —————— Sometimes —————— Almost Always

22. We factor future scenarios into today's decisions.

0 1 2 3 4 5 6 7 8 9 10

Never —————— Sometimes —————— Almost Always

23. We appoint a committed change sponsor for each organizational change.

0 1 2 3 4 5 6 7 8 9 10

Never —————— Sometimes —————— Almost Always

24. We work hard to enhance the personal credibility of organizational leaders.

0 1 2 3 4 5 6 7 8 9 10

Never —————— Sometimes —————— Almost Always

25. We tolerate mistakes in the interest of learning.

0 1 2 3 4 5 6 7 8 9 10

Never —————— Sometimes —————— Almost Always

26. We create systems and processes for sharing knowledge, information, and learning across boundaries.

0 1 2 3 4 5 6 7 8 9 10

Never —————— Sometimes —————— Almost Always

27. We encourage the formation of change agent networks to share best practices, tools, and research about organizational change.

0 1 2 3 4 5 6 7 8 9 10

Never —————— Sometimes —————— Almost Always

28. We focus on stringing together an ongoing series of momentary competitive advantages.

0	1	2	3	4	5	6	7	8	9	10

Never ——— Sometimes ——— Almost Always

29. We provide key change projects with enough resources to get highly visible, public successes.

0	1	2	3	4	5	6	7	8	9	10

Never ——— Sometimes ——— Almost Always

30. We listen to, encourage, and reward mavericks and trailblazers.

0	1	2	3	4	5	6	7	8	9	10

Never ——— Sometimes ——— Almost Always

31. We value conflict and use it to achieve understanding and creativity.

0	1	2	3	4	5	6	7	8	9	10

Never ——— Sometimes ——— Almost Always

32. We provide responsive and proactive training and education in support of specific organizational changes.

0	1	2	3	4	5	6	7	8	9	10

Never ——— Sometimes ——— Almost Always

33. We debrief people after important organizational changes with a focus on learning from experience.

0	1	2	3	4	5	6	7	8	9	10

Never ——— Sometimes ——— Almost Always

34. We create and communicate a change friendly identity both internally to our employees and externally to our customers and partners.

0	1	2	3	4	5	6	7	8	9	10

Never ——— Sometimes ——— Almost Always

35. We shelter breakthrough ideas with their own budgets and people.

0	1	2	3	4	5	6	7	8	9	10

Never ———————— Sometimes ———————— Almost Always

36. We create a climate of trust, honesty, and transparency.

0	1	2	3	4	5	6	7	8	9	10

Never ———————— Sometimes ———————— Almost Always

Part 2: Scoring & Interpretation

1. Next to each questionnaire item number below, record your rating from Part 1 of this questionnaire. After you have entered your rating for each question, calculate the average score for each dimension.

Item	Score	Item	Score	Item	Score
1.	______	2.	______	3.	______
7.	______	8.	______	9.	______
13.	______	14.	______	15.	______
19.	______	20.	______	21.	______
25.	______	26.	______	27.	______
31.	______	32.	______	33.	______
TOTAL =	______	TOTAL =	______	TOTAL =	______
Total / 6 =	______	Total / 6 =	______	Total / 6 =	______
Facilitative Culture		*Supportive Infrastructure*		*Different Change Approaches*	

Item Score	Item Score	Item Score
4.________	5.________	6.________
10.________	11.________	12.________
16.________	17.________	18.________
22.________	23.________	24.________
28.________	29.________	30.________
34.________	35.________	36.________
TOTAL = ______	TOTAL = ______	TOTAL = ______
Total/6 = ______	Total/6 = ______	Total/6 = ______
Ongoing Strategizing	*Sufficient Resources*	*Willingness and Ability to Change*

2. Which of the six major dimensions of change capacity is highest? Why?
3. Which of the six major dimensions of change capacity is lowest? Why?
4. Which of the six major dimensions of change capacity should be your top improvement priority? What specifically could be done to increase change capacity along this dimension?

CHAPTER 6

THE USE OF METAPHOR IN CONSULTING FOR ORGANIZATIONAL CHANGE

Deborah Colwill

Metaphors "are central to human discourse and understanding" (Cornelissen, Oswick, Christensen, & Phillips, 2008). Organizational theorists and practitioners have discovered the potential of metaphor and have sought to more deliberately employ its use in theory building and practice. Drawing on these perspectives, the focus of this chapter is to examine how organizational change consultants can use metaphor to help guide their work with clients.

The chapter is divided into three parts. It begins with a brief exploration of insights about metaphor from recent literature. The chapter then turns to four organization metaphors:

1. the machine;
2. the organism;
3. the "human brain" (Morgan, 2006, p. 223); and
4. the energy wave.

Consultation for Organizational Change. pages 113–135
Copyright © 2010 by Information Age Publishing
All rights of reproduction in any form reserved.

The fourth metaphor, the "energy wave" will be introduced as one possible way of looking at postmodern organizations. The final part of the chapter focuses on the implications of metaphor for the practice of organizational change consulting.

INSIGHTS ABOUT METAPHOR

Within the literature on organizational studies, there has been a steady increase in the use of metaphor for both theory building and practice (Cornelissen, Oswick, Christensen, & Phillips, 2008). Research suggests that "metaphors constitute one of the primary ways by which scholars frame and understand the world of organizations" (Cornelissen & Kafouros, 2008b, p. 365). In addition, practitioners are also discovering the applied power of metaphor (Barrett & Cooperrider, 1990).

There is, however, a wide variety of opinion that exists with regard to the use of metaphor in organizations (Cornelissen, et al., 2008; Short, 2001b). Yet, rather than exploring the philosophical differences that lie beneath these opinions, this section highlights salient portions of the literature on metaphor that has the potential to aid organizational change consultants in their work with clients. In light of this focus, a "common sense" (Coghlan, 2009) view of metaphor will be used in which ideas from different philosophical viewpoints will be highlighted and integrated into this work.

Understanding Metaphor

Metaphorical language is commonly used to describe situations in organizations as well as organizations themselves (Basten, 2001; Morgan, 2006). Paying attention to the use of metaphors can help a consultant understand both the individual's mindset and the collective culture of an organization. To this end, at least a cursory understanding of metaphor is essential.

Analogies that Illuminate and Clarify

Stated simply, metaphors draw an analogy between the features of two unrelated entities in order to suggest a resemblance. In creating or examining a metaphor, the mind is challenged to move into new vistas of thought by aligning two previously unrelated objects, concepts, or experiences with the intention of comparing, contrasting, or promoting interaction between them. Metaphors, in effect, have the capacity to open up and illuminate a way of seeing and thinking that stretches the imagination. In other words, metaphors bring to light new aspects of the familiar.

In addition to illuminating new thought, metaphors are also used to bring clarity to difficult concepts or experiences. Metaphors are "mental pictures used to conceptualize, understand, and explain vague or unfamiliar phenomena" (Sackmann, 1989, p. 463). Marshak (1993, p. 45) further suggests that "metaphors are often the medium for understanding and presenting ideas, insights, and intuitions" that cannot be easily accessed through "analytic reasoning and discourse." Not only do metaphors have the potential to illuminate the familiar and clarify the unfamiliar, they also guide perception.

Images that Guide Perception and Action

Metaphors focus attention on certain aspects of our experience, and in doing so they act as "a way of organizing perceptions" (Barrett & Cooperrider, 1990, p. 222) or structuring "a person's conceptual system" (Palmer & Dunford, 1996, p. 699). A classic example of a metaphor intentionally being used to guide perception in organizational change is Lewin's unfreezing-movement-refreezing image (Basten, 2001). In this example, people intuitively understand the change process as depicted by the need to "unfreeze" the initial situation, preparing the system for change. As such, metaphors "provide vivid images which make future actions more tangible" (Sackmann, 1989, p. 464). By providing a framework for perceptions, metaphors serve as a guide for future action. As Lakoff and Johnson (1980, p. 145) state:

> New metaphors have the power to create a new reality. This can begin to happen when we start to comprehend our experience in terms of a metaphor, and it becomes a deeper reality when we begin to act in terms of it. If a new metaphor enters the conceptual system that we base our actions on, it will alter that conceptual system and the perceptions and actions that the system gives rise to. Much of cultural change arises from the introduction of new metaphorical concepts and the loss of old ones.

When allowed to repeatedly guide perception and action, metaphors may in a sense become "self-fulfilling prophecies" (Lakoff & Johnson, 1980, p. 156). In short, metaphors have the capacity to influence our conceptual systems which in turn will "affect how we perceive the world and act on those perceptions" (Short, 2001a, p. 302).

While a metaphor may focus attention in a certain direction, the implication is that it also limits the scope of what is seen by omitting what is not encompassed in the metaphor (Morgan, 2006). In this sense, metaphors are also "filters that screen some details and emphasize others" (Barrett & Cooperrider, 1990, p. 222). In selecting certain aspects of experience as a focus, metaphors paradoxically expand one's perspective while at the same time limiting the scope of what is seen. One way that metaphors expand what is seen is through surfacing tacit knowledge.

A Catalyst that Surfaces Tacit Knowledge

Metaphors can also serve as "the windows into the soul, if not the collective consciousness, of a social system" (Burke, 1992, p. 255). In paying attention to the use of metaphor in the language of an individual or group, tacit knowledge can be brought forth (Srivastva & Barrett, 1988). The idea of tacit knowledge simply means that "we know more than we can tell" (Polanyi, 1966, p. 4). As an example of tacit knowledge, Polanyi (1966, p. 4) suggests that:

> We know a person's face, and can recognize it among a thousand, indeed among a million. Yet, we usually cannot tell how we recognize a face we know. So most of this knowledge cannot be put into words.

Through metaphor people are better able to put into words tacit knowledge that might be otherwise difficult to access. Marshak (1993, p. 53) argues that "the metaphors and images used by people in publicly describing a situation are usually a strong indicator of the private, underlying assessments and promises from which they are operating." The value of understanding tacit knowledge unearthed by metaphor is that it brings the latent knowledge of the person, group or organization to the surface and helps to uncover what may be at the heart of dysfunctional "habits of thought" (Isaacs, 1999, p. 52), relational discord, or ineffective action.

As previously stated, metaphors can openly represent people's guiding perceptions—including their tacit assumptions. Rather than being merely a rhetorical devise, at their core "metaphors are conceptual, not linguistic" (Johnson & Lakoff, 2002, p. 253). In other words, "metaphors are viewed as primarily conceptual constructions that play a central role in the development of thought and intersubjective meaning making; they can allow actors to reframe their perceptions" (Jacobs & Heracleous, 2006, p. 209). Metaphors "connote meanings on a cognitive, emotional, and behavioral level in a holistic way" (Sackmann, 1989, p. 464).

In sum, there are three core ideas from the literature on metaphor stated above. Metaphors are:

1. analogies that illuminate and clarify;
2. images that guide perception and action; and
3. catalyst that surfaces tacit knowledge.

The next section examines the contrast between "projecting metaphors" and "eliciting metaphors" (Cornelissen, et al., 2008).

Two Types of Metaphor

Cornelissen and associates (2008, p. 9) contrast two types of metaphors that are used in the process of organizational change: "projecting" and "eliciting." In short, the projecting metaphor is "imposed onto organizational reality," whereas the eliciting metaphor is allowed to naturally emerge "within the talk and sensemaking of individuals" (Cornelissen, et al., 2008, p. 9). As they point out, a majority of the work on organization theory has a projecting metaphor focus.

Projecting Metaphors

One of the meanings of the word "project" is to thrust an object forward. A projecting metaphor carries this sense of being propelled forward. Projecting metaphors are promoted by the leadership of an organization to provide guidance to people in a directed change process. Sackmann (1989, p. 464) names this type of metaphor a "targeted metaphor," one that suggests "a transformation process toward pre-specified goals." The "deductive metaphor" (Palmer & Dunford, 1996) is another term used for metaphors that are deliberately applied to organizational situations.

In situations where "directed change" (Kerber & Buono, 2005) is the best option for an organization, a projecting metaphor is most suitable. OD practitioners often use projecting metaphor as an intervention device for change, typically selected "based on their diagnosis of the organizational situation and on the desired organizational outcomes" (Heracleous & Jacobs, 2008, p. 71). As Marshak (1993, p. 53) notes:

> One way to help people align themselves with an intended change effort is to insure first that everyone is operating from the same metaphor/image system, and then that the metaphors and images are congruent with the intended change. If people seem confused about what to do, changing or altering the implicit and explicit metaphors may either free up their thinking, or cast the situation in a new light.

The advantage of using a projecting metaphor to guide organizational change is that it puts the metaphor selection and application in the hands of the leadership. The limitation is that it does not allow the latent potential of the collective organization to own the metaphor by creating it themselves.

Eliciting Metaphors

The word "elicit" means to draw out or bring forth. The eliciting metaphor emerges naturally from the context of the organization. Whereas the projecting use of metaphor "involves the application of a generic, preexisting set of metaphors to organizational situations" (Heracleous & Jacobs,

2008, p. 71); the eliciting metaphor "operates on the assumption that organizational members can generate and employ novel metaphors in view of their context and experience, that can be tapped on for the purposes of system diagnosis and change; emphasizing the emergent, local, and contextual nature of metaphors" (Heracleous & Jacobs, 2008, p. 71). The "inductive metaphor" (Palmer & Dunford, 1996) is another term used for metaphors that are elicited. Sackmann (1989, p. 464) talks about the "adaptive metaphor" which underscores "the search for a direction since the outcome of the transformation cannot be clearly specified." (1989, p. 464) In short, elicited metaphors emerge from the collective thought of the group or organization.

The situation in the organization will determine whether or not a projected or an elicited metaphor would be most appropriate. The influence of social constructionism seems to be pushing the trend of metaphor use in organizations toward eliciting metaphors due to their collaborative emergent nature. However, each situation is different and the use of metaphor in the change process should arise out of what is most appropriate for the needs of the organization and its members. In other words, "building true organizational change capacity involves leading change in ways that are appropriate to the situation" (Kerber & Buono, 2005, p. 24).

In sum, metaphors are analogies that illuminate the familiar and bring clarity to the unfamiliar. They can serve as images that guide the perception and action of people and act as a catalyst that surfaces tacit knowledge. There are also differences between projected and elicited metaphors. Although much more could be said about the concept of metaphor, these insights should lay a sufficient foundation for the purposes of this chapter.

FOUR ORGANIZATION METAPHORS

This section examines four basic examples of organization metaphors: the machine, the organism, the "human brain" (Morgan, 2006, p. 223), and the energy wave. Although some of these metaphors have a longer history of use than others, they are all still represented implicitly and explicitly in organizations today.

The Machine Metaphor

A machine is "an apparatus consisting of interrelated parts with separate functions, used in the performance of some kind of work."[1] When applied to organizations, the machine metaphor emphasizes the same connotation, that people (as parts of the machine) perform select functions related to the efficiency and overall smooth running performance of the organization's production of goods or services. The machine metaphor is an example of a "projected metaphor" in that it is promoted by the leadership of an organization rather than emerging from the organizational members.

The concept of organization as machine was prevalent during the industrial revolution. At this time, organizations that were experiencing considerable growth were in the manufacturing business heavily supported by the disciplines of economics and engineering (Burke, 2008). In large corporations, the organizational charts were pyramid shaped and hierarchical to show lines of authority and accountability. Managing from the top of the organization downward was thought to insure a rational efficient operation and make communication clear and straightforward. Classical management theorists taught that "management is a process of planning, organization, command, coordination, and control" (Morgan, 2006, p. 18). Organizational members were expected to perform their duties a skilled workers and follow the direction of their supervisor. People were viewed as parts of a machine, "passive units of production" (Zohar, 1997, p. 69), treated like "cogs . . . removable, replaceable and expendable" (Ellinor & Gerard, 1998, p. 43). In essence, the individual role was shaped to fit the organization's needs (Oliver, 1989).

The compartmentalization of a large bureaucratic organization often caused fragmentation, competition, and conflict between departments, functions, groups, and individuals. If some sort of conflict or issue arose that caused a malfunction in production, the problem became the focus of attention until it was repaired and smooth-running performance was restored. Organizations were improved by identifying problems, analyzing causes, evaluating possible solutions, and developing action plans (Cooperrider, Whitney, & Stavros, 2003).

Overall, bureaucratic organizations have the best chance of working well in relatively stable environments (Hatch & Cunliffe, 2006). Not surprisingly, one of the biggest disadvantages of a mechanistic organization is the difficulty it has adapting to changing circumstances. Machines are built with predetermined goals in mind, to make a specific product or perform a service; they are not designed for innovation (Morgan, 2006). Likewise, the rigidity of the bureaucratic organization precludes its ability to quickly adapt or innovate, especially as information and knowledge do not flow effectively in an overly segmented hierarchical system (Morgan, 2006). The organization as organism metaphor, in part, arose out of the need to find a more adaptable organizational form.

The Organism Metaphor

The mechanistic approach to management set the stage for constructing organizations that were better able to react to their external environment. The rigidity that plagued many bureaucratic organizations propelled people toward a different view of organizations. Theorists turned to biology, more specifically ecology, to base their understanding of the organization as an organism in a living system. Ecology deals with the relations between organisms and their environments. Applied to organizations, the "social ecology" (Morgan, 2006, p. 34) of an organization implies there is a living system of relations between people, their small groups, and their communities.

The idea of population ecology in organizations takes its cue from the Darwinian catch phrase "survival of the fittest" where only the strong of a species will thrive. The realization that organizations must take their survival and competition seriously in the broader external environment (or ecosystem) moved some organizational theorists to view corporations as open systems. Reacting to the external environment is a "stimulus-response" implicit in the organism metaphor (Cornelissen & Kafouros, 2008b, p. 372). The open system framework not only sees the organization as part of a larger system, but it also sees an open system within itself, in that there are "integrated subsystems" in the organization (Morgan, 2006, p. 39). The systems are mutually interdependent and, in the ideal form, help one another maintain various vital processes.

Understanding the needs and vulnerabilities of an organism is essential for its survival; this is also true in the case of the organismic organization. The health and development of the organization will not only help it to survive in a competitive environment, but if an organization is healthy, it will also learn to adapt itself and make the changes that need to occur as the environment changes (Cornelissen & Kafouros, 2008b; Morgan, 2006). Change in the organismic organization happens through redesign. Scharmer (2007, p. 51) defines such "redesigning" as "changing the underlying structure and process" of an organization.

Contingency theorists argue that since there are several possible ways of organizing, management should focus on "achieving alignments and good fits" (Morgan, 2006, p. 42). The leadership must guide the members in thinking through the strategic, technological, cultural, structural, behavioral, managerial systems, and processes of their specific organization as well as its external environment (Jamieson, 2009; Morgan, 2006). Effective leaders of an open system organization are participative and democratic, in contrast to the authoritarian or autocratic styles of leaders in mechanistic organizations. In the best interest of the system, it is good to encourage alignment and active participation from the organizational members.

In this context, survival of the organization also depends on the health and development of its people. Concern for the needs of employees can be demonstrated by developing motivating jobs, and giving autonomy, responsibility and recognition (Hackman, 2002). These are only a few of the actions that leaders can take to keep their organization fit, trim, and healthy. Organizational members are to be treated with respect as valuable resources to the system.

One criticism of the organism metaphor is that it is excessively concrete and as such may lead to an overindulgent use of the metaphor (Morgan, 2006). For example, viewing organizational members as valuable resources to the survival of the system may subtly negate their humanity. The assumption underlying this view is no different than the "cog" view of persons in the mechanistic organization.

The organization as organism is largely influenced by the need to survive and adapt in a competitive environment. The main criticism of both contingency theory and population ecology is that they portray organizations as dependent on the outside pressures of the external environment as motivation for change rather than recognizing people are active participants in the construction of their world (Morgan, 2006). The organism metaphor is also a "projected metaphor" in the sense that it is put forward by the leadership of the organization to influence the thoughts and behaviors of the organizational members. The "human brain" metaphor for organizations, in part, arose out of the need to delve underneath the surface assumptions that governed the operations of both mechanistic and organismic organizations.

The Human Brain Metaphor

The transition from the industrial age toward the information age brought with it many changes to the leadership and management of organizations. The closed-system machine view of organizations does not accommodate the flexibility needed in the rapidly changing environment of the information age. To stay competitive, organizations need to become more flexible in order to respond to growing economic pressures, expanding globalization, the rapid pace of change, and the increasing influx of information and technology. The need to be flexible precipitates organizational structures that are flatter, leaner, and more collaborative (Colwill, 2005). One of the shifts in management of organizations came through the guiding metaphor of the organism. A very different organizational framework is encompassed by the metaphor of the "human brain" (Morgan, 2006).

In the two previous metaphors, change is viewed differently than in the brain organization. Change in the mechanistic organization was controlled at the action or task level. Redesigning processes and systems was the focus of much of the change in the organization as organism. Both of these ways of viewing organizational change are referred to as "single-loop learning" (Argyris & Schon, 1974). Single-loop learning means that the members of the organization are able to detect error in relation to a set of standard norms and make changes to correct the situation. Single-loop learning changes what happens at the level of action on the surface of things, not in "the governing variables" (Argyris, 1987, p. 94).

The metaphor of organization as a human brain involves "double-loop learning" (Argyris & Schon, 1974). Double-loop learning looks at the variables that govern action, that is, the deeper taken-for-granted assumptions underneath operation norms. People examine their own behavior, take responsibility for their own action or inaction, and surface uncomfortable information that could potentially lead to constructive change (Argyris, 1994).

Although the "learning organization" (Senge, 1990) works with both single and double-loop learning (Scharmer, 2007), the human brain metaphor is epitomized in the learning organization (Morgan, 2006). The brain is the information processing center for the human body. Decisions are made by the brain that have affect on the entire system. If poor decisions are made, harm or dysfunction can occur in the body's overall system. In the same vein, ineffective organizations are the result of poorly-designed systems; the learning organization enables people to rise above "cognitive biases" through "systems thinking" (Senge, 1990). Systems thinking is a framework for seeing patterns and interrelationships, while looking at the whole.

Learning organizations are self-regulating or self-organizing (Morgan, 2006). Organizations self-organize through "reframing," in essence "changing the underlying pattern of thought" (Scharmer, 2007, p. 51). The leaders in a learning organization facilitate reframing through collaborative learning. Leaders engage groups of "knowledge workers" in dialogue about issues that are crucial to the organization's development, fostering its ability to learn, and uncovering its "learning disabilities" (Senge, 1990). Dialogue literally means "flow of meaning" or "shared meaning" (Bohm, 1996). Generative knowledge is discovered through dialogue that leads to new applications of that knowledge (Isaacs, 1999). In this respect, both "projecting" and "eliciting" metaphors are used in the learning organization. The overarching dominant metaphor of the human brain implicitly or explicitly guides the organization, whereas, locally elicited metaphors could emerge throughout the organization fostered by collaborative learning.

The capacity for learning requires both openness and self-evaluation. As such, one limitation of the learning organization is that double-loop learning is difficult and often elusive (Morgan, 2006). It may be blocked as people engage in "defensive routines" when they feel threatened or vulnerable in order to protect themselves and others (Argyris & Schon, 1974). Another limitation of the brain metaphor is the actual practice of its self-organizing capacities. More specifically, "the increase in autonomy granted to self-organizing units undermines the ability of those with ultimate power to keep a firm hand on day-to-day activities and developments" (Morgan, 2006, p. 114). The role of the leader is to be a facilitator of learning, however, the responsibility for the growth or lack of growth an organization experiences still ultimately falls on the leader.

The Energy Wave Metaphor

The emergent laws of quantum physics are reshaping how people view and interact in human systems. Physicist David Bohm was one of the first individuals who applied what he was learning from quantum thought to the realm of human experience (Isaacs, 1999; Oliver, 1989). Since then, many organizational theorists have used the concepts from both quantum physics and postmodern philosophy to inform their perspectives (Cooperrider & Whitney, 2005; Hatch & Cunliffe, 2006; Isaacs, 1999; Scharmer, 2007; Senge, Scharmer, Jaworski & Flowers, 2005; Whitney, 2005).

Originating out of quantum thought, the concept of an energy wave could be used as a metaphor describing postmodern organizational processes. An organization that practices Appreciative Inquiry (AI) will be used below as an example of a postmodern organization. AI "has emerged as a process for social, organizational, and global change based on postmodern principles" (Whitney, 2005, p. 438). An organization shaped by the principles and practices of AI is an example of an energy wave organization.

Quantum Physics and the Energy Wave

Newtonian physics described the world in terms of time, space, energy, matter, and causation. In this view, an entity is *either* a particle or an energy wave, one or the other but not both (Zohar, 1997). Quantum physics teaches that an entity which appears to be solid has wave-like properties. In fact, quantum entities are concurrently particle-like and wave-like. However, it is only possible to look at the particle-like aspects or the wave-like aspects of an entity at one time. In other words, one must either focus on the "position or on the momentum" of an entity (Zohar, 1997, p. 62).

In the same way that a quantum entity has both particle-like and wave-like aspects, the same is true with the appreciative organization. The particle-like level revolves around the actual practice of AI in organizations, while the energy wave-like level represents the philosophical orientation and guiding forces of AI.

The Particle Detector View of the Appreciative Organization

The particle-like level view of appreciative organizations represents the here and now aspects of what AI looks like in practice. The local expression of an appreciative organization promotes positive attitudes, communication, actions, and relationships. An appreciative organization is "sustainable" in that it "creates value for its shareholders and its stakeholders" (Laszlo & Cooperrider, 2008, p. 18) by ensuring that multiple voices are heard and respected. Whitney (2005, p. 438) speaks of three "bold" implications of AI in organizations, that AI encourages people to be "radically relational", "dramatically creative" and "decidedly affirmative" (Whitney, 2005, p. 438).

Rather than being a problem-solver or decision maker, the leader of an appreciative organization is conceptualized as a designer (Avital & Boland, 2008). They see through a "positive lens" or, in other words, they have the "capacity to construct better organizations and technologies through discourse that encourages human strengths and participative action in leading organizational change" (Avital & Boland, 2008, p. 3). Appreciative leaders foster a positive climate, cultivate positive affirming relationships, promote positive communication, expand vision through a spirit of inquiry, nurture positive meaning, and value authenticity (Cameron, 2008; Colwill, 2009).

The Wave Detector View of the Appreciative Organization

The wave-like aspect of appreciative organizations is the discovery or unfolding of positive future possibilities and potential. AI seeks to illuminate the life giving "positive core" of an organization (Cooperrider, et al., 2003, p. 4). The theorists of AI assume that all organizations have something that works well and that these strengths can be the basis upon which the positive core unfolds. AI does not promote change in organizations in the traditional sense of reducing obstacles or solving existing problems. Rather, AI seeks to highlight the positive essence of the existing organization and move forward in regenerating that positive life giving core. As Maier (2009, p. 115) suggests, "by preceding the visioning process with an inquiry aimed at discovering moments of excellence, the stage is set to allow richer and more provocative possibilities to emerge." In other words, AI "focuses on change through the identification of positive forces within an organization" (Sharkey, Yaeger, & Sorenson, 2004, p. 521). These positive live-giving forces are the energy wave of the appreciative organization.

As a form of social constructionism, AI assumes that the shared interactions and experiences of the members of the organization have a primary influence on shaping the organization itself (Cummings & Worley, 2005). In other words, undergirding AI is the belief that people have the collective ability to create their own future (Seo, Putnam, & Bartunek, 2004). This belief is "apparent in the overt choice of various humanistic means and processes in initiating organizational change, such as stories, narratives and visions" (Seo, et al., 2004, p. 97). Life-giving themes are selected from the stories. Dialogical inquiry is initiated around the themes. Generation of shared images, metaphors or knowledge leads to articulating innovative avenues of realizing a preferred future state. Throughout the process energy is gained by focusing on the positive.

However, like any change intervention, if AI is not supported with strong follow through by the leadership, people may generate positive ideas and then have no way to express them—and the resultant disappointment will lead to frustration, and frustration to skepticism (Bushe, 1999). For some individuals, the intentional focus on positive questions might actually bring forth negative comments in an attempt to balance the situation (Bushe, 2009). In any case, AI is challenging and will require leaders who are both gifted but also wise.

A Summary of the Four Metaphors

The value of highlighting these metaphorical examples is that it gives the consultant an opportunity to see the formative power of a metaphor in guiding people's thoughts and actions. In addition, these metaphors also illustrate the difficulty organizations may have in changing a dominant metaphor due to the power these images create in the minds of people. Table 6.1 provides a comparison of the four metaphors side by side, drawing out some of their implications for organizations.

Table 6.1. Summary of the Four Metaphors

Guiding Metaphor:	Machine	Organism	Brain	Energy Wave
Type of Organization	Bureaucratic	Open System	Learning	Appreciative
View of Organizational Process	Mechanistic	Social Ecology	Self-Organizing	Unfolding
Predominant Change Process	Reacting	Redesigning	Reframing	Regenerating
Preferred Outcome of Change	Maximizes production	Survival, Adaptation	Knowledge is generated and acted upon	Positive potential is being realized
Level of Learning	Action, Task	Dynamic Interrelationships	Cognition and action	Innovation and creativity
Organizational Values	Efficiency, Production, Control	Health and development	Collaborative learning	Interconnected participation
Role of Leadership	Commander, Director	Participative, Democratic	Facilitator	Architect, Designer
Role of Organizational Members	Skilled workers	Valuable resources	Knowledge workers	Collaborators

METAPHOR AND CONSULTING FOR CHANGE

In spite of all the research on and practice of organizational change, "successful organizational change often remains an elusive quest" (Buono & Kerber, 2009, p. 1). The skilled uses of metaphor as part of the change process may be an additional advantage that a consultant can bring to the table in helping clients navigate change. Burke (1992, p. 256) agrees that "paying attention to language in general and to metaphors in particular is highly important for effective organizational diagnosis." The "creative and constructive" use of metaphor is especially valuable during organizational change (Marshak, 1993, p. 55). To this end, this section explores the use of metaphor in consulting for organizational change, serving as a "steering function" (Barrett & Cooperrider, 1990) and supporting organizational uniqueness. Limitations and cautions about the use of metaphor in change are also addressed.

A Steering Function

Within the context of organizations, metaphors provide "a steering function" for organizational change (Barrett & Cooperrider, 1990, p. 223). In short, "the choice of an organization's metaphoric image drives the degree and type of organizational change that takes place" (Ricketts & Seiling, 2003, p. 37). Yet, while Marshak (1993, p. 44) argues that the effective use of metaphors is a "critical competency for leaders and change agents," he (1993, p. 55) also cautions that in using metaphors leaders cannot allow:

> ... their change initiatives to be recast and/or misunderstood as a result of implicit or unexamined metaphors. Leaders must be clear in what they want and help shape and inform change through congruent use of literal and symbolic reasoning.

As Sackmann (1989, p. 465) states, "successful executives seem to make effective use of the power of metaphors in rendering abstract and vague ideas more tangible."

Regardless of whether an organization espouses projecting or eliciting metaphors, both types of metaphor can provide a steering function during a change process. In projected metaphor use, the selection of the metaphor is promoted and maintained by the leadership as a dominant metaphor. In the case of elicited metaphor, the creation and emergence of the metaphor comes from the broader organizational community; however, the metaphor could still be intentionally used to guide the organization through the change process. What follows below are several ways that metaphor can be used as a steering function by an organizational change consultant.

Influencing Direction

As argued above, metaphors are images that guide perception and action. The implication of this statement in the context of an organization is that metaphor has the capacity to influence the direction of a change process. The imaginative and cogent use of metaphor can intentionally shape how people conceive and think about the organizational change (Marshak, 1993). If carefully selected, metaphors can positively influence employee thinking, feeling and acting in ways that "facilitate organizational transformation" (Sackmann, 1989, p. 468). The conscious development and use of metaphor can "influence the direction and fate of the organization's growth and sustainability" (Ricketts & Seiling, 2003, p. 35).

Guiding Assessment and Diagnosis

Metaphors have the capacity to enhance organizational effectiveness, especially when used in organizational assessment and diagnosis (Cleary & Packard, 1992). Paying attention to the informal metaphors-in-use will give a consultant a window into what is familiar or taken-for-granted by organizational members and perhaps intentionally or unintentionally left unsaid. Metaphors-in-use are similar to the idea of "theories-in-use" (Argyris, 1994, p. 80), which underscore what people really believe to be true and what they generally act upon, especially when they are under stress.

Listening for the common themes of metaphors-in-use, along with other types of corroborating evidence will provide baseline information for the process of assessing and diagnosing organizations. Metaphors can be used to "chart morale and gauge an organization's health" (Brink, 1993, p. 370). Marshak (1993, p. 45) believes that "for diagnostic purposes, the way to approach and listen to metaphorical expressions is 'as if' they were literally true." For example Cleary and Packard (1992, p. 233) report the following metaphorical phrases in working with an organization:

> "this place stinks," "It's really rotten here," "I feel dead even before I get to work," and "this place makes me sick." These are the words of employees surviving in a decaying or dying organization.

This example of metaphor-in-use illustrates the natural ability people have to use metaphorical language to vividly describe the situation as painful and hopeless. The same could be true of a more positive situation in which the members of an organization had a more hopeful outlook on the future. For example, one distinct outcome of AI is the creation of metaphors that compel people to action (Bushe & Kassam, 2005). Cooperrider and Whitney (2005) speak of heliotropic plants that follow the light as a metaphor for appreciative organizations, a deliberate choice of a "life-giving image" that has the ability to "mobilize enormous energy" (Hart, Conklin, & Allen, 2008, p. 634).

Observing how people respond to a dominant projected metaphor that the leadership espouses is another way to provide insight into the organization's culture. Favorable, resistant or indifferent responses by organizational members provide clues as to whether or not the projected metaphor is internalized or merely outwardly espoused. In addition, as Basten (2001, p. 353) states:

> Dominant metaphors in organizations may be hidden from employees' awareness but can have a serious impact on how situations are perceived and problems are approached. Identifying those metaphors raises them to a level of awareness where they can be challenged and, if need be, altered.

Redirecting Focus

Metaphors have the power "to redirect and focus the energy of the people within an organization" (Ricketts & Seiling, 2003, p. 33). When an organization is "stuck" its members need to "deliberately change the prevailing metaphor(s) and image(s) as a way to get out of the box and induce new ways of thinking" and "guard against blind spots" (Marshak, 1993, p. 54). At times it is helpful to "take the frame of reference away from historic reality and into the realm of anticipatory reality" through metaphor (Barrett & Cooperrider, 1990, p. 228). Metaphors "catalyze our thinking and help us approach the phenomenon of organizations in a novel way or in a more constitutive way in setting up a conceptual scheme through which we interpret organizations" (Cornelissen & Kafouros, 2008a, p. 960). As (Ricketts & Seiling, 2003, p. 38) note, due to:

> nature and conceptualization that is involved in the intentional use of metaphors and imagination, there is a heightened opportunity and power to shift the awareness (and appreciation) that drives an organization's direction and development.

Facilitating Learning

Another way that consultants could use metaphor as a steering function in their practice is through facilitating the learning of new knowledge (Barrett & Cooperrider, 1990). Research has shown that "in confronting radically new knowledge, metaphor can be helpful" in bypassing resistance and bringing forth a "sudden transformation" into a new way of thinking (Barrett & Cooperrider, 1990, pp. 223, 224). Metaphors allow "us to frame existing realities into new opportunities, to reflect and design different, previously not thought of viewpoints, and schemas, while removing past contradictions and assumptions" (Ricketts & Seiling, 2003, p. 37).

Relieving Anxiety about Change

The use of metaphor also allows people to talk about uncomfortable issues in a less direct way. To the degree "that metaphor captures powerful emotional feelings in a way that explicit language is incapable, it provides face-saving ways to talk about important experience" (Srivastva & Barrett, 1988, p. 48). The example of the dying organization noted above is an illustration of this point. If consultants guide people in considering "difficult phenomena metaphorically" it could allow them "to be more accepting and open" (Srivastva & Barrett, 1988, p. 54). The use of metaphor invites "active experimentation in areas of rigidity and helps people overcome self-defeating defenses" (Barrett & Cooperrider, 1990, p. 223), helping to "reduce feelings of uncertainty and underscore the benefits to be derived from accepting upcoming modifications" and assisting "in understanding the need for change and the positive outcomes associated with its acceptance" (Armenakis & Bedeian, 1992, p. 247).

Supporting Organizational Uniqueness

Since divergent assumptions lay underneath the variety of ways organizations use metaphors (Palmer & Dunford, 1996), in designing a change effort consultants need to keep in mind the organization's uniqueness (Cleary & Packard, 1992). For example, bureaucratic organizations involved in relatively stable industries may successfully utilize "directed change" (Buono & Kerber, 2009, p. 3). In this type of approach, change is "driven from the top of the organization and relies on authority, persuasion and compliance" (Buono & Kerber, 2009, p. 3). Projecting (prefabricated) metaphors are often used in such directed change, focusing people toward a predetermined goal. The machine organization metaphor as described above would be an illustration of a dominant projecting metaphor used in directed change.

Open-system organizations or learning organizations, in contrast, might utilize "planned change," attempting to provide "a 'roadmap' that outlines a project management approach to the change process," attempting to "create the conditions for people to become more involved in the change process, identifying and encouraging key stakeholders to participate in both the form and implementation of the change" (Buono & Kerber, 2009, p. 5). Projected metaphors may still be communicated from the top of the organization, however, emergent eliciting metaphors may be created in pockets of the organization effecting local practice and possibly emanating to the whole organization. The organism metaphor and the human brain metaphor for organizations as described above would serve as illustrations of organizations that might use of a combination of both projecting and eliciting metaphors in planned change.

A postmodern organization might be likely to use a "guided changing" approach to change (Buono & Kerber, 2009, p. 5). This type of change is more egalitarian in that it can begin "at any location within the organization" and "it is based on the commitment of organizational members and their contributions to the purpose of the organization" (Buono & Kerber, 2009, p. 5). Guided changing is a spiral-like "iterative process of initial interpretation and design, implementation and improvisation, learning from the change effort, and then sharing that learning system-wide, leading to ongoing re-interpretation and redesign of the change as needed" (Buono & Kerber, 2009, p. 5). Eliciting metaphors would be most appropriate for the guided changing approach in that they would naturally emerge from the community of organizational members. The energy wave organization metaphor as described above would be an illustration of a metaphor that could be used in guided changing. Ironically, the energy wave as a dominant metaphor sets the stage for the emergence of multiple eliciting metaphors to occur throughout the organization as a whole. In this situation, metaphors may shift as the need arises.

Perhaps having the flexibility to use a combination of eliciting and projecting metaphors may be most effective; in the same way that it is advantageous to be able to employ more than one approach to change as needed. As Kerber and Buono (2005, p. 35) state, "the highest level of change capacity would be exemplified by an organization in which directed change, planned change, and guided changing are implemented as appropriate in different situations."

Limitations and Cautions

Although the use of metaphor in organizational change has many advantages, there are a number of cautions that should be considered. It is important, for example, to avoid excessive emphasis on the metaphor in a change process, in essence trying not to "confuse the map with the territory" (Palmer & Dunford, 1996, p. 707). Likewise, metaphorical analysis and construction is only one aspect of organizational change and not the sole basis for change (Cleary & Packard, 1992). As McCourt (1997, p. 511) adds, metaphor is an "epistemologically valid approach to making sense of organizations, although not at the expense of traditional literal language approaches."

A second very practical caution is to consider both the "constructive and destructive connotations of a metaphor" (Armenakis & Bedeian, 1992, p. 245) before putting it into practice. Similarly, leaders must "be sensitive to their own blind spots created by unthinking use of favored metaphors or images that may be limiting their own reasoning processes" (Marshak, 1993, p. 55).

A final more prominent caution has to do with guarding against the tendency toward confusion when using metaphor. To elevate confusion, having one common metaphor is thought to provide shared understanding. Marshak (1993, p. 52) notes that

> When different people in the organization share the same underlying metaphor(s) there is usually agreement and focus on what to do . . . . When the underlying metaphors are different, conflict over what to do and how to do it is common . . . people may fight over the causes and cures to the problem without ever realizing that their differing, unexpressed, metaphorical reasoning may be preventing them from really understanding one another.

However, people may also interpret the same metaphor in different ways, which typically leads to different conclusions and behaviors (Short, 2001a). Research has shown that metaphors that are more easily comprehended have "greater explicatory and generative impacts" (Cornelissen & Kafouros, 2008b, p. 375). Daley (2001, p. 330) adds that "Clarity and precision are . . . essential when using metaphors" in order to eliminate as much confusion as possible. As Kraemer (2001, p. 364) notes, "To aid dialogue on new metaphors, they need to be described fully, emphasizing how they generate new insights, questions, and behaviors, and also emphasizing the limitations or risks (e.g., from applying the new metaphor in inappropriate ways not intended by the generator)."

CONCLUSION

The focus of this chapter has been to highlight the importance of metaphor in organizational change. While many of the authors cited in the chapter would agree that using metaphor in theory building and the practice of organizational change is helpful, perhaps even essential, they also would likely say that the use of metaphor is "supplement to and not a replacement for other OD activities" (Cleary & Packard, 1992, p. 235). However, the use of metaphor touches on crucial aspects of the change process that are not addressed by traditional methods alone.

Given the prominent place that metaphor holds in contemporary language and its importance to the topic of organizational change, in closing, several implications will be named for further consideration. Opening dialogue about the use of metaphor in the change process can give clients an opportunity to address their questions regarding its usage. Discussing metaphors-in-use will help clients to identify and examine their assumptions about organizations and beyond (Kuchinke, 2001). As part of such discourse, clients will have the opportunity to re-examine their metaphors, potentially changing the dominant metaphor if it no longer provides a benefit in achieving their goals (Ardichvili, 2001). Branching out beyond the use of "known metaphors" also continues to bring in fresh perspectives and insights (Kraemer, 2001). Finally, change consultants "could consider identifying and analyzing their own metaphors-in-use for consistency and efficacy regarding the core values with which they approach their practice" (Shindell & Willis, 2001, p. 319).

Metaphors can be used as powerful tools in the hands of organizational leaders and consultants. Wise change agents will pay attention to the metaphors organizational members use, listening for emergent themes as if they were "windows" into the collective culture of the organization. In addition, leaders have the opportunity to craft constructive metaphors that inspire a compelling direction and, chosen carefully, metaphors have the capacity to guide organizational members toward an envisioned future.

NOTES

1. The definition of "machine" was drawn from the 2009 Dictionary.com.

REFERENCES

Ardichvili, A. (2001). Three metaphors for the lives and work of HRD consultants. *Advances in Developing Human Resources, 3*(3), 333–343.

Argyris, C. (1987). Reasoning, action strategies, and defensive routines: The case of the OD practitioners. In R. W. Woodman & W. A. Pasmore (Eds.), *Research in organizational change and development* (vol. 1, pp. 89–128). Greenwich, CT: JAI Press, Inc.

Argyris, C. (1994). Good communication that blocks learning. *Harvard Business Review, 72*(4), 77–85.

Argyris, C., & Schon, D. (1974). *Theory in practice.* San Francisco: Jossey-Bass.

Armenakis, A. A., & Bedeian, A. G. (1992). The role of metaphors in organizational change: Change agent and change target perspectives. *Group Organization Management, 17*(3), 242–248.

Avital, M., & Boland, R. J. (2008). Managing as designing with a positive lens. In M. Avital, R. J. Boland, & D. L. Cooperrider (Eds.), *Designing information and organizations with a positive lens* (pp. 3–14). Oxford: JAI Press.

Barrett, F. J., & Cooperrider, D. L. (1990). Generative metaphor intervention: A new approach for working with systems divided by conflict and caught in defensive perception. *Journal of Applied Behavioral Science, 26*(2), 219–239.

Basten, F. M. R. C. (2001). The role of metaphors in (re)producing organizational culture. *Advances in Developing Human Resources, 3*(3), 344–354.

Bohm, D. (1996). *On dialogue.* New York: Routledge.

Brink, T. L. (1993). Metaphor as data in the study of organizations. *Journal of Management Inquiry, 2*(4), 366–371.

Buono, A. F., & Kerber, K. (2009). *Building organizational change capacity.* Paper presented at the International Conference on Management Consulting, "The Changing Paradigm of Consulting: Adjusting to the Fast-Paced World." Management Consulting Division, Academy of Management.

Burke, W. W. (1992). Metaphors to consult by. *Group & Organization Management, 17*(3), 255.

Burke, W. W. (2008). *Organization change: Theory and practice* (2nd ed.). Thousand Oaks: Sage Publications, Inc.

Bushe, G. R. (1999). Advances in appreciative inquiry as an organization development intervention. *Organization Development Journal, 17*(2), 61–68.

Bushe, G. R. (2009). *Commentary on 'appreciative inquiry as a shadow process.'* Unpublished Article.

Bushe, G. R., & Kassam, A. F. (2005). When is appreciative inquiry transformational?: A meta-case analysis. *Journal of Applied Behavioral Science, 41*(2), 161–181.

Cameron, K. S. (2008). *Positive leadership: Strategies for extraordinary performance.* San Francisco, CA: Berrett-Koehler Publishers Inc.

Cleary, C., & Packard, T. (1992). The use of metaphors in organizational assessment and change. *Group Organization Management, 17*(3), 229–241.

Coghlan, D. (2009). Toward a philosophy of clinical inquiry/research. *Journal of Applied Behavioral Science, 45*(1), 106–121.

Colwill, D. (2005). *Dialogical learning and a renewed epistemology: Analysis of cultural and educational shifts from modernity toward postmodernity.* Deerfield, IL: Trinity International University.

Colwill, D. (2009). *Appreciative leadership.* Paper presented at the ISEOR-AOM: Lyon, France.

Cooperrider, D. L., & Whitney, D. (2005). A positive revolution in change: Appreciative inquiry. In D. L. Cooperrider, P. F. Sorensen, T. F. Yaeger, & D. Whitney (Eds.), *Appreciative inquiry: Foundations in positive organization development* (pp. 9–33). Champaign, IL: Stipes Publishing L.L.C.

Cooperrider, D. L., Whitney, D., & Stavros, J. M. (2003). *Appreciative inquiry handbook: The first in a series of AI workbooks for leaders of change.* Bedford Heights, OH: Lakeshore Publishers.

Cornelissen, J. P., & Kafouros, M. (2008a). The emergent organization: Primary and complex metaphors in theorizing about organizations. *Organization Studies (01708406), 29*(7), 957–978.

Cornelissen, J. P., & Kafouros, M. (2008b). Metaphors and theory building in organization theory: What determines the impact of a metaphor on theory? *British Journal of Management, 19*(4), 365–379.

Cornelissen, J. P., Oswick, C., Christensen, L. T., & Phillips, N. (2008). Metaphor in organizational research: Context, modalities and implications for research—introduction. *Organization Studies (01708406), 29*(1), 7–22.

Cummings, T. G., & Worley, C. G. (2005). *Organization development and change* (8th ed.). Mason, OH: Thompson South-Western.

Daley, B. J. (2001). Metaphors for professional learning. *Advances in Developing Human Resources, 3*(3), 322–332.

Ellinor, L., & Gerard, G. (1998). *Rediscovering the transforming power of conversation.* New York: John Wiley & Sons.

Hackman, J. R. (2002). *Leading teams: Setting the stage for great performance.* Boston, MA: Harvard Business School Press.

Hart, R. K., Conklin, T. A., & Allen, S. J. (2008). Individual leader development: An appreciative inquiry approach. *Advances in Developing Human Resources, 10*(5), 632–650.

Hatch, M. J., & Cunliffe, A. L. (2006). *Organization theory: Modern, symbolic and post-modern perspectives* (2nd ed.). Oxford: Oxford University Press.

Heracleous, L., & Jacobs, C. D. (2008). Understanding organizations through embodied metaphors. *Organization Studies (01708406), 29*(1), 45–78.

Isaacs, W. N. (1999). *Dialogue and the art of thinking together.* New York: Doubleday.

Jacobs, C. D., & Heracleous, L. T. (2006). Constructing shared understanding: The role of embodied metaphors in organization development. *Journal of Applied Behavioral Science, 42*(2), 207–226.

Jamieson, D. (2009). Strategic organization change: Overview (Working Paper). Benedictine University: Springfield, IL.

Johnson, M., & Lakoff, G. (2002). Why cognitive linguistics requires embodied realism. *Cognitive Linguistics, 13*(3), 245–263.

Kerber, K., & Buono, A. F. (2005). Rethinking organizational change: Reframing the challenge of change management. *Organization Development Journal, 23*(3), 23–38.

Kraemer, T. J. (2001). Generating new metaphors: Downsizing as cancer. *Advances in Developing Human Resources, 3*(3), 355–365.

Kuchinke, K. P. (2001). Metaphors and paradigms for HRD research and practice. *Advances in Developing Human Resources, 3*(3), 366–378.

Lakoff, G., & Johnson, M. (1980). *Metaphors we live by.* Chicago: The University of Chicago Press.

Laszlo, C., & Cooperrider, D. L. (2008). Design for sustainable value: A whole system approach. In M. Avital, R. J. Boland, & D. L. Cooperrider (Eds.), *Designing information and organizations with a positive lens* (pp. 15–30). Oxford: JAI Press.

Maier, T. A. (2009). Appreciative inquiry and hospitality leadership. *Journal of Human Resources in Hospitality & Tourism, 8*(1), 106–117.

Marshak, R. J. (1993). Managing the metaphors of change. *Organizational Dynamics, 22*(1), 44–56.

McCourt, W. (1997). Discussion note: Using metaphors to understand and to change organizations: A critique of Gareth Morgan's approach. *Organization Studies 18*(3), 511–522.

Morgan, G. (2006). *Images of organizations.* Thousand Oaks, CA: Sage Publications, Inc.

Oliver, D. W. (1989). *Education, modernity and fractured meaning.* New York: SUNY.

Palmer, I., & Dunford, R. (1996). Conflicting uses of metaphors: Reconceptualizing their use in the field of organizational change. *Academy of Management Review, 21*(3), 691–717.

Polanyi, M. (1966). *The tacit dimension.* New York: Doubleday & Company, Inc.

Ricketts, M., & Seiling, J. G. (2003). Language, metaphors and stories: Catalysts for meaning making in organizations. *Organization Development Journal, 21*(4), 33–43.

Sackmann, S. (1989). The role of metaphors in organization transformation. *Human Relations, 42*(6), 463–485.

Scharmer, C. O. (2007). *Theory U: Leading from the future as it emerges.* Cambridge, MA: The Society for Organizational Learning.

Senge, P. M. (1990). *The fifth discipline: The art and practice of the learning organization.* New York: Doubleday/Currency.

Senge, P. M., Scharmer, C. O., Jaworski, J., & Flowers, B. S. (2005). *Presence: An exploration of profound change in people, organizations, and society.* New York: Currency.

Seo, M.-G., Putnam, L. L., & Bartunek, J., M. (2004). Dualities and tensions of planned organizational change. In M. S. Poole & A. H. Van De Ven (Eds.), *Handbook of organizational change and innovation* (pp. 73–107). Oxford: Oxford University Press.

Sharkey, L., Yaeger, T. F., & Sorenson, P. F. (2004). Appreciative inquiry in a fortune 50 global organization: Extending the AI concept to Japan. In P. F. Sorensen, T. C. Head, T. F. Yaeger & D. L. Cooperrider (Eds.), *Global and international organization development* (pp. 517–524). Champaign, IL: Stipes Publishing L.L.C.

Shindell, T., & Willis, V. (2001). Analyzing HRD metaphor-in-use. *Advances in Developing Human Resources, 3*(3), 309–321.

Short, D. C. (2001a). Shining a torch on metaphor in HRD. *Advances in Developing Human Resources, 3*(3), 297–308.

Short, D. C. (2001b). Strategies for applying metaphor in HRD research, practice, and education. *Advances in Developing Human Resources, 3*(3), 379–396.

Srivastva, S., & Barrett, F. J. (1988). The transforming nature of metaphors in group development: A study in group theory. *Human Relations, 41*(1), 31–64.

Whitney, D. (2005). Postmodern principles and practices for large scale organization change and global cooperation. In D. L. Cooperrider, P. F. Sorensen, T. F. Yaeger, & D. Whitney (Eds.), *Appreciative inquiry: foundations in positive organization development* (pp. 425–440). Champaign, IL: Stipes Publishing.

Zohar, D. (1997). *Rewiring the corporate brain: Using the new science to rethink how we structure and lead organizations.* San Francisco: Berrett-Koehler.

CHAPTER 7

PEER CONSULTING IN THE NOT-FOR-PROFIT SECTOR

Dalitso S. Sulamoyo

How many times have we heard the terms the new millennium and the 21st century used to contextualize the challenges and opportunities organizations face today? How many changes have we seen proposed and implemented in the last twenty years as a result of the challenges and opportunities that were attributed to the dawn of the new century? Have organizations heeded the call for organizational change because the environment in which they operate has dramatically changed? Our environment has been defined by globalization, regulation in response to scandals, a fledgling economy, immigration, retiring baby boomers and the advancement of technology. The question is how do we address these environmental challenges while creating opportunities for organizational change and development?

In a time when a fledgling economy and budget cuts make it difficult for not-for-profits and the public sector to invest in organizational change and effectiveness, there is dire need for a model that is cost effective. This chapter examines the mutual benefits of peer consulting as a method of intervention to facilitate organizational effectiveness and learning in the not-for-profit sector and public sector and how those benefits have been ap-

Consultation for Organizational Change. pages 137–153
Copyright © 2010 by Information Age Publishing
All rights of reproduction in any form reserved.

plied to respective organizations for continuous improvement. The chapter also examines the limitations of this peer-to-peer model for consulting, concluding with a discussion of opportunities for this model of consulting to be utilized for organization development and change.

THE PEER MODEL

As organizations in the not-for-profit and public sectors face myriad capacity building challenges, a number of approaches and models have been used to mitigate their circumstances. These models are referred to as train the trainer, best practices, knowledge transfer, and peer-to-peer consultation. They represent an exchange of values, practices, strategies, ideas, knowledge, and skill among peers. These approaches to capacity building are valued by both the public and not-for-profit sector because of their cost effectiveness and mutually beneficial gains. A peer-to-peer model was developed by the Illinois Association of Community Action Agencies (herein referred to as the Community Action Association) as a means of building the capacity of its network of anti-poverty organizations to maintain compliance with their various government funded programs. The Peer model involves the utilization of peers within the Community Action network to function as consultants. These peer consultants can reflect the entire organization, from executive directors, fiscal officers and human resource managers to program staff. The peer consultants work with a "sister" agency in mitigating any capacity issues while utilizing that opportunity for learning to impact their own organizations.

Context and Challenges

Community Action Agencies like most not-for-profit and public sector organizations have to respond to the demands of a dynamic environment through internal capacity building for organizational effectiveness. Many not-for-profits are predominantly funded through governmental and private grant structures, which means many of their environmental challenges involve interfacing with funding organizations and changing priorities. In order to maintain compliance with their various funding sources, not-for-profits have to ensure that they have effective management systems, strong internal controls, mission effectiveness, strong leadership, structures aligned with their systems and mission, informed governing bodies and clear organizational strategies. Juxtaposed to the issue of compliance is the need for not-for- profits to build their capacity beyond compliance with funding sources. There is the need for them to develop a competitive edge in a world where demand for social and community services is on the rise. In essence, there is a need for them to strive for excellence.

More nonprofits are competing for government and philanthropic funds. Traditional forms of funding are becoming smaller and less reliable. New for-profit businesses are competing with nonprofits to serve community needs, and funders and donors are demanding more accountability (McNamara 2008). In the face of this new reality, leaders in not-for-profit organizations are reinventing themselves as social entrepreneurs, combining the passion of a social mission with an image of business-like discipline, efficiency, innovation, and determination to transform the lives of people in their communities.

In the early 2000s some of Illinois' Community Action Agencies began to experience organizational challenges that were systematic, programmatic, leadership oriented, and cultural in nature. At the same time, the state of Illinois was in a recession and was faced with a massive exodus of talent due to early retirements sought as a means to balance the state's budget. This state of affairs meant that state government was not well equipped to provide the required oversight of these community action programs. The Community Action Association was also not necessarily equipped with the infrastructure or methodology to respond to these organizational challenges faced by members of its network. The Community Action Association was haunted by a history mired with agencies that were shut down by the government because of their inability to effectively respond to organizational challenges. It was also faced with an administration, which at the federal level differed philosophically with the framers of community action. As such it became clear that the Community Action Association had to emerge as the caretaker of community action in Illinois if this network of agencies was to continue to fulfill its mission and vision of fighting and alleviating poverty. It became clear that the Community Action Association had to develop a process which would assist its agencies to mitigate organizational challenges for their continued survival. And finally, it became clear that the Community Action network needed a process that would act as a bulwark against political attacks launched against the community action movement and the "War on Poverty." Illinois needed its agencies to not only overcome these organizational challenges, but to excel as organizations of excellence.

Defining the Peer Model

The Community Action Association developed a process for intervention and capacity building based on internal resources. An underlying concern was that many not-for-profit organizations spent exorbitant amounts of precious resources on external consultants that often times told them what they already knew or suggested a process for their organization that did not directly address their challenges. The Community Action Association needed an approach that would assist its agencies in sustaining organizational progress and effectiveness.

It was resolved by Community Action's leadership (President & CEO and Board of Directors) that Illinois' framework would involve peers who were deemed experts within the network. After all, the challenges they would assist in addressing were challenges that they saw or were able to overcome within their own organizations. As Cho, Chung, King, and Schunn (2008, pp. 84–85) noted:

> Contrary to intuition, similarities among peers can actually facilitate knowledge refinement. When the intended audience consists of non-experts, a group of peers is often better than experts in providing evaluations and feedback on peer developed materials. Peers are more likely to share knowledgebase, experience, and problems; such socially shared cognition enables them to establish common ground that stimulates development of mutual knowledge, along with an error-correction mechanism. Because peers are closer to one another cognitively and behaviorally, they better understand what they need in a codified piece of knowledge than do experts.

Applying the Peer Model

On one level, the diagnostic framework for resolving identified organizational challenges was no different from what is utilized by many external consultants. What was different is the fact that practical experience on the part of the peer experts—in the common community action context—made their analysis more credible. This factor—common experience and the empathy it creates—is critical when dealing with organizations whose missions do not always enjoy public support. It was felt that organizations experiencing these challenges would be more open to the process if they knew that the peer experts understood what they were going through from their own experience. It was also felt that the challenged organizations would be open to the process because as a "family" of Community Action Agencies their future was interconnected (Cho, et al, 2008, p. 85):

When multiple peers participate in knowledge refinement, the aggregated benefits can be significant. One possible reason is that multiple peers create a larger search space for potential problems in the target knowledge; more reviewers find more problems. The probability of a serious problem being detected increases with the number of peer reviewers.

The Community Action Association designed a diagnostic tool that involved the evaluation of an organization's operating system, management structures, program effectiveness, and organizational governance by peer consultants from the Community Action network. The assessment itself was a week-long intensive process in which a peer team (1) interviews staff from all programs, clients, board members and external stakeholders, and (2) reviews program performance and management systems. The assessment is conducted on agencies experiencing difficulties, such as the loss of a long-tenured executive director, a dysfunctional board, new leadership in key management positions, and major issues in key program areas. There are also program assessments that are conducted for purposes of preventing agencies from falling into corporate instability. The methodology utilized involves:

1. confidential questionnaires from staff, the board and clients;
2. reviews of organizational documents;
3. focus groups;
4. interviews; and
5. observations.

An outcome of the diagnosis is a report that contains the assessed organization's strengths and weaknesses, and recommendations, with further resources and time frames for the recommendations made by the peer team.

The Community Action Association created a database—the Skill Bank—comprised of peer experts from all over the state and categorized them under particular areas of expertise. The process was a centralized statewide mechanism to collect, store and make accessible to member agencies any information related to management, operations, and programs. The Skill Bank also facilitated and supported certain types of training, technical assistance and peer exchange programs. The Community Action Association has utilized the peer approach to facilitate one-on-one technical assistance among the agencies. There are instances when agencies hire new program staff that may need training in specialized areas pertaining to their programs. In those instances, the agency needing the training is encouraged to contact the Community Action Association for peer training, which is conducted on a one-on-one basis at the recipient's site.

The Skill Bank is also accessed for board governance training, which is conducted by peers. Community Action Agencies (CAA) have a unique composition of at least one-third members from the low-income community, exactly one-third public officials and up to one-third members from the private sector. The average size of a CAA board is 25 people. This structure allows for maximum feasible capacity and participation of the affected populations. The structure also brings with it challenges that are unique and require a specialized approach. The peer training model to support these boards has been Illinois' response to these unique challenges.

LESSONS FROM THE FIELD: REFLECTIONS ON THE PEER MODEL APPROACH

According to Loughry (2002, p. 1) "peer monitoring has not been extensively studied and the positive effect on performance that is asserted in agency theory has not been empirically tested." Thus there are myriad question about the strengths and weaknesses of this approach, the successes and failures in the Illinois system, and whether this approach can be replicated in other states.

Strengths and Successes

Reflecting on my experience with the peer-to-peer model in the Illinois system, there are a number of advantages that this approach brings to the not-for-profit world. These advantages are discussed as strengths and successes in this section of the chapter.

Reciprocal Technical Assistance and Capacity Building

The peer model of consulting involves mutual exchange of knowledge. The individuals who serve on the peer teams gain more knowledge about their organizations or programs as they assist other organizations. They do so because, in most cases, the Community Action Association selects team members who have similar programs as the agency that is subject to the intervention. During the review, peer consultants share best practices, provide clarity in program guidelines and regulations, and obtain interpretations of statutes and not-for-profit guidelines. This process of sharing and obtaining information allows the peer consultants to learn more about guidelines and systems in the context of their own organizations as well as their "client." Peer consultants also have the opportunity to learn from the recipient organization, as it would have its own best practices and clarity on regulations and guidelines that can be replicated by the peer consultant's organization. The peer consultants thus leave a project with new information and knowledge, which can be utilized to improve their own operations. This reciprocal nature of consulting is cost effective because, if it is done effectively, the peer consultant's organization will be able to enhance its own capacity and improve operations without the need of a direct intervention. All interventions are thus capacity building opportunities for the recipient organization *and* the peer consultants.

Empathy and Interconnectedness

The biggest strength in this approach is the fact that the consulting is done by peers. They are able to offer expertise, experience, and empathy. These peers, for the most part, share their experience with the recipient organizations. In other words, if they have been in Community Action long enough, capacity issues or even strengthening of systems is something that is shared across the board. Every agency goes through program audits, independent audits and changing funding priorities. It is through sharing this experience that a level of trust is developed between the peer consultant and the recipient organization. Some of the challenges that outside consultants come across when they work with the Community Action Agencies are that their knowledge of the network is limited and thus their prescribed interventions are usually not sustained because they are not prescribed with the uniqueness of Community Action. The Community Action Association had to establish a high level of trust with its own members for agencies to voluntarily be open to their peer's scrutiny and criticism. It took some of the leading agencies having the courage to be open to this process for the rest of the network to buy into it. Trust is the binding factor that has led to this model's success in Illinois.

Confidentiality

When utilizing a peer model for consulting, confidentiality is a key ingredient to establishing trust among those involved. the Community Action Association requires that all participants on the peer teams sign confidentiality statements that forbid them from sharing any information obtained during the intervention with anyone outside of the recipient organization. Any breach of these statements would lead to disciplinary action by the Community Action Association's board of directors. In instances where the team uncovers deficiencies that could impact the integrity of the organization, such as fiscal operations, board governance, or even human resource management, that information is provided to the recipient organization in the form of a management letter addressed to the organization's board of directors and executive director. This is done so as not to create any further issues among the staff of the organization.

All materials utilized for the intervention, such as personnel policies, bylaws, fiscal operating procedures, personnel files, and other organizational materials, are returned to the recipient organization. No copies are allowed to be made by the team members and organizational material cannot leave the premises of the recipient organization without permission from the recipient organization. Finally, the report that was rendered as a result of the intervention is provided to the recipient organization and only one copy is kept on file by the Community Action Association. Team members are not allowed to obtain or keep a copy of the report. However, the team members do keep notes taken during the intervention, particularly pertinent information that can be utilized within their own agencies. The team members—if given permission by the recipient organization—may obtain copies of materials that they may deem to be best practices for use within their own organizations.

Reporting Recommended Changes

The peer team reports its observations using a format that consists of strengths, challenges, and recommendations, citing federal or state regulations as appropriate. As part of this process, the team identifies a recommendation as a "best practice" if it exceeds what is required by regulations. During an exit interview, the peer team provides a summary or preview of their observations to the agency. The peer team leaders also hold a private meeting with the executive leadership to share any sensitive issues the team may have discovered during the assessment process.

The report is organized according to the critical areas identified prior to the intervention and those found during the intervention, focusing on the agency's strengths, challenges and recommendations to meet those challenges. The Community Action Association provides a suggested timeline to help the agency identify which recommendations should be handled immediately, in the next six months and over course of the year.

The report is presented to the executive leadership of the recipient agency within 30 days of the review. If a board member is not present, the executive director is expected to present the report to the entire board at its next scheduled or special board of directors meeting. It is customary to schedule a date to formally present the report to the executive director and board.

The Community Action Association also schedules a follow-up review at the agency at least 2 to 3 months after the initial peer assessment. The purpose of the review is to see how the agency has implemented the recommendations made by the team and whether there are still outstanding issues that require additional training and technical assistance. The follow-up review does not have to consist of the entire team, but it may, depending on the size of the organization. The team is expected to use the report and the recommendations in the report to conduct the follow-up.

Training and Learning

The peer model of consulting offers training and learning through the reciprocal exchange of knowledge that occurs during interventions. There have been instances where the Community Action Association has utilized new executive directors and staff to the network as peer consultants. The mix of seasoned peer consultants and new peer consultants allows the training and learning to occur within the peer team. Although they may not have the deep experience in dealing with these program and issues, the new peer consultants bring a fresh perspective for dealing with organizations and programs. In turn, the seasoned peer consultants and the recipient organizations offer hands on training to the new peer consultants that they would otherwise not obtain in a workshop or seminar setting. As they bring this insight back to their own organizations, their own capacity is also developed through this reciprocal process.

Compensation

The Community Action Association has grant resources that are utilized to partially pay for the expenses involved with this model. The expenses involved usually cover stipends for peer consultants, per diem, mileage, and hotel costs. The stipend amount is determined by the Community Action Association and the per diem and reimbursement rates are based on the latest Internal Revenue Service (IRS) rates and guidelines. The agency is expected to pay for the cost of the hotel and the Community Action Association's administrative costs. Thus the costs borne by the agency are very reasonable, especially compared to the total costs to bring in a team of usually 10–12 people. Agencies are asked to share some of the costs to ensure buy-in into the process and to offset some of the Community Action Association's expenses, especially in years where there are several assessments conducted. The compensation, even though not enough to offset one's salary rate for a week-long project, also acts as an incentive for recruitment of peer team members.

Testability and Reliability

The peer model of consulting has benefited both the Community Action network and the state of Illinois in that no agencies have had to be shut down due to non-compliance and mismanagement. The state of Illinois, as a result of a poor economy and attrition due to retirements, has not had the capacity to provide the comprehensive monitoring and technical assistance that is part of its role as a funding source. Thus, the fact that no Community Action Agency has had to be shut down in the last ten years suggests that (1) the communities where these agencies provide services continue to benefit, and (2) the state of Illinois continues to save tax dollars as experience proved it to be very expensive to set up a new Community Action Agency in replacing an existing one. Another benefit is that the Illinois network itself has been brought closer through experiencing and working through challenging times.

This model of consulting has also saved both the Community Action Agencies and the state outside consulting costs as the expense to facilitate the peer consulting only costs a fraction of what could be spent on external consultants. It is important to note, however, that this method of capacity building is not the only model utilized by the Illinois agencies. There are areas of capacity building which are beyond the capacity of the peer model.

Challenges and Limitations

Even though this model has worked effectively for the Illinois network of Community Action Agencies, there are some weaknesses and challenges to the model. If these challenges are successfully addressed, the possibility exists that the model can be transformed into a broader framework for change.

Focuses on Gap Analysis

Even though the report that is rendered as a result of this process contains strengths, it is not purely a strength-based approach, as found in Appreciative Inquiry. The diagnosis focuses on problems with recognition of strengths and resulting recommendations, which are intended to become part of the organization's action plan. Part of the challenge with this approach is the fact that the organizations seem to focus on the challenges or weaknesses as their starting point. There have been organizations that have not followed through with their assessment because the weaknesses or challenges have been overwhelming to their staff. We have also had organizations that have used only the challenges to restructure their organizations—unsuccessfully.

Lack of Consistency

The peer consultants who work on these interventions have full-time jobs. Consulting is something that they do on an "as needed" basis. As a result, the body of knowledge they develop as peer consultants is not always consistently sustained, as their role in interventions may be erratic. As a network, the Community Action Association has to ensure that opportunities to work on these interventions are shared across the board in order to maximize on the model's potential.

Compliance versus Organizational Excellence

Another limitation with the Community Action peer-to-peer model of consulting is that much of the emphasis to date is placed on program guidelines and compliance as well as organizational systems within the framework of technical assistance and capacity building. There has not been any direct, sustained emphasis on organization development and change, with a goal of creating true excellence.

Cultural Challenges

Not all of Illinois' Community Action Agencies utilize this peer model of consulting. There have been Peer team members who have not been comfortable in utilizing peer services for their own organizations even after they have participated on teams for other organizations. No two Community Action Agencies are identical even if they share their mission and vision as it relates to fighting poverty. They are different on a sub-cultural level. In order for the Community Action Association to be effective in working with its member organizations, it has to understand organizational sub-cultures that are driven by leadership, region, urban versus rural, demographics etc. The Community Action Association has been successful with interventions where the Community Action Agency's culture was more open. Peer interventions have not been successful or accessed by organizations whose cultures can be classified as not being open.

Economic Challenges: The Downside of Increased Funding

Due to the downturn in the economy, many programs that provide relief to the poor were appropriated significant increases in the Economic Stimulus Package approved by President Obama and Congress in February 2009. Many of these programs, such as the Weatherization program, have been envisioned by the President and Congress to play a major role in facilitating the economic recovery strategy proposed by the administration. Weatherization is poised to help with green jobs creation, economic stimulation, and independence from foreign oil as it provides utility relief for many families through energy cost savings that the program helps to realize. The Weatherization program is one the many programs administered by Community Action Agencies. As a result of the stimulus budget, the Weatherization program is faced with a growth of 500% over a two year time frame. This network of agencies is now faced with managing and responding to significant growth over a short prescribed timeframe dictated by the economic stimulus package.

The challenge for the peer model will be the availability of peer consultants to assist other agencies with capacity building while they focus on their own organizational needs. The growth that is being experienced as a result of the stimulus is unprecedented and most organizations will be focusing on their own challenges. However, there could have not been a better time than the present for Community Action's peer consulting model to build the capacity of Community Action Agencies. During this period, the Community Action Association may have to bring in external organization development expertise to assist its agencies.

Federal/State/Audit Usage of Community Action Association's Report

Finally, the biggest potential challenge that could potentially derail the program is if a state agency or federal entity were to use the Community Action Association's report against an agency. The Community Action Association needs to maintain its role as the caretaker of the network and not be placed in a position where it could justify the demise of an agency. Currently, the process is partially funded through grants from the state of Illinois and, at the present moment, the Community Action Association has a partnership with the state which is built on trust. The problem with that arrangement is that the players within state government could change and thus the process could be compromised.

OPPORTUNITIES FOR ORGANIZATION DEVELOPMENT AND CHANGE

There are opportunities to transform this model of intervention into a change model. The framework for capacity building, which defines the peer model, can be redefined in the context of change and development.

This can be done through the training of peer consultants to become organizational change agents by exposing them to different methods and frameworks of change. Once trained, the peer consultants can be deployed as individuals or in teams to work with peer agencies to facilitate change. This process could also be applied as a reciprocal learning model. One of the tasks that consultants fulfill in a change project is familiarization with the organization they are engaged to facilitate the change. Peers bring this familiarization because of the similarities in the organizations and the programs they run.

This section of the chapter explores the peer model of consulting in the context of organizational change. As a way of framing the discussion, the analysis draws on Cummings and Worley's (2005) categorization of organization development and change interventions.

Human Process Interventions

Cummings and Worley (2005) define human process interventions as change programs which are involved in mitigating challenges related to interpersonal relations and group dynamics. This section will briefly discuss examples of human process interventions that can be facilitated with the peer model.

Executive Coaching and Mentoring

Executive coaching and mentoring could be done more effectively by peers as there would be mutual or reciprocal benefit. Pairing new executive directors with seasoned executive directors would allow the exchange of innovation and experience for organizational change initiatives. Many of the seasoned executive directors in Community Action are in most cases hanging onto survival strategies. This sometimes means that change is the farthest issue from their agenda as it is viewed as destabilizing and risky. Through coaching and mentoring, the Community Action Agencies and their leadership could become more change capable. A blended mix of newly trained leaders with experienced and tested leadership holds promise as a recipe for transformational change.

Training and Development

This area of intervention could be carried out by peers, though the peer consultants would have to go through appropriate training curricula, such as the programs offered by the National Training Lab or American Society of Training and Development. The training would also have to be focused on the leadership of organizations as well as their governing boards in order for the change strategies to be sustainable.

Process Consultation and Redesign

The delivery of social services and public services is becoming more sophisticated with the advancement of technology. Not-for-profits and public organizations are constantly exploring ways to effectively and efficiently deliver services just as their counterparts on the for-profit side. Funding sources and tax payers are demanding efficiency in these tough economic times because it is equated to responsibility and cost effectiveness. Efficiency approaches that both government and the not-for-profit sector are always striving to implement are "one stop shops," particularly for human services and programs that promote health and safety. These ensure that clients and the public are able to access services they are eligible for through one application process. The design of these "one stop shops" is an activity that could be facilitated by peers who have successfully implemented them within their own organizations.

Team Building

The development and management of teams is an area of organization development that is of interest to every organization and industry that hopes to be successful in a global economy. As such, a significant focus has been placed on how to make teams work effectively, how to lead teams and how to develop teams. In order for the Community Action network to continue to be relevant and effective in its mission and service delivery, its talent has to be developed into change capable teams. They would need to become teams that embrace positive organizational changes in a very dynamic and demanding environment. As D'Andrea-O'Brien and Buono (1996, p. 4) note:

> The demands of the 21st century will require business organizations to become more customer focused, using employee talent to create, share, and utilize information as part of a broad-based competitive strategy. Another part of this transition will see organizations undergoing significant structural change, developing horizontal networks of task-focused teams leading to "delayered," flatter organizational structures. The horizontal organization will be (1) organized around processes rather than tasks, (2) driven by customer needs and inputs, and (3) dependent on team performance.

A foundational step for utilizing the peer model to develop change capable teams in Community Action is Beckhard's (1971) model on enhancing team effectiveness. This approach focuses on the need to provide teams with clear goals and objectives, roles, and procedures and processes. Building on this framework, the peer model could create teams throughout the Community Action network by utilizing positive organizational and personal change models, such as Luthans, Youssef and Avolio's (2007, p. 3) Psychology Capital (PsyCap) paradigm:

> PsyCap is an individual's positive psychological state of development and is characterized by (1) having confidence (self-efficacy) to take on and put in the necessary effort to succeed at challenging tasks; (2) making a positive attribution (optimism) about succeeding now and in the future; (3) persevering toward goals and, when necessary, redirecting paths to goals (hope) in order to succeed; and (4) when beset by problems and adversity, sustaining and bouncing back and even beyond (resiliency) to attain success.

This approach has the potential to provide a framework for instigating positive organizational change among peers. As an example, when Community Action applies its peer model of technical assistance, an approach like PsyCap could be integrated into this model by having the individual team members utilize the exercises under each component of PsyCap with their peers—focusing on hope, efficacy, resiliency and optimism.

Strategic Change and Organizational Transformation

As indicated earlier, the peer model of consulting has focused primarily on ensuring compliance within programs that are operated by agencies. Although change has not been a focus of the interventions or capacity building efforts that are facilitated by the peer model, these organizations have to be prepared to respond to an environment that at times is very dynamic and unpredictable.

Organization Transformation

Cultural change within the context of not-for-profits or public organizations has to occur from within the organization to ensure that they respond effectively to the environment. The earlier discussion of transformations of not-for-profits and public organizations into "one stop shops," for example, requires a cultural shift. Peer consultants whose organizations have successfully managed, or at least embarked on, cultural shift initiatives could assist other organizations with appropriate methodologies, strategies and frameworks. The peer consultants would be in a better position to facilitate this process because they would be better prepared to deal with the reality of two types of culture within these organizations. The first type is the overall network culture of Community Action, which all of the organizations share. This culture is defined by history, structure, and common relationships with the environment. The second culture, which would be more challenging for the peer consultants, is the culture that is defined by the organization itself. This sub-culture is defined by location, size, demographics, leadership, programs and services. Peers understand the network culture because of their experience and their ability to identify with it, which could also come into play when dealing with the specific sub-culture of the organization in question.

A further illustration of this point is a statewide Information Technology project that involved the Community Action network in Illinois. This project was designed to implement software that would enable Community Action Agencies to conduct centralized in-take for all of their programs as well as report on all program outcomes through one system. The implementation involved the hiring of two external consultants to deal with project management and the programming side of the project. A challenge these external consultants faced was that they did not know or understand the culture of Community Action as organizations. They also did not understand the programs and services operated by Community Action. Even though they had expertise in software and project management, they were faced with challenges attributable to the culture of the organizations

A team of peers was assembled to assist the external consultants with project management as well technical assistance to other agencies. The team was assembled from agencies that were further along with their implementation and deployment of the software. These were the agencies that realized the need for an internal cultural shift, which involved cross training of their staff as a means of eliminating program silos within the organization. This was necessary to enable the software to facilitate the centralized in-take process. The peer consultants were better able to communicate the changes needed from an organizational basis than the external consultants. In some cases, the external consultants' suggestions were met with resistance because it was understood that they did not understand Community Action.

Large Group Interventions

"Large Group Interventions for organizational and community change are methods for involving the whole system, internal and external, in the change process" (Bunker & Alban, 1997, p. xv). Bunker and Alban go on to state that in order for this process to be effective, the issues being resolved need to be systemic and affect a large number of people across the board. "Although there are many differences and varieties of LGI methods, they all share in common the values that have informed OD theory and practice, particularly the imperative for inclusiveness and widespread participation in the change process" (Griffin & Purser, 2008, p. 261). Peer consultants could be as effective in facilitating large group interventions. Interventions such as Appreciative Inquiry summits could be facilitated by a team of peers. The structure of the summit would allow peers to go through the process of planning for transformational change together. Other large group process such as World Café, Future Search and Open Space could also be facilitated in the same way.

CONCLUSION

The peer model of consulting has been successful in ensuring compliance with a broad range of programs administered by not-for-profit organizations through technical assistance and capacity building. This model of consulting has also served as a learning model as the peer consultants have shared and adopted best practices from other organizations. However, due to the ever dynamic environment that not-for-profit organizations have to work within, it is necessary for this model to transition into a change assistance model where facilitation and guidance through change processes would be facilitated by peers. If not-for-profits are to effectively respond to changes from the environment and within the organization, they have to become change capable. The capacity to change could effectively be facilitated by peer consultants. These peer consultants would have to be trained in change strategies and curricula of organization development and change in order for them to become effective change agents. The learning component of the model, which is reciprocal by design, would increase the probability that interventions facilitated by peer consultants would be accepted and sustained over time. If peer consultants become change agents, the need and process of change would become less of a threat because of the familiarity of those facilitating it.

REFERENCES

Beckhard, R. (1971). Optimizing team building efforts. *Journal of Contemporary Business, 1*(3), 23–32.

Bunker, B. B., & Alban, B. (1997). *Large group interventions: Engaging the whole system for rapid change.* San Francisco, CA: Jossey-Bass.

Cho, K., Chung, T. R., King, W. R., & Schunn, C. (2008). Peer based computer-supported knowledge refinement: An empirical investigation. *Communications of the ACM, 51*(/3), 83–88.

Cummings, T. G., & Worley, C. G. (2005). *Organization Development and Change* (8th ed.). Mason, OH: Thomson South-Western.

D'Andrea-O'Brien, C., & Buono, A.F. (1996). Building effective learning teams: Lessons from the field. *SAM Advanced Management Journal, 61*(3), 4–10.

Griffin, T. J., & Purser, R. E. (2008). Large group interventions: Whole systems approaches to organizational change. In T. G. Cummins (Ed.), *Handbook of organization development* (pp. 261–277). Thousand Oaks, CA: Sage publications.

Loughry, M. L. (2002). Coworkers are watching: Performance implications of peer monitoring. *Academy of management best paper proceedings.* (pp. 1–6) Pace, NY: Academy of Management.

Luthans, F., Youssef, C. M., & Avolio, B. J. (2007). *Psychological capital: Developing the human competitive edge.* New York: Oxford University Press.

McNamara, C. (2008). Social Enterprise (Social Entrepreneurship). Free Management Library. <http://www.managementhelp.org/soc_entr/soc_entr.htm> Retrieved March 13, 2008.

CHAPTER 8

FROM THERAPIST TO EXECUTIVE COACH

Insight, Intervention, and Organizational Change

Judith A. Gebhardt

Over the past decade a significant number of clinical therapists have reinvented themselves as executive coaches while the executive coaching profession simultaneously burgeoned. Reflecting on the migration of clinical professionals to the coaching profession, several questions emerge: What are the differences between clinical mental health intervention and processes and coaching? How does an executive's "needs" differ from the classic "mental health" client? What are the necessary skills for a successful coach? What are the transferable skills of the clinical professional? What are the ramifications for the practice of executive coaching?

Many of these answers, of course, lie in understanding the amalgamation of the client's two distinct personas: the individual as a person, which includes personal development and relationship quality; and the person as an employee, which includes on-the-job behavior and organizational performance. The answers are simple, yet complex and examining the intimate

Consultation for Organizational Change. pages 155–180
Copyright © 2010 by Information Age Publishing
All rights of reproduction in any form reserved.

and intertwined relationship between the fields of executive coaching and clinical psychology can provide a foundation for future inquiry, intervention and training programs.

THE CHALLENGE AND THE IMPACT OF COACHING

According to the National Institute of Mental Health (NIMH) "more than 30 million Americans need help dealing with feelings and problems that seem beyond their control," while "one-third of adults in the United States experience an emotional or substance abuse problem [and] nearly 25 percent of the adult population suffers at some point from depression or anxiety shared" (American Psychological Association, 2004a, pp. 51–52). An underlying question, which is highly relevant for an assessment of coaching and clinical practice, concerns the extent to which such feelings are due to work-related issues and whether they might be addressed with coaching.

Looking at the workplace, the numbers suggest that employee problems and the concomitant work-related issues they create merit our attention. Data from the Center for Creative Leadership (Fisher, 1998), for example, suggest that 40% of new management hires fail within the first 18 months, and over 60% of unsuccessful new hires and promotions reflect the "individual's failure to build good relationships and teamwork with peers and subordinates" (Fisher, 2005, p. 48). Such failures are often expensive as senior manager replacement costs can exceed six figures (McCune, 1999). Another contributing factor is leadership's focus on the "bottom line" and consequent organizational strategies including downsizing, rightsizing, outsourcing, mergers, and acquisitions. The resultant breakdown of the psychological contract can readily contribute to such issues as low morale, limited motivation, and even sabotage (Morrison & Robinson, 1997). Additionally, today's organizational workforces are a conglomerate of generations (e.g., Traditionalists, Baby Boomers, Gen-X, Gen-Y) each bringing a different value system, sets of challenges and approaches to the work environment (see Buono & Nurick, 2008), which can also contribute to increased tension and stress.

Within this context, the focus and purpose of coaching engagements have changed significantly over the past decade (Coutu & Kauffman, 2009, p. 92):

> Ten years ago, most companies engaged a coach to help fix toxic behavior at the top. Today, most coaching is about developing the capabilities of high-potential performers... [Yet] survey results...suggest...the industry is fraught with conflicts of interest, blurry lines between what is the province of coaches and what should be left to mental health professionals, and sketchy mechanisms for monitoring the effectiveness of a coaching engagement. Bottom

line: Coaching as a business tool continues to gain legitimacy, but the fundamentals of the industry are still in flux.

Although the number of executive coaches grew at an annual rate of more than 35% between 1996 and early 2000 (Berglas, 2002) and industry revenues are in the $1 billion range (Sherman & Freas, 2004), more recent statistics provide mixed signals. A recent survey of 530 UK organizations found 78% made use of coaching and the Charter Institute of Personnel and Development (CIPD) found coaching to be the "fastest growing approach to training delivery" (Grey, 2006, p. 476). The International Coaching Federation's (ICF) membership statistics doubled between 2003–2005 to 7,000 members in 33 countries (Anonymous, 2005), and more recently May, 2008 figures indicate a doubling of that number to 14,000 members in 80 countries.[1] However, the use of executive coaching could be waning (Anonymous, 2007, p. 4) as 63% of organizations surveyed in 2007 reported a use of coaches, down from 79% in 2006.

The return on investment (ROI) for coaching is promising, but it has a significant spread, ranging from estimates of 10 to 20 times "what is spent" (Gaskell, 2007), to an astounding 689% ROI benefit according to Booz Allen's Center for Performance Excellence Executive Coaching Program (Parker-Wilkins, 2006). Similarly, Levinson's (2009, p. 102) recent study of 12 paired coach-coachee pairs indicated a mixed outcome and "showed varying degrees of impact of the coaching on business related outcome," results that were likely influenced by the executive's role and the relationship between the organizational environment and that executive's individual performance.

Although a "psychological consultation with executives [using] a clinical approach" is not new (see Glaser, 1958), both the professional shift and emergence of coaching as a profession should not be surprising given the "increasing frustration with the politics and economics of traditional mental health care, [which] has lead many… to shift or add executive coaching as a competency in their practices" (Berman & Bradt, 2006, p. 244). It follows then, that the practitioners must have the skills and tools necessary for providing the best interventions possible. More specifically a therapist, consultant or coach with training and knowledge of *both* OD and clinical psychology will have a significantly enhanced "tool bag." As such, a first step is a thorough understanding of the nuances between clinical psychology and executive coaching, the topic of this chapter.

In the introductory essay to this volume, Buono and Jamieson assert that "consulting for organizational change is a special type of management consultation, a complex field of endeavor" that requires a broad range of skills and competencies. This premise clearly reflects the challenge faced by clinical therapists and executive coaches. As part of the bridge between therapist and coach, understanding each other's paradigms would be a value-added for both clinical therapists and executive coaches, where old perspectives would be both reinforced and challenged and one's knowledge-base would be expanded.

CLINICAL THERAPISTS AND EXECUTIVE COACHES: A COMPARATIVE GLANCE

Although there are many similarities between clinical therapy and executive coaching, the differences are most noteworthy (see Table 8.1). This section focuses on the foundations of the two fields and professions, beginning with a brief historical and theoretical overview, followed by a presentation on roles, education/training and licensure, governance and ethical consideration, skills and reimbursement. These components set the stage for the next two sections, which focus on the clients and diagnosis/intervention.

The Professions: A Comparative View

The history of psychology spans more than a century (e.g., Heidbreder, 1933) progressing through "400 therapeutic schools of thought [and] five predominant conceptual thrusts" (Wachtel & Messer, 1997, p. ix). Although the coaching field, in contrast, is still "in its adolescence" (Lowman, 2005, p. 95), it "continues to gain legitimacy as a business tool despite the fact that fundamentals of the industry are still in flux" (Coutu & Kauffman, 2009, p. 92). Kilburg's (1995, p. 30) 17-dimention model of systems and psychodynamic theory, for example, helps to "navigate through the complex world that confronts individuals who do executive coaching," and Sperry's (2009, p. 36) work addresses the finer nuances between executive consultation, coaching, and psychotherapy. Indeed, despite its relative youth, coaching has already differentiated into numerous segments including work-related and OD-based executive coaching (see Kilburg 1996, 1997; Kilburg & Levinson, 2008; Lowman, 2005), including a four-category coaching model of facilitative coaching (FC), restorative coaching (RC), developmental coaching (DV), and executive consulting (EC) (Berman & Bradt, 2006).

Each field and its professionals also bring a different focus. The field of psychology considers an individual's mental processes and behavior while the subfield of clinical psychology focuses on the individual during psychotherapeutic sessions. The American Psychological Association (2004b, p. 52) defines psychotherapy as "a partnership between an individual and a professional such as a psychologist who is licensed and trained to help people understand their feelings and assist them with changing their behavior." Under this premise, Lowman (1993, pp. 7–8) concludes that the goal of psychotherapy usually includes a "major restructuring of personality... of the 'psychically impaired.'" Given this, clinical treatment times range from short-term targeted treatment to the lengthy classical Freudian psychoanalysis,[2] with the timeframe typically indicated by the diagnosis.

Coaching is an intervention option frequently embedded in OD initiatives such as action research. The process is typically focused on the individual-as-an-employee and is less invasive than a clinical psychology intervention. As one of the fastest growing areas of OD practice (Cummings & Worley, 2009), coaching is a "collection of advice and techniques with a focus on 'work dysfunctions'" (Lowman, 2005, p. 90), in the context of the organization and the individual's work-related roles and responsibilities. In this capacity, coaching addresses the development of "a person's skills and knowledge so that their job performance improves, hopefully leading to the achievement of organizational objectives." (Jarvis, 2004; see www.compass-coachingco.uk/info/buying.html).

A number of coaching definitions have been offered. For example, Kombarakarn, Yang, Baker, and Fernandes (2008, p. 79) define executive coaching as:

> ... a short-term process between a coach and a manager to improve leadership effectiveness by enhancing self-awareness and the practice of new behaviors. The coaching process facilitates the acquisition of new skills, perspectives, tools and knowledge through support, encouragement, and feedback in the organizational context.

Along similar lines, Kilburg (1996, p. 142) defines executive coaching as:

> ...a helping relationship formed between a client who has managerial authority and responsibility in an organization and a consultant who uses a wide variety of behavioral techniques and methods to help the client achieve a mutually identified set of goals to improve his or her professional performance and personal satisfaction and, consequently, to improve the effectiveness of the client's organization within a formally defined coaching agreement.

Finally, The International Coach Federation (ICF), a nonprofit, individual membership organization "formed by professionals worldwide who practice business and personal coaching and the largest worldwide resource for business and personal coaches, and the source for those who are seeking a coach,"[3] defines coaching as:

> ... partnering with clients in a thought-provoking and creative process that inspires them to maximize their personal and professional potential. [In]... an ongoing relationship which focuses on clients taking action toward the realization of their visions, goals or desires. [It] is an interactive process that helps individuals and organizations improve their performances and achieve

Table 8.1. Comparison of Clinical Therapist & Executive Coaching Professional Groups

	Professional Groups		
The Foundations	**Clinical psychology/therapist (T)**	**Coach (C)**	
History	Over 100 years old	In its adolescence	D[a]
Theoretical base	Over 400 therapeutic schools Five predominant conceptual thrusts Medical model Scientifically studied	Emerging; based on psychodynamic theory Borrowed from psychotherapy Lacks scientific base	S/D
Role	Change feelings, attitudes, emotions, behaviors	Advice & techniques to develop skills & knowledge related to job performance Focus on behaviors impacting work and may or may not include a change of attitude	D
Education/license	Formal education (BA/MS/PhD levels) followed by state exam for licensure; CEUs required	Certification and in some cases Credential; No CEUs; SME	D
Governing bodies/ confidentiality and ethics	State boards; confidentiality and abuse-reporting guidelines clearly identified	None; attempting to "legitimize" profession; no requirements for keeping confidentiality or reporting abuse	D
Skill set/core values	Clinical psychology/APA: Culture of the Assessment of Competence: www.apa.org/ed/graduate/ Introduction%20to%20Benchmarks%20Document.doc Competency Benchmarks Document (rubric): http://www.apa.org/ed/graduate/comp_benchmark.pdf Coaching/ICF: www.coachfederation.org/includes/media/docs/credentialing-requirements-chart-(9-2008).pdf		D
	Skills: Active listening; clearly defined roles and boundaries; predictable, reliable, respectful, empathetic, authentic, genuine; ability to make strong connection, professionalism, clear and sound methodology		S
	Insurance, third party payor, individual	Organization or the individual	S/D

The Client			
Social system referral sources	Non-work related: Society, family, friends, self	Work related: Organization, team, SBU[b], firm leaders, subordinates, co-workers, peers, self	D
Functioning status/ paradigm	Distressed by personal or social issues, "sick"	Psychologically well	D
Stigma/outsider's perception	"You/I must be crazy or having serious problems" if I need 'treatment for mental health services'	Range—"addressing issues" to personal development: "Finally, he's getting help" to "he wants to improve and become a better employee/manager/boss/supervisor"	D
Subsequent outsider support	Until recent individuals were "ashamed"/embarrassed and wanted to "keep it a secret"	Involvement of key [work-related] stakeholders Usually get more support, positive feedback for attempted changes	D
Treatment/ Intervention			
Diagnosis	DSM, based on medicine's ICD	No official guide rather practitioners' frame, background & experience; generic planned change model	D/S
Treatment focus	Weaknesses of individual	Individual strength Integrates individual psychology & organizational needs	D
Goals	"Feel better" and alleviate pain	Developmental: become better employee Improve work relationships	D/S
Commitment	If driven by others personal commitment is not as strong If self-motivated the opposite is true	Usually higher with buy-in and support from other employees including peers, subordinates and supervisors	S

[a]S: Same; D: Different
[b]SBU: Small Business Unit

extraordinary results. Professional coaches work with clients in all areas including business, career, finances, health and relationships. As a result of professional coaching, clients set better goals, take more action, make better decisions, and more fully use their natural strengths.

Although executive coaching typically targets the "high performance" individual and his or her improvement at work, it also has the potential to affect the person's private life—despite the fact that it has a significantly different focus compared to clinical therapy.

Education/Training and Licensure

The mental health practitioner's position, on the professional continuum, is frequently correlated with their educational level, while executive coaching is haphazard at best. The far end of the clinical psychology spectrum begins with paraprofessionals and includes the peer counselor, counselor, and sometimes clinicians followed with clinical therapists and psychologists. In comparison, the executive coaching profession does not have the clear continuum of the clinical psychology profession, rather it incorporates a variety of educational backgrounds, including professional subject matter experts and those calling themselves coaches.

Paraprofessional peer counselors usually have some basic "active listening" skills and the related ability to empathize. Although most have been through training, almost all have a basic education relative to their age and some have completed higher education classes at the college level. In almost all cases "street smarts" serve as a primary educational foundation. Continuing over the continuum is the "clinician" who may be working towards, or has completed, an advanced degree (usually a Master of Arts or Science) in a field such as psychology or social work. The clinical therapist and psychologist may become eligible to sit for state licensing exams after completing graduate degrees and a specified number of internship/practicum hours, which are segmented into specific content areas. It is noteworthy that in many cases, but not all, paraprofessionals work under the umbrella of a licensed professional, especially in (US) agencies funded by a city, county, state or federal entity.

As recently as 2002 there were "no standards of practice or widely recognized certification for executive coaches in the UK and Europe… and anyone can set himself or herself up as a coach" (Anonymous, 2002, p. 56). The training and education of executive coaching continue to be haphazard, far less stringent than the psychology profession, and can take a variety of forms. The "formal education" process of being a *certified* coach includes attendance at any one of a myriad of programs that offers classes and a certificate. Unlike the clinical profession, there are no specified guidelines and standards overseen by government entities. A next step, after certification, is the coaching *credential* that is awarded by the US-based International Coach Federation (ICF), the largest worldwide resource for business and personal coaches. According to ICF's Megan Thomas (personal communication), the Federation is the "only organization in the world that awards a coaching credential." ICF offers three credential levels, which includes "very specific coach training [that] has achieved a designated number of experience hours and has been coached by a mentor coach."[4] In addition to the ICF, the UK-based Chartered Institute of Personnel and Development (CIPD), which began in the early 1900s as the Welfare Workers' Association (WWA), functions as another "professional body for those involved in the management and development of people" [and] "largest body of personnel and development specialists in the world" (CIPD, 2008). It is noteworthy, however, that none of the credentialing options have a specified minimum academic criteria, suggesting that a high school dropout could be a coach.

The recent study by Liljenstrand and Nebeker (2008) of 2,231 coaches focuses on coaches' approaches and practices, including training and education which lends support to some of the aforementioned issues. The ramifications regarding educational, academic and practical backgrounds are profound since they establish a context for understanding the individual/employee relative to their environmental context. More specifically, the therapist usually addresses relationship issues within the context of "family" and non-work social networks while the executive coach focuses on employee- and organizationally-related issues.

Finally, like the legal profession, psychology is a tightly regulated field, with continually updated rules, regulations, and ideas. In order to keep abreast of these developments licensed professionals are required to complete a specified number of continuing education units (CEUs), in specific content areas. This is usually accomplished by attending meetings, conferences and sessions prior to licensure renewal, an event that occurs every several years. With respect to the field of coaching, in contrast, the, ICF offers a list of "Continuing Coach Education" (CCE) options that satisfy the renewal requirements relative to specific coach credentials. At the same time, however, they also post a disclaimer that "approval does not guarantee the ethical practices or effectiveness of the training program or organization."[5]

Skill Set, Core Values, and Roles

The basic skill sets of both clinicians and coaches are strikingly similar, with clinical psychology's offerings much more detailed and evolved, paralleling the profession and field themselves. An historical perspective on psychology's competency movement (Rubin et al., 2007) considers competencies within a framework of: ethical principles; accreditation practices;

competency-based education, training, and credentialing efforts; licensure; post licensure certifications; and board certification. Hatcher & Lassiter (2007) review the competencies in psychology's initial training, the practicum, while APA's Competency Benchmarks Document clearly outlines the expectations of the mental health practitioner.[6] The ICF ethical guidelines and professional standards are articulated in 4 clusters and 11 "core competencies."[7]

Governing Bodies and Ethical Considerations

Clinical psychology is a heavily-regulated field where ethics and confidentiality are paramount and any infraction could result in variety of punishments, ranging from a slight reprimand to licensure revocation to incarceration. In comparison, as noted earlier, executive coaching has no state oversight committees and no enforcement entities, and, except for the self-appointed ICF, there is no governing body to monitor credentials or oversee punitive sanction capabilities.

According to the American Psychological Association (2004a, p. 51), "psychotherapists consider maintaining your confidentiality extremely important and will answer your questions regarding those rare circumstances when confidential information must be shared," which often includes incidences of child and elder abuse (physical, sexual, and emotional), danger to self and danger to others. Monitored in different ways than confidentiality, ethical standards also receive attention and review by psychology's oversight entities. Undoubtedly, any infraction of the aforementioned standards would subject the practitioner to a review board that has the power to impose disciplinary actions ranging from a review to license revocation. And, in some cases, law enforcement may become involved and a conviction could result.

In comparison ICF publishes a list of four "Standards of Ethical Conduct" for coaches, which includes confidentiality.[8] Although the coaching profession "hopes that over the next five years an ethical framework will be agreed by the industry, followed by a set of core competencies needed by all types of coaches" (Sheppard, 2005, p. 11), it is yet to exist.

Several concerns emerge relative to the practices of therapists and coaches to which immediate attention is paramount. First, as licensed mental health practitioners transition to the "coaching" profession questions of governance, reporting, and reprimand need answers. In the event a "coach," who continues to be a licensed clinical practitioner, has an infraction of the APA standards, what will be the course of action? Will they be subject to a review board? What disciplinary actions might be taken or imposed? Would law enforcement become involved? Who is liable and will they be covered by their malpractice insurance? As for the individual coach and the coaching process itself, a client should be concerned with the current state of the profession. There is only one credentialing entity (the ICF), and it is not monitored by an official agency. While there are certification programs that are authorized by the unmonitored ICF, the reality is that there is haphazard education and training of coaches, with a lack-of-governance void to the point where coach "professionals" will never be penalized for ills caused in their consultations.

Reimbursement and Fees

Clinical psychology fees range from very little to hourly rates of hundreds of dollars (and sometimes more). Frequently, the low fees are at local mental health clinics, which receive subsidies from public funding sources—in fact, "Medicaid is the largest single payer for mental health care" (Carpenter, 2005, p. 32). For those with insurance, third party payers (e.g., insurance companies) are frequently used for private therapy clients, and usually include a co-pay fee. A dramatic shift occurred over the past decade, indicating an inverse relationship between the amount of paperwork filed (increased) and reimbursement (decreased). Additionally, some insurance companies now limit the number of reimbursable sessions, cover only certain diagnoses, fail to pay in a timely manner and require justification for treatment. Without doubt this crosses into ethical and legal arenas. According to Braun and Cox (2005, p. 425):

> Managed health care regulations affect the manner in which counselors provide and deliver services ...[they are] challenged by ethical and legal dilemmas when diagnostic codes in the Diagnostic and Statistical Manual of Mental Disorders are not honored for insurance reimbursement [which can lead to] intentional misdiagnosis of mental disorders for reimbursement.

Coaching fees, in contrast, range from minimal to tens of thousands of dollars. Although one of the country's top coaches, Marshall Goldsmith, does not charge a fee until (and unless) client progress has been duly noted,[9] *some coaches charge a retainer and others an hourly rate.* A recent survey by *Harvard Business Review* found costs range from $200–$3,500 per hour, with a median price of $500 per hour—or in the words of Coutu & Kauffman (2009, p. 92), "the cost of a top psychiatrist in Manhattan."

Summary

The differences between clinical psychology and coaching are especially noteworthy as the coaching profession evolves. A comparison of ICF's Core Competencies and APA's Competency Benchmarks (see Table 8.2) indicates significant differences in criteria. More specifically there are four main areas and eight specific issues ICF does not address when compared

Table 8.2 ICF's Core Competencies and APA's Competency Benchmarks Document[a]

ICF: Core Competencies	APA: Foundational Competencies	
	Reflective Practice Self-Assessment—Practice conducted within the boundaries of competencies, commitment to lifelong learning, engagement with scholarship, critical thinking, and a commitment to the development of the profession.	• Reflective Practice • Self-Assessment and Self-Care • Professionalism
	Scientific knowledge-methods—The ability to understand research, research methodology, and a respect for scientifically-derived knowledge, techniques of data collection and analysis, biological bases of behavior, cognitive-affective bases of behavior, and lifespan human development.	• Scientific Mindedness • Knowledge • Scientific Foundations
Setting the foundation—Meeting ethical guidelines and professional standards and establishing the coaching agreement **Co-creating the relationship**—Establishing trust and intimacy with the client, coaching presence **Communicating effectively**—active listening, powerful questioning, direct communication	**Relationships**—Capacity to relate effectively and meaningfully with individuals, groups, and/or communities	• Interpersonal Relationships • Affective Skills • Intradisciplinary Relationships • Expressive Skills
	Individual-cultural Diversity—Awareness and sensitivity in working professionally with diverse individuals, groups and communities who represent various cultural and personal background and characteristics.	• Self-Awareness • Applied Knowledge
Setting the foundation—Meeting ethical guidelines and professional standards and establishing the coaching agreement	**Ethical-legal standards policy**—Application of ethical concepts and awareness of legal issues regarding professional activities with individuals, groups, and organizations. Advocating for the profession.	• Knowledge • Awareness and Application of Ethical Decision-Making Model • Ethical Conduct

	Interdisciplinary systems—Identification and involvement with one's colleagues and peers. Knowledge of key issues and concepts in related disciplines and the ability to interact with professionals in them.	• Understanding the shared and distinctive contributions of other professions, knowledge of key issues and concepts related to the work of other professionals. • Multidisciplinary and interdisciplinary functioning: understanding the differences and ability to function in both contexts • Understands how participation in interdisciplinary collaboration/ consultation enhances outcomes • Respectful and productive relationships with individuals from other professions.
	Functional Competencies	
	Assessment-diagnosis-case conceptualization—Assessment and diagnosis of problems and issues associated with individuals, groups, and/or organizations	• Diagnosis: Normal/Abnormal Behavior & Skills • Assessment: Knowledge of Measurement and Psychometrics; Use of Methods (Interview & Tests/Measurements) • Integration (Site Specific; Communication of Results; Integrated skills)
Facilitating learning and results—Creating awareness, designing actions, planning and goal setting, managing progress and accountability	**Intervention**—Interventions designed to alleviate suffering and to promote health and well-being of individuals, groups, and/or organizations	• Knowledge of Interventions • Intervention planning • Intervention Implementation • Progress evaluation • Skills

(*continued*)

Table 8.2 Continued

ICF: Core Competencies	APA: Foundational Competencies	
Facilitating learning and results—Creating awareness, designing actions, planning and goal setting, managing progress, and accountability	**Consultation**—The ability to provide expert guidance or professional assistance in response to a client's needs or goals.	• Addressing Referral Question • Role Knowledge • Knowledge
	Research/evaluation—The generation of research that contributes to the professional knowledge base and/or evaluates the effectiveness of various professional activities	• Scientific Approach to Knowledge Generation • Application of Scientific Method to Practice
	Supervision-teaching—Supervision and training of the professional knowledge base and/or evaluates the effectiveness of various professional	• Supervision: Knowledge; Skills Development; Awareness of factors affecting quality; Participation in Supervision Process; Ethical and Legal Issues • Teaching: Skills
	Management-administration—Managing the direct delivery of services (DDS) and/or the administration of organizations, programs, or agencies (OPA).	• Leadership • Management • Effective Program Development

[a]http://www.apa.org/ed/graduate/comp_benchmark.pdf

to APA's competencies. This includes the foundational competencies of reflective practice self-assessment, scientific knowledge-methods, individual-cultural diversity and interdisciplinary systems and the competencies of assessment-diagnosis-case conceptualization, research-evaluation, supervision-teaching, and management-administration.

Reflecting on the current status of clinical psychology and coaching, it appears that there is a similar pattern to the 1970s, when clinical psychology eclipsed psychiatry. As the world renowned psychiatrist and family therapist Murray Bowen (1982, p. ix) observed:

> People with little professional background began calling themselves "therapists." The new rush made inroads into the time-honored discipline of psychoanalysis and into departments of psychiatry... New "experts" began touring the circuits and attracting followers with their own brand of gospel. The whole "therapy" rush was devoid of theory and similar to the great religions in which charismatic experts preach their own brands of gospel. ... The state of chaos is still with us, with bands of people of one persuasion competing with those of other persuasions. People pick up ideas and distort them to fit their own private gospels. ... The field of work and administrative systems is much smaller than the family 'therapy' field but it also participates in a milder version of distortions and misrepresentations.

More recently some observers (e.g., ; Koocher, 2007, p. 382; Sharfstein, 2006) concluded that "psychiatry is a profession on the demise" as the academic training model is outdated, focusing on psychopharmacology while excluding psychotherapy and psychosocial interventions. The combination of general practitioners prescribing psychotropic medication, jettisoning the need for a "specialist," and the lack of psychotherapeutic skills could very well cause psychiatry to "disappear as a medical specialty" (Koocher, 2007, p. 382). If history is indeed repeating itself, it seems appropriate to explore the lessons from the 1970s and psychiatry's more recent experience in our examination of the clinical psychology and coaching fields.

THE CLIENTS AND INTERVENTIONS: "PATIENT TREATMENT" OR "CLIENT SESSION"?

Both clinical therapy and executive coaching include the client's social systems and referral mechanisms, status, baseline perceptions, and outsider support. Clinical psychology frequently targets the micro-system, which usually encompasses the individual, couple, family, and small group. Referrals are usually a result of "symptoms" or "problems" of the respective person or system. Historically, the interventions were based on the medical model (of disease and illness) and more recently the ideas found in positive psychology.

Executive coaching clients also span the continuum of micro- to macro-systems, which sequentially manifests as the employee, business unit or team, the entire organization, and potentially even the industry (or several if it is a diversified company). Referral reasons usually include "work issues" or "problems at work," concerns that are analogous to the clinical psychology client seeking help, with one significant caveat—the person is usually psychologically well. This is noteworthy and in direct contrast to the clinical psychology/medical model of sickness and un-health.

Referral Mechanisms and Client Functioning Status

The psychology "patient" usually comes to a clinical therapist for help in dealing with "issues" or "problems" with society, family, friends or themselves. A myriad of emotions and thoughts frequently contribute to one's seeking help, which could include such feelings as out-of-control, depressed, angry, unhappy, frustrated, "torn," and confused. Frequently, an individual seeks treatment because they are "distressed by personal or societal issues" (CIPD, 2008) or comes to psychotherapy because "they are discouraged and demoralized about some aspect of their lives and psychotherapists engage in what is essentially a persuasive exercise that helps them overcome that demoralization" (Frank, 1973). The APA (American Psychological Association, 2004a, p. 51) suggests an individual consider therapy if they:

- ...feel an overwhelming and prolonged sense of helplessness and sadness, and ...problems do not ...get better despite ... efforts and help from family and friends;
- ...find it difficult to carry out everyday activities;
- ...worry excessively, expect the worst; [or]
- ... [their] actions are harmful to yourself or to others.

In addition to the individual, small systems such as families and couples may also seek treatment for similar issues including relationships. As the APA's (2004, p. 51) help center indicates:

> ... psychotherapists work with patients to change their feelings and attitudes and help them develop healthier, more effective patterns of behavior.... [They] apply scientifically validated procedures to help people change their thoughts, emotions, and behaviors. Psychotherapy is a collaborative effort between an individual and a psychotherapist. It provides a supportive environment to talk openly and confidentially about concerns and feelings.

Historically, coaching clients are referred employees, often "executives in trouble...who are technical proficient but exhibit poor management and leadership skills (Peak, 1997, p. 9). Focusing on leadership development, which includes modification of one's perspectives and behavior (Strickland, 1997) or role transition (i.e., from a project manager to people manager) (Hayes, 1997), the individuals referred for work-related matters bring a myriad of manifestations that have escalated to a noteworthy point. As noted earlier, although coaching can take on a variety of forms, the CIPD (2007) identified some general agreements among coaching professionals:

- It is essentially a non-directive form of development.
- It focuses on improving performance and developing individuals' skills.
- Personal issues may be discussed but the emphasis is on performance at work.
- Coaching activities have both organizational and individual goals.
- Assumption that the individual is psychologically well and does not require a clinical intervention.
- It provides people with feedback on both their strengths and their weaknesses.
- It is a skilled activity which should be delivered by trained people.

The fact that Kilburg (1997) addresses the core problems and basic approaches to coaching and executive behavior is noteworthy in that some employee behaviors and actions are more appropriate for psychological intervention. Although many employers are hesitant to make psychological referrals, some coaches may be put in situations where their skills are inadequate. This issue was not lost by Peterson (2009, p. 94) who reported that "more than three-quarters of coached report having gotten into personal territory at some time" and Grant (2009, p. 97) who asserts that "some executives will have mental health problems." At the same time, the therapist-turned-coach must be vigilant in *not* crossing the line, recognizing when a mental health referral is or is not appropriate. In other words, they should stay professional and *not* confound their clinical and coaching professions, setting and articulating the boundaries as they relate to their intervention responsibilities. As Grant (2009) concludes, coaching is the grey area between consulting and therapy, borrowing from both arenas. Thus, Lowman's (1993) decade-old work on the "counseling and psychotherapy of work dysfunctions" merits attention. More specifically, Lowman's "clinically useful taxonomy" (p. 43) clearly establishes the work-clinical and coaching-therapy links, which are clinically grounded in APA constructs and subsequent interventions.

Perceptions and Outsider Support

Another issue is the stigma of seeking mental health treatment. Although change has occurred over the past several decades, some clients still see themselves as deficient and feel ashamed of needing "professional help." Consequently, therapy was typically kept as one's "big secret." Given the changes in the US work environment over the last two decades, and the emergence of coaching, this paradigm shifted and it became increasingly acceptable to seek help for personal development and self-improvement (i.e., a coaching focus) to become a better employee (and person by default). As noted by Liljenstrand and Nebeker (2008, p. 58), the "shift from hiring coaches for struggling employees to focusing on the rising stars has decreased the stigmatization of receiving coaching series and has in turn increased the demand for such services.

Although the perception of coaching as "acceptable" has begun to spill over into the clinical arena, client support still differs. First, given the all-too-often negative undertones related to psychotherapy, including personal deficit, an individual is not likely to share treatment goals with potential external support systems, which could include family, friends and social groups. Second, the motives for seeking "professional help" or "seeing a therapist" is usually founded in the idea of "purging pain" as opposed to "making the good better." In combination, the clinical patient may inhibit his or her own growth by not sharing new learning and attempted changes including behaviors and feelings, thus, in effect, sabotage themselves. The coaching client, in comparison, frequently receives support and encouragement, resulting in a synergy in their growth process. As Goldsmith (2006, p. 16) writes, "co-workers are active participants in process" and by "sharing that you're in coaching usually get more support, positive feedback and support for your attempted changes."

Treatment and Intervention

The mental health profession's clinical treatment follows the medical model, beginning with an evaluation and subsequent diagnosis, followed by the treatment plan and intervention (See Gebhardt, 2009; Gebhardt & Olson, 2007). Similarly, executive coaching also closely follows a planned change outline (cf. Burke, 2008; Cummings & Worley, 2009). Yet, despite what may appear to be similar schemas, there are a number of embedded differences that merit attention.

Diagnosis and Treatment Focus

The roots of clinical psychology lie in medicine, and more specifically, diagnosis and coding. The beginnings of psychology's methodically tested and validated diagnostic tool, *The Diagnostic and Statistical Manual of Mental Disorders* (American Psychiatric Association, 2000) dates back to the 1880s, with a statistical classification system in place by 1917. In comparison, executive coaching's diagnostic tools are haphazard and are limited to a coach's personal repertoire and experience. These may include a 360-feedback measure and/or assessments related to personality, goal setting, leadership development, and development. The purpose of these tools may form the basis for the coaching engagement, but it falls to the coach and client as to when, if and how they will be implemented.

In comparison to the clinical psychology process, coaching is far less stringent, given the paradigm for change, and focuses on one's behavior and the employee/work relationship. As an example, Goldsmith's principles[10] for executive coaching consists of five activities, which are useful for establishing a baseline for the coaching process:

- Agreement on specific coaching goals based on an assessment of the leader's strengths and weaknesses by him/herself, and by colleagues who are best able to comment on his or her behaviors. In some cases, the client organization has already completed a leadership diagnostic; in other cases, the coach is asked to manage that process.
- Creation of a written development plan that includes agreed-upon goals, targeted outcomes, action steps, time frames, and measures.
- Syndication of the leader's goals with key stakeholders, and periodic feedback from this group [including]... input from six to eight of the leader's colleagues, including his or her manager, peers, and direct reports...[and] critical clients or customers.
- "Homework" assignments between coaching sessions.
- Progress assessment at the end of the engagement (and also at the midpoint for yearlong assignments)... [where]... we solicit stakeholders' perceptions of change against goals.

Inherent in both professions is the understanding that improvement in an individual's or employee's situation, which may include performance, is the ultimate goal. Although this concept can take on a variety of meanings and definitions it begs the question about the importance of an accurate diagnosis. Its significance is paramount as it sets the foundation for subsequent interventions at both the macro (i.e., organization) and micro (employee/individual) levels. On this pretext Grant's (2009, p. 97) conclusion that "coaches have some training in mental health issues" merits more than a cursory nod.

Positive Psychology: Implications for Executive Coaching?

As psychology eclipsed psychiatry in the 1970s, intervention strategies may also be shifting from the negativistic paradigm of the medical model to the emerging positive psychology (PP) paradigm. Seligman and Csikszentmihaly introduced PP in 2000 with the first taxonomy focusing on "Character Strengths and Virtues" (Peterson & Seligman, 2004). As the authors assert, although the "new field lacks a common vocabulary," it's clear classification of character is a step in the right direction (Seligman & Peterson, 2003) and already garners support with scientific-based studies and empirical validation of interventions (Seligman, Steen, Park, & Peterson, 2005).

The emergence of PP in clinical therapy is a current topic in the literature, as reflected by the series of articles in the *Journal of Clinical Psychology* (May, 2009). Included in the publication is Biswas-Diener's (2009) case-study of executive coaching, which builds on his earlier PP coaching book (see Biswas-Diener & Dean, 2007). Finally, as Seligman (2007, p. 266) has recently concluded, "positive psychology can provide coaching with an evidence-based framework, and defined scope of practice...[in order to] help set the boundaries of responsible coaching practice...and bring some order into the chaos of coaching."

Akin to the individual-level, PP has become integrated into organizational interventions, including OD initiatives that include executive coaching, appreciative inquiry (Cooperrider, 2005; Cooperrider, 1990; Cooperrider & Srivastva, 1987), appreciative intelligence (Thatchenkery & Metzker, 2006), positive organizational scholarship (Cameron, Dutton & Quinn, 2003) and Positive Organizational Behavior (Luthans, 2002a, b; Luthans & Youssef, 2007). More recently Wright and Campbell-Quick (2009) presented a thorough and comprehensive discussion addressing the "emerging positive agenda" in organizations.

The significance of these positivistic strategies is the focus on what is "right" and "good" in organizational life, removed from the focus of the traditional intervention ideology of what is "wrong." As such, the field and intervention techniques merit attention and possible integration into the realm of executive coaching.

The Fusion of Core Values

According to the CIPD (2008):

> It can be hard to draw a clear distinction between coaching and counseling, not least because many of the theoretical underpinnings of coaching are drawn from the worlds of counseling and therapy. For the purpose of managing coaching services the key distinction to be drawn is that coaching is for those who are psychologically well; a coach should be able to recognize where an individual is so distressed by personal or social issues that he or she needs to be referred to specialist counseling or other support.

Although Frank (1973) assets four features that are "shared by virtually all approaches to psychotherapy," they seem appropriate and fitting for the coaching relationship as well. In summary, the intervention, for either professional should be:

1. a relationship in which the patient has confidence that the therapist is competent and cares about his welfare;
2. a practice setting that is socially defined as a place of healing;
3. a rationale or "myth" that explains that patient's suffering and how it can be overcome; and
4. a set of procedures that require the active participation of both patient and therapist and that both believe to be the means of restoring the patient's health.

More recently publications on coaching in the *Harvard Business Review* included a "coach or couch" synopsis (Grant, 2009), noting the overlaps between the two professions. In fact, despite the differences in backgrounds, role and reasons for client referrals, both professions hold corresponding values and share features that are strikingly congruent.

Summary

Comparing the clients and subsequent intervention strategies, the label of "patient treatment" or "client session" might best capture the ideologies of the two camps. Both the client and treatment/intervention categories each included four areas (Table 8.1) where the most striking differences between the psychology and coaching lie in the client, which is driven by the non-work versus work environment. Consequently, the social system and referral mechanism, "mental health" status, stigma/outsider's perception and subsequent outsider support are different for each population. The treatment/interventions are strikingly similar relative to goals and commitment, but have differences that are remarkable. As discussed, psychology's foundation lies in medicine and is based on the medical model while coaching purports a "healthy" perspective. This mindset parlays into the treatment/intervention strategy, whereby psychology clients explore deeper emotional and personal problems in comparison to coaching where the sessions focus on work-related issues and is developmental in nature.

CONCLUSION: DIFFERENTIATING THE GREY AREA

The perceived similarities in the coaching and clinical psychology professions reflect the grey area between the two professions. In an attempt to highlight potential problems, this chapter introduced three primary areas where differences and similarities between clinical therapy and executive coaching are most noteworthy (see Table 8.1). As illustrated in Table 8.2, there are four areas where coaching and APA standards are not correlated. This includes the competencies of personal (self) awareness (i.e., reflective practice self-assessment and individual-cultural diversity); scientifically-based issues (i.e., scientific knowledge-methods and research/evaluation); education, training and development (where APA criteria includes training interdisciplinary systems, assessment-diagnosis-case conceptualization and supervision-teaching); and finally the business component (i.e., management-administration). In combination it seems these components fall under two main categories of personal development and formal education. As such, the education and training of coaches would benefit from more consistency and more stringent entry-level criteria.

Although respectable, life-lessons and personal experience are not formal education. Indeed, coaching's attempt to become "more professional" would benefit from a sounder education and training process. Assuming that basic skills (e.g., active/reflective listening) are already garnered, basic knowledge of psychology would be beneficial. This might include basic psychology, abnormal psychology, family constructs (which is somewhat emulated in the organization in terms of structure and relationships), group and/or team processes and ethics. A glaring omission in both coaching and clinical initiatives is also problematic. Most clinicians, and possibly coaches, lack a deep understanding of organizationally-related issues such as organization development, organizational theory and behavior, strategy, leadership, organizationally-focused group and team dynamics, power, politics and influence, and so forth.

As discussed in the chapter, the striking differences between the two roles generate a number of important questions: Will executive coaching clients expect professionals to have a working knowledge of these organizationally-related issues? Will the professionalization of coaching include the oversight of a credentialing agency? Will there be reporting criteria for a licensed therapist working as a "coach"? Will a client be able to bring a lawsuit against a licensed therapist who was working in the capacity of an executive coach?

Clearly, in order to better understand these issues each of the professions must better understand the paradigms of the other. As Maccoby (2009, p. 95) observes:

> Two particular kinds of shift in [engagement] focus...are dangerous and should be avoided.... When the behavioral coach...seduces you into a form of psychotherapy without making it explicit... [and] when the personal coaches morph into business advisors.

As psychiatry is failing to respond to the zeitgeist, and clinical practitioners and coaching comes closer and closer together due to the complexity of change in personal, professional and organizational life, it is imperative to consider and address the lessons learned, opportunities unfolding, and, at the very least, recognize the limitations of "carte blanche" when migrating into the domains of others.

NOTES

1. Information on the International Coaching Federation can be found at http://www.coachfederation.org.
2. See http://mentalhealth.samhsa.gov/publications/allpubs/SMA-02-3617R/model3.asp retrieved August 13, 2009
3. The quote was taken from the ICF (2008) homepage, http://www.coachfederation.org.
4. See http://www.coachfederation.org/includes/media/docs/Credentialing-Requirements-Chart-(9-2008).pdf.
5. See www.coachfederation.org/research-education/coach-training-programs/search-programs/.
6. See www.apa.org/ed/graduate/comp_benchmark.pdf.
7. The ICF ethical guidelines and professional standards can be found at: www.coachfederation.org/research-education/icf-credentials/core-competencies/.
8. The ICF's "Standards of Ethical Conduct" for coaches can be found at: www.coachfederation.org/about-icf/ethics-%26-regulation/icf-code-of-ethics/.
9. See www.marshallgoldsmith.com.
10. Goldsmith's principles are available at: www.marshallgoldsmith.com/Page.aspx?PageID=8.

REFERENCES

American Psychiatric Association. (2000). *The diagnostic and statistical manual of mental disorders* (4th ed.). Washington, D. C.: American Psychiatric Association.

American Psychological Association. (2004a). Finding help: How to choose a psychotherapist. <http://www.apahelpcenter.org/articles/article.php?id=51> Accessed March 28, 2009.

American Psychological Association. (2004b). How to find help through psychotherapy. <http://www.apahelpcenter.org/articles/article.php?id=52> Accessed March 28, 2009.

Anonymous. (2002). Why executive coaching is booming. *Career Development International, 7*(1), 56.

Anonymous. (2005). Coaching versus therapy in business management. *Development and Learning in Organizations, 20*(1), 23–25.

Anonymous. (2007). Coaching: Business savior or just a fad? *Human Resource Management International Digest, 13*(1), 26–29.

Berglas, S. (2002). The very real dangers of executive coaching. *Harvard Business Review, 80,* 87–92.

Berman, W. H., & Bradt, G. (2006). Executive coaching and consulting, Different strokes for different folks. *Professional Psychology,* 37(3), 244–253.

Biswas-Diener, R. (2009). Personal coaching as a positive intervention. *Journal of Clinical Psychology, 65*, 544–553.

Biswas-Diener, R., & Dean, B. (2007). *Positive psychology coaching: Putting the science of happiness to work for your clients.* Hoboken, NJ: John Wiley & Sons.

Bowen, M. (1982). Introduction. In R. R. Sager & K. K. Wiseman (Eds.), *Understanding organizations: Application of Bowen family systems theory* (pp. i–xii). Washington, DC: Georgetown University Family Center.

Braun, S. A., & Cox, J. A. (2005). Managed mental health care: Intentional misdiagnosis of mental disorders. *Journal of Counseling and Development, 83*(4), 425–433.

Burke, W. W. (2008). *Organization change: Theory and practice.* (2nd ed.). Thousand Oaks, CA: Sage Publications.

Buono, A. F., & Nurick, A. J. (2008). Reaching your next generation of employees. *Federal Ethics Report, 15*(9), 1–4.

Cameron, K., Dutton, J. E, & Quinn, R. E. (2003). *Positive organizational scholarship.* NY: Berrett-Kohler Publishers.

Carpenter, C. E. (2005). Financing mental health care. *Journal of Financial Service Professionals, 59*(6), 32–34.

Charter Institute of Personnel and Development (CIPD) (2008). Coaching. <http://www.cipd.co.uk/subjects/lrnanddev/coachmntor/coaching.htm?IsSrchRes=1> Accessed August 6, 2008.

Cooperrider, D. (1990). Positive image, positive action: The affirmative basis of organizing. In S. Srivastva, & D. L. Cooperrider (Eds.), *Appreciative management and leadership,* (pp. 91–125). San Francisco: Jossey-Bass.

Cooperrider, D. (2005). *Appreciative inquiry: A positive revolution of change.* NY: Berrett-Kohler.

Cooperrider, D., & Srivastva, S. (1987). Appreciative inquiry in organizational life. In R. Woodman, & W. Pasmore (Eds.), *Research in Organizational Change and Development* (vol. 1, pp. 129–169). Greenwich, CT: JAI Press.

Coutu, C., & Kauffman, C. (2009). What can coaches do for you? *Harvard Business Review,* (Jan.), 91–93.

Cummings, T., & Worley, C. (2009). *Organizational development and change* (9th ed.). Cincinnati : South-Western College Publications.

Fisher, A. (1998). Don't blow your new job? *Fortune,* 137(6), 162–163.

Fisher, A. (2005). Starting a new job? Don't blow it. *Fortune,* 151(5), 48–51.

Frank, J. D. (1973). *Persuasion and healing: A comparative study of psychotherapy* (Rev. ed.). Baltimore, MD: Johns Hopkins University Press.

Gaskell, C. (2007). HR Directors will gain if line managers take on coaching. *Personneltoday.com.*<http://www.personneltoday.com/articles/2007/04/17/40416/hr-directors-will-gain-if-line-managers-take-on-coaching.html> Retrieved August 6, 2009.

Gebhardt, J. A. (2009). *OD's lessons from the medical model: Reconnecting with our roots and moving forward.* Working Paper.

Gebhardt, J. A., & Olson, T. (2007). *Organizational diagnosis: Extending traditional concepts through psychology's DSM and positive psychology paradigms?* Academy of Management Conference Pre-conference Workshop, Philadelphia, PA.

Glaser, E. M. (1958). Psychological consultation with executives: A clinical approach. *American Psychologist, 13*(8), 486–489.

Goldsmith, M. (2006, June). Where the work of executive coaching lies. *Consulting to Management, 12*(2), 15–17.

Grant, A. M. (2009). Coach or couch? *Harvard Business Review, 87*(1), 97.

Grey, D. E. (2006). Executive coaching: Towards a dynamic alliance of psychotherapy and transformation. *Management Learning, 37*(4), 475–497.

Hatcher, R. L. & Lassiter, K. D. (2007). Initial training in professional psychology: The Practicum Competencies Outline. *Training and Education in Professional Psychology, 1,* 49–63.

Hayes, G. E. (1997). Executive coaching: A strategy for management and organizational development. In A. J. Pickman (Ed.), *Special challenges in career management: Counselor perspective* (pp. 213–222). Mahwah, NJ: Erlbaum.

Heidbreder, E. (1933). *Seven psychologies (Century Psychology Series).* Englewood Cliffs, NJ: Prentice-Hall, Inc.

International Coaching Federation's (ICF) http://www.coachfederation.org/.

Jarvis, J. (2004). *Coaching and buying coaching services. A guide.* London: CIPD.

Kilburg, R. (1995). Integrating psychodynamic and systems theories in organization development practice. *Consulting Psychology Journal: Practice and Research, 47*(1), 28–55.

Kilburg, R. (1996). Toward a conceptual understanding and definition of executive coaching. *Consulting Psychology Journal: Practice and Research, 43*(2), 134–144.

Kilburg, R. (1997). Coaching and executive character: Core problems and basic approaches. *Consulting Psychology Journal: Practice and Research, 53*(4), 251–267.

Kilburg, R., & Levinson, H. (2008). Executive dilemmas: Coaching and the professional perspectives of Harry Levinson. *Consulting Psychology Journal: Practice and Research, 60*(1), 7–32.

Kombarakarn, F. A., Yang, J. A., Baker, M. N., & Fernandes, P, B. (2008). Executive coaching: It works! *Consulting Psychology Journal: Practice and Research, 60*(1), 78–90.

Koocher, G. P. (2007) Twenty-first century ethical challenges for psychology. *American Psychologist, 62*(5), 375–384.

Levenson, A. (2009). Measuring and maximizing the business impact of executive coaching. *Consulting Psychology Journal: Practice and Research, 61*(2), 103–121.

Liljenstrand, A. M., & Nebeker, D. M. (2008) Coaching services: A look at the coaches, client and practices. *Consulting Psychology Journal: Practice and Research, 60*(1), 57–77.

Lowman, R. (1993). *Counseling and psychotherapy of work dysfunctions.* American Psychological Association: Washington, DC.

Lowman, R. (2005). Executive coaching: The road to Dodoville needs paving with more than good assumptions. *Consulting Psychology Journal: Practice and Research, 57*(1), 90–96.

Luthans, F. (2002a). The need for and meaning of positive organizational behavior. *Journal of Organizational Behavior, 23,* 695–706.

Luthans, F. (2002b). Positive organizational behavior: Developing and maintaining psychological strengths. *Academy of Management Executive, 15,* 57–72.

Luthans, F., & Youssef, C. M. (2007). Emerging positive organizational behavior. *Journal of Management, 33,* 321–349.

Maccoby, M. (2009, Jan). What can coaches do for you? *Harvard Business Review, 87* (1), 95.

McCune, J. C. (1999). Sorry, wrong executive. *Management Review, 88,* 15–21.

Morrison, E. W., & Robinson, S.L. (1997). When employees feel betrayed: A model of how psychological contact violation develops. *Academy of Management Review, 22*(1), 226–256.

Parker-Wilkins, V. (2006). Business impact of executive coaching: Demonstrating monetary value. *Industrial and Commercial Training, 38*(3), 122–127.

Peak, M. H. (1997). Peter principle at work. *Management Review, 86*(7), 9.

Peterson, C., & Seligman, M. E. (2004). *Character strengths and virtues.* New York: American Psychological Association and Oxford University Press.

Peterson, D. B. (2009). Does your coach give you value for your money? *Harvard Business Review, 87*(1), 94.

Rubin, N. J., Bebeau, M. J. Leigh, I. W., Lichtenberg, J. W., Nelson, P. D., Portnoy, S. M., Smith, I. L., & Kaslow, N. J. (2007). The competency movement within psychology: An historical perspective. *Professional Psychology: Research and Practice, 38,* 452–462.

Seligman, M. E. (2007). Coaching and positive psychology. *American Psychologist, 42*(4), 266–267.

Seligman, M. E., & Csikszentmihalyi, M. (2000). Positive psychology: An introduction. *American Psychologist, 55,* 5–14.

Seligman, M. E., & Peterson, C. (2003). Positive clinical psychology. In L. G. Aspinwall, & U. M. Staudinger (Eds.), *A psychology of human strengths: Fundamental questions and future directions for a positive psychology* (pp. 305–317). Washington, DC: American Psychological Association.

Seligman, M. E, Steen, T., Park, N., & Peterson, C. (2005). Positive psychology progress: Empirical validation of interventions. *American Psychologist, 60*(5), 410–421.

Sharfstein, S. (2006). How will psychologists practicing medicine affect psychiatry? *Psychiatric News, 41*(9), 3.

Sheppard, G. (2005). Coaches fight for credibility. *Training Magazine,* (September), 10–11.

Sherman, S., & Freas, A. (2004). The wild west of executive coaching. *Harvard Business Review, 82*(11), 82–90.

Sperry, L. (2009). Executive coaching: An intervention, role function or profession? *Consulting Psychology Journal: Practice and Research, 60*(1), 33–37.

Strickland, K. (1997). Executive coaching: Helping valued executives fulfill their potential. In A. J. Pickman (Ed.), *Special challenges in career management: Counselor perspective* (pp. 203–212). Mahwah, NJ: Erlbaum.

Thatchenkery, T., & Metzker, C. (2006). *Appreciative Intelligence: Seeing the Mighty Oak in the Acorn.* San Francisco: Berrett-Koehler.

Wachtel, P. L., & Messer, S. B. (Eds.). (1997). *Theories of psychotherapy: Origins and evolution* (pp. 227–272). Washington, DC: American Psychological Association.

Wright, T. A., & Campbell-Quick, J. (2009). The emerging positive agenda in organizations: Greater than a trickle, but not yet a deluge. *Journal of Organizational Behavior, 30,* 147–159.

CHAPTER 9

USING ENGLISH AS A FOREIGN LANGUAGE IN INTERNATIONAL AND MULTICULTURAL CONSULTING

Asset or Hindrance?

Kathrin Kordon

The professional world at the beginning of the 21st century seems to be undergoing a paradigm shift that resembles a constant process of change. Growing internationalization routinely brings about situations that require individuals to "switch" between different cultures on a daily basis, from multi-professional teams and interdisciplinary projects, to multiple professional identities, various work places, and so forth. Such transitions certainly imply personal and institutional enrichment, but they also raise new challenges, risks and potential for conflict—and, therefore, call for new forms of consulting in terms of professional counseling. "Diversity management," for example, has become one of the most prominent buzzwords of our times and one can observe a boom of intercultural trainings and seminars, which are often of highly disputable quality.

Consultation for Organizational Change. pages 181–205
Copyright © 2010 by Information Age Publishing
All rights of reproduction in any form reserved.

During encounters of people of mixed national and ethnical backgrounds, one of the key challenges is undoubtedly dealing with linguistic diversity. Given the widely acknowledged status of English as *the* world language (for detailed discussion see, for example, Crystal, 1997; Graddol, 1997; Phillipson, 1992), it has also become the most widely used language when it comes to professional counseling in intercultural contexts. For many coaches, supervisors, and trainers a certain command of the English language has become indispensible due to the growing demand of counseling processes in English. Consultants not only work with clients who speak different first languages and, therefore, have to rely on English, but the radius of their professional lives has long transcended national borders: conferences and international intervision groups are held in English, publications are expected to be written in English if one aims to address the international "scientific community,"[1] and so forth.

From a linguistic point of view, the question that arises concerns the "form" of English used in these contexts. Rarely, it is English native speakers who prompt a "multilingual" group to speak English. In most working contexts (and, thus, also in contexts of international or intercultural counseling), it is speakers, "none of whom is the mother tongue" (House, 1999, p. 74), who agree to use English as common code of understanding, i.e., *English as a lingua franca* (ELF).

The present chapter[2] examines the implications of the use of ELF in professional counseling processes, with a strong focus on supervision.[3] After a brief definition of ELF and its perceptions both from the perspective of linguists and consultants, a sample of extracts from an audio-recorded intervision group will be analyzed and used to propose some tentative observations and hypotheses about supervision processes in ELF. Having encountered many colleagues for whom working in ELF constitutes an insurmountable barrier—and at times even a reason for declining projects—I am motivated to make these professionals aware of the fact that a high level of proficiency in English (measured in accordance with native-speakers' norms) is not always be the main prerequisite to work on a global level. This certainly calls for a change of attitude, away from deficit-oriented thinking towards an understanding of the innovative and creative power of ELF.

ENGLISH AS A LINGUA FRANCA (ELF)

The discussion concerning the status and use of English has long pervaded our everyday life. The discourse has abandoned any distinction of being restricted to a study object of linguists or language policy makers, and is regularly discussed in media (cf. Baker, Resch, Carlisle, & Schmidt, 2001; Meinhart, 2001). The status of English as the world language is widely unquestioned, both from a popular and linguistic perspective (e.g. Graddol, 1997; Phillipson, 1992).

Popular and Linguistic Perceptions

Over the last couple of years, the discussion surrounding English as the global language has gradually started to involve questions concerning its linguistic "form." In the media, these assessments often involve issues regarding speakers' language proficiency. A 2006 *Newsweek* article, for example, laments the "...problem [that] many call centers [in the Philippines] can't keep up with the demand because they can't find enough employees who speak 'proper' English" (Vitug, 2006, p. 44). Although Vitug does not specify what she considers "proper" English, she is most likely referring to a language form spoken by native speakers, such as British English, American English, or Australian English. What has to be considered, however, is the fact that the number of non-native English by far transcends the number of native speakers (e.g. Crystal, 1997). In fact, English as a Lingua Franca (ELF) is the "most extensive contemporary use of English worldwide" (Seidlhofer, 2001, p. 134). It is, thus, questionable why English as a native language (ENL) is still widely viewed as the only point of reference for "correct" English use—as noted by Widdowson (1994, p. 385) who questioned any "ownership" of the English language:

> How English develops in the world is no business whatever of native speakers in England, the United States, or anywhere else. They have no say in the matter, no right to intervene or pass judgment. They are irrelevant. The very fact that English is an international language means that no nation can have custody over it.

Seidlhofer (2001, p. 134) argues that it has to enter people's consciousness that ELF—with its specific characteristics—is a use of language in its own right and that ELF speakers have to be recognized as "language users in their own right." She further calls for the need to counteract the "reproduction of native English dominance."

One of the prerequisites to realize this certainly revolutionary view is the need for empirical work in this field.[4] Drawing on a small-scale study of ELF in professional consulting, this chapter attempts to make a small contribution in this direction. The analysis of sample extracts during an international intervision process illustrates that counseling processes—or more specifically supervision processes—in ELF can be carried out successfully. Despite linguistic deviations from native English norms, the participants' different cultural backgrounds and different levels of proficiency, communicative goals can be reached without obvious indications of communicative problems or misunderstandings.

Perceptions of ELF in Intercultural Consulting Contexts

Just like any other profession, the field of professional counseling has been strongly affected by the socio-political changes that globalization has brought about. In fact, intercultural or international work experience seems to have a fairly long-standing tradition in the field of professional consulting. Freitag-Becker (2003, p. 74), for example, argues that a view of the history of the profession of supervision reveals the fact that its 100 years of existence is infused by frontier crossings and intercultural exchanges:

> Die Profession Supervision hat sich ... 'grenzüberschreitend' entwickelt und man könnte annehmen, dass die Reflexion und Gestaltung der Interkulturalität seit Anbeginn sozusagen zum Fächerkanon der Ausbildung und zum Rollenbewusstein gehörten. [The profession of supervision has developed "transnationally" and one could assume that the reflection and creation of interculturality has always been among the core subjects of trainings and has constituted an essential part of a supervisor's role awareness.]

A glance at international journals, for example, *Supervision: Mensch Arbeit Organisation*, mirrors the fact that the chances and challenges involved in working across national borders have become a central issue in the work of supervisors: in such issues as "Globalisierung" [Globalization] (4/2002), "Über Grenzen hinweg" [Across borders] (1/2003) and "Kultur belebt!? [Culture revitalizes!] (3/2006) professionals reflect on the implications of globalization on consulting processes.

Clearly, there is strong awareness among consultants for the issue of multilingualism in intercultural working environments (e.g., Gotthardt-Lorenz & Sauer, 2003, p. 3). There is, however, at least to my knowledge, not a single published work that looks *exclusively* at the impact of a lingua franca on consulting processes. Rather, the attitudes of consultants towards a lingua franca (which is, in most cases, English) can only be inferred from papers dealing with international and intercultural work experience in general. In these papers the issue of language is only peripherally touched upon, but never the focus of investigation itself. What seems most striking for the purpose of this chapter is the fact that these publications hardly ever mirror the resource-oriented perception of ELF mentioned earlier. Quite the contrary, they strongly focus on problems and negative issues involved in the use of a second or a third language. Indeed, an analysis of papers written by consultants suggests the following categorization of attitudes towards ELF.

ELF is a Simplified and Reduced Form of Language

ELF is often described in a pejorative way, as, for example, in the following quotation (Krainz & Lackner, 2008, p. 6, italics my emphasis):

> Die berufliche Welt ist von einer eigenen Logik durchdrungen und gebiert als nahezu universelle Verkehrssprache dieses *eigentümliche* Organisations-Wirtschafts-Magnagement-*Pidgin*-Englisch, mit eigenen Codes und eigenen Begriffen... [The professional world is infused with a specific logic and allows this *weird* Organization-Economic-Management-*Pidgin*-English with its own codes and terms to act almost exclusively as a universal lingua franca.]

A more concrete example of non-native speakers' reduced linguistic repertoire is given by Müller and Zvacek (2008, p. 23, italics my emphasis) when they discuss possible ways for executive managers to "solve" communicative problems:

> Weiters ist es hilfreich, bei Konflikten einen Blick auf mögliche Kränkungen zu legen, die Nicht-Muttersprachler oft allein aus der *Reduktion der Sprache* produzieren 'Can you... 'statt,' 'Would you like... [Moreover, it is helpful to throw a glance on slights which non-native speakers often produce merely due to a *reduction of language*, such as 'Can you' instead of 'Would you like...']

If we follow this line of thought, we must assume that an "inappropriate" use of a particular grammatical form (as in this case, the lack of the conditional form in a polite request) can cause interpersonal conflicts. The authors certainly raise an interesting point here, which relates to the question of politeness in intercultural encounters and I certainly do not wish to entirely object this claim. Also, the assumption that non-native speakers do not have the same linguistic repertoire at their disposal as native speakers is widely unquestioned. What descriptive investigation into ELF—and also the analysis of the intervision group—shows, however, is that grammatical deviations from standard norms or lexical gaps are no threat for positive interpersonal relationships between the interlocutors (see Kordon, 2006).

ELF Does Not Allow for Linguistic "Nuances"

It is often claimed that ELF speakers, most likely due to their supposedly restricted linguistic repertoire, do not have the ability to express themselves appropriately in more complex, emotional or even problematic situations. Müller and Zvacek (2008, p. 23, italics mine) state that a lack of linguistic subtleties can increase the likelihood of interpersonal misunderstandings:

> In einer anderen als der Muttersprache zu sprechen, erhöht die Möglichkeit von Missverständnissen. *Sprachnuancen* verschwinden, ein und dasselbe Wort wird unter Umständen mit verschiedenen Bedeutungen belegt. Themen werden vermieden, da die Gesprächsteilnehmer nicht rechtzeitig verstehen, was eigentlich relevant wäre oder sich nicht so ausdrücken können, wie sie es gerne möchten. Nichtverstehen führt schließlich zum Gefühl, ausgeschlossen zu sein. [Communicating in a language other than one's mother tongue increases the likelihood of misunderstandings. Language nuances disappear, the one word might take on different meanings. Topics are avoided because

interlocutors do not understand the relevant issues or cannot express themselves as they wish. Non-understanding eventually leads to the feeling of being excluded.]

A very similar line of argument was suggested by Suter (1997, p. 83, italics mine) in his description of a project which was conducted after a merger of an American and a Swiss company:

> und gerade in *anspruchsvollen, möglicherweise konfliktbehafteten Sitzungen und Verhandlungen* ist es ein wesentlicher Vorteil, wenn man sich seiner Muttersprache bedienen kann. Unadäquate Wortwahl sowie das Problem, *sprachliche Nuancen* richtig anzuwenden und zu verstehen, können zu Missverständnissen und Konflikten führen, vor allem wenn sie *emotional wahrgenommen* werden. [and specifically in demanding, *conflict-prone meetings and negotiations* it is an essential advantage if one can use one's mother tongue. Inadequate word choice as well as the problem of applying and understanding *linguistic nuances* can lead to misunderstandings and conflicts, particularly if they are *perceived emotionally.*]

The observation that emotions and feelings are (more) difficult to be expressed in ELF is also mirrored in the following claim brought forward by a group of supervisors after having worked together cross-nationally: "Englisch ist der Schlüssel zu Europa, die Muttersprache ist der Schlüssel zur Seele" [English is the key to Europe, the mother tongue is the key to the soul] (Tatschl, 2003, p. 7).

Being a Native Speaker Means Power

Consultants often work in settings that involve both native and non-native speakers of English. In Suter's example above, for instance, English was appointed the corporate language after the two companies had been united, which certainly provokes a noticeable cleavage between non-native speakers and native speakers of English. Suter (1987, p. 83) himself follows from this situation that "...Muttersprache [bedeutet] Macht" [...mother tongue [means] power].

Along similar lines, Müller & Zvacek (2008, p. 23) draw a direct relation between the (non-) native speaker status and his or her professional career:

> So wird aus der Sprachwahl (Konzernsprache, Teamsprache) geschlossen, wer in einer Organisation dominiert. Dies hat auch Auswirkungen auf die Kompetenzausschreibungen, die muttersprachige und nicht-muttersprachige MitarbeiterInnen bekommen. Teammitglieder, die nicht die Landessprache sprechen und aufgrund derer das ganze Team in einer Fremdsprache kommunizieren muss, geraten wegen dieser „Bevorzugung" unter Druck. Oder jene Führungskraft, die sich beim Besuch des Tochterunternehmens bemüht, dessen Sprache zu sprechen kann mit stärkerer Folgebereitschaft rechnen. [The choice of language (corporate language, team language) determines

who dominates within an organization. This also has implications on the competence descriptions of native and non-native staff. Team members who do not speak the national language and, therefore, prompt the whole team to communicate in a foreign language, are pressurized due to this privilege. Or a manager who, in the course of a visit of the subsidiary company, makes an effort to communicate in the local language is likely to be more respected.]

Likewise, the authors spot negative consequences for the native speakers by stating that the communicative problems of the non-native speakers are often hard to grasp for native speakers. They claim that native speakers are also challenged as they often perceive particular conversational settings, such as meetings, as redundant, slow and stultifying (cf. Müller & Zvacek, 2008, 24).

In linguistic studies there is also considerable evidence for the communicative "dominance" of native speakers. Due to the limited scope of this paper, however, this issue can not be dealt with in detail. As the extracts analyzed in the empirical part of this paper does not involve any native speakers it is also not of direct relevance. What has to be pointed out at this stage, however, is the fact that the "gap" between native and non-native speakers certainly has implications on group dynamics and the creation of "informal" hierarchical structures within a team or an organization. This is, thus, an issue that consultants also have to be aware of. When working with a group of both native and non-native speakers it might be relevant to employ certain methods of intervention which enable clients to "bridge this gap."

ELF is Free of Culture

As mentioned earlier, the use of a lingua franca in consulting processes is often only peripherally touched upon in papers dealing with the issue of intercultural working environments. Linguistic competence and intercultural competence are often considered as separate entities that can be clearly distinguished. Often, the command of a language is viewed as the prerequisite for the development of intercultural competence, as, for instance Lackner (2008, p. 79) states: "Erst durch eine gemeinsame Sprache wird multikulturelle Kommunikation möglich" [A common language is the prerequisite for multicultural communication]. And she continues, "[e]ine Lingua franca ermöglicht einander zu verstehen, verdeckt jedoch kulturelle Unterschiede" [a lingua franca allows mutual understanding, conceals however cultural differences] (p. 79). It can be inferred that a lingua franca dos not allow the speaker to get across his or her cultural values, as he or she is viewed as being detached from any cultural identity. Due to the complexity of this matter, this crucial question cannot be further pursued at this point. However, I would merely like to underscore the understanding that cultural competence and linguistic competence are clearly separable.

Summary

Quite clearly, the categories discussed above are closely interrelated or sometimes even mutually dependent. The underlying common message, and therefore the core issue in this debate, is the assumption that non-native speakers lack linguistic proficiency. Different levels of language competence are also presented as severe impediments to successful communication (see Krusche & Zillner, 2008, p. 54). The only legitimate point of reference according to which language competence is measured is the native speaker. The observations and hypothesis put forward in the empirical part of this chapter attempt to refute some of these arguments.

Based on the negative perceptions presented above, it might come as a surprise that actual reports on supervisors' working experiences in an international context (such as international intervision groups, meetings and working groups of members of different national associations, intercultural supervision processes) suggest the communication conducted in ELF was more successful. Tatschl (2003, p. 6), for example, stresses the creative power that work in intercultural (and mulitilingual) contexts brings about. As he argues:

> Vieles von dem, was Supervisoren und Supervisorinnen tun, was sie erleben, wofür sie eingesetzt werden, tritt bei der grenzüberschreitenden Europaarbeit, bei grenzüberscheitenden Supervisionsprojekten einfach viel deutlicher zu Tage. [Much of what supervisors do becomes even more evident in intercultural working contexts.]

He also points to a few resources that these "global players" have access to, such as the:

1. use of metaphors, images and body language;
2. capability to address taboos;
3. capability to ask "naive" questions; and
4. reduction of pace.

Some of Tatschl's arguments will be revisited in the following empirical section of the paper.

AN ANALYSIS OF AN INTERNATIONAL INTERVISION GROUP

The data analyzed in this chapter are part of an audio-recorded and subsequently transcribed[5] intervision process of approximately 42 minutes of total length. The discussion is between a Dutch female, an Estonian female, and a German male during an international conference for supervisors in Tallinn in summer 2007.[6] English was not the mother tongue of any of these speakers. As they did not share any other language than English, they had to rely on ELF as the only possible common code of understanding.

As mentioned earlier, the chapter attempts to show that supervision processes can be carried out successfully in ELF. This claim certainly calls for the necessity to define the term "successful" in this context. Is it possible to argue that the intervision was successful purely by listening to the recorded audio-data and looking at the transcribed data? Is it possible to evaluate the "outcome" of supervision as either positive or negative without being able to look into the speakers' minds or ask them about their perceptions and attitudes (similar to the research method that Möller (2001) presents in her book, *Was ist gute Supervision?* [*What is good supervision?*])? This issue relates to the big and widely unanswered question of how "good" or "effective" supervision can be defined (see also Petzold, 2007, p. 10), which can unfortunately not be further pursued at this point as it would clearly transcend the scope of this paper.[7] Caution, however, was taken to avoid making hasty judgments concerning the effectiveness of supervision in this exchange (see, for example, Steinhardt, 2003).

In the case of the present data, the following approach was used to tackle the challenge of "measuring" the success of the intervision process, which was subdivided into five different phases, each one serving a particular purpose:

- **Phase 1:** (~ 3,2'): Purpose—distribution of roles and decision on formal criteria such as method and time management.
- **Phase 2:** (~ 2,1'): Purpose—presentation of the case/problem and definition of working task.
- **Phase 3:** (~ 9,5'): Purpose—identification of possible explanations or reasons for the presented problem (starting with the first intervening question by the supervisor).
- **Phase 4:** (~ 6'): Purpose—"transfer": recognition and assurance of the working results and reflection on transfer into professional life.
- **Phase 5:** (~ 20.8'): Purpose: process reflection and meta-communication.

By attributing a particular purpose to each phase, we can retrace if that purpose was fulfilled by a discourse analytical analysis of the data. As language serves as a tool to achieve these goals in the respective phases, the data will also provide sufficient evidence to show that the intervision was communicatively successful (i.e., that the participants were capable of carrying out the intervision session successfully in ELF).

What is evident from the outline of the phases noted above is that Phases 1 and 5 obtain a very distinct position in the analysis as they are not part of the actual supervision process. Their purposes are, however, highly relevant for the analysis of the entire process. Phase 5 is not only language-wise but also content-wise highly significant for this analysis, as the speakers also carry out what can be termed "meta-communication" or "metalanguage" (i.e., "words used for talking about or describing language," Summers, 1998, p. 854). From the speakers' exchanges in these meta-communicative passages we might, therefore, gain insight into their attitudes towards ELF. Moreover, Phase 5 also contains a hypothesis explicitly mentioned by the speakers concerning possible explanations for the success of the supervision process.

Due to the limited scope of this chapter, only two episodes of the intervision—Phase 2 and 3—will be analyzed in detail.

Phase 2: The Case and the Work Task

In this phase of the process, the participants successfully manage to set all the necessary conditions for the supervision. They commonly decide that each of them would take on a different role in the process. The Dutch speaker (DS1) was willing to present a case arsing from her work with a client, takings on the role of the supervisee. The two other participants distributed the role of the supervisor (German speaker, GS3) and the observer (Estonian speaker, ES2) among themselves.

A supervision session is normally opened with the presentation of a problem by the supervisee. Ideally, this helps the participants to subsequently extract the main underlying question(s) or problem(s) and, thus, formulate a working task for the session. If we look at the following extract, it becomes clear that these conditions were met in the second phase, in which the supervisee (DS1) elaborated on a problem she encountered in a supervision session with a client who was trained to become a youth psychiatrist:

Extract (1)[8]

DS1: I can start hh er (.) it was a few weeks ago (.) and i had a regular session with (.)
erm (1) psychiatrist and training? (1) sorry
GS3: in a training? (.) <6> context? </6>
ES2: <6> <un> xx </un> </6>
DS1: in a tr- er it's er it was <fast> supervision context </fast> (.) is psychiatrist who's
(.) learning to be (.) a youth (.) psychiatrist so that's er (.) educational=
GS3: =yes (.) there's <7> one? </7> person or
DS1: <7> background </7> one person.=
GS3: = one person
DS1: <1> one person. </1> so it was an individual (.)
GS3: <1> okay mhm </1>

DS1: session
GS3: mhm (1)
DS1: <smacks lips> and er: (.) she? (.) is a she (.) she was telling me? (.) about a situation (.) with a family? (.) she she was encountering a family and (.) she was talking about it (.) and while she was talking about it (1) er (.) I felt (1) a great (.) distance coming. (.) i wasn't (.) really involved anymore (.) and that's rather unfamiliar for me (.) during a session. (.) **I was getting (2) yeah distanced.** (.) i think that's the good word (2) **and during the session I (.) I felt it? (.) But I couldn't find words to it or (.) I, I couldn't reflect DURING the session** (.) what really happened. (.) I remembered asking the questions? I remember (1) <smacks lips> asking her (.) what she wanted to do? what she wanted to learn about it. (.) I did all that (.) but (.) within myself I felt (.) great distance (.) er (.) about the story and to (.) my <pvc>superv- </pvc> (.) <pvc> -I see </pvc> (3) she (1) I didn't ask her (.) if she er: (2) noticed any of that? (.) but I reflected on it later. (.) **and I think? (.) it had something to do with the (2) with the (.) the family she talked about.** (.) <soft> **that's what i think.** </soft> (.)

With regard to the purpose described above, the supervisee (DS1) makes four points (steps) during the exchange. She:

1. presents her case (lines 1–25);
2. verbalizes the problem, distancing herself from her client during the supervision session (line 18) and did not ask the client if she felt the distance herself (line 23);
3. indirectly states the question she wishes to analyze in the supervision with ES2, to find out why she distanced herself (lines 18–19); and presents a hypothetical reason for the problem—her feelings had something to do with the family her client talked about (lines 24–25).

Having said that language serves as a tool for the participants to carry out their work successfully, we can infer from the observation that the purpose of this phase was fulfilled in that this exchange was *communicatively* successful.

There are number of relevant linguistic aspects that this phase contains. Bearing in mind that both DS1 and GS3 are non-native speakers of English, most readers probably have noticed the high level of language proficiency of DS1. DS1 manages to make herself understood without major grammatical, syntactical, or lexical inconsistencies. When listening to the entire recording, the different levels of linguistic proficiency of the three participants become evident: the Dutch speaker is certainly the most proficient and the German speaker has a better command of the English language than the Estonian speaker. Yet, a close analysis shows that these diverse levels of linguistic competence do not seem to be an impediment for the success of the supervision. Recent research into lingua franca communication in English provides an answer to this phenomenon: just like any spoken discourse, ELF talk is characterized by self-regulation and reciprocal negotiation (e.g., Seidlhofer, 2002, p. 20), which means that interactants mutually accommodate to each other's speech styles. ELF speakers' capacity to modify their language in such a way that they feel understood by their interlocutors appears to be more important than accuracy:

> ... it may well be that mutual accommodation ... will be found to have greater importance for communicative effectiveness than "correctness" or idiomaticity in ENL [English as a native language] terms (Seidlhofer, 2002, p. 18).

Extract 1 provides us with another interesting phenomenon with regard to language proficiency. Interestingly DS1's monologue in which she presents her case is immediately interrupted after her first utterance by GS3's question "in a training context?" (line 3). It is likely that GS3 is irritated by DS1's use of the preposition "and" in line 2. GS3, therefore, asks for clarification by replacing "and" with the preposition "in" and the article "a" in line 3, which is subsequently repeated by DS1 in line 5 before she further defines the term in line 5 and 6. It gradually becomes clear that the supervision was carried out within the framework of DS1's client's training as a psychiatrist as a case supervision (similarly to the German term "Lehrsupervision"). Eventually, DS1 coins the term "educational background" (lines 6 and 9) to define this setting.

GS3's request for clarification might be an indication that he does not feel intimidated by DS1's higher level of language proficiency. In his role as the supervisor, he obviously seems to consider it crucial to perfectly understand what his supervisee says. Uncertainty seems to be avoided by immediate interruptions or invitations to rephrase what was being said. Although this is one of the most relevant prerequisites in any consulting process (also among speakers of the same mother tongue), clarification processes of this kind are likely to occur more often in ELF contexts. This observation can be related to Tatschl's (2003, p. 6) hypothesis that it is easier to ask naïve questions in intercultural contexts: "Häufig wird argumentiert, dass man gerade wegen des Fremdseins auch die naivsten Fragen formulieren draf und dass dies für die jweiligen Supervisionssysteme hilfreich sei" [It is often argued that precisely being a stranger offers the opportunity to ask the most naïve questions, which often turns out to be helpful for the respective systems of supervision].

The observation that a lack of understanding in supervision sessions in ELF seem to be immediately bridged raises another hypothesis linked to one of Tatschl's (2003) arguments: interruptions and subsequent clarification processes or repetitions as in the first couple of lines of Extract 1 certainly slow down the process. Apart from the clarification process illustrated above, Extract 1 contains additional features that are also likely to contribute to the reduction of pace. Readers might have noticed that DS1's elaboration of her case is peppered with an amazingly high numbers of breaks. Although I cannot entirely refute the possibility that this is a specific characteristic of DS1's speech style, the high amount of communicative breaks in her monologue are likely to be caused by her efforts to express herself clearly in a second language.

The analysis also brings to light that ELF speakers sometimes struggle to find the right word(s), as, for example, explicitly stated by DS1 in line 18 with the utterance, "I think that's the good word." In fact, this phenomenon appears very frequently in the entire recording. It goes without saying that the speed of a process is reduced by this tendency.

Another contribution to the reduction of pace is the speakers' self-interruptions and self-repetitions, which appear numerously in the recording. Apart from a few minor interruptions and repetitions in DS1's monologue, this is more difficult to illustrate with Extract 1 (most likely due to DS1's high level of language proficiency). They are, however, omnipresent in the rest of the recordings.

In line with Taschl's (2003, p. 6) argument, I consider all factors which provoke a certain reduction of pace as a chance rather than a threat to supervision processes: "...Verlangsamung ist eine Chance gerade für Supervision" [...reduction of pace constitutes a chance, particularly for supervision"]. Reducing the speed of speech (or a more cautious handling of language) also implies a reduction of the speakers' sequence of thoughts. It, therefore, gives more room for the subtleties of the participants' observations. In fact, reducing speed is often the only way to achieve a satisfying working outcome in supervision.

Apart from the first couple of lines, this phase is rather monological. The analysis of phase 3, however, will show that ELF speakers are also capable of handling more interactive passages successfully.

Phase 3: "Peeling the Onion"

Given the above-mentioned complexity of supervision, it certainly cannot be assumed that there is always a "solution" to the problem(s) presented by a client. However, an analysis of phase 3 of the intervision process shows sufficient evidence that the supervisee (DS1) has (at least) gained a broader awareness for possible phenomena underlying her trouble. In the following extract, the supervisee makes explicit that the first intervening questions asked by the supervisor (GS3) prompted her to redefine the problem she presented and, subsequently, helps her to gain an understanding for the core problem herself:

Extract (2)

1 DS1: and MAYbe? (.) **now you are asking me?** (.) it had something to do (2) **no—now I'm talking**

2 **about it's coming?** (.) er maybe it had something to do (.) with the (.) unaffected way she talked

3 about it (2) she **was very distanced (.) too.** (.)

4 S3: mhm? (.)

5 S1: er (.) **as we speak? (.) I remember** <5> the feeling </5> and (.)

6 S3: <5> <clears throat> </5>

7 S1: **I remember how I (.) observed her?** (.)

This exchange is part of the phase in which the supervisee is still in the process of making the problem with her client explicit and, thus, is trying to grasp the problem herself. She argues that it is both the supervisor's questions (line 1) and the process of putting her feelings into words (lines 1 and 5) that enable her to identify the difficulties in the work with her client. This process constitutes, at least to my mind, one of the main purposes of a supervision process. The client enters into a state of self-reflection and is, thereby, able to identify the core issue of his or her problem, which, in the long run, is also one of the prerequisites to formulate a working goal and, eventually, to close a "formal" contract with the supervisee. The process can be compared with the peeling of an onion: one layer after the other is removed until finally the "real" problem is uncovered.

With the utterance "she was very distanced too" in line 3, it is likely that DS1 begins to gain awareness that her feeling of distance towards her client might have to do with *countertransference*, a phenomenon rooted in psychoanalysis (e.g., König & Staats, 1996; Münch, 1990; Oberhoff, 2005; Steinhardt, 2005). This hypothesis is further supported by the following extract in which she gradually realizes that it is the client's distanced attitude towards violence that eventually caused her to distance herself from the client:

Extract (3)

1 DS1: I observed her (2) maybe it was a *par- parallel (.) para- parallel (.) process* i don't know?
2 but (.) erm (1) I, I felt (1) **my distance?**

3 GS3: mhm

4 DS1: and I saw **HER distance.**

5 GS3: mhm=

6 DS1: =so maybe **I took that** (.)

Extract 4 below illustrates that the supervisor brings in an additional hypothesis, namely that her problem might be linked to a violation of her personal set of values and beliefs:

Extract (4)

1 S3: and wha- what what was it? was it more an irritation for you? or wa:- was it like that that
2 **you expected** (.) if somebody (1) er (.) presents er (.) something doing this (.) violence?
3 then it must er (.) be accompanied by (.) deep feelings. (2)

ES2's hypothesis is subsequently strongly approved by DS1:

Extract (5)

1 DS1: i think you are right. I think <6> that **I ex-** </6> (.)

2 GS3: <6> and (.) yes </6>

3 DS1: <7> that **in** </7> **my expectations.**=

In the course of the subsequent independent exchanges, which chronologically follow each other, it becomes evident that the supervisee begins to realize that there are two phenomena underlying her problem—countertransference (extract 6: line 7; extract 8: line 3) and the involvement of her own personal beliefs, values and experiences (e.g., extract 6: line 1; extract 7; extract 8: lines 1 and 2; extract 9: line 8; extract 10: lines 1,2 and 4).

Extract (6)

1 DS1: <5> I </5> **expected her** (1)

2 GS3: <5> mhm </5>

3 DS1: to: (.) to (.) give more insight (2) not just <6> facts </6>

4 GS3: <6> insight </6> to? (.)

5 DS1: to (.) to what it (.) <7> did with her? </7> (.)

6 GS3: <7> to give them words </7>

7 DS1: to gi- to put it in words. (.) but i did the same? (3)

Extract (7)

DS1: but maybe it is that even more? because (.) that has to do with **my own expectations**

Extract (8)

GS3: what the <un> xxx </un> (.) er (.) you are not a neutral in in this (.) way? **what do you expect you from yourself?** (.)

DS1: yes (.) yes an- an- an- <5> that's </5> double (.)

Extract (9)

DS1: and I **wasn't neutral to myself** (2) <6> <whispering> yes </whispering> </6>

GS3: <6> n- </6> **not neutral to her?** (.) is it exact or was that more? (.) because you expected that somebody (.) <7> is is </7> is able to: er: (.)

DS1: <7> no i </7>

GS3: to er (.) accompany: er: (4) an event no <Lnde> ein ein erlebnis? {an experience} </Lnde> (.) what that in english er this er this (.) to to to er (1) to give them a context of er (1) **feelings of er (1) values** of er (1)

DS1: mhm (2) yes. (.) it it has to do with er (3) the **values I set** (.) maybe. (2) know what I mean?

Extract (10)

GS3: er (.) your (.) that in this setting your belongs you believes there or er er (.)

DS1: that **my own beliefs** (.) are

GS3: mhm

DS1: **were were there.**

Given the complexity of this case, it is rather impressive that the participants manage to discover the underlying phenomena in an ELF. The analyzed extracts contain a number of linguistic inconsistencies and deviations from Standard English forms on various different levels of language (mainly uttered by GS3), for example:

- Grammar: Extract 4/line 2: 'something doing this (.) violence?' (use of gerund instead of infinitive); Extract 10/line 1: 'you believes' (3rd person 's' with 2nd person singular)
- Syntax: Extract 10/line 1: 'er (.) your (.) that in this setting your belongs you believes there or er er (.)' (incomplete sentences, self-interruptions, etc.)
- Lexis: Extract 10/line 1: 'your belongs' (coinages of new words); Extract 9/lines 5 and 6: 'to er (.) accompany: er: (4) an event no

<Lnde> ein ein erlebnis? {an experience} </Lnde> (.) what that in english' (lexical gaps)

None of these deviations, however, seem to be an impediment for the speakers to achieve their communicative goals. Rather, the interactants seem to be very creative and inventive to overcome potential trouble sources in their communication. One thing that has to be particularly highlighted with regard to their interaction in phase 3 is the speakers' ability to bridge lexical gaps. It is striking that they manage to discover and work constructively with such complex phenomena as countertransference without ever using specific terminology. Rather, they paraphrase what can be expressed by one single term with utterances such as "parallel process" (Extract 3), "I did the same"(Extract 6), or "that's double" (Extract 8). It can be concluded, then, that the interactants managed to work on a highly professional level without having a wide range of specific vocabulary at their disposal.

Often, the interactants did not pay much attention to lexical gaps as the example in Extract 9 (lines 5 to 6) exemplifies: GS3 does not find the right word for the German word "erlebnis" (experience). This, however, seems to be fairly unnoticed by his interlocutor. It seems as if DS1 is well aware of the fact that the term "experience" is not vitally important to grasp GS3's main message, namely his hypothesis concerning DS1's involvement of personal values.

This phenomenon might be explained by the widely acknowledged "let-it-pass principle" in ELF (Firth, 1996). House (1999, p. 75) describes this principle in the following way:

> .... ELF interactants ... "normalize" potential trouble sources, rather than attending to them explicitly, via for example, repair, reformulation, or other negotiating behaviors. As long as participants-to-the-talk achieve a certain threshold of understanding sufficient for their current conversational purpose, they seem to adopt a "Let-it-Pass" principle governing the way they handle ambiguously or overtly deficient utterances.

It may well be that this principle is linked to the observation that ELF is "overtly consensus-oriented, cooperative and mutually supportive" (Seidlhofer, 2002, p. 15).

Another outstanding linguistic features in this phase is the high amount of minimal responses (or feedback tokens) such as "mhm," "yeah," "yes," and so forth. In fact, all five phases of the intervision are infused with minimal responses of these kinds. These tokens do not only serve to signal agreement with what is said, but they are also used as "tools" to signal attention and listenership. They are, thus, an important feature for interlocutors to both establish and maintain interpersonal contact and to keep up the flow of the conversation (see also Kordon, 2003, 2006). As silence or longer pauses seem to be an intrinsic element in supervision, the latter function as feedback tokens does not seem to be so relevant. When looking at the extracts above, the minimal responses seem to primarily serve the former function (i.e., the establishment and maintenance of rapport). With the intensive use of these tokens, the supervisor seems to signal his active involvement and, likewise, strongly agrees to his supervisee's observation and ideas.

The establishment and maintenance of positive interpersonal contact is the prerequisite for any functioning supervision process, or as DS1 expresses it in the following extract (phase 5).

Extract (11)

1 DS1: and what you said earlier about our profession (3) i think is very true. **our**
2 **profession is about making connection.** (3)

In fact, in ELF-settings it often seems much more relevant than the correctness of the particiapants' language.

CONCLUSION AND OUTLOOK

Before attempting to formulate any concluding remarks or suggesting the practical consequences of this research, it is important to stress that the observations in this chapter are based on a small-scale empirical study. Therefore, the findings reflect this particular sample and should only be considered as a point of departure for further investigation on a broader empirical scale. With regard to the methodology employed in this research project, the discourse analytic examination of counseling processes are of great relevance as a way of assuring successful communicative processes in international or intercultural consulting. The central aim of this chapter was to show that supervisions in English as a lingua franca can be carried out successfully despite linguistic devations (on all levels of language) from standard native speakers' norms. The speakers in this exchange managed to reveal complex cognitive and emotional patterns within a very short period.

Reflecting on this analysis, a number of characteristics of a consulting process in ELF can be elaborated:

- Different levels of language proficiency are balanced by mutual accommodation of the speakers' speech styles.

- Problems of understanding are immediately repaired by requests for clarification.
- The pace of the process is reduced by the use of a lingua franca, which can have positive implications on the quality of the consulting process.
- The use of specialized terminology (such as the term countertransference) does not have crucial relevance for the achievement of the communicative goals. Speakers skillfully paraphrase what can be expressed with one single specific term.
- Lexical gaps are bridged by the highly cooperative and supportive speech style of the speakers.
- Speakers employ a wide range of different strategies to establish and maintain rapport (i.e., positive interpersonal contact) during the session. Positive interpersonal relationships seem to be of greater relevance for a successful working result than linguistic accuracy.

By juxtaposing these findings with popular beliefs of consultants about ELF (or the use of a lingua franca in general), the chapter has shown that many negative perceptions of ELF appear misguided, without sufficient scientific grounding. Although I certainly do not wish to entirely refute such observations as the reduced or simplified linguistic repertoire of non-native speakers of English or the power of native speakers, I do think that the implications of these phenomena for the cross-cultural consulting profession is overestimated or, at least, misleading. The belief that linguistic accuracy and a strong adherence to native speakers' norms are the most important prerequisites for successful international or intercultural work undoubtedly stokes fears among consultants and sometimes even prevents them from "climbing the global stage." Hopefully the empirical investigation of supervision processes in ELF will serve to motivate professionals to have courage to start working in ELF—even if they consider their English language competence as being far from being "perfect." As GS3 put it in phase 5: "**yes (.) it (.) it was not that not necessary to present me: as somebody who was perfect (.).**"

Hopefully the chapter will also raise the reader's awareness of the creative and innovative communicative strategies that ELF speakers employ in order to compensate for their linguistic deficiencies, to avoid misunderstandings and to bridge communicative problems. In fact, supervisions in ELF bring about certain insights into characteristics that even can enrich consulting processes, such as the reduction of pace (caused by breaks, self-interruptions, repetitions, clarification processes or the struggle to find the right words). This insight reflects Tastchl's (2003, p. 6) argument that we can learn a lot about supervision in general by carrying out intercultural supervisions in a lingua franca.

What seems most important for the consulting profession is the need to move away from deficit-oriented and fearful thinking to a more resource-oriented attitude. This can certainly not be reached by undergoing strict language training or by acquiring as much specific vocabulary or closed sets of grammatical rules as possible. Rather, it is important to develop sufficient communicative capacity that can enable consultants to converse in English with speakers of different cultural and first language backgrounds. One of the most efficient ways to reach this capacity is certainly "practical" training. As such, consultants are encouraged to expand their work to intercultural and multilingual settings, actively using their supposed "deficits" in ELF as tools rather than obstacles to their processes.

NOTES

1. As this chapter is meant to be descriptive rather than ideological, issues concerning language policy remain widely untouched. What should be stressed at this point, however, is the fact that I do not support the idea of monolingualism in science or any other professional discipline. Rather, I believe that linguistic diversity has to be maintained and strongly protected.
2. This chapter is a shorter version of the final paper of my academic training as a supervisor and coach at the University of Vienna (Universitätslehrgang für Supervision und Coaching der Universität Wien): http://www.univie.ac.at/lammgasse/ (Kordon, 2008).
3. The term "supervision" (and its derivatives) are used with the meaning and connotation attributed to it internationally among consultants and not in its Anglo-American meaning: "if you supervise an activity or a person, you make sure that the activity is done correctly or that the person doing a task is behaving correctly" (Collins Cobild English Dictionary, 1995, p. 1677).
4. A comprehensive overview of descriptive work undertaken in this field can, for example, be found in Seidlhofer (2004, 2005) and Seidlhofer, Breiteneder, and Pitzl (2006).
5. The audio recordings were transcribed according to transcription and spelling conventions that were developed for the compilation of a sizeable, computer-readable corpus of ELF at the English Department of Vienna University (Vienna-Oxford International Corpus of English (http://www.univie.ac.at/voice). The most important features of the conventions are given in the Appendix. 9-A.

Some changes to the computer-readable transcription key were made in order to make the analysis easily comprehensible. A transcription of the entire intervision is provided in Kordon (2008).

6. The intervision group analyzed in the chapter is only a small segment of a sizeable database collected for the author's PhD thesis.
7. Readers interested in this issue may wish to consult Möller (2002) or Petzold (2003).
8. The data extracts are chronologically numbered throughout this chapter. Please note that underlined exchanges refer to language-related issues while those in bold face point out issues related to the purpose of the respective phase and to content-related issues discussed in the analysis. When these two foci overlap (i.e., when an exchange is both linguistically and content-wise relevant), the comment is placed in italics.

APPENDIX: VOICE TRANSCRIPTION AND SPELLING CONVENTIONS

For the sake of readability of the transcripts analyzed in the chapter, the most important features of the transcription and spelling conventions are provided. Please consult http://www.univie.ac.at/voice for more detail:

1. DECAPITALIZATION

No capital letters are used except for marking emphasis (cf. mark-up conventions).	Example: S8: so you really can <@> control my **e**nglish

2. INTONATION

Words spoken with falling intonation are followed by a full stop "."	Example: S7: that's point two**.** absolutely yes**.**
Words spoken with rising intonation are followed by a question mark "?" .	Example: S1: that's what my next er slide**?** does

3. EMPHASIS

If a speaker gives a syllable, word or phrase particular prominence, this is written in capital letters	Example: S7: er internationalization is a very IMPORTANT issue

4. PAUSES

Every brief pause in speech (up to a good half second) is marked with a full stop in parentheses.	Example: SX-f: because they all give me different **(.)** different **(.)** points of view

Longer pauses are timed to the nearest second and marked with the number of seconds in parentheses, e.g. (1) = 1 second, (3) = 3 seconds.

Example:
S1: aha **(2)** so finally arrival on monday evening is still valid

Whenever two or more utterances happen at the same time, the overlaps are marked with numbered tags: **<1> </1>**, **<2> </2>**,... Everything that is simultaneous gets the same number.

Example:
S1: it is your best **<1> case </1>** scenario (.)
S2: **<1> yeah </1>**
S1: okay

5. LAUGHTER

All laughter and laughter-like sounds are transcribed with the @ symbol, approximating syllable number (e.g. ha ha ha = @@@). Utterances spoken laughingly are put between **<@> </@>** tags.

Example:
S1: in denmark well who knows. **@@**
S2: **<@>** yeah **</@>** **@@** that's right

6. NON-ENGLISH SPEECH

Utterances in a participant's first language (L1) are put between tags indicating the speaker's **L1**.

Example:
S5: **<L1de> bei firmen </L1de>** or wherever

7. SPEAKING MODES

Utterances which are spoken in a particular mode (fast, soft, whispered, read, etc.) and are notably different from the speaker's normal speaking style are marked accordingly.

Example:
S2: because as i explained before is that we have in the **<fast>** universities of cyprus we have **</fast>** a specific e:rm procedure

8. ANONYMIZATION

A guiding principle of VOICE is sensitivity to the appropriate extent of anonymization. As a general rule, names of people, companies, organizations, institutions, locations, etc. are replaced by aliases and these aliases are put into square brackets **[ ]**. The aliases are numbered consecutively, starting with 1.

Example:
S9: that's one of the things (.) that i (1) just wanted to clear out. (2) **[S13]**?

9. UNINTELLIGIBLE SPEECH

Unintelligible speech is represented by **x's** approximating syllable number and placed between **<un> </un>** tags.

Example:
S4: we **<un> xxx </un>** for the <7> supreme (.) three </7> possibilities
S1: <7> next yeah </7>

REFERENCES

Baker, S., Resch, I., Carlisle, K., & Schmidt, K. A. (2001). The great English divide. *BusinessWeek* <www.businessweek.com/magazine/content/01_33/b3745009.htm>. Accessed August 13, 2001.

Collins Cobuild English Dictionary. (1995). *Collins Cobuild English dictionary*. London: HarperCollins Publishers.

Crystal, D. (1997). *English as a global language*. Cambridge: Cambridge University Press.

Firth, A. (1996). The discursive accomplishment of normality: On 'lingua franca' English and conversation analysis. *Journal of Pragmatics, 26*(3), 237–259.

Freitag-Becker, E. (2003). Im Dialog mit der Andersartigkeit [In Dialog with the Otherness]. *Forum Supervision, 22*, 70–89.

Gotthardt-Lorenz, A., & Sauer, J. (2003). Supervision überschreitet nationale, sprachliche und kulturelle Grenzen [Supervision Crosses National, Linguistic and Cultural Borders]. *Supervision, 1*, 3–4.

Graddol, D. (1997). *The future of English?* London: British Council.

House, J. (1999). Misunderstanding in intercultural communication: Interactions in English as a *lingua franca* and the myth of mutual intelligibility. In C. Gnutzmann (Ed.), *Teaching and learning English as a global language* (pp. 73–89). Tübingen: Stauffenberg.

König, K. & Staats, H. (1996). Übertragung und Gegenübertragung in Institutionen [Transference and Countertransference in Instituations]. In H. Pühl (Ed.), *Supervision in institutionen. Eine Bestandsaufnahme* [*Supervisions in Instituations. A Stocktaking*] (pp. 60–76). Frankfurt: Fischer Taschenbuch Verlag.

Kordon, K. (2003). *Phatic communion in English as a lingua franca*. Unpublished Master's Thesis, University of Vienna.

Kordon, K. (2006). "You are very good"—Establishing rapport in English as a lingua franca: The case of agreement tokens. *Vienna English Working Papers, 15*(2), 58–82.

Kordon, K. (2008): *"...the strangeness is there in the language'" A discourse analytical view on supervisions in English as a lingua franca*. Unpublished Master's Thesis, University of Vienna/Universitätslehrgang für Supervision und Coaching.

Krainz, E. E., & Lackner, K. (2008). Editorial introduction. *Gruppendynamik und Organisationsberatung* [*Group Dynamics and Organisational Consulting*], *1*, 5–7.

Krusche, B., & Zillner, S. (2008). Stop making sense! Erfolgreiche Teamkooperation in globalen Kontexten [Stop making sense! Successful Team Cooperation in Global Contexts]. *Gruppendynamik und Organisationsberatung* [*Group Dynamics and Organisational Consulting*], *1*, 50–63.

Lackner, K. (2008). Expatriation: Entsendung ohne Wiederkehr? [Expatriation: Dispatching without Return]. *Gruppendynamik und Organisationsberatung* [*Group Dynamics and Organisational Consulting*], *1*, 64–87.

Meinhart, E. (2001). Can you English? *Profil, 31*, 101–106.

Möller, H. (2001). *Was ist gute Supervision? Grundlagen—Merkmale—Methoden [What is Good Supervision? Basics—Characteristics—Methods]*. Stuttggart: Klett-Cotta.

Müller, C., & Zvacek, L. (2008). Das internationale Führungsparkett—Herausforderungen, Haltegriffe und hilfreiche Schrittfolgen [Managing Internationally—Challenges, Grips and Helpful Step Rates]. *Gruppendynamik und Organisationsberatung* [*Group Dynamics and Organisational Consulting*], *1*, 17–35.

Münch, W. (1990). Zur Arbeit mit Übertragung und Gegenübertragung in Supervisionsgruppen für Lehrer: Die Abwehr ödipaler Verantwortung [About Transference and Countertransference in Supervision Groups for Teachers: the Defense of Oedipal Responsabilty]. In H. Pühl (Ed.), *Handbuch der Supervision 1 [Handbook of Supervsion]* (pp. 452–463). Berlin: Marhold.

Oberhoff, B. (2005). *Übertragung und Gegenübertragung in Supervision [Transference and Countertransference in Supervision].* Münster: Daedalus-verlag.

Petzold, H. G. (2007). Integrative Supervision, Meta-Consulting, Organisationsentwicklung: Ein Handbuch für Modelle und Methoden reflexiver Praxis [Integrative Supervision, Meta-Consulting, Organisational Development: a Handbook for Models and Methods of Reflexive Prxis]. 2nd edition. Wiesbanden: VS Verlag für Sozialwissenschaften.

Petzold, H. G., Schigl, B., Fischer, M. (2003). *Supervsion auf dem Prüfstand. Wirksamkeit, Forschung, Anwendungsfelder, Innovation* [*Supervision on Trial. Effectiveness, Research, Applications, Innovation].* Opladen: Leske + Budrich.

Phillipson, R. (1992). *Linguistic imperialism.* Oxford: Oxford University Press.

Seidlhofer, B. (2001). Closing a conceptual gap: The case of English as a lingua franca. *International Journal of Applied Linguistics, 11,* 133–158.

Seidlhofer, B. (2002). *A Concept of international English and related issues: From "real English'"to "realistic English'"* Strasbourg: Council of Europe.

Seidlhofer, B. (2004). Research perspectives on teaching English as a lingua franca. *Annual Review of Applied Linguistics, 24,* 209–239.

Seidlhofer, B. (2005). Englisch als Lingua Franca und seine Rolle in der internationalen Wissensvermittlung: Ein Aufruf zur Selbstbehauptung[English as Lingua Franca and its Roles in International Knowledge Transfer: a Call for Self-Asseration]. In S. Braun, & K. Kurt (Eds.), *Sprache(n) in der Wissensgesellschaft: Proceedings der 34. Jahrestagung der Gesellschaft Angewandte Linguistik [Language(s) in the Community of Knowledge: Proceedings of the Annual Conference of the Association of Applied Linguistics]* (pp. 27–45). Frankfurt/Main: Lang.

Seidlhofer, B., Breiteneder, A., & Pitzl, M.-L. (2006). English as a lingua franca in Europe. *Annual Review of Applied Linguistics, 26,* 3–34.

Steinhardt, K. (2003). Rezension von Möller: Was ist gute Supervision? Grundlagen—Merkmale—Methoden [Recension of Möller: What ist good Supervision? Basics—Characteristics . Methods]. *Supervision, 1,* 48–50.

Steinhardt, K. (2005). *Psychoanalytisch orientierte Supervision: Auf dem Weg zu einer Profession? [Psychoanalytical supervision: Towards a profession?].* Gießen: Psychosozial-Verlag.

Summers, D. (1998): *Longman dictionary of English language and culture* (2nd ed.). Harlow: Longman.

Suter, M. (1997). Kulturelle Aspekte bei der Übernahme einer Schweizer Firma durch einen amerikanischen Konzern: Ein Erfahrungsbericht[Cultural Aspects involved in a Merger of a Swiss and an American Company: A Field Report]. In Kopper, L. (Ed.), *Globalisierung: von der Vision zur Praxis* [Globalisation: from Vision to Praxis] (pp. 78–84). Zürich: Versus Verlag.

Tatschl, S. (2003). Wenn Supervisoren reisen: Was bei europäischer Arbeit von Supervisoren und Supervisorinnen entsteht. Erfahrungen und Reflexionen anhand des Projekts HASI [When supervisors travel: experience of European work of supervisors. Experience and Reflections based on the HASI project]. *Supervision, 1*, 5–12.

Vitug, M. (2006): Lost in Translation. *Newsweek*, May 29, 44.

Widdowson, H. G. (1994). The ownership of English. *TESOL Quarterly, 28*(2), 377–389.

PART III

REFLECTIONS ON CONSULTING FOR CHANGE

CHAPTER 10

CONSULTING PROCESSES FOR ORGANIZATION CHANGE

A Belief System, Situation Centered, Sensemaking Perspective[1]

Craig C. Lundberg

Anyone who closely observes the real world of organizations recognizes that it is loaded with confusion, stress, uncertainty, politics, trial and error, frustration, disappointment, and emotional disturbances (Mali, 1981). Interestingly, however, the literature on organizations implies a lot more stability, orderliness, systematization, and clarity than is commonly discovered when studied closely (Weick, 1982). Similarly the prevailing rhetoric about management and change is one in which rationality, logic and analysis dominate problem identification and solving, diagnosis, planning and design, and action intervening. Thus the rhetoric of rational goal achievement is often mocked by actual practice. If organizations are more ambiguous, only locally and intermittently cohere, and are less well understood than is usually assumed, management is really just a jun-

Consultation for Organizational Change. pages 209–232
Copyright © 2010 by Information Age Publishing
All rights of reproduction in any form reserved.

gle of ideas, techniques, practices and divergent justifications, and organizational members possess multiple allegiances, multiple identities as well as somewhat unique histories, competencies, needs and wants, how does anyone—especially organizational leaders and their consultants—make sense of joint action? This situation is especially the case if everything in and about organizations is always somewhat political, always somewhat emotional and symbolically laden, and constantly changing.

The answer to this question, of course, resides initially in the conceptual frameworks employed—in essence, how we make sense out of how managers and consultants make sense of organizational change. At the present time the hypocrisy of our conceptualizations about organizations, management and consultancy can in part be explained by three conceptual errors. One is that the constructs in common use are rather loosely defined and not very well linked to the discontinuities and nuances of behavior (Weick, 1987). Second is the unthinking adherence by managers and consultants to the ideology that promotes the survival and power of entrenched managerial elites (Stablein, 1988). Third is the reliance by managers and consultants on relatively simple, teleological, prescriptive models that extol the logic of consequence (March, 1994). What these three errors have in common is that they gloss over the phenomenon of interest.

Our arguments for reconceptualizing change consultancy in terms of beliefs and sensemaking will proceed in four sections. First, the chapter briefly characterizes organizational change consultancy and highlights the underlying conceptual strategy, theoretic criteria for reconceptualization, and the premises behind this work. Second, we will introduce and argue for the core ideas of our perspective. Third, we will outline intentional, generic organizational change as a sequence of sensemaking projects. The chapter concludes with a discussion of the opportunities for and functions of consultancy in these projects.

CONCEPTUAL STRATEGY, ASPIRATIONS, AND ASSUMPTIONS

In general, contemporary conceptualization about consultancy can be characterized as a set of relatively simple, linear, cognitively rational, and mostly normative models outlining a sequence of steps or stages which, if followed, will ameliorate any problem. These models aspire to be generally applicable across a wide variety of organized settings (i.e., they are nomothetic), and they tend to be primarily at one level of analysis (i.e., micro). In their efforts to be general, consulting models are relatively context and history indifferent. Most are etic (i.e., adopt an outsider's perspective). Also, as noted above, most consultancy conceptualization implicitly serves a managerial ideology while suggesting they are value free. Consultancy conceptualization thus appears to be captive of a mindset that unquestionably assumes the value of rational, analytic, calculative, consequence-oriented thinking to achieve organizational objectives under implicit preferences for stability and typicality.

If the above characterization of consultancy conceptualization, and its enfolding "pragmatic-normative" perspective seems to describe conventional thinking, it is instructive to inquire what it is not. While no doubt appearing overdrawn, we can also characterize consultancy conceptualizations as:

1. not ideologically free;
2. not sensitive to contexts or emotions;
3. not really concerned with time;
4. not very refined process-wise;
5. not portraying action from the point of view of organization agents; and
6. not acknowledging either client systems or consultants as continuously involved in sensemaking.

If so, these under-appreciated, under-conceptualized features of consultancy beg development. It may be instructive to attempt to construct a perspective that explicitly counteracts the prevailing conceptualization of consultancy.

Our reconceptualization effort is both general and focused. It is general in that it purports to encompass the behaviors of all persons who are engaged in all types of consultancy in all types of organizational change endeavors. It is focused in that the perspective eschews both overly essentialist, micro causes of behavior (e.g., individual needs and other personal attributes) and overly macro causes (e.g., socio-technical/political contexts or institutional and societal forces). Rather we have elected a more modest, "proximate" understanding that links change agents' perceptions of self and situation into an evolving sequence of personally meaningful realities that guide behavior.

As much as possible a reconceptualization of consultancy (and, eventually, the theory which could follow) should consciously reflect several theoretic criteria. Consultancy conceptualization, ideally, should be:

1. ideologically neutral, i.e., not be captive of any particular interest groups—neither economic elites, humanists, conflictualists, nor scientists (Stablein, 1988);

2. ontologically centrist, i.e., be consciously social constructionist—avoiding either extreme positivism or subjectivism (Morgan & Smircich, 1980);
3. contextually sensitive;
4. potentially applicable to several levels of analysis while initially avoiding excessive reifications (Rousseau, 1985);
5. applicable to both modal and extreme cases of consultancy (Pondy & Olson, 1977);
6. explicit about its tradeoffs among theoretic virtues, preferring face validity (plausibility) over accuracy, situational meaningfulness over generality, and phenomena warranted complexity over simplicity (Lundberg, 2001; Weick, 1979); and
7. able to be linked to the conceptualizations of most other forms of theory and schools of thought (Lundberg & Young, 2005).

These conceptual strategy and theoretic criteria aspirations constitute a daunting charge for the conceptualization of consultancy. While the degree to which the perspective explicated below meets these ideals remains to be seen, such ideals should probably guide any critique that aspires to reconceptualize any facet of organization studies as well as consultancy at the present time.

All conceptual efforts rest upon one or more assumptions (primitive statements) about the essence of the phenomena under scrutiny although they are rarely made explicit. Conceptual work intentionally either refines or extends or replaces extant theorizing. All new conceptual efforts therefore ultimately reflect foundational premises, some familiar, some new or different. The present work is no exception. The five premises listed below underlie our change and consultancy conceptualization.

Premise 1: Organizations, that is, purposive human systems that require coordinated, conjoint action by their members and agents, are constantly changing (albeit different components at different rates at different times).

Premise 2: Almost all external and internal circumstances that organizational members and their agents experience are more ambiguous, discontinuous, complex and less orderly than usually believed. Thus they are always emotionally charged and experienced as more or less distressful.

Premise 3: Ambiguity and uncertainty often lead to some degree of distress in persons and are universally avoided if at all possible. Organizational members and their agents prefer less to more distress.

Premise 4: Organization members and their agents naturally create, learn and share meanings about their circumstances (internal and external), and these meanings govern organizational behavior (within physical, biological, and language constraints).

Premise 5: Multiple meanings can be imposed by organization members and agents on all perceived circumstances, events, activities, things, and persons. Organizationally salient meanings will usually reflect the more or less shared values, beliefs and emotions, perceived situational features, and the relevant remembered history of any focused upon situation.

These premises are believed to be consistent with what is known about all complex, open, human systems and their participants (e.g., Bak, 1996; Cowan, Pines, & Meltzer, 1994; Miller, 1978; Thoits, 1989; Weick, 1987, 1995). Their generality is intended to be applicable to the domain of organizational behavior, and thus presumed to encompass those situations where two or more persons interact in joint action in an organization over time, as well as in client-consultant engagements.

Recapitulation

We have tersely argued that a new conceptualization of organizational change and consultancy might usefully exhibit a number of features that are either underappreciated or simply missing in contemporary thinking. An alternative perspective, we have suggested, should:

1. possess considerable face validity;
2. be descriptive rather than prescriptive;
3. embrace a range of types of consultancy, all types of change foci and change strategies;
4. give priority to action that reflects managerial/consultant beliefs and emotions and thus sensemaking;
5. encompass a wider vision of joint action beyond conventional problem solving;
6. be context-free while being situationally sensitive; and
7. not overly gloss either the client-consultant relationship or the process of consultation.

REFOCUSING CHANGE CONSULTANCY

Joining the foundational premises explicated above to our conceptual aspirations points us toward several core ideas.[2] The first is the process of *sensemaking*. Sensemaking is a core idea because meanings created and held by persons are believed to be what primarily guides behavior. A second idea is *mindset*, a system of beliefs and associated emotions that govern sensemaking. Beliefs are considered a necessary idea because they outline action preferences; emotions are likewise necessary because meanings are believed to be more or less emotionally charged and thus impactful. Third is the idea of *situations* and the process of *how they are known* to persons. This is considered a basic idea because meanings are presumed to always be more or less situationally relevant. The fourth core idea is *change recipe,* which includes preferred client and consultant roles, preferred strategies for going about change, and preferred change foci. Recipes are central to change endeavors because they form the proximate guides for change related activities.

On Sensemaking

While how to make sense of the world we inhabit and our experience of it has fascinated scholars for a very long time, it is only in recent decades that sensemaking has become important in management and organizational behavior (Weick, 1995). The attraction of sensemaking is that it permits a dynamic, actor-centered, situation, and social-cultural understanding for both individuals and human system inquiry. The main features of sensemaking may be summarized as follows:

1. Sensemaking is grounded in identity, i.e., who the sensemaker is and is becoming appears to be determinant.
2. Sensemaking is a process of human construction, which begins when a person notices something (a cue) in the ongoing flow of his or her experience.
3. A sensemaker uses his or her own social-cultural experience as a frame to retrospectively create a plausible, more or less coherent interpretation/speculation/explanation of the noticed cue.
4. Sensemaking therefore has three elements: a frame, a cue, and a connection. *Frames* are collections of past moments of socialization, learned precedent, and tradition. *Cues* are present moments of perceived experience. How a cue is understood in terms of the frame is the meaning-making *connection.*

Since experience is ongoing, we see that sensemaking brackets moments in the flow of life. Cues exist within and are noticeable in terms of a frame learned from first and/or second-hand experiences in social-cultural systems—these at least are partially creations of the sensemaker. Sensemaking is thus more about socio-cultural plausibility than factual accuracy. Cues are either symbolic or about interruptions, and, typically but not always, are perceived and processed out of awareness. Symbolic cues are those learned from repetitive experiences in situations where something is deemed significant. Interruption cues can be about when something expected to be there or happen did not, or when something not expected did happen. All cues are more or less arousing (i.e., become emotionally laden).

In general, arousal associated with interruptions is usually experienced as a negative emotion and arousal associated with interruption removal is usually experienced as positive. Cues can and do prompt organismic arousal in people and arousal (discharges in the autonomic nervous system) is known emotionally (Mandler, 1984). A person's socio-cultural experiences teach what a specific level of arousal means in terms of emotion type and strength (Thoits, 1984). Arousal and its associated emotional meanings may help or hinder cognitive processing (e.g., judgment, reasoning, and analysis) (Mano, 1992). Intensely experienced emotions tend to impact the efficacy of complex thought processes. Persons in positive affective states are more likely to rely on general knowledge structures, whereas persons in negative affective states are more likely to focus on the data in hand (Bless, 2001). Sensemaking generates meaning by relating an emotionally-charged cue to a socio-cultural frame; sensemaking is thus about how people generate that which they subsequently interpret.

On Mindsets

A mindset is comprised of a set of interdependent beliefs that condition most if not all managerial thought and behavior. For organizations it is the shared mindset of the dominant coalition (i.e., those one or more managers who make key decisions about the organization's purpose and direction and about how resources are allocated) that is significant.

Four general, action-specifying beliefs comprise a mindset. One is how the organization should compete in its markets and industry. A second is how the organization should go about satisfying its stakeholders. A third belief is about organizational governance, including how to relate to the organization's members. The fourth belief is about change, whether change is difficult or not, episodic or ongoing, and whether change should be either mostly reactive or proactive. These beliefs encompass the dominant coalition's assumptions (e.g., about time, environmental munificence, resource costs) and values (e.g., about power, rationality, social responsibility). The dominant coalition's mindset is often implied in their preferred metaphors, for themselves (e.g., captain of a ship, football quarterback, military commander, team coach) and their organization (e.g., besieged castle, polar expedition, dog sled, zoo). In general, mindsets direct attention, privilege some type of information, provide a common identity, and mobilize energy. Mindsets, of course, are typically out of the awareness of those who hold them but may also sometimes be surfaced and articulated. Whether known or not the mindset of an organization's dominant coalition functions as an ongoing, general frame for their sensemaking.

On Change Recipes

Managerial mindsets—as general sensemaking frames—shape our thinking about organizational change. In other words, mindsets lead to preferences about what could or should be changed (*change foci*), how change could or should be undertaken (*change strategy*), and who the agents of change could or should be as well as how they perform their roles. This set of proclivities is termed a change recipe.

In general, all organizations are engaged in three fundamental tasks (Lundberg, 1989):

1. they attempt to make acceptable internal adjustments;
2. they attempt to make appropriate external alignments; and
3. they attempt to anticipate their possible future.

Adjustments are changes in internal relationships, activities, and resource allocations so as to reduce, omit or prevent a perceived discrepancy among the organization's purpose, depicted goals, and actual performance levels. Consistency of adjustment efforts tends to preserve organization coherence and order. Alignment refers to the modification of the organization—environment dependency relationships and/or exchanges so that the organization's input and/or outputs more accurately enhance the achievement of organizational goals—typically through environmental scanning, restrategizing, and crisis management. Anticipation is the transformation of the organization itself so that it will more likely meet predicted alignment and adjustment requirements in the future. Operative managerial mindsets order the organization's beliefs for which of these three change foci will be viewed as most common or likely and thus deserve attention.

The second aspect of a change recipe has to do with the organization's beliefs about its preferred way of accomplishing change (i.e., its preferred change strategy). There are, in general, three basic types of change strategy: managerial change, guided change, and renewal facilitation.[3] Managed change is the engineering of intentions (i.e., most planned change), where managers impose their design for substantive changes (i.e., they use their authority to say what content should be changed). Guided change is the strategy emphasizing the improvement of organizational processes—that are assumed to lead to appropriate substantive changes). The third strategy, facilitation of renewal, brings about organizational change by encouraging learning by members and subunits. This strategy presumes that enhancing the competencies of change agents will enable them to consider and enact needed changes. Interestingly, all three beliefs about change strategies more or less claim to reflect humanistic values.

If we map the two change recipe components just discussed onto one another, we can see the wide variety of possible change choices that exist. Table 10.1 shows these alternatives as well as provides examples of change interventions for each.

The third component of a change recipe has to do with beliefs about preferred change competencies and hence roles of change agents. Each preferred change strategy suggests that different types of competency are required: competence about substantive things for a managerial change strategy; competence about processes for a guided change strategy; and competence about personal and organizational learning for a renewal facilitation strategy. In organizations that entertain change endeavors not everyone will be perceived as interested, concerned, or competent about change. Beliefs will vary as to whether change competencies should be part of every manager's job, only some managers' jobs (e.g., a task force), delegated to staff specialists or internal consultants, or contracted out to external consultants.[4]

TABLE 10.1. A Sample of Change Interventions that Illustrates Combinations of Change Foci and Change Strategy

	Preferred Alternative Change Foci		
Preferred Change Strategy	**Internal Adjustments**	**External Alignments**	**Anticipation of Future**
Managed Change (by engineering intensions)	• Problem solving • Organization development (OD) • Socio-technical system redesign	• Strategic planning • Crisis planning	• Transformational OD • High-involvement systems
Guided Change (by emphasizing process)	• Team development • Action research • Process consultation • Career planning	• Trans-organizational OD • Future search conferences • Triage teams	• Learning organization • Culture change
Facilitate Renewal (by encouraging learning)	• Training and development • Empowerment • Autonomous work units	• Executive self-modification • Bricolage enhancement	• Self-organizing systems • Double-loop learning

On Bracketed Situations and the Logic of Appropriateness

As already noted, people's experiences are ongoing, a flow without beginnings or endings. Given human limitations for cognitive processing and attention, the number of stimuli that can be experienced at any point in time is potentially overwhelming of a person's sensory and nervous systems. Thus people naturally bracket their experiencing in various ways, for example in terms of place, time, relationships, activities, goals, and the like, typically in some combination consistent with culturally learned language categories and social norms. Experience is, of course, always situational, more or less real and/or imagined, and thus bracketed situations focus and limit experiencing.

In organizations, members situationally bracket their experiences around work, social, and personal "projects" (i.e., a set of rule-guided related activities requiring certain knowledge and skills), a time duration, a locale, one or more identities, and a shared sense of appropriate technologies and purposes. Projects are thus the common basic contexts of meaning. Projects are recognized as well as understood by people through their shared mindsets, shared socio-cultural experiences, especially their shared language. Organizations may be conceived as dynamic networks of related projects—these projects varying in size, duration and importance. Of note is that projects are linkable in two ways—a given project can either embrace or be a part of another project, and projects can usually occur in sequences. It follows that organizational change may be conceived as a set or sequence of one or more projects.

Project members can and do understand their projects in many ways, more or less shared by project colleagues. Common views are that a project is more or less important, difficult or easy to accomplish, tightly or loosely organized, barely learned or over determined, and whether there are just one or several ways for project completion. These features are important because they influence project sensemaking. Organizational members will typically be engaged in several projects simultaneously, although just one will be salient to them at a point in time. Salient projects are presumed to be the result of responses to three ordered, orienting questions that people continuously ask themselves (usually implicitly but occasionally explicitly): What kind of situation is this? What kind of person am I in such a situation? What is a person like me in a situation like this supposed to do? These three questions—of situation recognition, situational identity, and actionable situational rules respectively—constitute a logic of appropriateness (March, 1994). The answers to these questions comprise a frame through which one's experience is made sense of. People have inventories of responses to these questions from their first-hand life experiences and especially from their vicarious ones, that is, people typically have a large number of situations, identities and rules (e.g., for what cues to attend to, for what is the called for emotional reaction to a cue, for how to think about relevant information, for how to behaviorally display what they think or feel) to draw upon and combine to define their projects.

A frame provided by a mindset and situational logic of appropriateness will, of course, vary as to clarity and completeness. The more clear and complete a frame, the easier sensemaking will be and the more surety accompanies action. Joint project action, however, requires that individuals have relatively clear and complete frames and that project members—including consultants—share significant portions of their frames. Shared frames thus give coordinated projects.

Recapitulation

There are two key relationships that link the core ideas introduced above. One is that the belief set of managerial mindset largely determines change recipes (i.e., the organization's preferences toward certain generalized change foci, change strategies, and change-related competencies and roles). The second is that change recipes, in turn, influence (through the logic of acquaintanceship) the bracketing of situations into organizationally relevant projects. Within this perspective, organizational change may be generically understood as a sequence of sensemaking projects[5]—which will be explicated in the next section.

ORGANIZATION CHANGE AS A SEQUENCE OF SENSEMAKING PROJECTS

As we have argued up to here, at a point in time one or more (usually more) persons share most of some managerial mindset as well as share most of some definition of their situation, their situational identities (and thus roles), and the situational rules that seem to be applicable. This sharing brackets and thus frames projects through which the goals and tasks of an organization get accomplished. Project frames enable organizational members to notice cues, symbolic and/or interruptive, and to interpret them thus giving them meaning.

We can now inquire about the types of projects that might constitute organization change. Clearly, organization change is a relatively abstract term and as such glosses over the real complexity of the process of change. How all organization changes are brought about (i.e., the general process) can, however, be outlined and further unbundled as to their sensemaking requirements. In outline, there are usually acknowl-

Table 10.2. The Phases and Sensemaking Projects of Organizational Change

	Sensemaking project: • Ongoing scanning
Focusing Phase	**Sensemaking projects:** • Initiating • Boundrying • Agenting
Analyzing Phase	**Sensemaking projects:** • Informationing • Diagnosing • Targeting
Actioning Phase	**Sensemaking projects:** • Action planning • Intervening • Stabilizing/Assessing

edged to be just three general, prototypical[6] phases—focusing, analyzing, and actioning. Each phase contains a set of sensemaking projects. In addition there is one, ongoing sensemaking project that is pre-change. Table 10.2 shows the sequence of change phases and the set of sensemaking projects each encompasses.

Sensemaking Project: Ongoing Scanning

The first project is really a pre-change one in which organizational managers or their agents, more or less continuously scan for factors that precipitate change, that is, factors that bring pressure to bear on an organization for change. The ongoing managerial mindset enables the noticing of cues about precipitating pressures, which are then interpreted as whether the organization's general health does or does not set the stage for members to be attentive to more specific cues that might call for changes.

Four types of precipitating pressures seem to occur. One is atypical performance demands on the organization—any greater or lesser level of performance expectations from the marketplace or the public tends to be pressureful if the organization is unprepared for them. A second precipitating circumstance is stakeholder pressures. Stakeholders, those claimants inside and outside the system with a vested interest in it (Mason & Mitroff,

1981), provide the main sources of organization purpose and strategy. One or more stakeholders can exert pressure on an organization to be different than it currently is. A third kind of pressure has to do with organizational growth or decrement. An organization can be either downsizing or growing in size, membership heterogeneity, or structural complexity. Each process creates pressures in which dysfunctions and dissatisfactions build up. A fourth precipitating source of pressure is in the real or perceived crises associated with environmental uncertainty, such as unpredictable competitor or consumer options as well as resource deprivations or excesses (e.g., skills, materials, ideas). Pressure is felt by organizational members with the accretion of preferred indicators.

The Focusing Phase

When scanning activities are interpreted as meaning that precipitating pressures imply some alertness is needed regarding potential change, an organization can eventually enter a phase of changing that focuses a change endeavor. Prototypically focusing embraces three analytically separable but operationally intertwined sensemaking projects.

Sensemaking Project: Initiating Change

The transition that initiates organizational change almost always begins in response to one or more triggering events. The now salient frame (managerial mindset and the perceived state of the organization's health) enables the noticing of cues that are interpreted as organizational difficulties and experienced as some level of distress. The image here is of tensions built up from pressures that can no longer be easily ignored: those tensions released through the stimulus of one or more events. Several types of such trigger events can be distinguished: environmental calamities and opportunities, internal and external revolutions, and business-managerial crises.

Environmental triggers are simply events that management believes cannot be ignored. Examples of calamities include all kinds of natural disasters, a sharp recession, or an innovation that jeopardizes the organization's product or services. Examples of environmental opportunities, like calamities because they appear suddenly and possess much potential, are technological breakthroughs, the discovery of a previously unknown or untouchable market niche, and newly available venture capital.

Revolutions can be triggering events too. Examples of external revolutions as triggers are events that have major consequences for the organization, such as being taken over by another organization or being subjected to political interference (e.g., nationalization of a foreign subsidiary or perhaps legislation of new and more stringent governmental regulations). Examples of triggers that stem from internal revolutions would be the installation of a new management team and a coup by the "young Turks."

Managerial-business crises are also potentially triggering events. Examples might be a shake-up among the organization's leadership, the fallout from an inappropriate strategic decision, a substantial misreading of the organization's markets, a foolish expenditure that loses reserve funds, and so on.

Trigger events, we recall, are interpreted as organizational difficulties and generate a felt distress (ranging from discomfort to upset to anxiety to panic), which initiate the processes of organizational changing and energizing the next sensemaking project whose outcome is to identify the boundaries of the change endeavor.

Sensemaking Project: Boundrying Change

The managerial mindset, especially its proclivity toward a general type of change foci, and the recognition of some difficulties/level of distress, combine to form the frame through which three sorts of information are noticed as cues that outline and give meaning to the anticipated urgency, scope, and time frame of change. One kind of cue information has to do with the existence or not of other changes currently being undertaken—which can act as either a constraint upon or serve to energize the change being indicated (Burke, Javitch, Waclawski, & Church, 1997). Another set of cueing information is perceived external enabling conditions that increase the likelihood of changes occurring. These are external in that they are in the environmental domain of the organization (or of a subunit) and are enabling in the sense that they indicate the environment will be supportive of change.

External enabling conditions, in essence, speak of the degree of difficulty an organization or subunit will likely experience if changes are attempted. Two conditions are: (1) domain forgiveness (e.g., conditions of scarcity or abundance, stability or instability, and the concentration or dispersion of resources which in combination determine the degree of perceived threat to an organization posed by its competition, input sources, and the economic cycling of its industry), and (2) the degree of organization-domain cultural congruence (e.g., too little or too great cultural congruence will make most organizational change seem overly risky, overly threatening, or unnecessary).

The third kind of cueing information is about internal permitting conditions—those propitious circumstances that must exist within an organization (or subunit). Four such internal conditions are:

1. the existence of a surplus of appropriate change resources or "slack" (e.g., priorities for managerial time and energy, financial

resources and the like which are available to the organization beyond those needed for normal operations);

2. system readiness, generally speaking the willingness of most members to live with the anxiety that comes with the anticipated uncertainties of change;
3. minimal coupling (i.e., the informational linkages and interorganizational dependencies that would make change difficult because of the additional coordinative and integrative work necessary if they are weak); and
4. change agent power and leadership since organizational changes puts extra demands on the management, formal and informal, of an organization.

While the agents of organizational changes may include consultants and/or staff, many are eventually and inevitably managers. The cues noticed from all of the above conditions are interpreted as meaning the difficulties and felt distress are more or less urgent, of narrow or broad scope organizationally, and probably will take a shorter or longer span of time to complete as shown below (see Figure 10.1).

Sensemaking Project: Agenting for Change

A third sensemaking project involves noticing any relevant cues about available change-related competencies and interpreting these as the potential cadre of agents. For example, who among the roster of managers and members are likely to become change managers and change agents? Who are likely to play change related roles, such as change champions, educators, and stewards? Are there particular kinds of third party roles (i.e., internal and/or external change assistance roles) that might

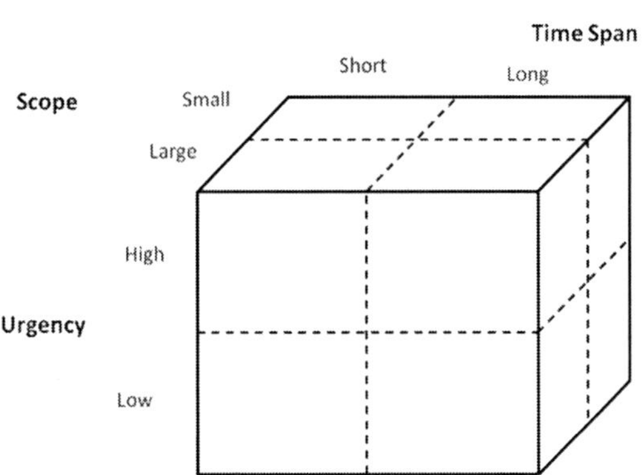

FIGURE 10.1. Boundrying Change Cues

have to be engaged? Who, if anyone, needs to authorize going forward? It is important to note that discerning the answers to these questions will be influenced by the preferred change strategy beliefs of the mindsets' change recipe.

We now see that for an organization to focus on change, three separate but possibly interwoven, sensemaking projects must occur—one which gives meaning about difficulties and distress; a second which outlines likely meanings of change urgency, scope, and time-span; and a third in which a general meaning of necessary change competencies is given.

The Analyzing Phase

The above described set of sensemaking projects bring organizational change(s) into focus. The next phase, termed analyzing, sharpens this focus through three additional prototypical sensemaking projects.

Sensemaking Project: Change Informationing

Here a frame composed of the managerial mindset and the meanings derived from prior projects enables management to (1) select one or more preferred organizational models (specifying organization components and how these components are related);[7] and (2) notice cues among available information ("presenting problems," symptoms of difficulties, and distress). The meanings interpreted from the model selected and noticed symptoms are informational, that is, they are responses to these questions: What kinds and amount of relevant data are required in order to diagnose these symptoms? Who should gather these data? Who should process them? The responses to these questions guide the acquisition of information useful for the next two sensemaking projects.

Sensemaking Project: Diagnosing the Need for change

Sensemaking in this project uses the frame provided by the managerial mindset and prior meanings to notice those cues in the data just acquired that indicate discrepancies between actual behaviors/ performances and described/intended ones.[8] Noticed discrepancies become meanings labeled either as problems (i.e., the over or underachievement of goals) or predicaments (i.e., interconsistency among goals within and among individuals, subunits and the organization itself), or the need for exceeding expected performance levels (i.e., positively deviant performance) (Spreitzer & Sonenshein, 2003). These, of course, are usually prioritized in terms of which must be dealt with immediately or later, which detracts from overall organizational performance, and those which can feasibly be dealt with given existing or possibly acquired competencies and resources.

Sensemaking Project: Targeting Change

The diagnosis and managerial mindset become the frame for a sensemaking project in which cues about system readiness for change and current beliefs about change urgency, scope, and time frame are used to designate meaningful change targets (i.e., those organization components and/or relationships which if changed would ameliorate identified problems/predicaments or expand performance goals, specify the nature of associated change goals, and develop some sense of the change related resources required).

The analysis phase, with its informationing, diagnosing, and change targeting sensemaking projects, moves organizational changing from its early focusing activities to the point of considering change actions.

The Actioning Phase

This final phase of organizational changing encompasses three sensemaking projects: planning, intervening, and stabilizing/assessment.

Sensemaking Project: Action Planning for Change

This sensemaking project prepares the organization for making desired changes. Noticed cues about available fiscal "slack," intellectual resources, manpower, target member commitment to changing, perceived system momentum, and the current state of symptoms are interpreted for their meanings about any inducements needed, an intervention plan, and any "sense-giving" needed, i.e., explanations to organization members of what will be happening and why.

Sensemaking Project: Intervening for Change

As the intervention plan gets enacted, managers and/or their agents pay attention to cues related to intervention activities as well as member reactions and levels of business functioning. These cues are interpreted for their meanings about the anticipated and unanticipated consequences of the intervention plan both for change targets and the organization as a whole. Usually this sensemaking occurs repeatedly throughout the time period in which intervention occurs.

Sensemaking Project: Stabilizing Change/Assessment

The final sensemaking project in the accomplishment of changing an organization embraces two concerns: 1) has the change become a normal, accepted part of the organization?; and 2) have the change goals been achieved? Cues of relevance to these concerns are about intervention effectiveness and whether the organization's operations have returned to an acceptable symptom-free level of operating. The meanings ascribed to such cue information takes the form of "lessons" (i.e., what seemed to have worked or not, whether the endeavor was worth the resource investment and effort or not, and what this change endeavor experience suggests for how future changes might be tackled).

Recapitulation

The process of changing organizations has been conceptualized as a sequence of ten sensemaking projects (summarized in Table 10.3). For each project, a frame composed of a managerial mindset augmented by a situational awareness (1) guides the noticing of relevant cues and

Table 10.3. The Sensemaking Projects of Organizational Change

Phase	Sensemaking Project	Cues	Meaning
FOCUSING	*Scanning*	• Precipitating pressures	• State of organization health
	Initiating	• Trigger events	• Organization difficulties • Member distress
	Boundrying	• Internal permitting and external enabling conditions • Other change endeavors	• Probable urgency, scope and time span
	Agenting	• Available change competencies	• Likely incumbents of change roles • Need for third parties
ANALYZING	*Informationing*	• Symptoms and preferred organizational model	• Needed type and amount of data • Who acquires and processes the data
	Diagnosing	• Model-actual performance discrepancies	• Problems and/or predicaments
	Targeting	• System readiness • Actual urgency, scope and time frame	• Identification of change targets, goals and resources
ACTIONING	*Action Planning*	• Fiscal slack, manpower, energy, commitment resources	• Need inducements • Tactics of intervening • Sense giving
	Intervening	• Intervention activities • Member reactions	• Target and system consequences
	Stabilizing/ Assessing	• Indicators of intervention effectiveness	• Change lessons

then (2) relates these cues to the frame to provide one or more meanings. Meanings both guide and energize the activities that follow each sensemaking project. Project meanings will usually combine with mindset beliefs to become the frame used in the subsequent project. Will every organizational change endeavor exhibit all 10 sensemaking projects described? This is unlikely because the sequence discussed above is prototypical, and because within phases some projects may be combined, skimped or even skipped in practice.

CONSULTING FOR ORGANIZATIONAL CHANGE

Changing organizations, in part or whole, as a sequence of sensemaking projects can and often is the sole province of an organization's managers and members. However, because organization change may require the utilization of sensemaking resources beyond those necessary for ongoing operations as well as distress management, assistance is sometimes sought and engaged. Assistance occurs when one or more members of an organization (nominally termed the client) express a request for help and one or more others located inside and/or outside the organization (nominally termed internal and external consultants respectively) offers to provide it (Lundberg, 2002). Assistance is, of course, always defined by the client. Consultants, just like the clients they serve, will have change recipe preferences (i.e., preferences about what sorts of change foci deserve attention, preferences about change strategy, and preferences about change competencies). Successful assistance almost always requires that the change recipes of client and consultant coincide.

Consultant engagement is either ongoing (i.e., the consultant has an open-ended relationship with the client) or for a limited period of time. In addition, consultants may be engaged to perform one or more roles:

1. as "doctors" who take on the responsibility for diagnosing issues and prescribing remedial measures (and, sometimes, for implementing change interventions);
2. as "suppliers" who provide information, knowledge, and/or technical services as designated by a client; or
3. as "facilitators" who are actively involved with helping clients do their own diagnostic and remedial activities (Lundberg& Finney, 1982; Schein, 1993).

Combining these features of engagement we see that there are many consultancy options (see Figure 10.2). Choice among these options will reflect considerations of costs and organizational politics and, especially,

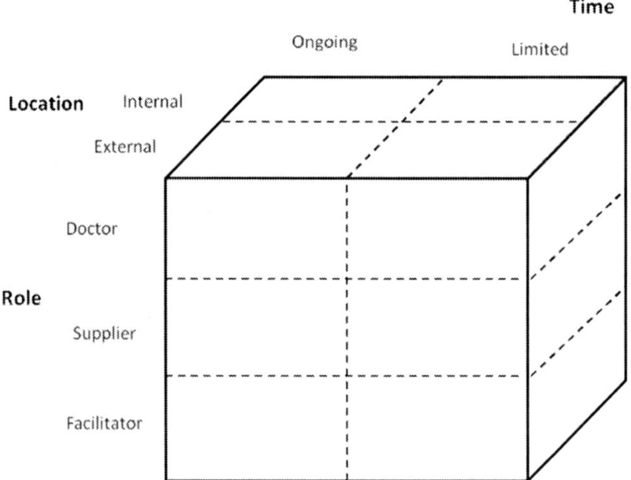

FIGURE 10-2. Consultancy Options.

managerial preferences about change strategy and the initial assessment of the likely urgency, scope and time-span of a change endeavor.

Change consultancy, as noted, will exhibit some combination of role-location-time and competencies (i.e., those of content, process and/or learning). Our belief system, situation centered sensemaking perspective, however, suggests that third-party change consultants will usefully proffer several types of expertise to the sensemaking projects of change, which are undervalued in the literature. Throughout all projects, consultants need to be able to facilitate their clients' noticing and weighing the importance of cues, to validate the interpretation of any meanings derived from noticed cues, and to coach about the sensemaking process itself.

In addition there are three kinds of enabling expertise heretofore largely ignored. One has to do with *reducing client distress* both in early sensemaking projects as well as throughout an engagement and, usually, the distress among other organization members and even outsiders as the change endeavor unfolds. A second expertise has to do with *managing the client-consultant relationship* (i.e., surfacing and negotiating it for each sensemaking project so that an acceptable matching of change roles and change strategy exists). The third enabling expertise has to do with the *process of sensemaking itself*. For one or more change projects, consultants will usefully surface and articulate the sensemaking frame of mindset and situation. For one or more sensemaking projects, consultants will usefully modify as appropriate the managerial mindset-project frame, presumably a re-educative effort. Enabling clients regarding change project sensemaking may, in fact, be the distinguishing feature of change consultancy.

CONCLUDING COMMENTS

This chapter has presented a new perspective on organizational change and change consultancy. Building on the core ideas of sensemaking, mindset, change recipes, and situationally-bracketed projects, organizational change was reconceived as a sequence of 10 belief driven, situational sensemaking projects. Consultancy was in turn reconceived as assisting with the sensemaking leading to organizational change—potentially applicable to one, several, or all sensemaking projects. Change consultancy as portrayed thus emphasizes enabling expertise in distress reduction, the surfacing, articulating, validating and educating of organizational change agent sensemaking, and managing the client-consultant relationship.

As an initial presentation of this perspective, our characterization of both organizational change and its consultancy are necessarily approximations. Further development of this work (i.e., its correction, refinement, and/or elaboration) could, at least initially, usefully embrace the following activities. Experienced organizational change consultants should be invited to first understand and then carefully assess the face validity of this work (i.e., does this perspective seem to reflect the reality of their positive and negative consulting experiences?). Similarly this perspective could be used to explain the behaviors of organization members and their consultants as described in detailed change cases or ethnographies of change success and failure (i.e., are these rich descriptions accurately reflected in our perspective?; do they clarify and/or ground the perspective's core ideas and sequences of sensemaking projects?). Also, extant theories of organizational change and consultancy might be translated into this perspective thus advancing the specification of contextual contingencies and parameters (i.e., are there domains where this perspective does not pertain?; are there circumstances in which the perspective is not applicable?).

Much work remains to be done. Several features of this perspective beg nuancing and development, such as the operationalization of the perspective's core ideas, how to devise methods for gathering relevant data that are less inference dependent, the dynamics of sensemaking by teams, the personal attributes associated with mindset changes, how sensemaking around organizational change can be derailed, how to measure the effectiveness of sensemaking based change endeavors, how to delay the premature prescriptionalizing of this work, and so on. The perspective advocated in this chapter, while promising in many ways, requires both extension and refinement by scholars and practitioners alike, hence we conclude with an invitation to use it and improve it.

NOTES

1. The helpful comments on an earlier draft by A. P. Raia, S. Shirley and W. W. Burke are gratefully appreciated.
2. Our exposition of sensemaking, situations and the logic of acquaintance borrows in part from Lundberg (2004).
3. There is one other, very rarely seen change strategy—the enhancing of natural, evolutionary drifts/changes (Torbert, 1991). Here change agents focus opportunistically on the everyday mending of the consequences of other actions thereby shaping events to some thematic movement.
4. We hasten to note that the internal–external choice is always in part a cost matter. As McKenna (2006, p. 13) has convincingly argued, "Consultants flourish where the benefits from economics of knowledge outweigh the costs of external contracting."
5. Sensemaking has been used before to explain organizational change albeit generally. Mills (2003) retrospectively examined two major organization-wide changes (i.e., culture change and business process re-engineering) at the Nova Scotia Power Corporation (1988–1995). In critiquing her own study, Mills argues that contexts, activities, and rules need to be added to sensemaking to make sense of change—these points reflected in this chapter through our emphasis on sensemaking projects.
6. "Prototypical" here refers to a first, early or general form from which others might be developed. The phases promulgated here intentionally resemble the sequence of distinct change conversations outlined by Ford and Ford (1995) and shown to exist by Barret, Thomas, and Hocevar (1995) (i.e., initiating, understanding, performance, and closure) and the cognitive-emotional stages postulated by Salerno and Brock (2008).
7. Examples of five well-known organizational models can be found in Chapters 8 and 9 in Burke (2002).
8. Diagnosis as sensemaking was first elaborated in Lundberg (2008).

REFERENCES

Bak, P. (1996). *How nature works: The science of self-organized criticality*. New York: Springer-Verlag.

Barrett, F., Thomas, G., & Hocevar, S. (1995). The central role of discourse in large-scale change. *The Journal of Applied Behavioral Science, 31*(3), 352–372.

Bless, H. (2001). Mood and the use of general knowledge structures. In L. L. Martia & G. L. Clore (Eds.), *Theories of mind and cognition* (pp. 78–93). Mahwah, NJ: Lawrence Erlbaum.

Burke, W. W. (2002). *Organization change: Theory and practice.* Thousand Oaks, CA: Sage.

Burke, W. W., Javitch, M., Waclawski, J., & Church, A. H. (1997). The dynamics of mid-stream consulting. *Consulting Psychology Journal: Practice and Research, 49* (2), 83–95.

Cowan, G. A., Pines, D., & Meltzer, D. (1994). *Complexity: Metaphors, models, and reality.* Reading, MA: Addison-Wesley.

Ford, J. D., & Ford, L. W. (1995). The role of conversations in producing intentional change in organizations. *Academy of Management Review, 20*(3), 541–570.

Lundberg, C. C. (1989). On organizational learning: Implications and opportunities for expanding organizational development. In R. W. Woodman & W. A. Pasmore (Eds.), *Research in organizational change and development* (pp. 61–82). Greenwich. CT: JAI Press.

Lundberg, C. C. (2001). Toward theory more relevant for practice. In M. A. Rahim, R. T. Golombieski, & K. D. MacKenzie (Eds.), *Current topics in management* (pp. 15–24). New York: JAI.

Lundberg, C. C. (2002). Consultancy foundations: Toward a general theory. In A. F. Buono (Ed.), *Developing knowledge and value in management consulting* (pp. 153–168). Greenwich, CT: Information Age Publishing.

Lundberg, C. C. (2004). Toward an emotion-nuanced, sensemaking perspective on organizational behavior. In M. A. Rahim, R. T. Golombieski, & K. D. MacKenzie (Eds.), *Current topics in management* (pp. 85–100). New Brunswick, NJ: Transaction Publishers.

Lundberg, C. C. (2008). Organization development diagnoses. In T. G. Cummings (Ed.), *Handbook of organization development* (pp. 137–150). Thousand Oaks, CA: Sage.

Lundberg, C. C., & Finney, M. (1987). Emerging models of consultancy. *Consultation, 6,* 32–42.

Lundberg, C. C., & Young, C. A. (2005). *Foundation for inquiry: Choices and tradeoffs in the organizational sciences.* Palo Alto, CA: Stanford University Press.

Mali, P. (1981). *Management handbook.* New York: Wiley.

Mandler, G. (1984). *Mind and body: Psychology of emotion and stress.* N.Y.: Norton.

Mano, H. (1992). Judgments under duress: Assessing the role of unpleasantness and arousal in judgment formation. *Organizational Behavior and Human Decision Processes, 52,* 216–245.

March, J. G. (1994). *A primer on decision making: How decisions happen.* New York: Free Press.

Mason, R., & Mitroff, I. I. (1981). *Challenging strategic planning assumptions.* New York: John Wiley & Sons.

McKenna, C. D. (2006). *The world's newest profession: Management consulting in the twentieth century.* New York: Cambridge University Press.

Miller, J. G. (1978). *Living systems.* New York: McGraw-Hill.

Mills, J. H. (2003). *Making sense of organizational change.* New York: Routledge.

Morgan, G., & Smircich, L. (1980). The case for qualitative research. *Academy of Management Review, 5,* 491–500.

Pondy, L. R., & Olsen, M. L. (1977). *Theories of extreme cases.* Paper presented at the American Psychological Association, San Francisco.

Rousseau, D. M. (1985). Issues on level in organizational research: Multi-level and cross- level perspectives. In L. L. Cumming & B. M. Staw (Eds.), *Research in organizational behavior* (pp. 1–37). Greenwich, CT: JAI.

Salerno, A., & Brock, L. (2008). *The change cycle.* San Francisco: Berrett-Koehler.

Schein, E. H. (1993). Models of consultation: What do organizations of the 1990s need? In R. T. Golembiewski (Ed.), *Handbook of organizational consultation* (pp. 653–661). New York: Marcel Dekker.

Spreitzer, G. M., & Sonenshein, S. (2003). Positive deviance and extraordinary organizing. In K. Cameron, J. Dutton, & R. Quinn (Eds.), *Positive organizational scholarship* (pp. 207–224). San Francisco: Berrett-Koehler.

Stablein, R. (1988, June). *Structure of debate in organizational studies.* Paper presented at the Australian Management Education Conference, Perth, Australia.

Thoits, P. A. (1984). Coping, social support, and psychological outcomes: The central role of emotions. In P. Shaver (Ed.), *Review of personality and social psychology* (pp. 219–238). Beverly Hills, CA: Sage.

Thoits, P. A. (1989). The sociology of emotions. In W. R. Scott, & J. Blake (Eds.), *Annual Review of Sociology, 15*, 317–342.

Torbert, W. R. (1991). *The power of balance.* Newbury Park, CA: Sage.

Weick, K. E. (1979). *The social psychology of organizing* (2nd ed.). Reading, MA: Addison-Wesley.

Weick, K. E. (1982, June). *The presumption of logic in executive thought and action.* Presented at the symposium on Functioning of the Executive Mind, Case Western Reserve University, Ohio.

Weick, K. E. (1987). Perspectives in organizations. In J. Lorsch (Ed.), *Handbook of organizational behavior* (pp. 10–28). Englewood Cliffs, NJ: Prentice-Hall.

Weick, K.E. (1995). *Sensemaking in organizations.* Thousand Oaks, CA: Sage.

CHAPTER 11

CONSULTING IN THE FAST LANE

W. Warner Burke

Management and organization consulting isn't what it used to be. As consultants, we no longer have the luxury of time. Helpful consulting takes time—to establish rapport with the client, to get the lay of the land (what we used to call diagnosis), to achieve some understanding of the organization's culture, the informal system, and the nature of politics in the organization. But clients want immediate action; they want to see some positive differences from consultation *now!* if not yesterday. In these times, it's as if most clients have some form of attention deficit disorder.

Core consultative activities such as meeting facilitation, process consultation, and team building, cornerstone interventions in the field of organization development (OD), are not passé, but now are apparently less common. If true, why might this be so? These activities take time, of course, and often are perceived as "soft." In other words, it is not clear just how these consultative interventions contribute to the bottom line, that all-important performance goal in today's business enterprises.

We also know the importance of organizational learning for long-term survival and ultimate effectiveness. To learn from mistakes, to take full ad-

Consultation for Organizational Change. pages 233–246
Copyright © 2010 by Information Age Publishing
All rights of reproduction in any form reserved.

vantage of successes by understanding why an intervention went well, and to learn more about how to learn, akin to Argyris's double-loop learning (Argyris & Schön, 1978), can be highly beneficial to organizational effectiveness. The U.S. Army, for example, has benefited greatly from their "After Action Reviews" (AARs), a process of learning from mistakes, from what went well, and learning more about how to learn. Corporations would do well to adopt the idea of AARs. But this activity and others like it take time. And it seems that endemic to the American culture is the notion of "let's get on with it, let's move on; been there, done that." In other words, our culture is intolerant of review, reflection, and going over "spilt milk." "It's done, nothing we can do about it; so let's move on." Obviously, however, there is something one can do about it—to learn from it.

To clarify these points about management and organization consulting today, let us consider a metaphor from professional baseball. In the major leagues it is most unusual for pitchers to pitch all nine innings. Somehow they seem to be programmed to about 100 pitches per game. Once they reach this stage, around the sixth inning, they seem to tire and make mistakes—walking too many batters, delivering wild pitches, and allowing too many hits. The manager calls time out, walks to the mound and takes the ball from the pitcher, now fatigued, and somewhat embarrassed by his performance. He walks slowly to the dugout with his head down, not looking at the fans who either applaud him for his valiant effort or rain on him a torrent of boos for poor performance. The manager then gives the ball to the relief pitcher who must now save the day. But, the bases are loaded and there are no outs. To say that expectations are high and the relief pitcher is under pressure to perform to the maximum is an understatement.

Management and organization consultation in the twenty-first century is not unlike being a relief pitcher entering the game in the sixth inning. The client has tried many initiatives for positive change, but none have worked very well. Performance remains a problem. Now the client wants the consultant to perform what may seem like a miracle: to stop poor performance, provide new ideas, and help turn things around. We must win the "game."

Before addressing some remedies for how to consult in this present state of time pressure and delivery demands, the main thrust of this chapter, let us consider one final problem—a most disconcerting one at that. The stimulus for addressing this final issue for consultants today came from an article by Matt Bai (2007). First, he pointed out that never before in American history had so many aspiring U.S. presidential candidates from both parties "been so dominated by relative newcomers." Moreover, the incumbent president at the time, George W. Bush, was the least experienced commander-in-chief in 24 years. Bai went on to emphasize that American politics, being deeply embedded in U.S. society, means that something more profound is happening. He claims that this shift is the result of the emergence of the Internet, which has been accompanied by a devaluing of expertise. Why spend valuable time, which may turn out to be relatively worthless, going to see your family doctor about a current ailment when you can go to WebMD, diagnose the ailment yourself and then tell your doctor what drugs you need for him or her to prescribe. There is less need for the expertise of a stockbroker when you can go to E*Trade and make decisions for yourself. So, in politics experience may be a liability. We need fresh thinking and change, not more of the same. And expertise may come across as too narrow and stale, not up to date.

For those of us in the consulting world who value grey hair, experience, and, in general, matters of intellectualism, this is not good news. So how can management and organization consultants in this fast-paced world cope with these comparatively new pressures and demands? How can we conduct an organizational diagnosis "on the run"? How can we assure the client that participating in initiatives for possible change in the organization is not irrelevant and a waste of time? How can we combat a growing trend of anti-intellectualism, particularly when we need to be as evidence-based as possible in whatever we recommend and initiate? Responding to these questions and related considerations is the purposes of the remainder of this chapter.

SUGGESTIONS FOR CONSULTING IN THE FAST LANE

What follows are some suggestions for how to consult with organizational managers and executives in our fast-paced world of the 21st century.

Organizational Diagnosis

I recently had the opportunity to interview ten executives who reported to the CEO, a person I had been working with for about two years. These one-hour interviews were one-on-one and were spread over a two-week period. Following the interviews, I provided feedback, consisting of a summary and brief analysis of the interviews to the CEO in private and then a few days later to the CEO and the ten executives as a group. Questions were raised and responded to and follow-up actions were planned. The entire time to get everything scheduled took about a month and the process seemed to have worked quite well.

Looking back on this process, it seemed like the good old days. It felt luxurious—I *had time* to conduct my diagnosis, deliver the feedback, and help with planning follow-up actions. This activity was not remarkable nor out of the ordinary. The process represents organizational consulting and team building with a top group. What was unusual, however, is that it was the first time I had conducted such a consulting process in over three years. Clients have not been willing to spend such a "luxurious" amount of time. My consulting life has become much more in the moment (e.g., quick conference calls) and on the run—working with clients on one time-limited project after another.

Any seasoned consultant knows the importance of diagnosis. Without this step, we can easily make mistakes by assuming we understand, by taking actions that are not sufficiently grounded in data, and by ignoring history. Incidentally, it might look as if the client is ignoring organizational history as well when everything focuses on the moment and long-range planning is limited to 90 days (i.e., the end of the next quarter). But the history is still there, deeply embedded in the client's unconscious. We simply don't seem to have time to learn deep, yet important behaviors on the part of the client that can be misunderstood.

What is the alternative? Actually Kurt Lewin (1947, 1951) told us a long time ago. To paraphrase, he stated, if you really want to understand an organization, try to change it. In other words, when change in an organization is introduced people react, some positively, some negatively. These reactions Lewin called responses to forces. It is these reactions to forces from the environment—internal and external—that are significant. They tell you volumes about organizational behavior that is culturally and politically based. Our diagnosis, therefore, is observing, recording, and understanding these responses to forces.

Take, for example, the team-building activity briefly described earlier. Instead of interviewing everyone, I might have facilitated a meeting of the group where the agenda was a proposal for significant change in the organization. Paying close attention to the executives' responses to the proposal becomes diagnostic. Continuing to argue for and debate the merits of the change proposal gradually brings out the forces that you, as a consultant, need to understand and analyze.

Organizational diagnosis today therefore needs to be more "real time." It's a bit like jazz music—improvising on a theme. The theme is Lewin's behavioral reactions to external forces.

Executive Coaching

This form of consulting provides opportunities for quick responses to client issues and problems since it is usually "in the moment" and can lead to organizational level interventions for change. For example, in a coaching session recently with a CEO, it became clear that she was in need of information about the organization as a whole. She had been CEO for roughly a year and had been focusing primarily on financial issues since the organization was running into a serious operational deficit. Needing to understand in more depth what some of the causes might be for these money problems, I suggested that we conduct an organization-wide survey. This intervention was helpful and led to significant additional changes in the organization, both in terms of strategy and structure.

Executive coaching also lends itself to teachable moments that can lead to organization change. For example, working with a chief learning officer whose responsibilities included talent management, I found an opportunity to tell him about the research associated with self-awareness, that the greater the degree of congruence between how one sees oneself and how others perceive and rate the person on leadership behavior, the greater the likelihood that the individual will be a high performer as a manager or executive. My client believed that this domain of research was very important and relevant for his organization. This insight on his part led to a series of two-day workshops on "self-awareness for enhancing leadership" that were targeted at high-potential individuals who were being considered for development for higher responsibilities of leadership. These workshops were successful and have become institutionalized in the organization.

The point is that consultants these days need to find ways to add value when time is limited and elaborate planning for large-scale organization change is not likely to be tolerated by clients. Finding opportunities via executive coaching is a way to be helpful when quick responses are expected.

Have a Point of View

In this day and age of consulting it is not wise to emulate Carl Rogers (e.g., Rogers, 1951). Clients don't have patience with a question that is a response to their question. "And how do you feel about that?" is not typically appreciated. Clients are more likely to appreciate when the consultant has a point of view—whether they may end up agreeing with it or not.

The following are five examples of what I mean by having a point of view.

Use an Organizational Model

Around 1990 when I was being considered by the CEO, Bob Bauman and his executive colleagues, to be a consultant for the merger of SmithKline Pharmaceuticals (Philadelphia) and Beecham, Ltd. of London, I was asked questions about my approach to organizational consulting. A centerpiece of my responses was a brief explanation of what was a working model of organizational performance and change that George Litwin and I had crafted from our work with British Airways in the mid- to late-1980s. I explained that the framework was my way of understanding how organizations work (or not as the case may be), and what the primary dimensions of an organization are, how they interact, and what is key to understanding change. I also explained that the model was normative or causal not merely descriptive. The way the model was laid out meant that certain aspects of an organization had a direct, causal impact on other aspects, and in a particular order. This working model was later published as the Burke-Litwin Model of Organizational Performance and Change (Burke & Litwin, 1992).

Briefly, the model (see Figure 11.1), grounded in open system theory, consists of two significant categories: *transformational factors* (external environment, mission and strategy, leadership, and culture) and *transactional factors*—the remaining subcategories or boxes (structure, management

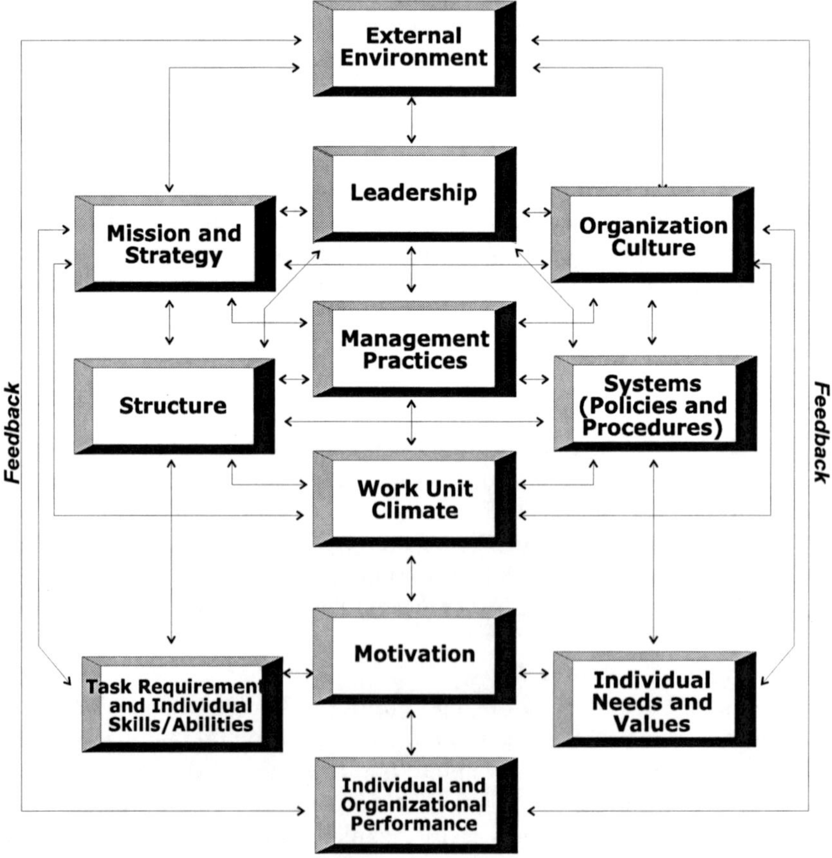

FIGURE 11.1. The Burke-Lewin Model of Organizational Performance and Change

practices, climate, etc.). The transformational factors of mission, and so forth, are more directly influenced by the external environment and therefore have more impact throughout the organization than do the transactional factors. In other words, regarding significance of influence, think top-down. Transformational, meaning change, are the driving factors for revolutionary or discontinuous change and the transactional factors are more operational and evolutionary (e.g., continuous improvement). Culture change is revolutionary (or needs to be) and structural or systems change is evolutionary. When considering change, we therefore begin with the transformational factors. If they seem to be in order, we then, but only then, move to the transactional or more evolutionary factors.

The twelve boxes represent the primary dimensions of an organization with eleven of them in the order presented driving performance, the twelfth, dimension. One should bear in mind, however, that the arrows are more important than the boxes, meaning that everything is interdependent (notice that the arrows go in both directions).

This brief explanation of the model is only a synopsis and much more could be explained. For more see the original article (Burke & Litwin, 1992) and my more recent coverage (Burke, 2008).

The CEO, Bauman and his colleagues, hired me, and I enjoyed three and half years of significant consulting work. Two surveys, a time 1—time 2 comparison, based on the model were conducted during that time, and the model continued to frame decision making, especially concerning change (Bauman, Jackson, & Lawrence, 1997). Bauman told me later that what influenced their decision to hire me was my point of view represented by the model.

Understand the Nature of Culture Change

I often use the statement, "You can't change culture by trying to change the culture." Like former President Clinton's phrase when running for president the second time, "It's the economy, stupid," it's the *behavior*. Yes, we need to first determine what the culture should look like, its norms and values, but then one should concentrate on the behaviors that will help us realize those values not on the values per se. Even though executives may say something like, "We must change people's mental sets," that should not be the focus. A mental set is a thought, a cognition. The presumption is that for change to occur, thought precedes behavior. Once people are clear about the desired new culture (i.e., the vision), they will behave accordingly—when rewarded in kind. There is sound theory and considerable evidence that the opposite is superior for effective change, that is, behavior change needs to precede mental set. In other words:

> to account for how the linkage typically occurs for organizational members between vision or mission (concepts, cognitions) and action (behavior), we

> must not assume that it is primarily a conscious, deliberate, and rational process. It is primarily the opposite. With a set of values and goals declared, we then quickly move to action: behavior that enacts these values and implements these goals without assuming that organizational members have made the linkages. As appropriate movement (behavior) continues over time, the proper attribution can eventually be made, for example, "We are doing this because we believe it is the right (value) thing to do." Behavior is followed by cognition (Burke, 2008; p. 131).

For the theory and research supporting the statements above, see the section "Organization Change Theory" in Burke (2008, pp. 126–133). It should be noted that use of a multi-rater feedback system can help to focus on the appropriate behaviors for culture change.

Develop Expertise in Multi-Rater Feedback Processes

It is difficult to find a large organization today—either profit or nonprofit—that isn't involved or considering involvement in a multi-rater feedback system. At least this is largely true for U.S. organizations. The Chinese, for example, may not be ready, if ever, to adopt such system. Their culture is not likely to support this type of process. In the U.S., however, multi-rater (or "360 degree" as it was called initially) feedback is alive, and sometimes well—but often not so well. Since multi-rater feedback is so widespread and frequently abused, it is highly important for organization and management consultants to understand in some depth how these processes work and don't work—to have perspective and a point of view.

The most important question to be addressed when considering a multi-rater feedback system is one of purpose. The feedback system is supposed to serve what purpose? Two critical more specific questions immediately follow: (1) Is the system to be used for individual development or individual performance evaluation?; and (2) Is the purpose for individual development or organization development?

With respect to the first question of development versus performance, there are significant implications and consequences that emerge from this choice. If individual, personal and professional development are proprietary for the person, then it should be made clear that the organization's subsidization of such a process, it is being generous. Although this approach may have payoff for the organization, there is little evidence to support this assumed outcome. So, it can be illuminating and helpful to the individual, and what the organization gains may be a more productive and satisfied employee, but this is not obvious as an outcome. The opposite could also be true.

If the choice is for individual evaluative purposes, then we have an entirely different situation. The system becomes much more of a political process. "You scratch my back and I'll scratch yours." In other words, when how I am rated by my direct reports and my peers (and, of course, my boss, but that's more "normal" than from the other two sources) determines my rewards (pay increase, bonus, promotion, etc.) or the lack thereof, then I will operate differently with others than if the information was for "my eyes only." By operate differently, I mean that, for example, I am not as likely to be as open and forthcoming with others as I might otherwise be. Caution, if not retribution, may prevail.

Regarding the second question, individual versus organization, it really doesn't necessarily have to be versus. If we are attempting, say, a culture change then the multi-rater feedback process can be used for behavioral change objectives and both individual and organizational development purposes (for an example, see the Dime Bancorp case in Chapter 11 of Burke, 2008).

Not long ago I was asked by a former client to come back to help him understand this "360 stuff," as he called it. This individual was an executive vice president in a very large organization reporting directly to the president. He had received his feedback and had been "coached," but he was not satisfied. I did the best I could to help him understand the feedback, the messages he was receiving, which were largely positive incidentally. But he wasn't quite sure what it all meant. I asked him what the purpose of the multi-rater feedback process was. Was it to support a strategic change for the corporation? Was culture change underway? Or was it just for his individual professional and personal objectives? Why was the corporation spending all this money and time with such an endeavor? His reply startled me. He said that as far as he could tell, they were doing this "360 thing" because most of their competitors were doing it. I realized once again how important purpose was. He also told me that the "coaching" he received was a complete waste of time. The coach essentially asked one question, "Was he surprised by any of the ratings?" He replied that there were a few. Then the coach handed him a notebook with an extensive list of training programs and explained that for the "surprises," he should find a program or programs that would match the content of this surprise and attend it (them).

This example illustrates abuse of an approach that has potential for enhancing either or both individual and organizational effectiveness. Even though this coaching example was grossly inept, good, professional coaching can be helpful.

The research about multi-rater feedback shows, in general, that it does not harm individual performance. But does it help? By itself, apparently not. Further research, however, has shown that with effective coaching it can improve individual performance (Luthans & Peterson, 2003; Seifert, Yukl, & McDonald, 2003; Smither, London, Flautt, Vargas, & Klucine, 2003).

Being up-to-date about multi-rater feedback processes is imperative in today's world of management and organizational consulting. Knowing such details as (a) eighty percent of us typically rate ourselves higher than others rate us and (b) that the greater the degree of congruence between self and others' ratings of self, the greater the likelihood will be that the individual being rated is a high performer (see, for example, Church, 1997). Clients in the midst of a multi-rater feedback process will find this kind of information highly relevant and useful.

Develop Expertise in Talent Management

The war for acquiring and holding on to talented organizational members—both in terms of technical, professional expertise, and experienced managers and leaders—is real. The demographic data are clear—there is a growing supply-demand gap. Helping client organizations battle effectively for talent can be extremely beneficial to them. What does having expertise in this domain of consulting mean? There are three primary areas: assessment, selection, and development.

With respect to *assessment*, we need to be aware of useful tools and techniques. In addition to tests and questionnaires that assess technical ability (e.g., computer literacy), there are instruments that measure general mental ability (e.g., the Wonderlic test), cognitive ability (e.g., Watson-Glaser), career preferences (e.g., Strong-Campbell), and a legion of questionnaires that address personal and interpersonal characteristics, two of my favorites being the *Myers Briggs Type Indicator* and the *FIRO-B*. While we do not need to be an expert in the administration and interpretation of these instruments, we do need to know that they exist, the categories of these tools, and the advantages and possible disadvantages of each. One useful source for instruments and their qualities is the book by Goodstein and Prien (2006).

Selection follows from assessment, which essentially means placing the right person regarding skills and abilities in the right position, which means what the job (or project) requires for effective performance (i.e., job-person match). Although there are assessment tools that help to select and place people in the appropriate position, this process is not fool proof. In the end, such placement decisions require judgment, especially about the person's work experience thus far and the degree of political and cultural fit. Even though those of us who serve as external consultants may not be as knowledgeable about the organization's politics and culture as the client, we can provide a certain amount of judgment that may be more independent and objective than the client's judgment and perspective.

Finally, *development*, which involves planned job experiences (job rotation), training and coaching. A common belief is that most learning in the workplace occurs on the job. This belief is no doubt true, but the more random the process the less learning is likely to occur. One does have experiences, but not necessarily a *learning* experience. For learning to happen, reflection is necessary. Planned job experiences can be highly beneficial, that is, creating opportunities for organizational members, particularly those with high potential, to rotate through a variety of work responsibilities and positions so that they can learn a lot about themselves—what they are good at and where they may have some limitations—and learn about the organization's business and its many facets. The "icing" on this cake of learning on the job is training programs and workshop opportunities for:

a. acquiring new skills that the organization needs that it did not need five or ten years ago;
b. learning about new trends technically and in the marketplace; and
c. becoming more socialized in the broader culture of the organization.

Coaching is key to all of the above regarding development because of the need for reflection, that is, linking experience that one has with a thought, an idea or a concept. Without this linkage, learning (e.g., how to use one's experience in a new situation) is not likely to occur. With a coach, one has the opportunity to reflect on—to test one's understanding about—recent experiences and to discuss future possibilities for growth and development.

The three areas—assessment, selection, and development—are not new nor are they mutually exclusive. Sometimes all three should be considered at the same time. What is newer is simply the term, talent management. The notion emerged due to the recognition that talented people have become harder to find, attract, and hire not to mention retain. We consultants can serve as battlefield advisors, strategists, and developers in this war for talent.

Expand Perspective about Executive and Leadership Development

When advising clients about what they need to be doing concerning the development of executives and leaders in their organization, it is important, I think, to be clear about your own perspective and point of view about leadership. With so much to consider (just go to your local bookstore, for example, and look at the volume of books on leadership and management), clients need to have consultants "boil it down" for them. What is important and what is really fluff? Let me suggest just four aspects of leadership that I believe are important for developing a clear point of view.

First, leadership (also important for management but less so) is very much about relationships. No follower, no leader. Leadership is reciprocal. When considering individuals for leader potential, a question to ask is "To what degree does the individual being considered pay attention to and treat people with respect when they are in a follower role as opposed to more of an imperialistic attitude and approach concerning the leader role?"

Second, it seems clear now that people around the world see a sufficient difference between a leader and a manager to warrant serious consideration when choosing and developing individuals for these roles (Bass, 1997). Management is more about position and formal organizational authority, whereas leadership is more about the person with authority being based on trust and how the individual comports him or herself in times of conflict and uncertainty. Development decisions need to be based on this distinction. Management can be taught. It is much more difficult to teach someone how to be a leader. It is much more personal (i.e., how the person understands and uses him or herself) rather than how to accomplish a task or master a function such as marketing or finance.

Third, is leadership more about the person or the situation? It is about both, of course, but are we clear about how much is about personality and how much is about circumstances? The so-called "great man" theory that emerged in the late nineteenth and early twentieth centuries is now considered to have no validity. But the importance of personality has roared back in recent times, that leaders and their personalities indeed make a difference either for good or for bad. This return is based on more sophisticated research and theory about personality than was true a hundred years ago (see, for example, Hogan, 2006).

Fourth, what determines leader effectiveness? What should be measured? Most of the literature on leader effectiveness is based on the behavior of the leader (e.g., whether transformational or transactional, the degree of charisma, amount of attention paid to task accomplishment), in essence getting results as compared with how those results are attained. More recently, however, followers' accomplishments are coming into focus. In other words, perhaps leader effectiveness should be a function of what *followers achieve*, with less attention being paid to what the leader actually does. This consideration should not, of course, be either/or. The important point is that more emphasis should be placed on what followers accomplish as a group, as a team, than has been true in the past.

These four aspects of leadership are ones that I consider important. Although other aspects could have been addressed, for consulting purposes, it is simply a matter of being clear about what we consider paramount when advising a client about leadership and executive development.

SUMMARY

With the rapid, complicated, if not chaotic array of forces from the external environment having immediate and powerful impacts on the way organizations operate today, it is no wonder that decisions need to be made in kind, that is, rapidly and without as much organized and analyzed information as one might want. Management and organization consultants experience more pressure than ever before to respond to clients needs for immediate action and fresh ideas. We are like relief pitchers in the sixth inning with the bases loaded and no outs. Much is expected with little time to deliver. How do we as consultants cope with these kinds of expectations?

Suggestions have been made in this chapter for surviving in our fast-paced world:

- Diagnose in real time—initiate change without having a complete diagnosis and observe carefully how organizational members react to change, as these reactions become the diagnosis.
- Executive coaching—usually conducted "in the moment," which can provide opportunities for follow-up actions that may lead to organization change.
- Have a point of view about....
  - an organizational framework or model;
  - how to bring about cultural change;
  - multirater feedback processes;
  - talent management; and
  - executive and leadership development.

If I have not been sufficiently clear about my bias in writing this chapter, let me conclude with this thought: In today's fast-paced world, consultants must respond more quickly than ever before—and what might help with this need to respond rapidly is knowing how to diagnose "on the run," how to coach in meaningful ways, and having clear points of view that help to explain who we are and how we consult. These approaches have served me well in my own career as a consultant.

REFERENCES

Argyris, C. & Schön, D. (1978). *Organizational learning: A theory of action perspective.* Reading, MA: Addison-Wesley.

Bai, M. (2007). The way we live now. *New York Times Sunday Magazine,* (July 15), 9–10.

Bass, B. M. (1997). Does the transactional-transformational leadership paradigm transcend organizational and national boundaries? *American Psychologist, 52*(2), 130–139.

Bauman, R. P., Jackson, P., & Lawrence, J. T. (1997). *From promise to performance: A journey to transformation at Smith Kline Beecham.* Boston: Harvard Business School Press.

Burke, W. W. (2008). *Organization change: Theory and practice* (2nd ed). Thousand Oaks, CA: Sage Publications.

Burke W. W., & Litwin, G. H. (1992). A causal model of organizational performance and change. *Journal of Management, 18,* 532–545.

Church, A. H. (1997). Managerial self-awareness in high-performing individuals in organizations. *Journal of Applied Psychology, 82,* 281–292.

Goodstein, L. D., & Prien, E. P. (2006). *Using individual assessments in the workplace.* San Francisco: Pfeiffer/Wiley.

Hogan, R. (2006). *Personality and the fate of organizations.* Mahwah, NJ: Erlbaum.

Lewin, K. (1947). Frontiers in group dynamics. *Human Relations, 1*(1), 5–47.

Lewin, K. (1951). *Field theory in social science.* New York: Harper & Row.

Luthans, F., & Peterson, S. J. (2003). 360-degree feedback with systematic coaching: Empirical analysis suggests a winning combination. *Human Resource Management, 42,* 243–256.

Rogers, C. (1951). *Client-centered therapy: Its current practice, implications, and theory.* New York: Houghton Mifflin.

Seifert, C. F., Yukl, G., & McDonald, R. A. (2003). Effects of multisource feedback and a feedback facilitator on the influence behavior of managers toward subordinates. *Journal of Applied Psychology, 88,* 561–569.

Smither, J. W., London, M., Flautt, R., Vargas, Y., & Kucine, I. (2003). Can working with an executive coach improve multisource feedback ratings over time? A quasi-experimental field study. *Personnel Psychology, 56,* 23–44.

CHAPTER 12

INTO THE RABBIT HOLE

Variation on Traditional Approaches to Diagnosis and Discovery

Dale Ainsworth

The rabbit hole went straight on like a tunnel for some way, and then dipped suddenly down, so suddenly that Alice had not a moment to think about stopping herself before she found herself falling down what seemed to be a very deep well.
—*from* Alice in Wonderland[1]

The most famous of rabbit holes is, of course, the one used by Alice when entering the alternate reality referred to as *Wonderland*. As a metaphor, *entering the rabbit hole* has come to mean a number of things, but is frequently used when referring to a shift in one's immediate environment—a shift so substantial that one's concept of reality is challenged or even changed. In the world of consulting, I have often heard the term used to describe a situation where the consultant unwittingly gets pulled into the client's system and loses objectivity, also widely known as getting "hooked." Both refer to a situation where consultants become so immersed in the client's system and reality they can no longer observe the system from an outsider's point-of-view. This results in the consultant becoming just another character in the organizational drama.

Consultation for Organizational Change. pages 247–268
Copyright © 2010 by Information Age Publishing
All rights of reproduction in any form reserved.

Being pulled into the drama, however, is not always so bad. O'Neill (2007) writes about getting hooked as one of the possible perils of executive coaching. In these instances, she recommends the coach, when able and aware of their plight, stay in the system for a bit and get a bird's eye view of the forces and dynamics the client is encountering—to actually stay in the rabbit hole for a while and look around. It's a subtle shift of perspective with hefty consequences. No longer is the coach outside looking in, but inside looking around. These perspectives, argues O'Neill, offer rich insights for both coach and client that can be gained *in no other way*. Although O'Neill was speaking about coaching, it does not require a leap of faith to apply this approach to consulting for organizational change. Rather, I argue that there are times in the consulting relationship when this approach is most appropriate in gaining unique and insightful perspectives that will bring added benefits to the clients we serve.

In this chapter, I make a case that there are times when it is most appropriate to jump into the rabbit hole—to enter the system and allow it to carry you off as a consultant, to let yourself get swept up in the drama we find in the world of our clients. Then, just as Alice ultimately did, emerge from the rabbit hole and use the experiences and knowledge gained to tell your client a more comprehensive story. This experiential approach as a means to gain insight is a common approach used countless times in everyday life to gain or deepen perspective.

The chapter examines three distinct helping roles that use such immersion as a means to deepen understanding. Two of these come from the research tradition—the cultural anthropologist or ethnographer, and the heuristic researcher. The last is brought to us by the ancients—a practice found around the world, and dating back to our hunter/gatherer history as a species—the shaman. These approaches to gaining knowledge and insight will be modeled toward the management consultant focused on organizational change. As the chapter will illustrate, there are times when this immersion approach is most suitable as a valid diagnostic methodology. Using a case study to illustrate this approach, the discussion will draw out the implications and key learnings from these experiences. Finally, I will show that through the use of the immersion method, consultants themselves are transformed along with the systems in which they work. This builds on the "self-as-instrument" paradigm to include a "self-as-transformed" perspective.

CONSULTING MODELS AND THE DIAGNOSTIC PHASE

"I think I could, if I only knew how to begin."
—Alice

Many of the generally accepted consulting models articulate a phased approach to the consulting engagement or relationship (Block, 2000; Burke, 2002; Cummings & Worley, 2001; Schein, 1999). Though not an exact science, these models put forth a linear, sequential approach to the consulting relationship. The argument is that one phase must be considerably (not totally) and adequately completed before the next phase can begin. Hence one starts with entry and contracting, moves to diagnosis and discovery, then on to analysis/feedback followed by intervention. These stages are followed by an evaluation phase. Each phase is constantly informing the orientation of both previous and subsequent phases. For example, a finding that occurred during analysis and feedback could highlight an oversight in diagnosis, and one might return to the discovery phase for additional information. Moreover, during diagnosis one might uncover information or facts that lead to amending the original contract, and so on. In the end, if all goes well, changes are institutionalized into the organization and we are off to our next engagement. The basic model is illustrated in Figure 12.1.

These models also suggest that each phase must be done suitably in order for the project to functionally proceed. If one phase is not completed, or is finished insufficiently or improperly, each subsequent phase is jeopardized as the omission, error, or oversight is carried through the remainder of the project. This notion is similar to child development models, which argue that each phase of human development must be brought to some level of fruition before subsequent phases can be undertaken (Berk, 2000). If not, the incompleteness of an early phase pervades each of those that follow and the child becomes an ill-formed and dysfunctional adult. One could argue that constructing a structure offers a similar metaphor—any structure, not matter how soundly and beautifully assembled, is imperfect if it sits on a faulty foundation.

Although this discussion suggests that each phase is equally important, I admit to a considerable bias that the diagnostic or discovery phase is by far the more important. This bias is born out of experiences and beliefs, which hold that problem identification and articulation constitute the bulk of problem-solving work. Once one can clearly see an issue, we can then clearly articulate it—and then crafting solutions becomes much easier. If

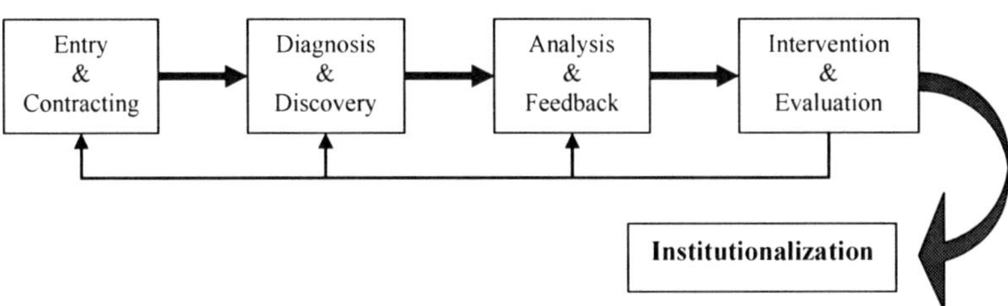

FIGURE 12.1. Basic Model of a Phased View of the Consulting Relationship

the core issues behind any problem are not clearly understood, this vagueness creeps into all solutions. Thus, ill-defined problems often end up with ill-defined, reactive solutions. Worse, well-designed interventions could be applied to poorly-understood problems. This may partially explain why the vast majority of consulting interventions do not accomplish their intended results (Cummings & Worley, 2001). Maybe we have applied well-thought out solutions to problems that are not fully comprehended or understood.

THE CONSULTANT AND THE RESEARCH TRADITION

"Oh, you foolish Alice!" she answered herself.
"How can you learn lessons in here?"

Organizational and management consultants are social scientists, looking to understand, describe, and explain the worlds our clients invite us to enter with the idea that we can help them through an issue, or illuminate a path toward wholeness and increased effectiveness. We are grounded in many traditional research methodologies, and many of these call for researcher objectivity. This idea of objectiveness or separateness from the object or thing we are evaluating or examining often permeates our ideas of how to conduct a proper inquiry or diagnosis—we believe we must be "outside" of something to objectively know or understand it. Braud and Anderson (1998, p. 5), in describing this conventional view of research, comment:

> A researcher's ideal stance is to be neutral, uninvolved, and as distant as possible with respect to what is being studied. Because researchers' qualities are irrelevant to their objective observations, researchers may be interchanged. Virtually identical findings are expected from all researchers who repeat the research procedures, provided they are appropriately skilled and have been properly trained.

As consultants we are trained to stay objective and avoid getting "hooked." Moreover, we consider it a lapse when we do, and feel as if we are deficient in our roles as helping agents. This obsession with objectivity, of staying on the outside while looking in, is in part due to the early research practices in which much of our work is grounded. Many of these earlier traditions, and those that carry them forward, are reticent to embrace a mindset beyond that of the physical sciences view of how the world works—a place where reductionism and objectivity rule the day.

This illusion of, and debate around, objectivity abounds in the world of research, and speaks directly to many consultants that frequently engage in social and action research. Two distinct camps stand in contrast to each other—the older modernistic or positivistic paradigm and the more recent post-modernistic, naturalist point of view. Creswell (1994) labels these the *quantitative* and *qualitative* paradigms, respectively. The positivistic view says that universal laws can be uncovered in each nook and cranny of life; that real things are visible and tangible (thus the invisible and intangible are unreal); and that we can and should reduce something down to its smallest of units to better understand it (and control it). The post-modern view stands at the other end of the spectrum and suggests that there are no universal, irrefutable laws—existence is contextual and what law applies in one domain will not necessarily apply in another; that the unseen is as real as the apparent (and often more influential); and that when something is torn down the essence of its meaning is lost. Post-modern, qualitative-oriented researchers thus call for the opposite of researcher objectivity, noting that it is never possible for one to be objective in the first place.

This humanistic perspective on epistemology declares that researchers cannot remove themselves and their experiences from the process of inquiry. Bentz and Shapiro (1998, p. 4) say it this way: "We believe that the person is always the center of the process of inquiry—that you will always be at the center of your own research, which in turn will always be part of you." Here, researchers immerse themselves into their inquiries in order to fully experience, internalize, and understand the phenomenon they are investigating.

Which of these perspectives or paradigms is more correct? Which is the most effective approach? As in all situations, it depends, and wise researchers choose methods of inquiry that are more effective in illuminating their paths toward deepened understanding of the phenomenon they are investigating. What all researchers seem to agree on is that the research question—the essence of what one is seeking to understand and explain—should determine the approach one takes. Chatman and Flynn (2005) argue that the rationale of which approach to use works like this: Early in the life of a theory, when conceptual models and hypotheses are just being developed and phenomena are not understood, more qualitative approaches are used. These are the equivalent to the early explorers that headed out into the wilderness to follow a river, to find a mountain pass, or to see what lay beyond the next horizon, never sure where exactly they were going the next day, or what they would find around the next bend. As a theory matures and becomes more robust, more experimentally-oriented methods from the quantitative paradigm are thought to be best. This is more akin to a mapping team creating a precise, detailed rendition of that terrain the early explorers traversed. Said another way, the less we know about a phenomenon, the more open-ended our research approach following the qualitative paradigm. We ask a lot of questions and follow the energy of the moment, remaining open to any and everything that may inform our search. Alternatively, the more we know about a topic, the more deliberate

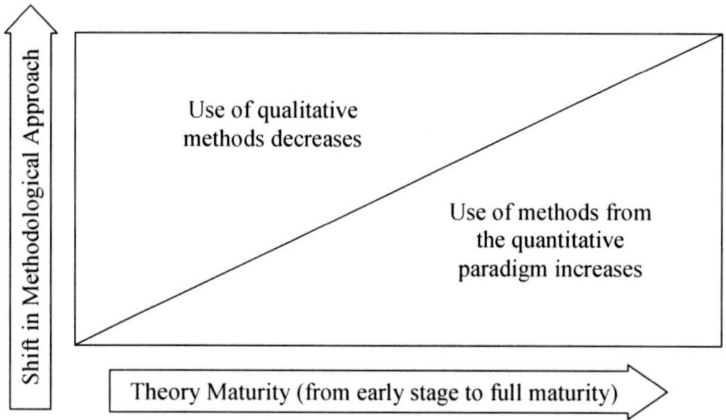

FIGURE 12.2. Relationship between Maturity of Theory and Method

and focused our inquiry is, often exploring a small corner of the larger theory that we are examining, trying to uncover causality while isolating and manipulating variables and control for outside influences. Conceptually this movement or evolution from one type of inquiry to another over the life of a theory can be seen in Figure 12.2.

How can we apply these principles from the world of research to our trade? What does this mean for consultants working with organizations? Wearing our social scientist research hat, it means that during diagnosis and discovery, different approaches are better suited for different situations. It means that sometimes objectivity is called for, but only when most appropriate. It means that there are times when subjectivity is needed, even required, like trusting one's intuition, following hunches and instincts, and even plunging head-first into the system we are observing. The more defined an issue—say a dysfunctional team in a larger, functional unit—a more structured approach is probably best. However, when the situation is ill-defined, a more qualitative approach to diagnosis is more suited. One such approach might include immersing oneself into the client's system to get a first-hand view of what's going on "behind the scenes." This tactic, in essence, reflects leaving the reality of our world and jumping into the rabbit hole to get first-hand experience in the systems in which our clients live and work.

Traditional data collection tools at the disposal of the consultant are generally thought to include questionnaires, interviews, observations, and "unobtrusive" measures or secondary sources like company records and archives (Block, 2000; Cummings & Worley, 2001). Through the use of these tools we extract raw data from the systems we are observing. We collect these data and reduce them into meaningful patterns of knowledge, packaging them into bundles of orderly, logical facts and presenting them to our clients during the feedback phase. These analyses become the critical and important stakes in the ground around which we build everything that follows. There are, however, other techniques for data collection that are not so readily articulated in the consulting literature—but are no less valid. One could consider these less traditional approaches to data collection that occurs during diagnosis. In the right situation, these approaches are often more effective than the traditional, "go-to" ones. What are these? One can turn to the research traditions of anthropology and heuristics, and the practice of Shamanism, to explore and understand these different approaches to diagnosis.

The Ethnographer, Heuristic Researcher, and the Shaman

Ethnographers, heuristic researchers, and shamans share several commonalities. Each is keenly interested in deepening understanding of a particular phenomenon, a culture, an experience, or group of people. Each immerses themselves directly into their topic of interest to obtain experiential information. Finally, each reports their findings in the first person—as one who has been there, one who knows first hand.

Each of their perspectives is unique, yet all share the element of gaining knowledge about a particular phenomenon experientially. Consider the shift that transformed the discipline of anthropology over a century ago. The early cultural anthropologists were at one time solely reliant on second-hand accounts of the societies they studied. They relied on information supplied to them by others who had visited the societies. Imagine the depth of knowledge and resulting shifts these first scientists experienced when field research by immersion became the norm. Second-hand reporting (e.g., surveys, interviews, company documents), the sort that we consultants often rely on in making our diagnosis, often lacks the context and perspective that fully conveys the depth and richness of the lived experience. It is no different than reading about a place compared to visiting it in person, for all experience is contextual; that is, one's experience is embedded in the totality of existence. When one is immersed in the totality of existence, one can go beyond the spoken or written word, and one can experience the context in which these are set. One can feel, smell, hear, taste, and see, in addition to cognitive, imaginative, and interpretive exploration. Listen to the words of Weber (1986, p. 68) in discussing the unfolding dynamics that occur during a one-on-one interview that illuminate this "contextualness" of existence:

> We cannot and should not be unaffected by what is said…On the contrary, it is only in relating to the other as one human being to another that interview-

> ing is really possible...when the interviewer and the participant are caught up in the phenomenon being discussed.

This experiential element brings a depth to the information we consultants use to draw conclusions and craft interventions. This added depth, or breadth of information, may be the difference in crafting solutions that work versus those that miss the mark.

Ethnography and the Consultant

What does diagnosis and discovery look like from the lens of ethnography? What might change agents and consultants take from this research tradition that could help in the discovery process, especially when dealing with complex, multi-layered, and ill-defined phenomena? Most know something of the anthropologist, and some are familiar with cultural anthropology. Ethnography can be considered an approach or technique to understanding a particular human society used by cultural anthropologists. It is "a description and interpretation of the culture and social structure of a social group" (Robson, 2002, p. 186). It is an approach that requires complete immersion into the everyday life of the people who are the subject of the study, often for extensive periods of time. There are stories of cultural anthropologists "going native" and fully joining the communities in which they live. It is also an approach to inquiry that produces what Geertz (1973) calls a "thick description."

As noted earlier, it was not always this way. Early anthropologists often relied on second-hand reports from travelers, missionaries, and colonial administrators for information on their subjects. However, in the early 20th century, anthropologists began staying in the field for prolonged periods of time. While doing so, they realized that the data gathered from this method held a uniquely personal element to it—one that enhanced the richness and deepened the understanding of the anthropologist, that transformed the scientist through participation in the culture. This level of knowing stands in contrast to that gained by second hand accounts. The famous anthropologists and ethnographers, Margaret Mead and Ruth Bunzel (1960, p. 3), spoke of this contrasting point-of-view when writing about anthropology's perspective on the colonization of Native Americans:

> Humanitarians lament the spectacle of the reservation Indian, riddled with tuberculosis, eking out a miserable existence on grudging federal rations, debauched or apathetic, withdrawing further from—rather than becoming more adjusted to—white civilization. This spectacle was far more vivid to anthropologists than to casual humanitarians who were concerned with Indian rights and had a sentimental view of Indian ceremonial. For anthropologists realized just how dependent Indian cultures had been on the balance between men and land, weapons and quarry, sun and rain and corn, and they

> recognized that in the meeting of two cultural systems so contrasting in technology and point of view, the Indian cultures had no chance of survival.

An important characteristic of ethnography is its production of data free from imposed external constraints and ideas (Robson, 2002). Said another way, there are no preconceptions at work in the ethnographer that guide their inquiry; hence they seek to produce descriptions of a culture from an insider's view. This, of course, flies in the face of conventional consulting wisdom that argues for the use of existing diagnostic models to guide one's inquiry during the discovery phase. However, the over-reliance on existing diagnostic models may pressure one to search "only where the light is good."

Heuristic Research and the Consultant

While ethnography is aimed at understanding the social structure of a group, heuristic research is pointed toward gaining insight into the perspectives of the individual. As an approach to research within the qualitative tradition of phenomenology, heuristic research is characterized by the researcher's personal immersion into the topic or phenomenon of interest. It seeks to describe one's lived experience. For example, in a path-breaking study into the nature of loneliness, Moustakas (2001) threw himself into the topic by studying his own loneliness. In his self report on the journey he articulates, "I found loneliness everywhere in my waking life...I walked the streets at night and noticed especially isolated stars, clouds, trees, and flowers." When commenting on his approach to the study of his topic, he says, "Loneliness, for a while, was the mainstream of my life and colored everything else or influenced the meaning of everything else." An important part of this research is the ability to approach a topic from a fresh perspective. Creswell (2007, p. 60) speaks of *transcendental* phenomenology as a method in which the researcher sets aside his or her views and beliefs about the phenomenon being examined and seeks to perceive it "as if for the first time." Like ethnography, heuristic research is intended to produce a description rather than an analysis or explanation.

Of all the research traditions, the heuristic method and approach is arguably most aligned to the concept of "self-as-instrument," an important value of the consulting profession. Self-as-instrument entails self knowledge, awareness, regulation, and development. In the words of Moustakas (2001, p. 263):

> From the beginning and throughout an investigation, heuristic research involves self-search, self-dialog, and self-discovery. The research question and methodology flow out of inner awareness, meaning, and inspiration...When I consider an issue, a problem, or a question, I enter into it fully...I search introspectively, meditatively, and reflectively into its nature and meaning...I

> begin the heuristic investigation with my own self-awareness, and explicate that awareness with reference to a question or problem until an essential insight is achieved, one that will throw a beginning light on a critical human experience.

Heuristic studies have included deeply personal topics like growing up in a single-parent home, the experience of feeling unconditional love, of being shy or sensitive, and being of a certain racial heritage.

Interestingly, other than the works of David Whyte (2001), there appears to be no heuristic studies published in the organizational sciences literature. Here research seems to support (or reflect) the chasm that exists between the study of organizations in an impersonal, dispassionate, modernistic manner, and examining these from the views of the emoting, frail, faulted, yet glorious and magnificent beings that comprise these systems—humans. And how better than heuristic exploration to delve into important diagnostic questions such as "What is it like to work for this organization?" and "Why do our employees quit so often?" or "Why hasn't the workforce embraced our new vision?" There is much to be learned from examining an issue from the individual's perspective.

How can explorations at the individual level be used to explore phenomenon occurring at the group or organization level? In discussing various systems models in his book *Rethinking the Fifth Discipline* (1999), Flood may offer insight into this question. In his work, he describes the principle of *recursion.* This is the idea that the whole can be found in each of the parts. If this principle applies to any system, as Flood argues, then couldn't we infer the nature of the overall system by understanding what it is like to be a part, be it an employee or member of a group? And what better way to gain this perspective than to become an employee or group member?

Shamanism and the Consultant

"A shaman is a man or woman that enters an altered state of consciousness—at will—to contact and utilize an ordinarily hidden reality in order to acquire knowledge, power, and to help other persons" (Harner, 1990, p. 20). I remember the first time I read this sentence in anthropologist Michael Harner's (1990) classical work *The Way of the Shaman.* It was several years ago as I was just entering consulting practice. The definition resonated with me to my core, for it seemed to grasp the essence of how I wanted to practice our craft as consultants. I read it again and again, and to this day often think of this perspective when working with clients. In shamanic practice, shamans consciously and intentionally move into alternate realities or worlds to gain knowledge. While in these "non-ordinary" realities, they make contact and communicate with other entities and beings. They gather important information from the ordinarily "hidden" realities in order to acquire knowledge to help the sick and afflicted restore health. The shaman then returns to "ordinary" reality and uses the gathered information to prescribe healing and a return to wholeness. With each journey, the shaman enters into a Shamanic State of Consciousness (SSC). This is not always a trance of sorts—no lying unconsciously on the floor in convulsions. Rather, this is a deliberate shift in perception to see what others cannot. In each encounter, the shaman is changed by the knowledge and insight gained.

Arthur Colman is a clinical professor in the Department of Psychiatry at UC San Francisco and an accomplished group relations theorist, author, and consultant. In his consulting work he often refers to the shamanic paradigm as a means to affect change in small groups. It is not hard to generalize his approach to the organization level. He describes the consultant entering the reality of the client and becoming a part of the consciousness of the group, "retaining only enough individual observing ego to be able to give words to the emotions, images, and myths of that collective experience" (Colman, 1995, p. xvii). To describe this powerful and often fearful journey of immersion, he evokes the imagery of crossing a fog-covered river in a small boat, "unable to see the other side, yet moving in faith that it exists…of moving forward in the face of fear and anxiety of not knowing if a way home will be found." He contends that those of us who serve our clients in the spirit of helping will face these fears, and in doing so, become transformed by our experiences. As he notes, "In the healing of others, you too will heal. If the journey is worth taking, you too will change. No one who has really crossed over ever returns the same."

PRINCIPLES AND PRACTICE OF IMMERSION

In another moment down went Alice
after[the rabbit], never once considering
how in the world she was to get out again.

There are certain attributes and characteristics needed for those who journey to the other side, or plunge headfirst into the rabbit hole. There are the dangers of getting forever lost or "going native" while visiting these alternate realities. And, who knows what type characters and challenges one might encounter while immersed in the client's system? There are techniques one can use, as Colman (1995) suggested, to retain "only enough individual observing ego to be able to give words to the emotions, images, and myths of that collective experience," and afterward emerge from this altered state of consciousness to return to ordinary reality. Like the shaman who moves into alternate realities and returns, consultants must be able to transition into and out of the systems we are examining. Keeping one foot in this reality, while letting go of self enough to enter another, requires skills.

The concept of "marginality" has been discussed as a trait or characteristic found in successful consultants (Brown & Cotton, 1975; Cummings & Worley, 2001). Consultants that exhibit this trait are those who can effectively "straddle" or traverse the boundaries of two different worlds—say the world experienced by leaders and that experienced by front-line employees in the same organization; or the reality encountered by administrative personnel in a large healthcare system versus a patient of one of their hospitals. In doing so, one has to have a great deal of tolerance for the wear and tear brought on by the emotional roller-coaster one is destined to ride for life. It can be taxing to be the type that watches movies and constantly finds empathy for both the pro- and antagonist; or watches a soccer game and cannot choose a side, even to the end. In finding empathy and understanding for all of the players in the systems into which we are immersed, we often begin to feel groundless and uncertain, washed over in shades of grey, unsure of right or wrong, and unable to distinguish mediocrity from greatness. In the end we run the risk of immobilization, sunk in the mire of neutrality.

In the marginal role one must possess a tolerance for ambiguity and the ability to "sit quietly with the question" while the forces of organizational life slowly reveal themselves. The state of dissonance and uncertainty is intensely uncomfortable for our species, and, considered an adaptive trait, it is a natural tendency for many living beings to resolve questions and puzzles with great haste (Inglis, 2000). But staying in the system requires patience while we allow the organizational dramas to play out each of their scenes, up until the last act. This difficulty is compounded by clients who often begin to question our competence when we respond to their "what's next" questions with "I don't know" or "I'm not sure where this is going at present." Here, client relationships are put to the test.

Ambiguity and the tension it generates have a role in the creative process. Pritzker (1999) demonstrates a parallel between Zen training and creativity by showing how Rinzai Zen students are trained to reach transcendental states. Each student is given a challenging puzzle to meditate on. They sit for hours in a state of dissonance, unable to resolve these complex riddles. Eventually, after sitting in these intense states of ambiguity for prolonged periods of time a satiation effect occurs and their perceptions of reality dissolve, or melt away, and this opens up the possibility for new ways of seeing the world. Balancing on the edge of being overwhelmed by uncertainty has also been linked to the well-known state of *flow*, sometimes referred to as "being in the zone." Here, when one's competence and skill is matched with an off-setting challenge to the point where an outcome becomes uncertain, the psychological experience can become transcendental (Csikszentmihalyi, 1990).

One has to be adept at living not only in the question, but in the fact that it will seldom be answered, if ever at all; that the answers we do get we recognize to be temporal; that "institutionalizing change" is an oxymoron; and that our intuition and transcendental side is as reliable, trustworthy, and durable as our cognitive rational selves. It is easy to say this, but it is difficult to prevail in a debate with your client, or worse, your boss, using the "trust me, my gut is telling me this is right" argument, when there are no rational signs that you are. Organizational life is one rigidly dedicated to rationality. It professes to worship objectivity, and values the suppression of "silly things" like emotions. As consultants, going into these systems with our hearts in our hands is not only dangerous—it is downright foolish. Knowing how to translate the words of the spirit into business speak requires some thought, skill, and a lot of effort.

Immersion requires one going out and becoming a part of the system. Many times this requires us to be with employees, customers, and other organizational stakeholders. Like the anthropologist conducting research by living among other cultures, one must leave the comforts of the office, and be with and around different people. This, of course, speaks to the essentialness of cultural competence. Entering a different culture, be it on the other side of the world or company cafeteria, can be daunting. One must relish these immersion experiences and not get overwhelmed and fearful of them. Fear can cause one to close down and go into survival mode. This is the opposite of being in the moment and taking in the fullness of an experience.

Trust in one's intuition as a navigation tool is an essential skill for immersion. Following the energy of the moment requires sudden, unplanned turns. While good diagnostic models inform one's basic orientation to the systems we study, they can also constrain. Like many roadmaps, these models we use often do not show all the little streets and trails we so often encounter while in the rabbit hole, and a good sense of direction is a must.

Staying grounded while in the system is important, and grounding or anchoring techniques abound. A passion for self-development is always a requirement. Equally important is having a network of colleagues with whom you can discuss your immersion journeys, especially when they have a basic understanding of your engagement, and are willing to ask probing questions that help ground you. I liken this approach to tying a rope around your waste before you descend into the rabbit hole, while handing the other end to a trusted colleague. At any time either of you can jerk the rope signaling the other to start pulling or climbing. This may be a simple as having coffee with a colleague weekly while immersed in a system and talking through your experiences, allowing your colleague to challenge and question your thoughts and interpretations of your experiences. Likewise, interval or regular reporting to the primary client is helpful. It causes you to emerge, to come up for air, reflecting on what you have found and consider where you think things are heading. This reflection is a technique that seems to lessen the natural pull of the system.

Last, and most importantly, one must have a willingness to undergo growth and transformation, which is often painful, uncomfortable, exposing, and unpleasant. Shaking up our mental models and constructs creates cognitive dissonance at a number of levels, and one must be committed to life-long learning. But learning is never easy. Building massive structures or bodies of knowledge takes time and effort, and we become rather protective over our creations. When they are challenged we often resist these remodeling opportunities.

Having discussed the general idea of immersion as a diagnostic method, some situations to which this approach is suited, and characteristics of those who engage in this approach, we now apply these principles in a case study. The case that follows is one that I experienced as a consultant several years ago. Of course I have changed all the distinguishing characteristics of the organization and the industry in which it functions in an effort to preserve my client's privacy. The experiences as articulated, however, are based on an actual engagement.

A CASE IN POINT

I almost wish I hadn't gone down that rabbit hole; and yet—and yet—it's rather curious you know, this sort of life!

My first inkling that I was in the rabbit hole came to me while sitting in a portable toilet on a cold, rainy, windy afternoon in Northern Arizona. Something I had eaten for lunch from the "roach coach" that stopped by the jobsite earlier had my stomach in knots. Waves of cramps cascaded through my body. I was longing for the warmth of my cozy office while shivering in the cold. As I sat hunched over hugging my stomach, the words spontaneously erupted from my mouth, "what in the hell am I doing here?" I was working as a junior member of a crew of six on a construction site. We were in the process of installing an elaborate petroleum storage system. As a part of my consulting arrangement, I had convinced my client that I needed to work in the field *as an employee.* From this perspective, I reasoned, I could better arrive at an accurate diagnosis of key issues we needed to address in our intervention.

Entry and Contracting

The engagement was with a new owner of a medium-sized (over $10M in annual revenue) commercial construction company that had been around for over four decades. With just under 30 full-time employees, the majority of these individuals were non-exempt (paid by the hour), non-union, highly trained, and specialized workers. The average tenure of the workforce was nearly a decade. In early contracting conversations, the new president/owner simply told me, "Things are so broke I don't know where to start." The company was on the brink of financial collapse when my client purchased the majority share from its founder and his daughter. Beyond the obvious financial woes (the presenting problem and symptom), the causes of the firm's failings were not evident. The industry in which it functioned was booming; the company's competitors were busy and allegedly profitable; and the barriers to entry from new competitors were extremely high. These helped to maintain a healthy book of future contracts for the firm. Further, the state in which the firm operated had legislated new laws requiring massive upgrades across the industry, and this firm was one of a few with the proper licensing, certifications, and highly-skilled employees who could perform the delicate upgrades. The future, therefore, looked very rosy.

On paper, the firm should have been thriving. The client and his several competitors in the area worked for a cluster of less than a dozen customers, who were themselves competitors of each other. All projects were competitively bid, and all projects were awarded to the lowest bidder. Further, all competitive bids were known to all bidders, so everyone knew the basic cost structures of everyone else. Everyone purchased materials from the same few specialty vendors, and all paid the same prices for the same parts and supplies. Labor costs across the industry were also similar. In other words, no one had an apparent advantage over their competitors. Within this small, close-knit segment of industry, everyone appeared to run profitable companies—everyone but my client. For him, projects routinely ran over schedules and budgets; employees seemed disengaged and overly protective of their reputations and perceived performance; customer relations were hostile; and everyone constantly worked at a frantic pace as if bailing water out of a sinking boat.

The mandate by the owner was simply to "help me fix things"—not exactly the clarity of objectives one would hope for. To make matters worse, we had an existing relationship. We had worked together several years earlier in a large corporation, and we had a high degree of trust and respect for one another. I was flattered that he called me to help, but also felt an enormous amount of pressure to perform. Of course, this clouded my judgment and permeated my contracting discussions. I didn't feel I could say "no," nor demand the clarity of objectives I desperately wanted. Additionally, I had only one other engagement that was about to conclude, so my financial need was also a consideration. I thought the best I could do was to contract with him to help sort things out—to help him figure out why he was losing money. I found comfort in the wisdom of Schein (1999, p. 5) who noted:

> In my experience, however, the person seeking help often does not know what she is looking for and indeed should not really be expected to know. All she knows is that something is not working right or some ideal is not being met, and that some kind of help is therefore needed.

In the end, we contracted through the analysis and feedback phase, which included diagnosis, with the option to continue with intervention and evaluation if we both agreed. I drew up a contract, created a project plan, timeline, and budget, submitted my first invoice, and we were off.

Diagnosis and Discovery

I have always thought diagnosis starts with a blend of the obvious and the intuitive. So, early into the engagement I decided to trust my instincts on a few key items. It was obvious there were efficiency issues in the organization's core activity—operations. What wasn't obvious is why these existed in our firm and not in others. What made us unique? What were we doing, or not doing, that competitors were or were not? In such a highly-structured, rigid environment, where everyone's basic organizational DNA looked the same, I reasoned that these differences had to be subtle. I became convinced that I needed to more fully understand what it was like to work for the organization, and in the industry, to pick up on these subtleties. I was confident that by working along side workers at all levels of the organization I could, like an anthropologist, gain a perspective that I simply could not get conducting surveys and interviews in the company's headquarters.

Not that I didn't try this traditional approach early on. I administered an employee survey, talked with key employees, and conducted extensive management, vendor, subcontractor, and client interviews. I learned, but knew that I had only scratched the surface of what was happening in front of my eyes. The employee survey had revealed little, and even provided the contradictory evidence that all was rosy in this downward spiraling organization. Vendors and clients had both praise and criticism for the firm, but nothing revealing. Management interviews were uncomfortable, deliberate endeavors where I got short, non-descriptive, succinct answers to open-ended questions. I thought that people were hiding things. After all, this was an industry not accustomed to consultants poking around and asking questions.

In a casual conversation with a key subcontractor who had worked with the firm for decades, I had the proverbial breakthrough moment that led me to believe that immersion was necessary. We were speaking about the firm's financial woes (a widely-known fact), and he blurted out, "well, they've been losing money for 40 years and it hasn't slowed us down yet." I half-heartedly asked if he were serious, after all no organization can sustain itself for decades with consistent losses. "Yeah," he replied, "they tell us what they want us to hear, trying to get us to work harder and cheaper. They pocket all the profit while we barely get by."

As soon as I could, I found time with my client to discuss the flow of performance information in and through the organization. I wanted to know how the company's performance (including financial) was communicated to the workforce in general, if at all. I found out that job supervisors, the point-person on any job-site, received weekly reports that indicated up-to-date performance on the job for which they were responsible. These tidy reports told most of story—performance relative to financial budgets and schedule (excluded were quality indicators, as this feedback came directly from clients). These reports did indeed tell an accurate story. Each and every week job supervisors reviewed the report, and each week they often saw mounting financial losses and project timelines that extended beyond established milestones and deadlines.

The question was: what effect did these reports have on performance? If theory held, then supervisors and workers, once aware of sub-standard operations through feedback mechanisms (like the weekly report), would alter their behavior and practice in order to improve overall performance to meet basic standards. Why did this not seem to be the case? What forces were holding this system in its dysfunctional state? Did the workforce simply not care? Were the reports not taken seriously? Was the apparent apathy based in ill-will toward the company, the former or new owner? Of course I questioned job-site supervisors about their views and perspectives on the information presented in the report. Although they complained that it was too complicated to have a lot of meaning, for the most part they admitted that they understood the basic measurements it communicated. When questioning the impact this information had on their views of their performance, I was offered ambivalent responses, excuses, questions of the report's validity, and a host of other reasons why the information was meaningless, unreliable, and otherwise a nuisance.

Going Native

Determined to get to the bottom of things, I joined a crew of workers as the junior-most member of the team. In essence this meant I operated cleaning equipment like brooms and vacuum cleaners, hauled heavy construction materials to and from storage, dug trenches with shovels, and anything I was told to do by virtually anyone on the job site. Work schedules began at sunrise, which meant a sudden shift to my established sleep pattern. Food availability was limited as we often worked in remote, isolated locations, so my diet shifted as well. Safety requirements had me wearing synthetic attire that I was unaccustomed to and found cumbersome and uncomfortable. During my first week as a crew member I became increasingly sore from using muscles I hadn't used in years. During week two I fell in a trench and gashed open my leg, (which I hid from everyone due to peer pressure). I had splinters, blisters, and cuts on my hands and arms. Fortunately, I had always maintained a fairly fit condition and this, along with the enormous pressure I felt to succeed and not succumb to the physical demands of the work, saw me through the initial shock of adaptation. I was also the brunt of every joke and prank one could imagine, but I took these in stride. Through it all, and after several weeks, I began to find some level of rapport with the crew of which I was a part.

More than anything, I learned. I learned what it was like to not only work for the company, but to work in the industry. During slow times, lunches, and occasional breaks, through genuine and honest interaction, I learned what life was like on the wages the company paid. I saw and heard of the lifestyles of these employees, the cars they drove, where they lived and played, and how they spent their spare time. I found that many of the workers were on their way to somewhere else—that they viewed this hard life as temporary and transient, and a means to stay afloat while looking for better and easier work. I learned a great deal about the industry overall.

One day, a temporary employee and I were assigned to scoop gravel into the bottom of an endlessly long trench, a task that took us most of the day. The employee had worked in the industry for years, and we talked non-stop to break up the boredom of the mundane task. He talked of working for competitors over the years and the distinctiveness between each company; how each differed in wages paid, work practice, management style, and orientation toward customers (some more friendly than others). He talked of how different companies interacted with their respective workforces, and his take on the pros and cons of each. He also gave me a unique perspective on our firm, the oldest in the industry. The company was considered old, inflexible, set in its ways, and conceited—virtually a clique. Only friends and relatives were eligible for hire when a job became available, which was seldom. We were, in essence, the old country-club set behind a gated entrance, where old men in blue blazers sat and smoked cigars, drank brandy, and talked for hours at a time.

I began to ask around about the weekly report, how each worker got feedback on his or her performance, and if any had a sense of how the company was performing overall. Some mentioned the update report the job supervisor received weekly, however, most did not. I also poked around about the crew's perspectives and views on the company's plight. What I found was what I was ultimately looking for. In essence, the workforce maintained a mercenary orientation toward the organization. Performance of the organization was viewed as secondary to the workforce's stability of income, not as contingent upon it. This was largely due to the perception of job availability beyond that offered by the company. Further, organizational performance as articulated in the weekly report was considered flawed, unreliable, and inaccurate—a report "made by folks in the home office to tell us what they want us to hear." This also illuminated an inherent suspicion I found that ran throughout this industry, as in many: management simply cannot and should not be trusted.

Climbing Out

I stayed immersed as a part of this crew for nearly a month. Honestly, I was elated to climb out of the rabbit hole, and wasn't sure I could have stayed in much longer. It felt good to wear my clothes again, and to sleep past 4:00 a.m. in the morning. Eventually my digestive system got back on track as well. During my immersion, I had maintained a good relationship with a colleague, and we had often discussed my experiences. Further, I had maintained a weekly meeting with my client to discuss my findings. Between these two, over the course of the immersion I had developed a good idea of what I had come across, and did not require much further analysis to make sense of everything.

I believe I discovered a depth of understanding of this firm and what it was like to be a part of it that could not be obtained in any way apart from this approach. No survey, interview, or observation could have produced the breadth of knowledge I developed about this system. In the words of Geertz (1973), I found a "thickness" of contextual factors that I would have never witnessed if I had not ventured into the rabbit hole.

I consolidated my findings into a very short report and delivered it to my client (along with a well-deserved invoice). We had already begun to discuss findings during our weekly visits, and now we continued to try to make more meaning of all this data that sat in front of us. We naturally began to craft and design interventions. Before I knew it, I had agreed to proceed into this phase of the consulting relationship, which itself turned out to be more challenging and exciting than what I had experienced up to this point.

Most importantly, the experience deeply affected me. I grew more empathetic for the employee body. I developed a deep appreciation for the type of work that occurs outdoors and requires the use of the body as a matter of course. This sense of empathy substantially informed the interventions that we crafted and implemented. In my view, the perfect intervention is not something that is "inserted" into the system from the outside; rather it is something that allows existing forces, those that are often sitting latent in the system—employee motivation, the inherent drive to do a good job, pride in what one does, the need to be a part of something greater than self—to burst forth and gush out. The best interventions ignite dormant energy, and channel it in a constructive and generative way. The crafting of these type interventions requires a depth and breadth of knowledge about the system that many times can only be attained through immersion.

CONCLUSION

> *So she sat on, with closed eyes, and half believed herself in Wonderland, though she knew she had but to open them again and all would change to dull reality—the grass would be only rustling in the wind, and the pool rippling to the waving of the reeds—the rattling teacups would change to tinkling sheep bells, and the Queen's shrill cries to the voice of the shepherd boy—and the sneeze of the baby, the shriek of the Gryphon, and all the other queer noises would change (she knew) to the confused clamor of the busy farmyard—while the lowing of the cattle in the distance would take the place of the Mock Turtle's heavy sobs.*

As consultants, we owe a great debt to the research traditions. Science has not only produced a great deal of knowledge from which we draw, but has also refined methods of gaining insight and information from phenomenon that, on the outside, appear confusing and difficult to understand. As consultants we should take full advantage of these tools and practices.

Throughout this chapter I have shown that research offers us many models we can use in diagnosis, and many of these are widely known and used in our trade. However, the research traditions also show us that one's selected method of inquiry is determined not by one's level of comfort or expertise with that method, but by the nature of the question. The more complex and ill-defined these questions are, the more researchers rely on methods from the qualitative paradigm. Here, we can learn again from the lessons of science.

There are times when one must leave the office and become a part of the system. The consultant must experience firsthand and report findings in the first person. Like the ethnographer, the heuristic researcher, and the Shaman, one must enter the realities of our clients and the systems of which they are a part to deepen the understanding of the forces and dynamics at work in these systems. In the end, this may be the best way we can help.

The firm that was the focus of the case study above is still around. I have maintained a good relationship with my client, and we visit from time-to-time. After diagnosis, we crafted several interventions designed to spread performance information more comprehensively throughout the system. More importantly, my client began to reward performance based on much of this information. This triggered an ongoing dialog between leadership and the workforce, one that took a generative, constructive tone. The vast majority of the workforce embraced and welcomed this approach, although a few senior workers committed to the old ways got frustrated and left. The workforce seemed to come alive and thrive. Company performance began to be a common concern and ongoing discussion. Workers appeared to become more engaged in the organization and its performance. In the end the company found its groove and the profits followed shortly thereafter.

Recently the owner told me that they had set an industry record in timeliness of completion of a multi-million dollar project that finished on budget. Their client was ecstatic with their performance. He also told me the same job set a company record for profit, as well as, bonuses paid to employees. That's called win-win-win.

NOTE

1. All epigraphs in the chapter are from Lewis Carroll's *Alice in Wonderland.*

REFERENCES

Bentz, V. M., & Shapiro, J. J. (1998). *Mindful inquiry in social research.* Thousand Oaks, CA: Sage Publications.

Berk, L. E. (2000). *Child development* (5th ed.). Needham Heights, MA: Allyn & Bacon.

Block, P. (2000). *Flawless consulting* (2nd ed.). San Francisco: Jossey-Bass Pfeiffer.

Braud, W., & Anderson, R. (1998). Conventional and expanded views of research. In W. Braud, & R. Anderson (Eds.), *Transpersonal research methods for the social sciences* (pp. 1–32). Thousand Oaks, CA: Sage Publications.

Brown, P. J., & Cotton, C. C. (1975). Marginality: A force for the OD practitioner. *Training & Development Journal, 29*(April), 14–18.

Burke, W. W. (2002). *Organization change.* Thousand Oaks: Sage Publications

Carroll, L. (1946). *Alice in wonderland & through the looking glass.* New York: Grosset & Dunlop, Inc.

Chatman, J. A., & Flynn, F. J. (2005). Full-cycle micro-organizational behavior research. *Organization Science, 16*(4), 434–447. Retrieved September 18, 2008, from Business Source Elite database.

Colman, A. D. (1995). *Up from scapegoating: Awakening the consciousness of groups.* Wilmette, IL: Chiron Publications.

Creswell, J. W. (1994). *Research design: Qualitative and quantitative approaches.* Thousand Oaks, CA: Sage Publications.

Creswell, J. W. (2007). *Qualitative inquiry & research design* (2nd ed.). Thousand Oaks, CA: Sage Publications.

Csikszentmihalyi, M. (1990). *Flow: The psychology of optimal experience.* New York: Harper & Row.

Cummings, T. G., & Worley, C. G. (2001). *Organization development and change* (7th ed.). Mason, OH: South-Western College Publishing.

Flood, R. L. (1999). *Rethinking the fifth discipline.* New York: Routledge.

Geertz, C. (1973). *The interpretation of cultures.* New York: Basic Books.

Harner, M. (1990). *The way of the shaman.* New York: Harper & Row.

Inglis, I. R. (2000). The central role of uncertainty reduction in determining behavior. *Behaviour, 137,* 1567–1599.

Mead, M. & Bunzel, R. L. (1960). *The golden age of American anthropology.* New York: George Braziller.

Moustakas, C. (2001). Heuristic research. In K. J. Schneider, J. F. T. Bugental, & J. F. Pierson (Eds.), *The handbook of humanistic psychology* (pp. 263–274). Thousand Oaks, CA: Sage Publications.

O'Neill, M. B. (2007). *Executive coaching with backbone and heart* (2nd ed.). San Francisco: Jossey-Bass.

Pritzker, S. (1999). Zen. In M. A. Runco, & S. R. Pritzker (Eds.), *The encyclopedia of creativity* (Vol. 2, pp. 745–750). San Diego, CA: Academic Press.

Robson, C. (2002). *Real world research* (2nd ed.). Malden, MA: Blackwell Publishing.

Schein, E. H. (1999). *Process consultation revisited.* Reading, MA: Addison-Wesley.

Webber, S. J. (1986). The nature of interviewing. *Phenomenology and Pedagogy, 4*(2), 65–72.

Whyte, D. (2001). *Crossing the unknown sea: Work as a pilgrimage of identity.* New York: Riverhead Books.

CHAPTER 13

FORGETTING TO PUT ON NEW SKIN

Enabling Healthy Closure

Judith R. Benson

Death, according to an African myth, came into the world through the carelessness of one old woman; when the season of universal skin-casting came round again (for in those days people renewed themselves by casing off their skins like snakes), she was absent-minded enough to put on her old skin instead of the new one, and in consequence died .
—Jung 1956, p. 348

In the African myth quoted above, death is believed to have come about because an old woman forgot to put on new skin therefore she could not regenerate herself. How similar is this to companies, individuals or consultants who become locked into either a non-viable business model or an unattainable career objective? They too cannot regenerate themselves and therefore die, not a physical death, but the end of a dream—a thriving business or a productive career.

The intent of this chapter is to provide useful information to professionals engaged in helping clients deal with the ending of one part of their career path or company's life so that they are able to regenerate themselves,

Consultation for Organizational Change. pages 269–292
Copyright © 2010 by Information Age Publishing
All rights of reproduction in any form reserved.

move on, or, in other words, reach healthy closure. The ability to skillfully enable healthy closure is particularly important today because of the rapid pace of 21st century change—we will not only experience more closures, but perhaps most importantly, be faced with new and different opportunities. The chapter begins by briefly setting the context—global, national, cultural and psychological. Elements of these concepts are then rolled up into a model composed of four levers that can be used to enable individuals, groups, and organizations reach healthy closure.

CONTEXT: GLOBAL, NATIONAL, CULTURAL AND PSYCHOLOGICAL PERSPECTIVES

The first decade of the 21st century ushered in a literal tsunami of unsettling and turbulent events that arose from a variety of factors, including the globalization of the economy, off-shoring, September 11th, the wars in Iraq and Afghanistan, and the quandaries of the Bush Presidency. They joined together to create a perfect storm experienced locally and globally as the real estate bust, banking crisis, credit crunch, and high unemployment became the new reality. In an opinion piece in the *Wall Street Journal*, Noonan (2009, p. A11) describes how all of this adversity can also generate innovation and dynamism:

> This isn't like the stock market crash of 1987 or the collapse of the dot-com bubble in 2001. People are not feeling passing anger or disappointment, they're feeling truly frightened. The reasons: this isn't stock market heebie-jeebies, it's systematic collapse. It's not only economic, but political. It wasn't only mortgage companies that acted up and out, so did our government, all the governments in the West, spending what they didn't have, for a decade at least. In the center of this drama is your house—its worth, or its ability to see you through retirement, or your ability to hold onto it. An extra added bonus: those thinking now about retirement are just old enough to remember America before the abundance, before everyone was rich, rich being defined as a place to live, and some left over for fun and pleasure. For them, the crash has released old memories. And it's spooking people.... I end with a hunch that is not an unhappy one. Dynamism has been leached from our system for now, but not from the human braid or heart. Just as our political regeneration will happen locally, in countries and states that learn how to control themselves and demonstrate how to govern effectively in time of limits, so will our economic regeneration. That will begin in someone's garage, somebody's kitchen, as it did in the case of Messrs. Jobs and Wozniak. The comeback will be from the ground up and will start with innovation.

As Noonan describes, the world as we know it is changing and evolving. Change and disruption—words that are unsettling because they evoke a fear of the unknown. These pressures, however, are also exactly the forces that cause cultures to change and evolve. Toynbee (1974) in his *Study of History* describes the rise and fall of twenty-one civilizations that collapsed, stagnated, and then evolved into different forms of cities, states and cultures. They did not entirely disappear; they changed. In the same way, institutions and ways of life that have become familiar will also evolve into something new.

The Cultural Context: "Chicken Little, the Sky is Falling"

Whether it's individual, organizational, or societal—a job loss, re-organization, promotion, or demotion—what is familiar and expected is ending. Individuals, groups, organizations, and societies adapt to the changing circumstances of their lives by consciously or unconsciously modifying their culture. Culture is hard to define. It has been said that trying to define culture is like trying to "nail jello on a wall"—it's squishy and it keeps moving around, an analogy that itself is cultural. Only those familiar with what jello looks, feels land tastes like can understand what this analogy means. Jello is an artifact of a western culinary experience. Those outside the influences of western advertising and culinary experiences will have no idea what jello is. Culture is a shared human experience; it is changeable, stable and unique all at the same time. It has been explained as a phenomenon that is "constantly enacted and created by our interactions with others" (Schein, 1992, p. 1). It can also be described as a "situational model for behavior and thought" (Hall, 1981, p. 13); as such it is an important part of how individuals, organizations and communities adapt to changing circumstances.

While there are cultural rules of interactions in every organization (Schein, 1987, pp. 78–91), perhaps the most significant point of pressure comes from executive leadership and most powerful is the influence of the person at the top—the Chief Executive Officer (CEO) and sometimes the company's founder. Even though I had read all about leadership, it was only after personal experience in consulting to organizations that I was able to fully appreciate leadership's true impact on organizational behavior. While many situations come to mind, the one that stands out is my experience working as an internal consultant for a commercial aircraft company. The company had been in existence for over twenty years and enjoyed the highest degree of success during and right after World War II. Since that time it had been struggling financially, and the time period I worked for them was near the end of their company existence.

One of my tasks was to design, organize, and support an integrated product team development program. This involved training and coaching team leaders, observing team meetings, and coaching senior executives. The program was put in place to increase organizational alignment and decrease costs by placing individuals from different functions on teams working toward a common goal. After observing team meetings, I found myself asking questions such as "Why did people from different functions have such difficulties working together?" "Why was I hearing so many stories with strong themes of use versus them?" "Why was there so much emotional tension between functions?"

The answers to these questions were found by looking at the impact of company history, style of leadership, operations, and cultural norms on workplace communities (Benson, 2000). What I observed in team meetings was the product of an organizational culture built upon the founder's values. As an engineer explained:

> The founder of the company set the tone. He said, "It is for engineering to design it and for manufacturing to build it." He set the stage for the division into separate functions and into different camps. The truth is that the best designs are collaborative. That was one of the initial strengths of the original organization that somehow got lost.
>
> Silos we have now—production, engineering, quality, product support, supplier management—have always been there. That's been the tradition.

Leaders model behaviors that influence not only how organizations function but also the very character of communities. A clear example of how leadership impacts community culture is described by Isbell (1978). The stronger the pressure for cultural and economic incorporation into the Peruvian mainstream, the more intensified were the efforts of the leadership of the Chuschinos, an indigenous Andean peasant community, to defend their communal holdings and ethnic identity. They closed in on themselves socially, economically, and symbolically, in order to strengthen their defenses against the outside world. The leaders of this indigenous Andean peasant community made conscious efforts to preserve characteristics of their way of life, which they felt were important to the group's cultural survival.

One might ask about the relevance of the leadership of a remote Andean indigenous community to 21st century organizational consultants. The point is how leadership made conscious choices that effectively maintained the cultural integrity of their community. In contrast to this group of Andean peasants, whose patterns of culture were consciously defended and maintained by their leadership in spite of political and economic pressures from the outside, there are other examples that illustrate how leadership decisions can disintegrate a community.

In small towns that rarely attract visitors, for instance, festivals give communities a sense of pride and bring in revenue. These small town festivals, however, are getting crunched by the economic crisis. Events are being cancelled or downsized as their leadership—represented by local governments, and community groups and corporate sponsors—pull back their economic support. The impact can be devastating, as Steve Schmander, president of the Boise, Idaho-based International Festivals and Events Association, explained "It's so important for these communities not to risk losing their events, which become often the brand for a community" (Gamerman & Carlton, 2009). For communities, such as these whose identity and economic well-being has been wrapped up in events dependent on a previously stable economic base, closure of one community identity will result in a conscious or unconscious cultural change to another community identity or perhaps to the disintegration of the community itself. In contrast, as shown by the example of the indigenous Andean community, leadership can play a strong role in maintaining the culture identity of a group.

The point of bringing culture into this discussion of closure is that culture sets up the expectations or norms of how individuals, groups, and organizations handle loss. In organizations, leaders model culture (Schein, 1992, pp. 211–228); therefore consciously or unconsciously leadership plays an important role in defining how closure is experienced. The question for leadership concerns how well they manage cultural elements that support healthy closure, or the extent to which they are sufficiently distracted by the onslaught of immediate problems they will be unable to take action. Within this context, counselors to the decision makers—coaches and consultants—can play an important role in helping leaders develop patterns of behavior that will result in a culture capable of managing through the stresses of economic and political change, a culture capable of closing one business model, supporting its healthy closure, while performing the midwifery duties of enabling the death of one and the birth of another.

Psychology of Closure

Structures of which we are unaware hold us prisoner.
—Senge, 1990, p. 160

Beginnings and endings, closings and openings are normal events in the life of a person, group, and an organization. The ebb and flow of economic forces are reflected in the growth and decline in the business environment—creating, on the upswing, opportunities for company formation, departmental expansion, and job creation; on the downswing, decline is experienced as waves of company failures, downsizing, and a slowdown of consumer demand. For an individual, the experience of starting a new job, beginning a new company, forming or being a member or leader of a new group, are all part of the normal career track right along with the experience of a demotion or job loss due to company reorganization or lay-off. Organizational development (OD) consultants serve as mediators, midwives, coaches, and supporters to individuals, groups, and organizations in all phases of their work lives. Most common and widely practiced are interventions aimed at the beginning and middle phases—alignment, re-direction, integration, and development—hence the popularity of team building, strategic planning, coaching, redesign, and process consultation. Less commonly practiced, but most likely in more demand in the future, are interventions designed to support individuals, groups, and organizations before, during and after a loss. To design effective interventions OD consultants, counselors, and coaches will be using elements from the psychological processes and dynamics underlying closure.

How people deal with closure—an ending, a death, or a loss—is culturally determined. The fact that Neanderthals buried their dead with items such as flowers shows the antiquity of these patterns of behavior. Rituals allow participants to act out, express feelings and thoughts in ways that are culturally prescribed. Any aspect or behavior or ideology may lend itself to ritualization. Even meetings are considered by some as a form of ritual enactment (Schwartzman, 1989).

In the workplace, rituals reflect organizational culture. In some there is a ritual lunch to welcome new employees, birthdays are sometimes honored and marked by sharing a meal; when employees decide to leave the company or retire there can be a variety of activities to honor the employee and at the same time provide a place for others to share memories and feelings of sadness and loss. In all business environments, organizational norms, or expected patterns of behavior, determine the manner in which companies close their formal relationship with individual employees. With an increasingly difficult economic environment, layoffs, downsizing and company closures are more common in the first decade of the 21st century resulting in the modification of once expected norms or cultural practices. During times of economic stress when large numbers of employee are leaving, when whole departments or organizations close down, the resulting confusion leaves little time for leadership to plan for anything other than immediate needs. In these situations, employees use informal ways of surfacing and acting upon their feelings of loss; these might be expressed by reminiscing about the past, regrets whispered in hall ways, the taking of tokens, or more negatively, active sabotage. This is the time when management needs the most support in being able to prepare their organization and this is exactly when they are less inclined to spend their resources on it. The one thing known for those affected individuals, groups, and organizations is that their future will be different than their past. For them the end is clear, a new beginning hazy, and the middle uncertain. For those still remaining in an organization, there is uncertainty about the end, middle, and the new beginning.

There have been different approaches and definitions of how people handle closure, the grieving process, and then move on with their lives. It is helpful to review a few of these ideas because they will form the basis of determining how to best support clients in these turbulent times. The grieving process, rituals, and patterns of behavior associated with closure of relationships have been compared to the psychological processes, thoughts and patterns of behaviors individuals go through in the process of dying. Descriptions of how individuals handle endings, such as the death of an individual, range from the loosely structured to an orderly process of moving from stage to stage. Edwin Schneidman wrote many books on the topic of death. He described the end of life as "a nexus of emotions… a hive of affect, in which there is a constant coming and going" (Curwen, 2009, p. A16). On the structured side, Kubler-Ross (1969) identified the stages individuals pass through in the process of dying—denial and isolation, anger, bargaining, and finally depression. Hanna (1985) found that individuals who were either going through or had gone through a substantial loss of life's meaning passed through a series of stages similar to those described by Kubler-Ross.

McWhinney (1980) applies a staged approach to describe how people in organizations handle a major upset. He proposes that organizations go through four phases. First a *retreat* that often begins with anger and feelings of guilt. This first phase also encompasses a *letting go* of prior goals, attitudes, and structures of beliefs. Then there is a *founding*—a rebirth of new ideas—and finally a *return* which involves a re-engagement of the organizational entity with its environment. Marris (1974) conducted research on the effects of bereavement among widows in the East End of London, slum clearance in Nigeria and America, students' experience of university education, African businessmen, and America experiments in social reform. What he found was that in each situation the anxieties of change centered on the struggle to defend or recover a meaningful pattern of relationships. In this struggle individuals go through conservatism, bereavement, and finally innovation. Yet another perspective on the unsettled feeling that uncertainty brings is from the psychoanalyst Schachtel (1959, p. 195) who explains that "man is afraid that without the support of his accustomed attitudes, perspectives and labels he will fall into an unknown abyss or flounder in the pathless…. But it is this very letting go that often arouses the greatest amount of anxiety."

Re-packaging these concepts, Tannenbaum and Hannah (1985) suggest that change follows the universally repetitive patterns of homeostasis (holding on), dying and death (letting go), and rebirth (moving on). The transitional states encompasses not only a loss of footing and security, there is an even deeper more primordial basis for this time of extreme stress. There is a term for that state of uncertainty and ambiguity—liminality (Turner 1977). A *limen* is a threshold, a corridor, or tunnel between one state to another. It is a place of transition, of uncertainty. One's sense of identity dissolves to some extent, bringing about disorientation. Liminality is a period of transition and, as such, for those very accustomed to structure, routine, and orderly process, can be extremely difficult to manage and stress-provoking. So, the need to hold on can be seen not only as a clinging to the familiar, but also a struggle not to fall and remain in a state of uncertainty or liminality. Bridges (1991, pp. 5–6) terms this state of being not here and yet not quite there the *neutral zone*, cautioning that:

> It's important to understand it for several reasons. First, if you don't expect it and understand why it's there, you're likely to try to rush through it and to be discouraged when you cannot do so. You may mistakenly conclude that the confusion you feel is a sign that there's something wrong with you.

Of all these approaches, explanations, and explorations into the human and organizational processes related to endings, one of the most useful for OD consulting is Tannenbaum and Hannah's (1985) piece on "Holding On, Letting Go and Moving On." Its main points are summarized below.

Holding On

"The feeling and emotion associated with the need to hold on draws from several thematic paths that bring back memories and their associated feelings and emotions" (Tannenbaum & Hannah, 1985, pp. 106-107):

- *Change is loss.* Every change in our situation requires us to give up or let go of something familiar, and predicable. Our past experiences with loss and how well they were accepted and integrated through a mourning process determine the strength and variety of negative emotions stored away in the unconscious, with the threatening potential to be stimulated by thematically similar change in the present. Some of the emotions and feelings typically associated with loss are anger, guilt, grief, helplessness, Kubler-Ross (1969) and depression.
- *Change is uncertainty.* All change requires us to move from the known to the unknown. Our past experiences with surprise and ambiguity and how well they were confronted and integrated through external support and patience determine the strength and variety of negative emotions stored away in the unconscious, with the threatening po-

tential to be stimulated by thematically similar change in the present. Some of the feelings typically associated with uncertainty are fear, panic, dread, and anxiety.

- *Change dissolves meaning.* All change causes the dissolution of some past meaning, which may or may not be replaced by new meaning. Some of the feelings typically associated with meaning loss are confusion, anxiety, frustration, boredom, apathy, and depression.
- *Change violates scripts.* Individuals have in their minds scripts, the unconscious life plans we make throughout our lives. Sometimes in our childhood we imagine how our lives will be when we grow up, our occupation, our life style, our life's companion. Life's journey causes these scripts to be rewritten. An unexpected modification of our college dreams can be unset by not being able to enter into the profession of our dreams; our sweethearts sometimes choose others as their life's mate; our children follow pathways that are in direct conflict with what we would have wanted for them. If the related negative emotions stored in the unconscious are too powerful to experience, we directly or indirectly sabotage changes that violate our script.

Letting Go

"When we are confronted by situations that cause us to make a change in how we construct reality, there is a need to hold on" (Tannenbaum & Hannah, 1985, p. 108). To be able to get past the need to hold on depends upon how much individuals understand it as part of our construction of reality, the strength of the negative emotional charge it is connected to and the ability to experience feelings and emotions that surface in attempting to let go of it.

The process of letting go and moving on encompasses three steps: conscious raising, re-experiencing, and mourning. In the first step—*conscious raising*—individuals first acknowledge what it is that they are holding onto and become aware of their own unique set of reasons for holding on. In experiences with facilitating this step at National Training Lab (NTL) sessions, individuals were asked to note their repetitive personal patterns, often using journals for this purpose. The pattern of seeing and doing things that most easily comes to the surface reveals that holding on can:

- Provide an illusion of security, stability, or predictability;
- Provide often obscure secondary gains in painful situations (for example playing the sick role gains sympathy);
- Ensure that some personal needs will be met;
- Continue the personal and/or social functionality of a way of seeing or doing things; and

- Permit one to avoid the work and frustration of breaking old habits and ingrained patterns.

On a deeper level, there are more powerful reasons for holding on. Individuals tend not be aware of them because they are rooted deeply in the unconscious and have a strong and threatening emotional component. These reasons for holding on fall into three groups:

1. The influence of childhood injunctions absorbed during societal enculturation, such as threats of rejections, loss of love in family socialization, and humiliation.
2. The influence of critical decisions, beliefs and assumptions that were formed in childhood to help bury any painful feelings and emotions and to avoid situations and actions that might resurrect them.
3. The influence of catastrophic expectations and fears, dread, and panic related to the unknown.

The second step in the process of letting go and moving on is called *re-experiencing*. To be made conscious and truly understood, these reasons for holding on must be re-experienced, often painfully (Jung, 1968; Miller, 1981). The deeper and more powerful reasons for holding on were discovered in NTL workshops during the quiet moments of journal work or meditation and then listening to how other's deal with their own childhood issues related to holding on. The first indicator that you have hit something significant from the unconscious is usually a vague or uncanny feeling, body sensation, or physical symptom. When this signal is recognized and given full attention despite the anxiety it might provoke, and with external support and encouragement, feelings rapidly surface and often erupt into cathartic emotional release. At other times, with the appropriate support, even deeper layers of feelings and emotions can surface. After a time, hours or days after emotional release, awareness moves into clarification of how an early traumatic experience can foster a painful belief about oneself, others, or life. At this point one can understand how a pattern of behavior was put into place that helped to cope with an intolerable situation. Most important, that pattern of behavior is now understood as the reason why adaptive changes could not be made in the present. To the degree that the process of re-experiencing can be felt and expressed, they are now freed to begin the process of letting go.

The third step is called *mourning*. The loss of the old ways of seeing reality, even though they may have been distorted or simplistic, is expressed with sadness and grief. The death of attachments begins. With the forgiveness of others and themselves it is possible to come to an appreciation and acceptance of what was and is.

Moving On

"The three phases of letting go—consciousness raising, re-experiencing, and mourning—make it possible to move on to new possibilities and new ways of thinking" (Tannenbaum & Hannah, 1985, p. 113). Techniques such as guided visualization (Korn & Johnson, 1983; Peale, 1982) or directed affirmation (Ray, 1976; Spangler, 1983) are ways to lay down a new track or pattern. The degree of ability to stick to these new patterns depends upon not only the strength of intention, but the inner ability to recognize triggers that encourage a retreat. The same can be said for the ability of some to give up harmful behaviors such as smoking cigarettes, abusing alcohol, or drugs; moving on means consciously avoiding situations that encourage a return to old ways of thinking or harmful patterns of behavior.

ENABLING HEALTHY CLOSURE

After undergoing a loss, individuals unconsciously select a pathway they will follow as they go through the experience. Will the path selected result in positive and healthy closure that will bring about a transformation, an adaptation, or a defeat interpreted as a life's lesson? Or will it cause an individual to lose confidence, give up on life's possibilities leading to a series of negative actions. The direction depends on four simultaneously operating factors that can be used as leverage points enabling healthy closure: meaning, inherent conservativism, the need to grieve, and the pull toward the future.

First Leverage Point: The Management of Meaning

Individuals interpret events based on their unique perception drawn from prior experiences in similar situations, stories they have heard from others facing similar situations, and other influences from their past. According to Kelly (1963) individuals formulate or attach meaning to events through the operation of their Personal Construct System (PCS). How an individual attaches meaning to an event is psychologically channeled by the ways they anticipate events rather than the ways they react to them. These patterns, called constructs, are the key to understanding and changing how events are interpreted.

Different individuals can experience the same event yet interpret and draw totally different meaning from it due to differences in their Personal Construct Systems. This dynamic system of creating meaning is continually adjusted by the individual in an attempt to satisfy personal needs and reduce conflict and anxiety (Marris, 1974). For example, in times of economic stress when front-line employees witness an unusual event, for instance their supervisor having more than the usual number of meetings with executive management, different meanings can be attached to the event depending upon their prior experiences. Do they anticipate a lay-off? Do they anticipate a change in their management? Or do they anticipate an opportunity to take advantage of a potential opening for a supervisory position? What action will they take based on the meaning they have attached? Will they be mentally preparing to leave the familiarity of their jobs? This situation presents an opportunity for leadership and management to provide credible explanations, particularly in challenging times, which can help manage meaning formulation (Ambrose, 1996; Noer, 1993).

Attaching meaning is the beginning of the process of creating healthy closure. It is at this point that the conditions for the road to be followed are put in place. The leverage point for consultants and executive management is to elicit from individuals, groups, and organizations the meaning they have attached to the events experienced. In the face of an actual lay-off, what meaning will that hold for the affected individuals? Does this represent yet another confirmation of their strengths or their weaknesses? These questions as well as many others, particularly for the unemployed, are discussed in length by Broman, Hamilton, and Hoffman (2001), Feather (1990), and Newman (2008).

The sense of meaning created by employment, for example, is captured in a quote from a GM auto worker after a lay-off (Broman, et al, 2001, p.161):

> It used to be that working for GM gave you a sense of meaning. You worked for the number one auto company. What more could you want? But now—after all of this—we have nothing left.

There is an opportunity to support individuals, groups and organizations by not only eliciting their own meaning, but by stimulating thought and discussion in such a way that reframes how they anticipate upcoming events so that their meanings might become more positive, healthy, and proactive.

Second Leverage Point: Inherent Conservatism or "Holding On"

Holding on feels safe even when the situation is not ideal, as described in the popular expression "better a devil that's known than one that's not." However, clinging to the familiar can be dangerous. In the simplest terms holding not only prevents trial and error, and it can cause physical, economic, and social harm. Holding onto feelings of insecurity and worthlessness are sometimes the product of chronic unemployment. They can also manifest in holding onto substance abuse or other forms of unhealthy behavior, as illustrated in the following quote from an individual who attended a support group for people with diabetes living on Skid Row. In the quote below he explains the attraction of the drug environment he knew so well and explains his inability to release himself from it (Benson, 2009, p. 9).

> I want to break from that place, but that's all I know. What can I do? It's lonely. I have tried to get off parole for 24 years but as soon as I get out, I get back into the old way because that's all I know. It's depressing there. I see the same people; they all smoked up and gettin' high. I feel like I don't fit in now but that's all I know since I was 12–13 years old. If they are not dead or shot, they are doing the same thing—drugs and gangs. It's better for me not to be there, to go to meetings, but I am lonely and don't know any different life. I have no friends not drugged out. I need to meet some people who will help me through. That's all I know, I keep coming back to the "homies."

The challenge for consultants and counselors is not only to help bring about awareness of holding on behaviors, but to help surface the underlying reasons, and then to surface the perceived benefits and the risks from the client's perspective. Holding-on behaviors can be extremely difficult to break through. In the case of the individual quoted above, the pressures to hold on to a known way of life that he knew were self-destructive exceeded his will to build a new one.

Third Leverage Point: The Need to Grieve

He that lacks time to mourn lacks time to mend.
—William Shakespeare

There are cultural norms that set in place expected ways of expressing emotions and behaviors associated with a loss. Mourning rituals, which include emotional displays of grief and have a programmed mourning period, are said to limit excessive or pathological mourning. They provide a way for people to act and this restores a sense of order and continuity to their lives enabling the bereaved to adjust to the fact of death (Michalopoulou & Michalopoulou, 1992, p. 6). In social settings, behaviors such as anger, sadness, depression, and confusion are expected and considered normal. However, in organizational settings people also grieve, but in contrast to the allowance given to individuals experiencing a loss in a social setting, there can be less forgiveness and tolerance for acting out behaviors thus creating additional stress on the affected individuals.

Bridges (1991, pp. 24–25) provides some advice on how to deal with these emotions in the workplace. He cautions that:

> ... you need to get people to recognize that they can accept the situation and move forward if they can work through these emotions. If you suppress the feelings and push people to get over them, you'll be handicapped with people who never "mended."

He also adds that it is not only individuals who can fall prey to the syndrome of never mending, but groups and whole organizations. In the rush to move forward, there is a strong tendency to hurry individuals through their process of mourning the loss of the familiar. Individuals need time to process the dynamics of a recent loss; the time needed depends on personal characteristics, the extent of their support system, relationships, their past experiences, and, when the context is organizational, the environmental culture of that company. Leadership plays an important role in facilitating healthy closure by:

- Acting with honesty and integrity;
- Communicating clearly and with expressions of genuine concern for the welfare of employees remaining and those leaving;
- Providing time and space for expressions of loss by taking steps to actively surface and acknowledge its presence rather than gloss over or ignore symptoms of organizational stress;
- Developing methods to help employees who are leaving exit with grace and respect; and
- Being conscious of the variation in response within the workforce and inviting professionals to work with staff who may need additional support.

In times of loss, consultant support can enable management to recognize not only their own symptoms of grief but support others as well by giving information, checking for understanding, defining the limit of the loss, developing an appropriate way to mark endings, honoring the past, helping individuals remember how they successfully handled challenging situations, and, most important, helping them see how the skills they gained will serve them well in the future.

Fourth Leverage Point: The Pull toward the Future

> *We must be willing to get rid of the life we planned so as to have the life waiting for us*
> *—Joseph Campbell, 1949 (quoted in Osbon, 1991, p. 18)*

In business, success is measured by financial outcome. Therefore, the pull toward the future for a company is contained in its plans to ensure viability. Life for a company is simple, it means financial success; death is financial failure. For individuals success is measured in more than economic terms; it can signify attainment of career goals. As noted by Goldschmidt (1990, p. 109), the term career is used broadly to signify more than a job:

It is the public aspect of the life of a person, entering in his or her activities in productive work, as a result of this work he/she attains a measure of social standing and through which he/she is rewarded the satisfactions of life. In this sense, every person in society has a career. In small homogeneous/traditional societies these careers tend to fit into a standard pattern for members of each sex, for the job expectations and social satisfaction are more or less the same. The ultimate reward is prestige or more basically in psychological terms, the satisfactory sense of self.

Success for the individual affirms self-worth, and self-esteem. It does not matter what type of work an individual performs—executive leadership, middle management, union or non-union, front-line staff—job loss, being laid off, being unemployed all mean the same thing—the disruption of plans for the future, the worry that they could end up "under a bridge with a shopping cart." The problem is that while individuals and companies are dealing with a potential or actual loss, their ability to take action, to pull a company or oneself out of their emotional morass is difficult. To quote a well known character—Mr. Spock from Star Trek—"fear is a mind killer." At this point, how able are individuals to re-shape or re-frame their career ideas or a company's business model to be able to explore new possibilities? The capacity to move on for both individuals and companies is more than just their internal capacity for resilience and reinvention. It is also about understanding something that Miller (2009) calls "the tyranny of dead ideas." This term refers to a set of ideas that made sense in the past but are on a collision course with social and economic developments of the 21st century. Peggy Noonan, quoted in an earlier section of this chapter, wrote about the dynamism that will bring the United States out of its current economic woes. To be able to participate in this dynamism and stream of creativity, individuals and companies have to be able to let go of the past and act upon their pull toward the future. Enter the skilled trusted advisor, organizational development consultant, career counselor.

Interventions to help individuals and companies move past their loss and take positive steps toward new opportunities are similar in many ways to those described in many articles and books describing methodologies for consulting and coaching (cf. Argyris, 2000; Block, 1981, 2001; Cummings & Worley, 1993; Goldsmith, et al, 2000; Koestenbaum, 1991; Olson & Eoyang, 2001; Reddy, 1994; Schein, 1987, 1988; Senge, 1990). The key to success in enabling clients' healthy closure lies in the counselor's or consultant's ability to help the client manage meaning, understand the tendency toward conservativism or holding on, and create a space for grieving, while shoring up the client's pull for the future. By helping clients process their loss using these four levers their experience can be transformative and adaptive leading to healthy closure.

Next Steps: Transformation, Adaptation and/or Defeat

Senge, Scharmer, Jaworski, and Flowers (2005, p. 93) call this process "letting go and letting come":

> In ancient Jerusalem, there was a gate called "the needle," which was so narrow that when a fully-loaded camel approached it, the camel driver had to take off all the bundles before the camel could pass through. Referring obliquely to this well-known image of his day, Jesus said, "It is easier for a camel to go through the eye of a needle than for a rich man to enter the kingdom of God." Sometimes we have to drop the baggage we've acquired on our journey in order to see clearly what's emerging.

As illustrated in the Figure 13.1, going through a job loss, ending a career path can be thought of as a passage through a "ring of fire." The analogy of fire to job loss takes into account not only the capacity of both to destroy and cleanse, but also the fear and pain associated with their approach. The destruction caused by fire permits re-birth and subsequent transformation, as captured by the legendary phoenix that arose from the fire renewed and transformed. For the person going through a job loss or for a company threatened by closure, going through this experience can result in a transformation, adaptation or defeat. For an individual, the transformation could mean entering a new and different career path; for a company it means a total change either in the way business is transacted

Passing Through A Ring of Fire

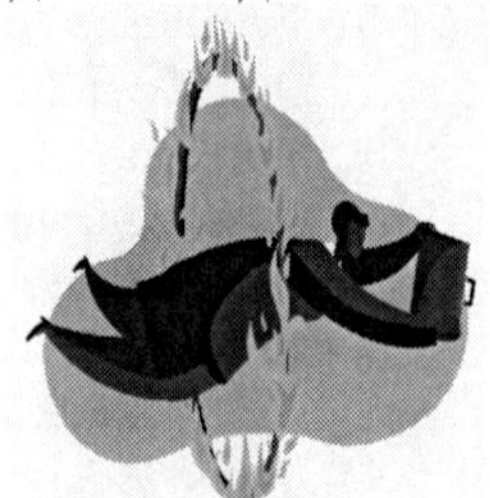

Enter **Test** **Emerge**
Willingly or Unwillingly Cleansed or Defeated

FIGURE 13.1. Passing Through a Ring of Fire

or the creation of a totally different business. However, in order to be transformed, individuals and companies have to drop some of the baggage they have acquired on their life's journey and be able to reinvent or transform themselves or their companies. Bridges (1994), for example, describes ten rules for living in an age of joblessness that are helpful to reframe notions not only about what jobs mean, but also how individuals can reframe how they think about their job skills. Sometimes this baggage is made up of ideas about the right job or the right business to be in. If the loss can be thought of as a transforming fire, than its cleansing action can bring the clarity, innovation and dynamism needed to move quickly in this challenging economic climate.

In times of trouble, obstacles can be or seem insurmountable; on the other hand, they can be powerful pressures enabling individuals, teams, organizations and communities to devise adaptive mechanisms. A very good example is described by Flandez (2009, pp. B1, B5):

Small businesses, squeezed for cash and unable to get loans are turning to an ancient payment system—barter. For example, the Atlanta Refrigeration Service Company worked out a deal with a local sandwich shop that was 90 days overdue on a $1,500 bill. The sandwich shop paid $500 and agreed to cater lunch to Atlanta Refrigeration's office five times over the next six months. "Bartering is critical to us in this recession," says Dave Brautigan, chief operating officer in the Atlanta-based refrigeration company. "As more and more of our clients find themselves in positions where they cannot pay the bill in full, it becomes our responsibility to figure out how to get that money in."

Individuals, during their careers, also exhibit varying degrees of ability to adapt their skills. We all know people who trained in one area or received university degrees in one field and found jobs in completely different occupation than what they were originally prepared to do. Even more amazing are those who because of personal choice and/or company decisions, find themselves moving from field to field as they nimbly move across a changed occupational landscape. While the impact of a job loss can be transformative and adaptive, it can also be destructive if individuals or companies cannot rid themselves of failed business plans, career objectives, or the guilt associated with the circumstances of the loss. As was described in this chapter, consultants and counselors often find themselves—and their clients—looking for ways of navigating turbulent times. Consultants also face canceled or deferred contracts, yet as Pile (2009) notes it's not the time to hide out; it's time to move on:

> We tell the clients, "seize the day, now is the time to act!" Yet most retreat to a predictable pattern of pulling in creative pursuits, downsizing, going HR-control freak crazy—and the biggest challenge of the day is going through the sock drawer before work. But look at Apple, Aeropostale, Cisco, Amazon,

> and the like, launching new products, expanding, making things happen. Oh yes, they are trimming too, but it ain't the same.

Enabling healthy closure, particularly while going through tough times oneself is not easy, but the consultant, counselor, coach and client all occupy the same space and share the same challenges in managing through tough times. With recent economic news and the prospect of downsizing and layoffs, OD and HR professionals are faced with challenges in how to lay off people in ways that preserve the culture for those continuing to run the business. Research and practice have given some insights to potential ways to downsize with dignity and avoid sabotage and destructive behaviors (Feyerherm, 2009)

I have selected examples from my own practice situations to illustrate how the four levers (managing meaning, holding on or inherent conservativism, the need to grieve, and the pull toward the future) can be applied to enable healthy closure in two very different settings.

Sample Applications

> *It is not the critic who counts; not the man who points out how the strong man stumbled, or where the doer of deeds could have done them better. The credit belongs to the man who is actually in the arena.*
>
> —Theodore Roosevelt (1910)

When thinking through one's consulting practice there are situations when everything you learned from seminars, workshops, school, your practice, and your own life seems to pull together and you are able to accomplish more than what you set out to do. In agreement with Harrison (1995), sometimes those situations are far and few between. Here are two examples from two very different segments of life, economics and environment that illustrate how to enable healthy closure.

Intervening in a Biotech Company

Some years ago, I was selected by the CEO of a small biotech company to work with two vice presidents whose conflict was impacting the organization's ability to function effectively. As a result of an intervention I call a "conflict laboratory," the two vice-presidents were able to successfully collaborate with each other. Some time later, one of the two vice presidents, Brenda, decided to accept an appealing position from another division of the same company. She had seven direct and four hundred indirect reports. After making her decision to leave the company, Brenda called and asked for help in dealing with the complex feelings she had about leaving the people with whom she had formed such a strong relationship.

As a first step, I suggested keeping up with the journaling of her thoughts and emotions as part of the process I had recommended earlier in our consulting relationship. As a result of her journaling, she recalled a time in her life when she had left a personal relationship without closure. This was six years ago when, without explanation, she left a romantic relationship. The incident had weighed on her unconscious ever since then. She called and arranged a meeting with the individual and spent an evening discussing their lives and the emotions of that time. She explained why she left and he explained the impact her leaving had on him. This was a powerful moment for Brenda because she was able to understand how her abrupt departure from their relationship impacted both of them; they both felt the effect of incomplete closure. This represents the first lever of the process of enabling healthy closure—the management of meaning. By re-connecting with this individual Brenda was able to manage meaning both for the individual she broke off a relationship with and then she was able to put together ways of managing the meaning of her departure for her staff. Because of how well she handled her personal relationship, she wanted very much to apply the lessons to her immediate problem of how to successfully achieve closure with her staff. We talked through a variety of options; she decided that the best would be for her meet separately with the ten people whom she felt would be most impacted by her loss.

When Brenda made the announcement to her whole staff their response was "why are you leaving us." Her response was two sided. She explained very honestly that the move was beneficial to her career aspirations. She also asked her staff to consider how their careers had been positively impacted by the opportunities she provided for them. She further told them how they could maintain contact with her if they wished. The ten people who worked most closely with her put together an album that reflected the milestones they had attained together and gave it to her. I asked her what her plans were for them. She cried and then said she would replicate the album and give a copy to each of them.

In a sense what Brenda accomplished through her actions was to manage the meaning of her departure both to herself and to the people who worked for her. Rather than leave them to fill silence with conjecture, she not only provided them with an explanation for her departure, she went further by preparing outlets for grief and the expression of feelings thereby preparing them and herself for a healthy closure. Coaching her through the application of the four elements of the healthy closure model (meaning, inherent conservatism or holding on, the need to grieve, and the pull toward the future) made her see how important it was for her to spend time with her direct reports and clearly address their sense of personal loss.

OD in Overlooked Communities

Interventions such as coaching, facilitation and team building are not only useful to the people who work for corporate America, but can also can help those of more modest means. The opportunity to use these techniques differently arose out of the results of a user-focused evaluation of the effectiveness of chronic disease management programs used at two downtown Los Angeles community healthcare clinics that provide services to the homeless population. Los Angeles has been called "the Homeless Capital of the United States." On any given night, approximately 75,000 people are homeless in Los Angeles County (Institute for the Study of Homelessness and Poverty, 2004, p. 3). Approximately 5,000 of those live on the 50 square-blocks that comprise Los Angeles's Skid Row (Inner City Law Center 2009, p. 1). Many of people who live there are diagnosed as having a mental health or substance abuse problem. This hard-to-reach population has a difficult time accessing services and following up with appointments and recommended treatment regimens. Diabetes is on the list of chronic illnesses that disproportionately impacts this population. It also is one of the chronic diseases that respond to self-management; however, in this population the skill and will for self-management tend to be low. The results of the user-focused survey uncovered specific areas for improvement, such as a need for greater social support and ability to use self-management strategies (Benson, 2009, p. 3).

Drawing on my experiences with community healthcare workers I organized a peer-peer support group for people living on Skid Row with diabetes as a means to promote social support and build the skill and will for self-management; I selected and trained an individual, I will call Paul, to be the group facilitator. He is a resident of Skid Row, a person with diabetes, and a former drug addict. He knows the community and is, therefore, very able to build connections, speak the language, and understand the life, needs and background of the people attending the group. Since June 2008, I have been observing with great delight how he has learned to facilitate. Together we are not only building community within the group (Block, 2008), we are enabling a slow migration from hopelessness, loneliness, and lack of knowledge to a sense of goal accomplishment, greater capacity and will for diabetes self-management, desire for connection, and hope for a healthier and more comfortable life—in essence, a pull to the future.

The model for enabling healthy closure has found a different expression within the peer-peer support group in Skid Row. Closure for some has meant not being able to work in their former occupations because of their diminished physical capabilities; others have gone through difficult drug recovery, while a few have suffered the violent loss of family members. Building healthy closure, reconstructing meaning, accepting the grief of personal loss, and appropriately holding on, becomes the informal content of every session of this support group. Paul calls it "putting on a new pair of glasses." During meetings each person tells their own story of the daily struggle to reconstruct fear to possibility thereby managing their diabetes within the circumstances of their life; their stories are then met by another member of the group's words of support, acknowledgment, and respect. A poignant example of how participants help each another came out during the check-in (Benson 2009, p. 21). As one of the participants who works at night as a security guard night noted:

> I have been working for the last 3 days at a job right by Denny's and I have been enjoying the Grand Slam breakfast. I get it for half price. I have not been taking my pills for 60 days. I have been peeing a lot and I know my sugar is high, but I just don't want to take it.

One of the ladies in the group told him:

> You make a conscious decision—do you want to live or die. You just think about your pills every day. Once upon a time in you life you were doing OK. It's a conscious decision in your life. You say you want to lose weight, but you are not working out or doing anything about it? You can't eat once a day when you are diabetic. What's going on with you? Do you eat to live or live to eat? It's life or death. The consequences are pretty awful. It makes me feel no good to hear you say that. It's life or death.

In this example the expression of holding onto self-destructive behavioral patterns was strongly countered in a way that not only showed the concern of the participants for each other, but their own frustrations in the difficulties of making meaningful changes even if the consequences are life-threatening. Thus each member of the group variously applies levers of the healthy closure model in a way that makes sense to each individual's situation. Success is measured on two dimensions; one the one hand by stories of success that serve as models for others, on the other it's measured by changes in quantitative health indicators.

SUMMARY AND REFLECTIONS ON ENDINGS

Endings, transitions and beginnings are all part of a natural cycle. Rock formations, a career path, or a human life pass through cycles that have a beginning, transitions, an ending and sometimes from the remnants, or after a death, new life arises—there are new beginnings. The cycle repeats through time and space. This chapter set out to provide a foundation of concepts and applications from which human resource professionals, counselors and OD consultants could devise ways to not only help clients, but also themselves as they go through the cycles of their own lives.

The passage through a traumatic event, such as an unexpected or expected loss, is compared to a ring of fire. The results can be transformative, adaptive, or destructive. How the four levers of loss are managed—how meaning is processed, the need to grieve, inherent conservatism, and the pull of the future—determine how healthy closure can be achieved. Unhealthy closure, the inability to evolve, to let go, to continue to hold onto unhealthy or unproductive patterns of behavior, a failed business plans, or career paths that offer little hope of a future, also can follow the trauma of loss and passage through the ring of fire. For some people holding on to what is familiar is so comfortable it overrides the pull of the future. This is the place for the skilled professional to help leadership, individuals, and groups as they go through personal loss—the trauma of a lay-off, downsizing or a declining business—so that transformation, adaptation, and resilience can be achieved and the destructive behaviors of substance abuse, sabotage, depression, diminished self-esteem, faulty decision making, and lack of motivation can be averted. The key to success in enabling clients' healthy closure lies in the counselor's or consultant's ability to help the client process meaning, manage the tendency toward conservatism or holding on, and create a space for grieving, while at the same time shoring up the client's pull or motivation for the future.

REFERENCES

Ambrose, D. (1996). *Healing the downsized organization.* New York: Harmony Books.

Argyris, C. (2000). *Flawed advice and the management trap.* Oxford: Oxford University Press.

Benson, J. R. (2000). *It takes a village to build a company: The operation of workplace communities on organizational growth and development.* Unpublished research project for the Master of Science in Organizational Development, George L. Graziadio School of Business and Management, Pepperdine University.

Benson, J. R. (2009, January). *Community, health and social support: A model to improve self-management of patients living with diabetes on skid row.* Paper presented at the 2009 Annual Symposium: Health Care for the Underserved: Excellence in Collaboration, Anaheim, California

Block, P. (1981). *Flawless consulting: A guide to getting your expertise used.* San Diego: Pfeiffer.

Block, P (2001). *The flawless consulting fieldbook and companion: A guide to understanding your expertise.* San Diego: Pfeiffer.

Block, P. (2008) *Community: The structure of belonging.* San Francisco: Berrett-Koehler.

Bridges, W. (1991). *Managing transitions: Making the most of change.* Reading: Addison-Wesley.

Bridges, W (1994). Where have all the jobs gone? *OD Practitioner, 26*(2), 11–18.

Broman, C. L., Hamilton, V. L., & Hoffman, W. S. (2001). *Stress and distress among the unemployed: Hard times and vulnerable people.* New York: Kluwer Academic Press.

Cummings, T. G., & Worley, C. G. (1993). *Organizational development and change.* Cincinnati: South Western College Publishing.

Curwen, R. (2009). Waiting for death, alone and unafraid. *Los Angeles Times,* (February 28), A1, A16–17.

Feather, N. T. (1990). *The psychological impact of unemployment.* New York: Springer-Verlag.

Feyerherm A. (2009). *What's New: Downsizing with dignity.* Graziadio School of Business and Management, Pepperdine University, Webinar, April 3.

Flandez, R. (2009). Barter fits the bill for strapped firms. *Wall Street Journal,* (February 17), B1, B5.

Gamerman, E., & Carlton, J. (2009). Due to the economy, there will be no celebrating the cackling goose. *Wall Street Journal,* (February 17), A1, A12.

Goldschmidt, W. (1990). *The human career: The self in the symbolic world.* Cambridge: Basic Blackwell.

Goldsmith, M., Lyons, L., & Freas, A. (2000). *Coaching for leadership: How the world's greatest coaches help leaders learn.* San Francisco: Jossey-Bass.

Hall, E. T. (1981). *Beyond culture.* New York: Bantam Doubleday Dell.

Hanna, R. W. (1985). Personal meaning: Its loss and rediscovery. In R. Tannenbaum, N. Margulies, F. Massarik, & Associates (Eds.), *Human system development* (pp. 42–66). San Francisco: Jossey-Bass.

Harrison, R. (1995). *The consultant's journey: A dance of work and spirit.* San Francisco: Jossey-Bass.

Inner City Law Center (2009). *The homeless.* Retrieved from http:/www.innercitylaw.org/homeless.htm.

Institute for the Study of Homelessness and Poverty (2004). *Homelessness in Los Angeles: A summary of recent research.* Los Angeles: The Weingart Institute.

Isbell, B. J. (1978). *To defend ourselves: Ecology and ritual in an Andean village.* Austin: Institute of Latin American Studies.

Jung C. G. (1956). *Symbols of transformation.* New York: Bollingsen.

Jung, C. G. (1968). *The Archetypes and the Collective Unconscious. Collected Works* (vol. 7). Princeton, NJ: Princeton University Press.

Kelly, G. (1963). *A theory of personality: The psychology of personal constructs.* New York: W. W. Norton.

Koestenbaum, P. (1991). *Leadership: The inner side of greatness.* San Francisco: Jossey-Bass.

Korn, E. R., & Johnson, K. (1983) *The uses of imagery in the health professionals.* Homewood: Dow Jones-Irwin.

Kubler-Ross, E. (1969). *On death and dying.* New York: Macmillan

Marris, P. (1974). *Loss and Change.* New York: Pantheon books, Random House.

McWhinney, W. (1980). Paedogenesis and other modes of design. In T. G. Cummings (Ed.), *Systems theory for organization development* (pp. 273–306). New York: Wiley.

Michalopoulou, A. M., & Michalopoulou, E. (1992). Social handling of death. *ICUS NURS WEB J, 11,* 1–7.

Miller, A. (1981) *The drama of the gifted child.* New York: Grove Press.

Miller, M. (2009). *The tyranny of dead ideas: Letting go of the old ways of thinking to unleash a new prosperity.* New York: Times Books- Henry Hold and Company.

Newman, K. S. (2008). *Laid off, laid low: Political and economic consequences of employment uncertainty.* New York: Columbia University Press.

Noer, D. M. (1993). *Healing the wounds: Overcoming the trauma of layoffs and revitalizing downsized organizations.* San Francisco: Jossey-Bass.

Noonan, P. (2009). Remembering the dawn of the age of abundance. *Wall Street Journal,* (February 21–22), A11.

Olson, E. E., & Eoyang, G. H. (2001). *Facilitating organization change: Lessons from complexity science.* San Francisco: Jossey-Bass.

Osbon, D. K. (Ed.) (1991). *Reflections on the art of living: A Joseph Campbell companion.* NY: HarperCollins

Peale, N. V. (1982) *Positive imaging.* New York: Fawcett Crest.

Pile, S. (2009). *MSOD conference: I could not let this one slip by.* MSOD List Serve correspondence. Quoted with permission.

Ray, S. (1976). *I desire love.* Millbare: Les Femmes.

Reddy, W.B. (1994). *Intervention skills: Process consultation for small groups and teams.* San Diego: Pfeiffer.

Roosevelt, T. (1910). *Citizenship in a republic.* Speech at the Sorbonne, Paris April 23.

Schachtel, E. G. (1959). *Metamorphosis: on the development of affect, perception, attention and memory.* New York: Basic Books.

Schein, E. H. (1988). *Process consultation: It's role in organizational development* (vol. I). Reading: Addison-Wesley

Schein, E. H. (1987). *Process consultation: Lessons for managers and consultants.* (vol. II). Reading: Addison-Wesley.

Schein, E. H. (1992). *Organizational culture and leadership.* San Francisco: Jossey-Bass.

Schwartzman, H. B. (1989). *The meeting: Gatherings in organizations and communities.* New York: Plenum Press.

Senge, P. (1990). *The fifth discipline: The art and practice of the learning organization.* New York: Doubleday.

Senge, P., Scharmer, C. O., Jaworski, J., & Flowers, B. S. (2005). *Presence: An exploration of profound change in people, organizations and society.* New York: Currency/Doubleday.

Spangler, D. (1983). *The laws of manifestation.* Findhorn, Scotland: Findhorn.

Tannenbaum, R., & Hanna, R. W. (1985). Holding on, letting go and moving on: Understanding a neglected perspective on change. In R. Tannenbaum, N. Margulies, F. Massarik, & Associates (Eds.), *Human system development* (pp. 95–121). San Francisco: Jossey-Bass.

Toynbee, A. J. (1974). *A study of history.* New York: Oxford University Press.

Turner, V. (1977).Variations on a theme of liminality. In S. F. Moore, & B. G. Myerhoff (Eds.), *Secular ritual* (pp. 36–52). Amsterdam: Van Gorcum.

CHAPTER 14

KURT LEWIN'S PROMISE[1]

Implications for Organization Change Consultancy

Kurt Motamedi

The contributions of Kurt Lewin (1890–1947) to twentieth-century applied behavioral sciences are consequential. As we weigh his influence some sixty years after his death, it is apparent that his work and ideas have impacted—and continue to inspire—the development of the field of applied behavioral sciences across a broad array of institutions and methodologies. The breathtaking contributions of so many who followed his path have led to improvements in quality of life, productivity and social justice through action research, participative problem solving, intergroup relations, community development and field theory.

Yet there are forces at work today that push in the opposite direction to which Lewin's work and values would point. We are continuing on the path of the last century of massive change, innovation and prosperity but in juxtaposition with war, violence, poverty and hopelessness for many. We have gained a great deal through change, but we have incurred the associated costs and dilemma of change as well. Thus, as we go forward in this millennium, it is worth remembering Lewin and his work. It is especially

Consultation for Organizational Change. pages 293–308
Copyright © 2010 by Information Age Publishing
All rights of reproduction in any form reserved.

valuable considering whether and how his legacy can be furthered in the face of the competing and contentious pressures of globalization, technology, overpopulation, social problems (e.g., poverty, violence), ecological exploitation, tyranny and war. The promise is to extend Lewin's values and methods as we continue to move forward.

LEWIN: THE PERSON AND HIS CONTRIBUTIONS

Lewin was a humanitarian, philosopher, scholar, psychologist, teacher, social activist, and mentor. His intellectual powers were joined by his demonstrative concern for people and appreciation for self-understanding and learning. His life work reflects a developmental progression through the study of the person, field theory, group dynamics, inter-group relations, work organization, community action, industry practices, sensitivity training, and social problem solving. His perspective was both broad and deep, ranging across many levels of inquiry, from the individual to the group to the societal and global.

Lewin developed many novel concepts, schema, research approaches, and methods specific to the situation and appropriate for the phenomenon in his investigations of human systems and dynamics. They included field theory (Cartwright, 1951), topological psychology (Lewin, 1936), action research (Lewin, 1946a), group dynamics (Lewin, 1945, 1946b), sensitivity training (Lewin & French, 1948), community development (Lewin, 1949), and cultural reconstruction (Lewin, 1948a). At a time when the prevalent attitude of practical and scientific domains of research and learning excluded emotions and sentiments, he developed a keen interest in human emotions. His approach validated human feelings and emotions as important facts for understanding human conduct and human systems development.

Believing that there is nothing so practical as a good theory, Lewin's research and practice were directed toward discoveries that involved theory building grounded in real-world action. He cared about generating the kind of knowledge that would be useful in improving human condition. For Lewin, theory building was purposeful and was intended to enhance the understanding of human-relations phenomena such as conflict (Lewin, 1949) and racism (Lewin & Radke, 1946). In turn, that understanding could lead to a course of action that would bring change. Lewin was not a neutral bystander. As a social activist, he strived to improve the human condition and life experience. He believed in the practicality of democracy and cared about advancing human rights and social justice. He believed work plays a central role in people's lives, and a person's work is an important contributor to one's life satisfaction. His research and contributions in industrial relations emphasized improving the understanding of human relations so that there would be an improvement in the quality of everyday work life. Many of Lewin's personal characteristics and values have become embodied in the study of human systems development and their applications run across the applied behavioral sciences, especially in organization development (OD) and change. His influence is felt through numerous streams of thought, research and application—and that influence will continue.

The centerpiece of Lewin's approach was his ability and willingness to attend to the particulars of everyday human experiences. He invented action research, whereby he would transform a life problem into a controllable experimental design and study it. He advocated learning through observing facts and behaviors in the situation and uncovering the complex reality of attitudes, motivation and feelings (Lewin, 1946c). By taking into account both the phenotypic and genotypic aspects of change, he endeavored to understand the dynamics of adaptation and resistance in human systems change.

Holding that behavior can best be understood in the context of the situation and attributes of the person [Behavior = *f* (Environment, Person)], he was interested in the concept of life space and social space and their relation to felt tension and behavior (Lewin, 1948d). His action research experiments validated that participation in fact finding and decision making by those who would be impacted by change reduces their resistance to that change. His approach of involving supervisors and workers in group problem solving—as well as the practice of self-examination, openness and feedback—led to higher commitment to and successful implementation of planned changes.

At MIT, Lewin founded the group dynamics research project, which led to significant findings in group productivity, communication, perception, decision making, leadership, membership, cohesiveness, conformity, and intergroup relations. Caring as he did about fairness and social justice, he was committed to taking a strong stance in resolving unfair cultural practices and establishing a broader understanding of social justice. His articles on "Bringing Up a Jewish Child" (Lewin, 1948b) and "Self-Hatred among Jews" (Lewin, 1948c) are poignant and clear about the plight of minority groups. In an era of blatant discrimination against minority groups, he created processes and approaches intended to expose the associated injustice of such practices and enlighten bigots of their unethical conduct. In the last years of his life, Lewin sponsored numerous programs addressing a variety of social justice matters, including integrated housing, integrated employment, fairness laws and ethical social change.

Throughout his life Lewin also paid attention to his own development. He was able to integrate his work and move to the next stage of development of ideas and research projects. The discovery and development of sensitivity training was his last contribution to the field. Sensitivity training, based on the integration of his previous work, offered a method of changing people's attitudes through self-observation and consciousness raising. The approach helped people to gain new insights into their reasons for resisting change. It used feedback-generated valid information about their conduct as participant observers. In 1947, shortly before his untimely death, he founded the National Training Laboratories (NTL) for further investigations into the applied behavioral sciences.

THE EVOLVING VALUE DISPARITY IN USING LEWIN'S WORK

The world has changed considerably since Lewin's death. World population has increased dramatically. Technology has made global communication instantaneous and travel to any part of the globe within a day a reality. It has diminished geographical distance, if not social distance. Globalization and technological imperative have gained dominance and have become a significant fact of life. Meanwhile, many of Lewin's innovations have been absorbed into the infrastructure of industrialized nations, businesses, governments, and not-for profits. In many places there is greater participation in governance processes, more tolerance of individual differences, and greater appreciation of diversity. There is greater concern for many broad, macro-level issues, such as the need to preserve the ecological systems, the related rights of future generations, and the preservation of natural resources.

It is paradoxical that his work has also been distorted and abused in directions opposite to Lewin's values and approach. There is an increasing concern among applied behavioral scientists steeped in the Lewinian approach that the fundamental values and ethics of the field have been violated by opportunistic practitioners. As Warner Burke (1997, p. 7) observed:

> A number of senior practitioners in OD, i.e., those with 20 or more years of experience, believe that the profession has lost its way—that its values are no longer sufficiently honored, much less practiced, and that the unrelenting emphasis on bottom line has taken over. . . . it does seem true that OD has lost some of its power, its presence, and perhaps its perspective.

The fields of human systems development, organization development, applied behavioral sciences, community development, and consumer behavior have incorporated applications of Lewin's approach. However, the fact that knowledge exists offers no guarantee of how it will be used. Lewin understood that. He knew that the knowledge of human systems did not necessarily mean that the values he espoused would be the guiding principles for its application. Understanding group dynamics may allow one to manipulate group activities and participation toward some predetermined end counter to democratic values. Some so-called behavioral scientists imposed their own short-sighted self-fulfilling agendas doing action research, participative social problem solving or sensitivity training. They have made use of Lewin's methods but counter to his values. They followed Lewin's model, but have instead created circumstances which ignore and demean Lewinian values. For example, rather than serving as a means of helping people to appreciate and understand others (Elvin, 1996) for humanitarian social problem solving, they further alienate and de-humanize human processes and communities. As an illustration, the U.S. efforts in "winning minds and hearts" waged following the invasion of Iraq used many of Lewin's methods and ideas, but these applications stood in contrast to Lewinian values of creating dialogue, discussion and social problem solving. In this instance, Lewin's methods were used void of their values and if not contrary, without regard, to effective democratic social problem solving.

Counter Lewinian values and frameworks exist, even within the ranks of those who claim to practice his techniques in the larger society as well as in the applied behavioral sciences. Part of this paradox involves the question of what basic assumptions are made and what values are at work in bringing about change. Lewin would lead the choice against democratically clothed autocratic action in wars, socialism, and blatant capitalism where human rights are compromised. He would seek to balance ideologies that hold market economics as the solution to all social issues and problems with humanitarian considerations. His humanitarian approach to social concerns differs from the contemporary "laissez-faire" culture that is so widely practiced in our businesses. He understood and supported the need for businesses to make a profit in order to survive and grow, but maximizing the bottom line without regard for the unabated human and societal costs was not acceptable in his value system.

People and their lives mattered to him, and he believed that enlightened communal action is required to deal with inhuman actions. He advocated that livable societies are not just an aggregation of individual people each maximizing their own narrow economic welfare and self interest. His work and personal conduct exemplified his values by successfully building and maintaining communities where people valued civility, caring and concern for the common life. He would have diligently put to work his innovative humanitarian applied behavioral science approach to address societal and global problems and prevent the emergence of what Kaplan (1996) referred to as the emerging societal and global anarchy. He would have found ways to study and learn the dynamics underlying the paradox of humanitarian and counter-humanitarian tension through democratic processes for furthering social understanding and outcome.

THE FUTURE CONTRASTING CHOICES: ECONOMIC OPPORTUNISM AND SOCIAL ENLIGHTENMENT

Reality is more complex than an either/or choice. Dialogue of contrasting choices often helps in the discovery of new choices, bringing about resolution, synthesis, and optimized action. In this context, there are two contrasting choices to realizing the means and ends chains of change and their far and wide-ranging effects. Both reflect our Western values and assumptions about reality and the preferred future. One is driven by consumption, a survival of the fittest morality, self-interest expressed by dominance and material accumulation for survival. The second choice stresses humanitarian values, good will, benevolence, community support, and enlightened self-interest in serving the community. The first may be called an *Opportunist Approach* and the second an *Enlightened Approach.* Lewin's contributions could be used in either approach with significant differences in their outcome. For example, Lewin used social change approaches to increase the consumption of animal organs during World War II. By systematically collecting data on reasons for citizens' resistance to eating kidney, liver, and other consumable parts of livestock, he engaged in a successful mass persuasion project supported by the government to reduce malnutrition among populations and reduce waste. Similar Lewinian methodologies, however, have been used by advertising agencies to market cigarettes to our youth. The Joe Camel promotion of Camel cigarettes is a familiar case. Use of propaganda and public relations campaigns regardless of their underlying values is problematic and quite common.

The economic and political ideology that has become dominant in much of the world through globalization is quite consistent with the opportunistic approach. The champions of this approach advocate the *economic man* view of humanity making decisions based on rational economic self-interest. Impersonal economic forces are assumed not only to be the dominating factor, but a positive force. They contend that the competition in the marketplace will require people to be productive and necessitate competitiveness to survive. Accessing the planet's resources and human work and life are seen as positive forces toward production efficiency and material consumption. Life is assumed to be competitive and individuals pursuing their own self interest are responsible for what happens to them. Those who survive the competition and do well will be rewarded. Those who don't win, for whatever reason, will have to survive as best they can—if they can. The bottom line is an important measure of success. Charity is optional and viewed as largely ineffective.

Opportunist choice purports that communities must discover their own way finding prospects for their development and in coping with the economic requirements of market efficiency, competition, and survival. Human conditions and ecology are viewed as an economic externality in the game of competition. As a result, human rights violations and worker abuses have flourished with growing domination by opportunistic global institutions and firms. They have enabled firms to capitalize on comparative economic advantages (regional and national) produced on the back of defenseless workers unprotected from abuses. As Roberts and Engardio (2006, p. 50) observe,

> For more than a decade, major American retailers and name brands have answered accusations that they exploit "sweatshop" labor with elaborate codes of conduct and onsite monitoring. But in China many factories have just gotten better at concealing abuses... Chinese factories keep double sets of books to fool auditors and distribute scripts to employees to recite if they are questioned. And a new breed of Chinese consultant has sprung up to assist companies like Beifa in evading audits. Tutoring and helping factories deal with audits has become an industry in China.

Many Chinese companies pay their workers less than China's minimum wage. With the help of consultants, they build and operate firms that abuse workers by not compensating them fairly and hiding violations of minimum wage, overtime, and labor laws. Such practices, of course, are not limited to China. Firms in most, if not all, countries, including Western industrial nations, abuse worker human rights in countless ways hidden from public eyes in their attempt to make more profits.

Opportunists espouse that when ecological disaster becomes near term and obvious enough, the market will create sufficient incentives to encourage people (and firms) to deal with externalities and the environment. Until then, it is rational to capitalize on opportunities and pursue any available path for gaining economic advantage. It is justified that resistance to efficiency-driven change must be overcome expeditiously to avoid and eliminate economic inefficiencies. Top-down means are facilitated by human relations specialists with appropriate attitudes who design, focus, align and develop productive workplaces for competitive economic advantage. It is assumed that people affected by change should be adaptive to absorb the costs of change and development.

The enlightened choice, in contrast, builds on humanitarian values, collaboration, social problem solving, sensitivity to human needs, and the study and understanding of human systems dynamics. Lewin's work is a precursor to this approach; it attempts to improve human understanding of events and choices through the social sciences, social learning and social problem solving. Enlightened consulting strives to make the unobserved observable and the tacit explicit by improving the awareness of values, assumptions, attitudes, social constructions, behaviors, and outcomes. It gives emphasis to participation in social problem solving and realization of stakeholder needs for discovery, learning and development and their participation in diagnosis, choice making and actions. It appreciates that the planet itself is a gift to be valued, preserved, and shared with the rest of creation—not a stockpile of resources to be exploited for opportunistic gain. It acknowledges that maximizing wealth is not necessarily the highest good. There is concern for the effect on the commons, with emphasis on preventing events that cause the tragedy of the commons. Life has more meaning than money, and not every problem is amenable to a market solution. The enlightened approach is directed towards supporting and enhancing humanitarian values.

Consistent with this approach, Korten (1996, p. 277) refers to a "healthy" society as one that demonstrates expanded capacity for love, tenderness, cooperation, and compassion, and makes life easy to live in balance with the environment. However, in the face of recent overpowering trends towards globalization and technology, the enlightened approach is on the defensive or simply quiet in much of the societal arena. The vision remains, however, and there are examples of caring being expressed in various ways throughout the larger community. The continued war in Middle East can serve as a reminder of our inability to apply social problem solving to end the suffering of so many. The plight of the oppressed in many parts of the world including Darfur, Sudan, Palestine, Bangladesh, and Afghanistan are examples of the global impact of arms trade and the formation of externally supported political hands serving inhuman causes. The deforestation of Brazil and unabated industrial pollution in developing countries are further examples of uncontrolled aspects of globalization in the hands of powerful, economically motivated forces. As cultures are coming in closer contact to one another and cultural differences in values and life styles are squeezed into each other, there is a greater need for social problem solving and an appreciation of the value of tolerance and of constructive ways to resolve differences. However, at times it seems that we are moving in opposite directions as indicated by the U.S. invasion of Iraq and the untold numbers of deaths, injuries and displacements suffered by innocent people. In a world where the powerful neglect the rights of the weak and disenfranchised, globalization can and does shift the burden of proof of injustice to those who have no seat at the table.

The Two Approaches in Organization Change Consulting

Of more direct concern in this essay, especially for those who teach and practice organization change and management consulting, is the way in which these approaches apply in the field in which Lewin was directly involved: the practice of applied behavioral science and action research.

Opportunist Choice

In the opportunist approach, the primary focus is on using the techniques and methods of the profession for materialistic gains. Opportunistic management consultants may choose to discard, minimize, or strip away the accompanying humanitarian values if economic gains are possible. They may ignore the fundamental processes of careful data collection and diagnosis, turning applied human systems research into a commodity product in pursuit of bottom-line results. It would be justifiable to promote and sell solutions without diagnosis of problems and needs. As long as the bottom line is enhanced, the time-consuming process of actually listening to people and encouraging their participation may be bypassed. Such processes may be viewed as time wasting—after all people are dispensable, profits are not. These practitioners may view humanitarian values as conflicting with wealth maximization and as causing economic inefficiency. Recommendations are based on the manipulation of people rather than on their genuine participation and involvement.

While this view may seem extreme, the opportunistic approach has gained popularity among many business-minded practitioners. Many consulting firms and private practitioners have capitalized on the opportunities to sell products and services to clients without a real diagnosis of what might be needed. Others have joined the marketing approach of packaging, advertising, networking, and selling human relations interventions as a commodity to buyers of all sorts for a price. Success is measured in billable hours, revenue, and profits accrued to the consulting firm or the consultant. The measure of client satisfaction is the consultants' generated income from the client. In this view, marketing and serving clients are viewed as opportunities for generating economic gains for the consultants.

This opportunist wave has impacted organization change and management consulting. Many consulting firms, for example, see themselves in competition with one another and are fully involved in the competitive strategies of developing market-driven programs. They promote and sell their products and services to generate revenues and profits—even if the clients are not well served. They strategize and compete to gain market share, size, revenue, and profits. They produce and employ celebrity names (speakers) to promote their programs and wares. The traditions and values of human systems development are often lost in marketable capsules, brochures, and glittery modules that make their offerings look glitzy and attractive to potential clients—justification for the high prices that are often extracted. What is lost in the marketing, promotions, competitive rankings, and revenue generating shuffle and scuffle is the teaching and the practice of ethics and morality and a commitment to the underlying assumptions of Lewin's humanitarian approach—the drive to improve the human condition through participatory democratic action research and methods.

Within this context, Lewin's work is narrowly and opportunistically used, stripped of its humanitarian traditions. As an example, Lewin's force-field model has gained popularity and is used to manage change, but his rigorous and disciplined methods and humanitarian values are often bypassed in the competitive rush for economic gains. It is not uncommon for managers, consultants, and change agents to use Lewinian force-field analysis to design interventions that usurp resistance to accepting change even when such resistance may have moral and ethical merits. Inducing thought leaders to lessen or abandon their opposition to change is not unusual. When Lewinian methods are used to persuade and even dictate outcomes regardless of their underlying values there is cause for concern. Without full awareness of implicit and explicit moral and ethical concerns, force-field analysis may be misused to perpetuate values contrary to the concern for human costs and suffering.

Action research, a cornerstone of Lewin's work, requires consultants to facilitate clients to obtain valid and reliable knowledge about their circumstances. The consultant's role is to educate the client on collecting valid data and to process the data using the participation of the community. For example, in dealing with bigots in Boston, Lewin required them to visit and interview black families to collect first-hand data about their lives and work circumstances as well as their views on segregation and prejudice. The bigots were then asked to share the data with one another and through discussion and facilitation their views were transformed. They became aware of their own assumptions and conduct as well as their contributions to segregation and alienation. According to Lewin, action research requires first-hand experience and data about the events and conditions by the participants in a setting. The consultant's role is to educate, design and facilitate, but not necessarily take part and impose his views on the situation.

In the present day, action research consultants often take the central role. They collect the data, they evaluate the data, they draw meaning from data, and then they present it to their clients. As the data are fed back to the client, the client and consultant jointly make a decision on the diagnosis and interventions without the involvement of the people whose data was gathered. Considering the remunerating dynamics of employment, the consultant takes the role of protecting the client. Such practices are a far cry from Lewin's model of action research, which is supposed to empower the client to generate its own valid, reliable and pertinent data through sharing, analysis, diagnosis of critical issues, generation of action options, selection of a prudent course of action, and implementation. Most action research projects do not reflect Lewin's philosophical stance and, in fact, are contrary to it.

The opportunist approach may promote quick fix consulting and interventions for immediate gratification and gains. It may shun meaningful research, diagnosis, and problem solving that generate and apply appropriate theories and concepts for understanding the dynamics of a specific situation and the short- and long-term problems and solutions. Performance is viewed as an economic objective to be improved for extracting profits. On a macro scale, the opportunist approach has also penetrated national and international policymaking. Arrow and associates (1995) point out that national and international economic policies (e.g., GATT and NAFTA) have usually ignored issues of the environment, working conditions, and community development. The presumption is that economic growth and liberalization are good for the environment, ecology, and people. In his well-documented work, Korten (1996) argues that global corporations are continuing to gain power beyond nation states and are moving beyond their monitoring and control regulations. They are contributing to ecological damage in developing nations and the widening of the gap between the haves and have-nots. The economically-motivated policies and interventions of opportunistic practitioners tend to weaken the quality of life of local economies and communities and increase alienation and hopelessness, while achieving greater economic prosperity for the larger economic entities. Opportunist approaches that myopically maximize economic variables without meaningful system-wide diagnosis and sound intervention tend to increase these systems' risks by increasing visible and hidden human costs, social inequality, ecological deterioration, and economic dislocations in the short and long term. When Lewin's work is used by consultants in such contexts, there are increased risks for value conflicts. The consulting effort is directed at addressing the client's opportunistic concerns and those present. The value laden issues of the broader context, distant from the immediate setting, are ignored and left out of the consulting agenda. The opportunistic planned change outcomes that may be satisfying to the immediate client may in fact have negative humanitarian values consequence for broader stakeholders and violate Lewin's humanitarian goals and intentions.

Estes (1996) argued that corporations have lost the perspective of accountability to their broader stakeholders. Recent executive pay and severance packages, such as at the home improvement specialty retailer Home Depot (Lubin, Simmerman & Terhune, 2007), provide examples of opportunistic abuses where stakeholders' interests are compromised through questionable maneuvers and actions. There have also been countless revelations of criminal corporate abuses and illegal actions by self-serving opportunistic executives, consulting firms, lobbyists, and public employees, ranging from excessive executive pay, accounting frauds, managerial misconduct, self dealing, bribes, and other illegalities. Opportunist-approach advocates are engaged in change-management programs designed to improve short-term profits and executive compensation. They advocate changing corporate cultures to extract personal economic gains in line with their self-serving values. Their operative values portray the disparities of haves and have-nots in terms of winners and losers—rewards go to the best and the fittest even if the means are dehumanizing. They view themselves as a part of the winning class in a global competitive economy that rewards the winners and shuts out losers. Kaplan (1996) discerns a global trend toward anarchy resulting from unethical opportunistic values and processes: scarcity, crime, overpopulation, tribalism, disease, and destruction of the social fabric of the planet. There is abundant evidence that the opportunist approach has been damaging to human societies. Clark (2006, p. 55), for example, impervious to the damages and evolving disastrous war in Iraq, proudly writes about her consulting efforts in bringing about public opinion change:

> "The essence of communication plan is to flood the zone with information," I explained, "information dominance." The communications plan was nearly as exhaustive as the war plan, and its centerpiece was embedding of journalists with military units on a scale never seen before. Embedding … had been in the works for months…

In effect, one can argue that the reporters were cleverly used to gain leverage over the opponents of the invasion by co-opting them to gain information dominance. The setting here, although not a corporation, illustrates the ramifications of how one-sided management of change on behalf of a client at the cost of open exchange of information deviates from Lewin's prinicples. Similarly, when a CEO client was asked his reasons for wanting a team building intervention, he asserted forcefully that he wanted an involved team that would perform his wishes and get done what he wants them to do. He went on to discuss his desire for the "right people on the bus" and he does not buy into participative management. The consultant who was subsequently hired viewed himself as a hired gun—with the belief that the client is always right and his job is to deliver what the client wants. Team interview data were collected by the consultant and shared confidentially with the client, and the change plan was designed in the privacy of the two and executed top down.

Technological innovations are also used to exploit, obscure, and frustrate efforts to develop and renew human systems potentials. For example, re-engineering change programs aimed at increasing organizational efficiency borrow survey techniques from the more enlightened Lewinian action research methods, but they are used for purposes counter to humanitarian values. The focus is on improving short-term productivity, taxing human systems, community development, quality of work life, and employee participation in problem solving. For example, Lewin's work on the force-field model of change is used to strategize and implement top-down management decisions through autocratic processes. Those using them impose individualistic rather than collectivist cultural approaches (Ramamoorthy & Carroll, 1998) that emphasize short-term individual performance, individual incentive schemes, formal performance appraisal schemes and individual results-based rewards, promotion, and hiring. These operationalize a unilateral shift of social contract and employment practices toward competition and survival, further reinforcing opportunistic values.

According to Lewin (1946a, p. 38), changes in values will finally lead to changes in social conduct. It is equally correct that changes in action patterns and actual group life will change cultural values. Hence, within this orientation, Lewinian approaches are used with a short-sighted view and contrary to the values of the field. Such pseudo-practices have already resulted in major failures, which are often erroneously attributed to action research, organization development and applied behavioral science fields. They have angered and frustrated many employees as well as lowered their morale and damaged their self esteem.

Enlightened Choice

This approach is the extension of the humanitarian and applied scientific orientation of Lewin, which attempts to mutually optimize both sets of values. It promotes consulting processes that emphasize the democratization of organizations. Change in any society can only have a lasting effect when the change processes themselves are conducted in a manner that is consistent with democratic values and processes. Lewin invented action research as a means of resolving social problems through democratic processes, inter-group fact finding, valid and reliable data, free choice and collaboration (Burnes, 2004). It continues to be a powerful method in stakeholder and community work with technology further enhancing its use and application

Action research also introduces new challenges to social systems. Along with globalization comes a greater appreciation of the diverse cultures and environs that humans have created and sustained over time. New challenges of how to learn about one's own cultural and social orientation in a global context and how to build bridges to other cultures and human systems are exciting and necessary. A great deal of new innovations and developments are needed to raise the ability of people to solve social problems though democratic and scientific processes. Effective social problem solving offers solutions to wars, terror, and dysfunctional societal dynamics. Enlightened practitioners strive to mutually optimize a number of competing variables and factors specific to the situations. In the twenty-first century, new innovations in theory, concepts, methods, processes, and interventions are needed to deal with the ever growing dynamic complexity of human systems and living.

Institutions such as National Training Laboratories and Case Western Reserve University have advanced the Lewinian approach with care. They emphasize humanitarian values in collaborative social problem solving, inter-group relations, sensitivity training and essential competencies for training action researchers and practitioners

The enlightened approach offers real possibilities for transforming the field through the next stage of changes for the millennium. It is possible to innovate and find new ways of dealing with human systems opportunities and problems through enlightened consulting approach. The integration and extension of current knowledge could open the path to a new renaissance in social sciences that Lewin envisioned and initiated. Perhaps more importantly, it could also help raise the consciousness of both those in academia and the larger society to the humanitarian concerns that are often lost in the rush to make a profit.

NEXT STEPS

To create a synthesis of the opposing choices, Kurland and Egan (1996) propose that the Internet, consisting of vast, loosely coupled systems of electronic forums—under the right conditions—can enhance democratic participation and overcome barriers to realizing democracy. However, to be effective, we need to apply the total package—values and all. The opportunistic techniques by themselves devoid of humanitarian values can be horribly counter-productive.

We struggle with questions as to why people seem to have less and less loyalty to their work or community, why they question the value of work itself, and why issues of ethics, honesty, and even civility seem so strangely irrelevant to many. Perhaps we need to look no further than the choices underlying what we model and our actions in bringing about change. If our major concern as management consultants, applied social-science practitioners and scholars is simply the bottom line and increasing wealth in the short term, regardless of the consequences to people or the environment, then we are simply reaping what we sow. And, if we fail to go beyond economic factors and productivity concerns in short- and long-term initiatives, we are simply perpetuating a world in which even basic human needs for ever growing populations are likely to go unmet. The Lewinian transformation of applied social sciences offers understanding of prudent synthesis and a balance of choices for more effective social problem solving and action in our emerging complex world. The enlightened organization change and managerial consulting of Lewin offers time-tested promise for a better future world for all. Lewin would have used the new communication tools and plethora of technologies to generate real-time social data, develop social network models for dialogue among diverse views to educate publics and stakeholders of the nature and power of accurate diagnosis of root problems, and generate and implement elegant and enlighted interventions improving human conditions globally.

NOTE

1. An earlier version of this paper was presented at the Kurt Lewin International Colloquium, Rutgers, New Jersey, September 12, 2008.

REFERENCES

Arrow, K., Bolin, B., Costanza, R., Dasgupta, P., Folke, C., Holling, C. S., Jansson, B., Levin, S., Maler, K., Perrings, C., & Pimentel, D. (1995). Economic growth, carrying capacity, and environment. *Carrying Capacity Briefing Book, 2*, 520–521).

Burke, W. (1997). The new agenda for organization development. *Organizational Dynamics, 26*(1), 7–20.

Burnes, B. K. (2004). Lewin and the planned approach to change: A re-appraisal. *Journal of Management Studies*, (September), 977–988.

Cartwright, D. (Ed.). (1951). *Field theory and social science: Selected theoretical papers by Kurt Lewin.* New York: Harper Brothers.

Clark, T. (2006). *Lipstick on a pig.* New York, NY: Free Press.

Elvin, J. (1996). Crusade for 'correctness' goes from insult to injury (Federal government's sensitivity-training programs). *Insight on the News, 12*(38), 21.

Estes, R. (1996). *The tyranny of bottom line: Why corporations make good people do bad things.* San Francisco: CA: Barrett-Koehler.

Kaplan, R. (1996). The coming anarchy. *Carrying Capacity Briefing Book, 3*, 56–81.

Korten, D. C. (1996). *When Corporations Rule The World.* West Hartford, CT: Kumarian Press.

Kurland, N. B., & Egan, T. D. (1996). Engendering democratic participation via the net: Access, voice, and dialogue. *The Information Society, 12*(4), 387–406.

Lewin, K. (1936). *Principles of topological psychology.* New York: McGraw-Hill Book Company.

Lewin, K. (1945). The research center for group dynamics. *Sociometry, 8*, 126–136.

Lewin, K. (1946a). Action research and minority problems. *Journal of Social Issues, 2*(4), 34–46.

Lewin, K. (1946b). Techniques for research in group living. *Journal of Social Issues,* 2(4), 55–61.

Lewin, K. (1946c). Behavior and development as a function of the total situation. In L. Carmichael (Ed.), *Manual of child psychology* (pp. 791–844). New York: John Wiley & Sons.

Lewin, K. (1948a). Cultural reconstruction. In G. W. Lewin (Ed.), *Resolving social Conflicts* (pp. 34–42). New York: Harper Brothers Publishers.

Lewin, K. (1948b). Bringing up a Jewish child. In G. W. Lewin (Ed.), *Resolving Social Conflicts* (pp. 169–185). New York: Harper Brothers Publishers.

Lewin, K. (1948c). Self-hatred among Jews. In G. W. Lewin (Ed.), *Resolving Social Conflicts* (pp. 169–185). New York: Harper Brothers Publishers.

Lewin, K. (1948d). Experiments in social space. In G. W. Lewin (Ed.), *Resolving Social Conflicts* (pp. 71–83). New York: Harper Brothers Publishers.

Lewin, K. (1949). *Training in community relations.* New York: Harper Brothers Publishers.

Lewin, K., & French, J. R. P. (1948). Research and training: The research program on training and group life at Bethel. *The Group, 10*(2), 11–15.

Lewin, K., & Radke, M. (1946). New trends in the investigation of prejudice. *Annals of American Academy of Political and Social Science, 6,* 167–176.

Lubin, J. S., Zimmerman, A.. & Terhune, C. (2007) Behind Nardelli's abrupt exit. *Wall Street Journal,* (January 4), A1.

Ramamoorthy, N., & Carroll, S. J. (1998). Individualistic collectivism orientations and reactions toward alternative human resource management practices. *Human Relations, 51*(5), 57–75.

Roberts, D., & Engardio, P. (2006) Secret, lies and sweatshops. *BusinessWeek,* November 27, p. 50.

ABOUT THE AUTHORS

Dale Ainsworth is a managing partner for a consulting firm in the Northern California area. He has worked in both industry and government in leadership and consultant roles focused on transition and change planning, implementation, and management. He is an accomplished team builder and group facilitator with experiences in a variety of cultural settings. He has also served in leadership roles where he was involved in direct hands-on management of the transitions of several critically challenge organizations. He holds a Master of Science degree from Pepperdine University in Organization Development, and a Ph.D. in Organizational Systems from Saybrook University. He also serves as an adjunct faculty member at a local university.

Terry R. Armstrong is an organization development educator and consultant primarily interested in consulting practice, ethics, and change strategies. Besides being a professor he has served as the: Director of the Arrupe Program in Social Ethics for Business, Woodstock Theological Center, Georgetown University; Director of Graduate Education in Communications, Emerson College; and Director of the MBA Program at the University of West Florida. Terry advises, coaches, and mentors CEOs, senior execu-

Consultation for Organizational Change. pages 309–315
Copyright © 2010 by Information Age Publishing
All rights of reproduction in any form reserved.

tives, managers and OD Professionals on a wide range of personal and organizational issues. He has worked or consulted in 14 countries to over 50 organizations. Terry is active in the Academy of Management and has been Chair of the Management Consulting Division. He has served several stints as editor of the *Organization Development Journal* and edited or co-authored several books on change. Currently he is a professor of management at Colorado Technical University's Institute of Advanced Studies in Colorado Springs, Colorado.

Judith R. Benson has been an internal and external consultant focusing on team building, user-focused evaluations, ethnographic research, leadership development, workplace community development and support of cultural alignment for over twenty years providing support for clients in the United States and Latin America. She has published over a dozen articles in the social science field. Current interests are in research and consulting using organizational development tools for community development and healthcare for underserved populations. She has a Ph.D. from UCLA and an MSOD from Pepperdine University, Graziadio School of Business and Management.

Anthony F. Buono, series editor, has a joint appointment as Professor of Management and Sociology at Bentley University and is Founding Coordinator of the Bentley Alliance for Ethics & Social Responsibility. His many books include *The Human Side of Mergers and Acquisitions: Managing Collisions Between People, Cultures and Organizations* (Jossey-Bass, 1989; Beard Books, 2003) and *A Primer on Organizational Behavior* (Wiley, 7th ed., 2008). His current research and consulting interests focus on organizational change and interorganizational alliances, with an emphasis on mergers, acquisitions, and strategic partnerships, and developing organizational change capacity. He holds Ph.D. with a concentration in Industrial and Organizational Sociology from Boston College.

W. Warner Burke is the E. L.Thorndike Professor of Psychology and Education, coordinator for the graduate programs in social-organizational psychology, and Chair of the Department of Organization and Leadership at Teachers College, Columbia University. His publications include twenty books and over 150 articles and book chapters. He is a Diplomate in Business and Consulting Psychology, American Board of Professional Psychology, a Fellow of the Academy of Management, the Association for Psychological Science, and the Society of Industrial and Organizational Psychology, and past editor of both *Organizational Dynamics* and the *Academy of Management Executive.* Among his awards are the Public Service Medal from NASA, the Distinguished Scholar-Practitioner Award from the Academy of Management, and the Distinguished Professional Contributions Award from the Society of Industrial and Organizational Psychology. His latest book is *Organization Change: Theory and Practice* (2nd ed., 2008).

Léon de Caluwé is senior partner of Twynstra, management consultants and professor at the Vrije Universiteit in Amsterdam (the Netherlands). He is social psychologist. He is one of the best-known consultants in the Netherlands. He heads the Centre for Research on Consultancy. He has more than 120 publications to his name, many of them in English. He received several awards for his writings. He teaches in many postgraduate management courses and is editor of journals. He is an active member of the Academy of Management.

Deborah Colwill serves as an Adjunct Faculty Member of Trinity International University (TIU) and Northern Theological Seminary teaching in both the Masters and Doctoral Programs. She teaches in the areas of leadership, organization development, and philosophy of education. In addition to her teaching roles, Deb has served in a variety of leadership and consulting roles within both profit and non-profit organizations. Her educational background includes a BA. in Psychology from the University of Minnesota, an M. Div from TIU, and a Ph.D. in Education from TIU. She is currently pursuing a second Ph.D. in Organization Development at Benedictine University.

Judith A. Gebhardt is on the faculty of the University of Maryland's Smith School of Business in the department of Management and Organization. A former full-time faculty member at Pepperdine University, she has also taught at the University of Southern California, California State University-Los Angeles, Freiberg University of Mining and Technology (Germany), and Catholic University of America. Judy practiced as a bilingual licensed family therapist (LMFT) in East Los Angeles and has consulted with both public and private sector organizations including the Department of the Navy, Chief Information Office and Heineken Technical Services, The Netherlands. Judy's current research interests and consulting focus on coaching, intangible capital, behavioral due diligence in the M&A/change management process, and leadership development. She holds a Ph.D. in Organizational Psychology from the California School of Professional Psychologyand four Master of Science degrees.

David W. Jamieson is president of the Jamieson Consulting Group and an adjunct professor in the Masters of Science in Organization Development Programs at Pepperdine University and American University/NTL. He is a past national president of the American Society for Training and Development (1984), and past chair of the Management Consultation Division and Practice Theme Committee of the Academy of Management. He has over

40 years of experience consulting to organizations on leadership, change, strategy, design and human resource issues. Dave is co-author of *Managing Workforce 2000: Gaining the Diversity Advantage* (Jossey-Bass, 1991), *The Complete Guide to Facilitation: Enabling Groups to Succeed* (HRD Press, 1998) and *The Facilitator's Fieldbook* (AMACOM, 2006). He also serves as editor of *Practicing*, an OD Network on-line journal, and the "Reflections on Experience" section of the *Journal of Management Inquiry*. He holds a Ph.D. from the Anderson School of Management at UCLA with a concentration in Organization Design and Development.

Kenneth W. Kerber is an organizational psychologist, management consultant, and trainer. His clients include EMC Corporation, Boston Scientific, Harvard Pilgrim Health Care, MITRE Corporation, Wells Fargo, MIT Lincoln Laboratory, Harvard Clinical Research Institute, Avid Technology, and Cognex. Prior to starting his consultancy, Ken was a Management & Organization Development specialist with Data General Corporation, Director of Training & Organizational Development at Chipcom Corporation, and, most recently, Director of Training & Development at 3Com Corporation. He is also an adjunct faculty member at Bentley University and Simmons College. Ken has published articles in a variety of professional journals, most recently in the *Organization Development Journal* and *Revue Sciences de Gestion*. He holds a B.S. in psychology from Loyola University of Chicago, and an M.A. and Ph.D. in psychology from the University of Illinois at Urbana-Champaign.

Kathrin Kordon is a university assistant at the Department of English and American Studies at Vienna University and works as an external lecturer in professional consulting and linguistics at various universities, *Fachhochschulen* and other organizations for adult education. She is also working as a free-lance consultant (supervision, coaching, organizational development) in various professional contexts, with a strong affiliation to the *beraterInnengruppe naschmarkt* (Vienna). Her major research interests are issues dealing with the interrelatedness between intercultural communication and professional counseling. She is currently pursuing her research into the pragmatic use of English as a Lingua Franca (ELF) in working on her PhD thesis.

Gina Lavery partners with leaders to create environments that unleash the human spirit, resulting in breakthrough results, relationships and strategies. She brings a broad, real-world perspective to her clients as a result of two decades as a business leader with a Fortune 100 health care giant, and study, work and travel to over 35 countries around the globe. She is a contributing author to the third edition of *Practicing Organization Development* (2009) and *Awakening the Workplace* (2006). Gina is passionate about personal transformation and impact on organizations, communities, creativity and innovation. She holds a Master's degree in Organization Development from Pepperdine University.

Craig Lundberg recently retired from Cornell University where he held the Blanchard Chair of Human Resource Development. He has published widely on management, organizational behavior, culture and change, consulting, and alternative inquiry practice. He works with managers on change and teamwork, serves on several editorial review boards, and is a Fellow of the Academy of Management. His current scholarship focuses on enhancing pedagogies for management education, differentiating organization change models, and learning systems. He is an ardent fly fisherman and the steward of a cattle-timber ranch.

Michael D. Mitchell is an independent organization consultant. He was corporate director of OD at Kaiser Aluminum and Chemical Corporation, an adjunct and core professor in Pepperdine University's MSOD program, an assistant professor at CSU, Chico, and has consulted with many organizations, including AT&T, US Army, Martin-Marietta, Intel and Kaiser Foundation, among many other high tech and manufacturing companies. He was a principal for some years in American Productivity Group, and on the Executive Board of the OD Network. He has two books in publication at present, *The Four Houses*, a book of new organization theory, and *Straw Into Gold*, a book that explores and explains the approach in his chapter in this volume. He holds a Ph.D. from Purdue University in Industrial Psychology.

Kurt Motamedi is Professor of Strategy and Leadership at Pepperdine University. He served as board member, key executive and consultant in a variety of industries and organizations. Kurt authored numerous publications on topics of transorganization development, creativity, T-groups, adaptability, and leadership. He received his M.B.A. and Ph.D. from UCLA-Anderson School and MS in Electrical Engineering from University California. He is a former chair of the Management Consulting Division of Academy of Management and served on its board.

Elsbeth Reitsma is partner of C3 consultants and managers in Leusden (the Netherlands). She studied Sociology at the University of Leiden (Master of Science) and followed a postgraduate course on management consultancy and change management. She is preparing a Ph.D. She does research on interaction between clients and management consultants in simulated environments. Her consulting practice focuses on innovations in Health Care.

John J. Scherer was co-creator and core faculty for the first competency-based graduate program in applied behavioral science at Whitworth College. Prior to that, he served a tour of duty as a Combat Officer in the U.S.

Navy, followed by graduate school in theology, and a posting to Cornell University as Lutheran Chaplain. In 1982 he started his leadership and organization development work with an international client list that includes many U.S. Fortune 500 companies. Founder of The Scherer Leadership Center in Seattle, John is also Strategic Partner with Pathways Polska, a Krakow-based firm introducing OD to Eastern and Central Europe. His writing on leading change has appeared in many publications, and his latest book, *Five Questions that Change Everything* explores the internal path to leadership development.

Dalitso S. Sulamoyo is the President and CEO of the Illinois Association of Community Action Agencies, Illinois' largest anti-poverty network of 40 organizations. He has presented on peer consulting at state, regional and national Community Action conferences. He also presented on this subject internationally in 2009 at the 4th International Conference on Management Consulting in Vienna, Austria. His current research interest is on the measurement of hybridized OD success rates in Africa. He holds two masters degrees in Political Science and Public Administration from the University of Illinois and is pursuing his PhD in Organization Development from Benedictine University.

Roland Sullivan, noted as one of the original 100 change agents, coined the phrase "whole system transformation" (WST) in the mid-1970s. He has conducted literally hundreds of WST initiatives since in over 30 countries in every major industry. Recently he co-edited the third edition of *Practicing Organization Development*, considered by some as the "bible" in the field of organization development (OD). Based in Minneapolis, MN, Roland has been a tireless force in developing OD awareness and capability in Asia, especially Singapore, China, India, Thailand and the Philippines, through an organization he co-founded, www.AODN.org. His web site is www.RolandSullivan.com.

Elizabeth Vales is the Director of Organization Effectiveness in the Technology and Operations Business Unit of Allstate Insurance Company, the United States largest publicly held personal lines insurer, located in Northbrook, Illinois. Since joining Allstate in 2004, Elizabeth and her team have increased the effectiveness of the Technology and Operations organization through developing leadership capabilities, increasing individual capacity for change, and creating a diverse and inclusive environment that enables everyone to do their best work. Elizabeth is currently responsible for leading a Whole System Transformation effort focused on holistically transforming the Technology and Operations organization. Prior to joining Allstate, she was a Senior Manager in Accenture's Human Performance Practice. During her eight years at Accenture, Elizabeth consulted with clients in the areas of change management, learning and development, competency modeling, and culture change. In 2008, Elizabeth was named to *Leadership Excellence Magazine*'s Top 100 practitioners in Leadership Development. She holds a M.S. in Organization Development from Pepperdine University.

Ginger Whitson is a Senior Organizational Effectiveness Consultant at Allstate Insurance Company. Over the past several years, she and a team of internal and external consultants have led a successful whole system transformation effort. She is passionate about helping leaders and leadership teams transform themselves, which makes organizational transformation possible. Her current focus is on strategy development and leadership team effectiveness. She holds a MBA from Central Michigan University and is a graduate of the Becoming an Effective Intervener (BEI) program at the Gestalt Institute of Cleveland.

LaVergne, TN USA
30 September 2010
198969LV00002B/24/P